TALKING ADHD

ESTHER GOLDBERG

Producer & International Distributor
eBookPro Publishing
www.ebook-pro.com

Talking ADHD
Esther Goldberg

Translation from Hebrew: Jonathan Boxman

Contact: goldberg.esther@gmail.com
ISBN 9798362567279

In memory of my father David Albert Silliman, a loving, good, sincere, genuine, honest, witty, charismatic, gregarious and extremely intelligent man who did not realize his enormous potential and did not enjoy his life to the full – because, I believe, he was grossly misunderstood. He inspired me to understand myself, and others, and explore the subject more and more.

Thanks to all the parents and children who have shared countless invaluable insights, thoughts, and feelings with me and enabled me to break up this complex phenomenon, and represent it in an authentic, precise, down to earth, simple, and practical language.

Special thanks to my loving and caring husband Avner Goldberg, who is always unconditionally by my side.

TALKING
ADHD

THE BREAKTHROUGH GUIDE TO:

Understanding, Empowering,
and Communicating without Judgement

ESTHER GOLDBERG

CLINICAL AND EDUCATIONAL PSYCHOLOGIST

CONTENTS

Recommendations 9

Preface 21

Introduction 25

Chapter 1 From the story of my life to the principles of
the therapeutic approach *Talking ADHD* 33

Chapter 2 The Development of the *Talking ADHD* Approach.................... 49

Chapter 3 *Talking ADHD* — Who is the Child With ADHD? 61

Chapter 4 *Talking ADHD* With the CHAMP Model................................. 77

Chapter 5 *Talking ADHD* — Hyperactivity... 107

Chapter 6 *Talking ADHD* — Impulsivity... 157

Chapter 7 *Talking ADHD* — Wandering Attention.................................. 199

Chapter 8 *Talking ADHD* — Executive Attention: 257

Chapter 9 *Talking ADHD* — Compensatory Attention............................ 305

Chapter 10 *Talking ADHD* — Emotional Therapy.................................... 349

Appendix A Developmental Deviations: Temperament and
Learning Difficulties... 439

Appendix B Diagnosis of ADHD 457

References 479

RECOMMENDATIONS

Prof. Iris Manor
Senior child and adolescent psychiatrist
Director of ADHD clinic Geha Mental Health Center
Associate professor, Sackler School of Medicine, Tel Aviv University, Israel
Head of Israeli Society of ADHD
Advisory board, APSARD
Chair of the ADHD section, World Psychiatric Association

The book *Talking ADHD* is a refreshing and innovative book in its field. While one might think that everything that could be said regarding this disorder has been said, defined and explained, this remains a complex disorder that is not fully understood even by professionals specializing in the field. Furthermore, in spite of the accumulating evidence to the contrary, public perception of the disorder still regards it as something of an indulgence, a 20th century invention and an outcome of the digitalization taking over our lives. Worse, its treatment, particularly medicinal, is perceived as something between "drugging the child" and "profit-raking by the pharmaceutical companies," for the purpose of "securing peace and quiet at school." This perception continues despite accumulated knowledge, scientific evidence and results in practice, all of which point to the exact opposite. This combination of ignorance and stereotypes prevents diagnosis and treatment, and funnels the loving parents, who are anxious to secure their child's wellbeing, into various futile approaches and therapies and countless books on the topic, which only confuse and make it harder for both parents and children to find their way. In contrast to these, this book is characterized by a wealth of information, deep and inner nonjudgmental understanding and seeing individuals with ADHD eye to eye, albeit from the expert therapist's position of knowledge and authority.

The approach in this book is creative, unique, fascinating and full of metaphors. It avoids any inappropriate judgment and criticism—indeed, it disqualifies and excludes them.

Esther herself constitutes the unique and vital combination of someone who has lived with the ADHD disorder and has coped with it to this day, while being a first-class professional therapist, who for years has treated and guided parents and children with ADHD. She therefore can observe with empathy and subjective understanding, while applying objective external analysis together with the expert guidance of the therapist.

ADHD, as Esther herself testifies, is invisible to the external environment. Children with ADHD all too often experience the world and themselves in a manner which is not understood, but instead, is harsh, punitive and vindictive. The emotional, social and behavioral difficulties associated with this disorder are an inseparable part of it, but often are not identified as such and so do not receive the treatment they need. The parents are also often left without support and suffer loneliness and helplessness, as many testimonies make clear. Esther has aided parents and their children for over 40 years in how to see this invisible disorder, identify it and treat it. Esther provides the required solutions with an attitude of acceptance and creativity, along-side her knowledge and professionalism. This book, *Talking ADHD*, is aptly named, for it forms a unification of Esther's rich professional experience and day-to-day experiences with the disorder, incorporating professional knowledge and clinical experience of many years in treating children with ADHD and advising their parents. This is, therefore, an important text for these parents, one which can accompany them during the diverse scenarios they have to manage in their daily lives. It is also an important text for the children themselves (in accordance with their ability to handle reading the book), and for teachers who work with such children, who might feel isolated and burdened with the extent of the responsibility, but lack the tools, training or backing to meet it. This book provides many specific solutions, while emphasizing the need for management strategies and therapy, just as for any other medical condition.

I enthusiastically recommend that every home or workplace with an individual that is coping with ADHD (be they child or adult) include this book in their library. This book can serve as an important educational aide, and no less importantly, as a relief for the loneliness that so many people dealing with ADHD feel.

Godspeed and my deepest appreciation,
Prof. Iris Manor

Dr. Yoram Sandhaus

Specialist in pediatric neurology and child development. Senior neurologist and clinical lecturer in several Israeli universities and former director of child development, Israel

I have known Esther for a very long time, and I have learned over the years to recognize her professional distinction as a therapist with a broad and comprehensive approach within the enormously varied field of ADHD and associated conditions.

Esther and I were both influenced by a great teacher, Prof. Dov Aleksand-rowicz, of blessed memory, whose personal and professional contribution continues to accompany us to this day. Esther specialized in ADHD and assisted many families over the years. She served for me as a safe destination to refer my patients and their families—a place where they would receive instruction, therapy and comprehensive consultations that would help them with the complex day-to-day management of their condition at home, in school and in broader society.

The vast field of attention disorders, with or without hyperactivity, can sometimes raise professional controversies. The diagnostic topic is multidimensional and sometimes inconclusive. A biological basis for the disorder exists, but it varies from one individual to another. Even within a nuclear family, there are differences between individuals. Each has their own path in life in connection with attention and hyperactivity, and each individual is a world unto himself. The ability to recognize this and to see the individuals as they are, with compassionate understanding about their specific conditions, is the basis for Esther's personal and professional work over the years, and is reflected in the text before you. This book is presented in a clear and friendly manner, and I am certain it will find its place among the leading professional books in the field.

Dr. Yoram Sandhaus

Mrs. Ariella Helvig-Daniel

Director of support centers for students with learning disabilities

Beit Berl and Sapir Academic Colleges of Education

Esther Goldberg's book, *Talking ADHD*, is a fascinating, clear and innovative text. It serves as an important manual for parents and educators who work with children with ADHD.

It is innovative in several ways: It offers a means of therapeutic and counseling instruction based on "psychological education." This approach emphasizes conveying broad, up-to-date knowledge in the field of ADHD – both in its physiological aspects and in the psychological, or emotional, aspects of the child's life. The working assumption is that expanding the knowledge base of the parent or responsible adult will enable them to form insights, to get to know the child in his myriad characteristics and to accept and understand him optimally. However, the power of this knowledge is primarily in enabling the child to become his or her own expert, and therapist.

This book further emphasizes the dialogue between child and adult that comes from a great respect for children and from a faith in their ability to change and evolve, and in their wisdom and sensitivity.

In the first chapter of the book, Esther reveals to the reader her fascinating life story and the path she has traveled, including her pain and personal confrontation with attention disorders. Thanks to this personal journey, she grew and became an expert in the field of ADHD. Through this personal and authentic story, it is apparent that what is right for Esther as an individual, and what has been implemented in her life, out of acceptance and understanding of herself, also holds true for Esther as a professional.

The book is divided into chapters based on a clear format that eases navigation through the topics and coalesces the professional knowledge of the reader. It is interwoven with many examples taken from Esther's encounters with children of various ages. It also bears the marks of Eastern philosophies (for Esther was born and raised in India) as well as up-to-date Western research. The delving into concepts such as acceptance, compassion, and informed and meditative observation is also conspicuous. The learning-therapeutic construct Esther proposes is based on the principles of the CHAMP model that she suggests, whose central purpose is for the child to learn about, and understand, herself. One of the CHAMP principles is the rich and extensive use of metaphors. Unique metaphors are dedicated to each component of attention, hyperactivity and impulsivity, in order to explain the condition and help regulate it. The many metaphors illustrate the understanding of both the challenges and their solutions.

As someone who assists many students in advanced education institutes who deal with attention and hyperactivity disorders, I am interested in how this model can be implemented in their lives.

Tal Kringel

Senior clinical and educational psychologist, supervisor and mental health coordinator of the National Health Maintenance Organization

The book *Talking ADHD* constitutes a new and important contribution to the therapeutic literature on ADHD and is warmly recommended to parents and professionals specializing in therapy. In clear language, rich in metaphors and examples, Esther makes her therapeutic approach accessible. This is an approach which she has developed and applied throughout most of her professional life as a psychologist and mentor to people and children dealing with ADHD and as a professional instructor in the field.

Esther's approach blends Eastern and Western methods (in a manner which also reflects the movement in her life between India, the United Kingdom, the United States and Israel), as she explains the subject matter holistically and teaches the parent how to become the expert therapist of her own child. The first step, according to Esther, is meticulous study of the specific characteristics of ADHD and their direct influence on the personality of the child, in a manner which enables vital therapeutic intervention by the parents and the educational environment.

The purpose of this approach is to study the subject and learn to talk a new language, to assist the child to acquire the skills she needs to become her own expert therapist, and to strengthen the feeling that she is understood, both by herself and by those in her environment. This is how we can make a change in her emotional, behavioral, functional and educational world.

I had the great privilege of getting to know Esther and witnessing the effectiveness and success of her unique approach which is transmitted via the CHAMP model, to treat children and adults that are managing ADHD. Using the language of her approach, many parents have learned how to know their children more completely, and using the approach has enabled them and their children to grow together, despite their difficulties.

Tali Abend
Senior clinical psychologist and supervisor

Sincere congratulations for a profound, innovative and thrilling book, which illuminates ADHD from a new and different angle, posing a significant contribution to the professional literature in this field.

Esther has dealt with ADHD from the unique perspective of a woman who has dealt with ADHD for her entire life, as well from her rich experience as a clinical and educational psychologist, an expert in the field for some 40 years. Her experience is an encouragement to the parent, teacher, instructor, coach and therapist to show interest in her therapeutic approach, which is both unique and creative, in teaching how to *Talk ADHD* using the the CHAMP language.

This language, which is based on pure observation, is simple, human, empathic, direct, positive, criticism-free and nonjudgmental. It enables us to speak eye to eye with individuals coping with ADHD, and can be incorporated in every encounter with them.

Esther explains this concept to adults who are responsible for these children, teaching them a language with which they can help such children develop consciousness, understand themselves, improve their self-image and channel their unique skills into effectively handling their difficulties. I was particularly impressed with the way in which Esther breaks up the concept of ADHD into a broad variety of expressions, which are seen in day-to-day life, and shows how innate neurological conditions are linked to emotional, cognitive and behavioral expressions. The theoretical explanations are translated into simple and easily understood language, which is integrated with plenty of examples and exact metaphors. These provide a broad base of understanding for parents, teachers and therapists to facilitate therapy, enable change and, most importantly, to build respect for the child, empowering her and enabling her to improve her self-understanding and to develop in the way that is right for her.

Warmly recommended,
Tali Abend

Tirza Sani
Personal and business coach

Esther presents a groundbreaking, illuminating approach that is brilliant in its simplicity.

I avidly read the theoretical approach and the therapeutic toolkit, asking myself: "Where were we before today?" I recommend reading this book to every child and adult—parents, as well as educators and therapists. For me, on a personal and professional level, Esther is nothing less than a guide to the perplexed.

Thank you, Esther, for professional and in-depth clarification of the field of ADHD from a new and innovative angle, and for permitting your readers to experience the leveraging of it for a better quality of life, success and fulfillment.

Dr. Smadar Ravid
Communications and Education expert
Holocaust, history, and literature teacher

During my time as a teacher, I have frequently faced difficulties that have been created by certain students, who were resistant during classes, lacked the ability to concentrate or were serially disruptive. I did not, at that time, know the name of the underlying condition—ADHD. In my own way, I tried to bring those children to cooperate, and to include them in classroom activities, but without much success. In out-of-class discussions, they responded to my requests without difficulty, as well as to my attempts to form personal bonds. They understood the desired conduct in class, but it seemed that from the moment the class began, all our previous understandings would be discarded.

Esther Goldberg's book answers my need, and that of many other teachers, to understand the children who deal with hyperactivity, impulsivity and attention deficiency, and to develop a closer bond with them that will enable them to enjoy a more significant learning experience. This is a comprehensive yet focused solution to the difficulties which frequently occupy teachers, and with it, we can reach effective results.

This book presents a broad yet detailed tapestry of all the phenomena clustered under the definition of ADHD. But beyond the detailed descriptions, this book is written based on Esther's deep familiarity with many children and teenagers, each of whom have experienced various, unique manifestations of the phenomena. Her work with individuals, parents and groups have enabled children to undergo a process of effective attention management, bringing about change in their functioning and their feelings of self-esteem. The many examples of children Esther recounts, out of her rich experiences, enable readers to achieve understanding of the child, their emotional world and the difficulties which they must face.

The critical starting point to understanding the difficulties these children cope with is the fact that they lack the ability to regulate and control their attention and impulses. They also lack the basic ability to comprehend how their behavior is perceived by the environment. They do not control their attention deficiency, just as they cannot control their outbursts. Their disruptive chatter in the classroom stems from their inner restlessness and unease, and their inability to follow and focus on the class.

That is why my sincere attempts to talk to them heart to heart could not have had any impact within the classroom.

The structured, informed therapeutic approach Esther proposes, based on her broad and deep knowledge of ADHD, and particularly based on her practical therapeutic work, over 40 years of experience with children and their parents, constitutes a coherent and very precise road map. It enables teachers seeking to assist their students dealing with ADHD to study the unique characteristics of each of them and to understand the needs deriving from them. Of course, consultation with the additional parties that assist the child is required, but the teacher who wishes to aid these students, to enable them to progress towards a more productive and satisfying mode of functioning, will find an inexhaustible treasure trove of information in this book. Educational advisers may also derive a considerable advantage from this book. It can serve as a useful aid in learning and expanding their understanding of the ADHD disorder and serve them to enrich their arsenal of therapeutic approaches and coping strategies, regardless of whatever experience they have acquired in the field. Its primary importance, however, is in proffering a practical, didactic and structured therapeutic approach in very clear and accessible language, that is based on the profound knowledge it contains. This approach is based on the unique model Esther has developed, whose purpose is to enable children with ADHD to feel they are understood, and to reach self-awareness and control in their lives.

PREFACE

Dr. Mali Danino

CEO of the Nitzan Society — The Israel Association for the Advancement of Children and Adults with Attention Deficit Disorders, Learning Disabilities and Difficulties in Adaptation and Functioning.

The book *Talking ADHD* offers a unique approach to treating ADHD, an approach quite unlike those common in the field and one that is not represented in other books. This approach is based on the use of dedicated therapeutic language—the CHAMP language. Esther explains the life experiences of a child with ADHD, leans on a rich world of imagery and provides a gallery of metaphors to help parents find a creative, nonjudgmental and criticism-free way to connect with their child.

Children with ADHD experience the world very differently from other children, in a manner that is often unfamiliar even to themselves. The experience of being not understood is harsh and, if left untreated, can also manifest as emotional and social difficulties. Esther, by her own testimony, was a child with ADHD who went undiagnosed. She felt lonely and misunderstood by an environment that was not attentive to her and did not know how to deal with her. She accordingly underwent harrowing formative experiences, which led her to eventually become a leading psychologist and mentor in the field. It seems that Esther experiences the children's difficulties from a place of personal pain and understanding—full identification.

Esther has helped thousands of children for over 40 years to cope with ADHD. It is for them that she created the language presented here in this book. Her desire is to transmit that language onwards to parents in Israel and the world, and to spare them and their children much frustration and disappointment, while helping them realize their abilities and be happy. The book *Talking ADHD* incorporates Esther's professional knowledge and clinical experience of many years in treating children and helping their parents. It is an important document for parents, for it provides them with support in the form of varied coping mechanisms in their daily lives. The ability to go back and read the chapters of the book, whenever a parent runs into difficulties or problems, will help the parent derive the insights they require to connect to their child and help them.

The book is written in a user-friendly language and represents the up-to-date literature dealing with the topic. Esther explains the scientific basis of ADHD and provides examples from daily life regarding how this disorder is expressed. One of the expressions she uses to describe a surplus of vigor is "you are foamy like waves in a stormy sea." This is an example of non-judgmental and criticism-free imagery, which enables reflection about the opposite condition—a situation of control: "Now you are as calm as a still sea without any waves. The stormy foam is gone."

Esther teaches parents to implement what they have learned and practiced with this language, to improve the ability of children to cope with different life situations. We often react to the result of the behavior, and thereby direct anger and guilt at the child. Esther instead seeks out the source of the behavior, seeing it as the key to understanding how to help the child prevent its recurrence in the future.

She says that this is a difficult stage for the child, for they are not always aware and cannot explain—and, besides, it is difficult for them to regulate themselves or stop their own behavior. Therefore, the role of the adult is to teach the children a new way for them to identify, stop, think about what has happened, successfully connect their emotions with what has happened and – later – successfully connect the different situations in which they are unable to stop themselves. Esther's goal is to help children achieve self-awareness, to understand themselves and to be understood. She claims that there is no way we can reach the children without developing our own consciousness—a process which requires investment, keen observation and delving into details.

This book helps children with ADHD, as well as professionals. Parents who read this book will have the opportunity to embark on a journey of learning "in motion," helping them deal with their child in their daily lives. Professionals will be inspired and will receive creative ideas which will help them in their work with parents and children dealing with ADHD.

With great appreciation,
Dr. Mali Danino

INTRODUCTION

Written with great love and passion for All Who Seek to Understand and Be Understood

This book was written **first and foremost** for you—the thousands of loving and worried parents, lost and confused, who are seeking guidance regarding how best to help your child. Its purpose is to present to you a unique therapeutic approach intended to help you understand the phenomenon known as ADHD, with all its characteristics, and to "Talk ADHD"—to accept, comprehend, embrace, and teach your child a language with which they can identify their difficulties, understand and develop awareness of them, and explain themselves. Through this, they can gradually learn how to control the expressions of their ADHD and reroute themselves in a desired direction. At the same time, this book is intended for teachers, therapists and physicians who are seeking to enrich their knowledge and receive practical tools that will empower them to help themselves and others.

The therapeutic approach proposed in this book is not an alternative to medical treatment or any other type of treatment. I do not oppose medication, but I do believe that one must learn the subject in order to make an informed decision that balances potential gains with potential losses. I believe that any therapy should be accompanied by an explanation, so that the child will understand what is happening to them, to connect with their strengths and to develop along the path they have chosen. We, parents, and responsible adults, need to learn the subject thoroughly to teach children about themselves.

The purpose of every treatment is to **lead the child to understand himself and become his own expert.**

This process takes time, and the way to achieve this purpose is long and complex. A young child cannot help herself on her own. She requires constant, intentional assistance by her parents, teachers, and instructors until she becomes aware of herself and can take responsibility for herself. This is why the parents and adults responsible for the child must learn about this subject and develop an eye-to-eye dialogue with her. This dialogue is generated out of a precise understanding and observation of ADHD phenomena. We can generate a friendly language, the language of CHAMP, a language which enables parents and other adults assisting the child to understand her experiences, identifying with them and communicating with the child efficiently and productively.

I wrote this book inspired by a deep feeling of purpose. It was written with great love, and out of respect and empathy for both children and adults—teachers, parents, instructors, therapists and any individual interested in ADHD. Understanding the subject and developing awareness of it will enable looking directly at the human soul of people with ADHD—and respecting it, just the way it is.

Over the past few decades, the topic of ADHD has become increasingly prominent in the media; we have been deluged by articles, studies, conversations, facts, opinions, data and "discoveries" conveyed by various media. And yet, despite the great interest around the topic, it remains **insufficiently understood**.

The medical establishment focuses on treating the symptoms of ADHD, little relating to the pain and hardship it causes. In this book, I seek to explain the disorder from a wider context and take into consideration the emotional injury associated with those living with it—as well as of those around them. At the same time, I seek to address the many "benefits" it provides. Through this book, I am seeking to outline for you the way to the hearts of these children and adults, regarding how you can expose and understand their hidden pain and help them feel better about themselves.

A dominant characteristic in ADHD is the pain. It is the direct product of the frustration children and adults with ADHD feel. The source of the frustration is the gap between their understanding of the tasks required of them and their inability to perform them. It is also the product of the vast dissonance in their ability to function, which they are unable to explain to their satisfaction. This pain is the result of a feeling of vulnerability, under-performance, emptiness and lack of fulfillment in their lives. It derives from the combination of lack of control and helplessness. This pain "shatters" the parents, frustrates the child and serves as a daily source of conflict between her and her surroundings.

Nonetheless, it is important to recall that for many people with ADHD, the associated traits are a blessing. They intuitively take advantage of these traits, rerouting their form of expression to their benefit, and thereby achieve success and fulfillment. That is why ADHD should not be viewed as a dispar-aging term; it should be seen as a collection of traits that should not be judged as "good" or "bad". Rather, their practical significance should be assessed—do they help the individual with ADHD to lead a happy, fulfilled life, or are they obstacles? When these inherent traits disrupt the life of the child, they should be seen as an obstacle to be treated in order to improve the child's quality of life. It is important to avoid perceiving such traits and the gaps that are formed by them as fundamental flaws of personality or parenting.

This book was written after an experience of many years of successful work in the field, countless talks with parents and children, and in-depth, long-term follow-ups. It includes various topics relevant to the ADHD dis-order, and every chapter contains scientifically validated information along with suggestions for practical, easy-to-understand tools. Therefore, each chapter is self-sufficient, enabling integrated and holistic understanding of the specific topic discussed therein. It is also possible to use each chapter as a framework in group guidance of children and parents. Since this is an instructional and didactic guidebook, it has incorporated case descriptions for illustration. The names of all the patients and their details have been changed to preserve their privacy. I wish to emphasize that this book pres-ents a unique language and teaches it. It is a prolonged process of developing self-awareness, and we should not therefore expect that reading the book in one go will enable us to develop this awareness and acquire the language of the CHAMP model which it presents. I suggest reading the book in "small helpings"—first, look through the entire book, and then, read each chapter or section separately. It will thereby be possible to understand, internalize, consider, digest, experiment and practice, just as is right to do when studying a new language. Every individual can study at their own pace—I don't expect you to immediately speak the language fluently. It will be enough for me that some people will understand the subject in a general manner, that some will change their perception regarding their child, that others will select a few concepts and cleave to them, and that others will seek to learn and implement more and more. My hope is that this book will be accessible at home, and that every individual will know that the chapters relevant to them can be selected to return to repeatedly, in order to remember, deepen or clarify the way the language is used.

I feel an obligation to put this therapeutic approach to writing, for it is unique in its authentic and respectful attitude towards the experience of frustration and helplessness of parents and other responsible adults who are struggling to assist children with ADHD. Its presentation here is meant to provide them with a language that will enable them to become emphatic therapists of their own children. Children with ADHD tend to intuitively feel misunderstood by their environment. An environment that does not understand them tends to criticize, judge, be angry, reject and punish. These children and adults are extremely sensitive but, for the most part, find it difficult to explain themselves and respond powerfully when they feel misunderstood by those around them. The frustrations with coping that they experience result in hardships surrounding their self-image and a severe sense of loneliness. Under such situations, the use of the language of the CHAMP enables children and adults diagnosed with ADHD to feel the rare sensation of "Bingo! I am understood." I believe that precise understanding accompanied by empathy makes for fertile ground for the child who is forming a connection with their environment—be it the parent, the teacher, the therapist or a friend.

The rare feeling of "I am finally understood" is the decisive turning point which enables the process of change and helps the child relax, observe, understand and defend herself.

This book was written over many years, but throughout these years, I was unable to bring myself to publish it. In 2016, I met with my dear mentor, Prof. Dov Aleksandrowicz, of blessed memory. I asked him to express his opinion about the manuscript *My Mind Races,*[1] which I had written together with Keren Zagury-Cohen. Keren, a talented mother who participated in one of the workshops I facilitated, was so inspired by the approach that she translated the metaphors I used into exact, catchy and friendly poems that parents could use for initiating conversations with their children. I explained that the book represents my therapeutic approach of "making the parent into the expert." He was deeply impressed and was happy to write a recommendation, telling me that he himself wrote a psychoanalytic book titled *The Injured Self*[2], in which he described the "injured self" feeling of children and adults with developmental difficulties. We concluded that I had come full circle. He convinced me to write another book and recommended that I expand and explain the therapeutic approach, because he found it to be creative, interesting, new and unique. Its uniqueness, he said, was in that it explained to the child what was happening to her in simple language. It spoke **to** the child rather than **about** the child. I had devoted my entire professional life to precisely understand and explain the enigma, first to myself, and then to parents and children, as well—so that they would understand themselves.

Reviews of *My Mind Races* were enthusiastic, describing the approach underlying it as "pioneering," "revolutionary" and "sophisticated in its simplicity." This enthusiasm, as well as the desire to hear more of my lectures in many forums following the publication of the book, convinced me that I had to concentrate the many drafts I had written prior to my retirement and transform them into a complete and comprehensive book, despite the great difficulties I foresaw in writing it.

As I deliberated how to overcome my writing obstacles, I overheard, completely by happenstance, the name Oshrat Gazal. I thought of my dear friend

Ditza Gazal, of blessed memory, who I met as an intern in a psychiatric hospital, and with whom I stayed in close contact for many years. I recalled the smiles that had lit up her face, and her heart that swelled whenever she spoke in admiration and pride about her daughter, Oshrat, who very successfully occupied herself in diagnosis and adaptive teaching. I immediately called Oshrat and asked her to perform the scientific editing of the book so that I could publish it. Oshrat told me that she was writing her Ph.D., for which she was studying the link between ADHD and difficulties in written language, and agreed to perform the task of editing the book. I knew I could entrust myself into her hands. And from there, the rest is history …

Comments and recommendations for optimal use of the book:

- Use of the terms "ADHD" and "attention deficit and hyperactivity disorder" is performed alternatively but refers to the same condition.
- The description, explanations and characterizations relating to the expression of ADHD refer to both children and adults, even when only children are mentioned.
- Each chapter in the book is self-sufficient. Accordingly, repetitions of certain details sometimes occur.
- The book has a clear and systematic format. The poems at the end of each chapter were originally written in Hebrew by Keren Zagury-Cohen and jointly published by her and me in a book titled *My Mind Races*. The entire book, including the 30 poems therein, was translated into English by Barbara Sutnick—into a yet unpublished book. This illustrated guidebook enables parents to communicate with their children on the subject of ADHD. I have selected one relevant poem at the end of each chapter of this book to help adults mediate and communicate with their children about these various issues – and perhaps to encourage others to write their experiences in prose or poetry.
- My therapeutic approach is presented throughout the 10 chapters of this book. Nonetheless, as I have frequently been asked by professionals and parents regarding issues associated with the phenomena, I chose to add two appendices meant to expand the scope of the book a bit beyond the approach I developed. The first deals with developmental variance—temperament and learning disabilities. The second—with diagnosis of ADHD.
- The gender pronouns in this book are mostly female but are, of course, intended for both genders.

CHAPTER 1

From the story of my life to the principles of the therapeutic approach *Talking ADHD*

What is different about me? Why am I different to others?

For as long as I can remember, I have sought out ways to understand myself and other people. I was particularly challenged and intrigued by dissonances I could not understand: the dissonance between different human beings, the dissonance between myself and society, and the dissonance within myself— between my potential and its realization. I repeatedly asked myself: "What is different about me?"

I was born on the festival of Purim, 1952, in Calcutta, India. I was a chubby baby, bursting with energy. On my first birthday, I somehow managed to crawl to a spiral staircase and roll down five flights of stairs. Fortunately, I was well-padded and suffered no great harm. This "padding" won me the title "fattest baby in the city" and a silver trophy (one of the only prizes I have ever won). Later, as my difficulties emerged, I was told I had "minimal brain damage," and I believed that this fall was the cause of this "brain damage."

When I was three, I was sent to a Catholic convent school. The education was British, among the best in India. I remember how I learned and absorbed both from the nuns in the convent and from everything around me beyond the convent gates: I learned to accept otherness and "the other." Bursting with energy, I gathered all the information I could, scampered about, observed everything and experienced life. India was the first school of life for me. Without understanding too much, I learned and adopted the holistic approach. I became acquainted with the world of mindfulness and spirituality and began to realize that everything is possible and that each individual must take charge of his or her own destiny.

As a young girl, I was very active socially. I was confident in myself and in my abilities; but at the same time I hid, as much as I was able, a "terrible" secret from the world.

In spite of my fierce desire to learn and succeed at my studies, I repeatedly failed. I was unable to study and adapt myself to the requirements of the school and the convent. When I asked repeatedly why I did so poorly in exams, I was told: "You are an intelligent child but have a hard time passing exams. We will pray for you." But, good intentions were of no avail, and my exam grades failed to improve. My parents decided to send me to a branch of this convent in England when I turned 15. The reason they gave me, which I never managed to understand, was to prevent me from marrying a non-Jew. That was how I found myself alone in England. It did not take me long to understand how incredibly accepting and accommodating India and the Indian people were to me. In the Western World, my life was much more difficult. I had a very hard time in school, and I was constantly judged, reprimanded and chastised for inappropriate behavior. I became known as "that wild, uninhibited child." I used to climb over fences, run away from the convent and hitchhike wherever anyone would take me. Through hitchhiking, I began to discover the world and explore it—first in England, and later on, upon discovering the success of this method of travel, in continental Europe, and eventually to India. My behavior resulted in repeated expulsions from studies in the school. Only with great difficulty was I able to graduate from high school in England. Despite my great efforts, I was never able to become a good student. I hitchhiked with my brother (who had also been sent to England) across Eurasia, all the way to Calcutta, where we met up with my cousins. My brother and cousins completed their studies with excellent grades and were planning to study in prestigious universities in the United States.

"What do they have, that I don't?" I repeatedly asked myself. I did not know, and I did not understand why it was so hard for me to study.

I also wanted to travel to the United States and study there. I did not give up and tried every possible way. Eventually, as a Jewish girl from India, I was able to secure a scholarship to Wellesley College, Massachusetts. In spite of being a prestigious Ivy League institution, it did not demand any entrance exams. As a Jewess from India, I was expected to contribute to "cultural diversity" by wearing a sari, participating in ceremonies and reading Bible verses in Hebrew. I did so willingly and joyfully. This distinctiveness helped me lead the other Jewish students on campus. It made me a well-known figure on campus and certainly strengthened my self-image.

Nonetheless, I kept my terrible "secret" hidden—that I could probably never be more than a mediocre student who flopped her exams. During my years in college, I never told anyone about my difficulties during exams or my fear of them. Instead of sharing and taking the exams, I always asked to present seminars or prepare significant projects on the pretext of cultural differences between India and the United States and my "language difficulties" (I claimed my native language was Hindi, rather than English, which was my mother tongue). These excuses were obviously baseless, but they enabled me to graduate Phi Beta Kappa without passing a single exam.

Despite this success, I was troubled. I knew I could not continue to advanced studies in the United States without passing exams. I decided to make Aliyah to Israel, where I might be able to continue using the "language difficulty" card to avoid exams. This is precisely what happened. I immigrated to Israel, and in spite of many difficulties, I graduated with distinction in 1976 from the Hebrew University with a clinical psychology degree. A few years later, I concluded two internships—educational psychology and clinical psychology.

My life path and the hardships I endured charted my academic course, leading me to seek out answers to the questions which had troubled me over the years.

Professionally, I was occupied initially with diagnosing and treating gifted children, and children suffering from learning disabilities. In my 30s, during my clinical psychology studies, I interned in a psychiatric hospital, where I found myself drawn to patients suffering from attention and hyperactivity disorders. They kept on coming to me, because my own life experience enabled me to understand their individual innermost experiences and connect to them.

ADHD—the Diagnosis Which Changed My Life

Prof. Aleksandrowicz, a psychiatrist and psychoanalyst specializing in developmental difficulties and their emotional consequences, and a world-class physician, was the chief of the department where I worked in the psychiatric hospital. He was the one who mentored me and identified my difficulties with attention, restlessness and lack of learning habits as the source of my difficulties. This informal diagnosis changed my life. Suddenly, my life story became more comprehensible to me. I had received an answer to the incessant flood of troubling questions that had plagued me. I now began to understand my academic difficulties, my difficulties in tests and my wild behavior. I understood my difficulties with rigid environments. I now understood the dissonance between my considerable abilities and insights, and my difficulties in securing matching academic and professional achievements. **I began to realize the significance of my diagnosis. I began to understand my difficulties with hyperactivity, impulsivity, and attention.**

Prof. Aleksandrowicz also proposed I leave the hospital framework, a strict work environment involving considerable paperwork and bureaucracy, and work as an independent clinical psychologist in the private sector. At the time, I was happy to accept his recommendation, and yet … my inner child was hurt by it. Badly. I was being rejected, once again—failing to fit in. Once more, in spite of my many efforts, I was not good enough. My feelings were hurt, but I had no choice but to leave the hospital. At the time, despite the diagnosis, I felt the people around me - even those closest to me, including my colleagues - did not really understand me—not my feelings, not my abilities and certainly not my limitations. The psychological therapy I underwent as an intern made clear to me the basic lack of empathy towards me from my surroundings, accompanied by the empathic failures, which had left me alone, once again (by the term "empathic failures," I mean situations in which the environment fails to respond to the needs of the child/person in a suitable manner). Over the years, I enjoyed the support of a bosom friend that I had met in the hospital, Ditza Gazal, of blessed memory. I spoke to her a great deal about my feelings and drew much strength from her. Ditza helped me understand that there had to be another way for me. Over the following years, I found myself seeking this path, drawing knowledge from within, and from every theory and therapeutic approach I could find. My investigations and field experiences led me to develop my own approach to treat children with attention and hyperactivity disorders. This approach was developed with consideration of my understanding about the emotional experience of ADHD patients, an experience seared into my very flesh. It was clear to me that the emotional dimension was central and significant to the essence, ability to function, abilities in general and development of any individual. This was why it was so important to recognize and understand the characteristics and impact of ADHD-derived emotional experiences— this was the only way ADHD patients could be better assisted and treated.

I learned love of my fellow man, the joy of giving and compassion at the knees of the nuns; and it was they who gifted me with the foundations of this worldview. Mother Theresa particularly influenced me. She was first posted to Loreto House, the very convent in Calcutta in which I studied, and established an improvised hospital in the street adjoining the school. Through the power of her unique personality, her enthusiasm and abiding faith, Mother Theresa was able to mobilize the entire city to help her in her mission. We, too, little nine-year-old girls, were recruited to assist. We stood on the church stairs, holding and stroking day-old infants abandoned by their parents. I will never forget this experience. Mother Theresa would instruct us little girls, alongside older people, saying: "First, we will pray for she who abandoned her infant on the stairs. She did so out of desperation and lack of choice. She knew that we would provide the infant with what she could not currently give her..." I received my first psychology lessons in those years. One sentence by this great woman was particularly etched in my memory—it has accompanied me throughout my life and echoes in my head to this day: "*To understand is to stand under.*"

If you want to experience and understand the experience of another individual, you must place yourself in their place, 'Live ADHD', and talk, their experience. I, therefore, called the therapeutic approach around which this book centers *Talking ADHD*.

In India, I learned of the incredible power of acceptance; and it, as far as I am concerned, is the first, essential step—accepting the phenomenon as it is, in all its "glory" and hardships. This is the essence of Eastern therapeutic approaches, which champion acceptance, observation, contemplation, understanding and learning. Deep holistic observation, deriving from observing the world of the child as a whole, is required in order to reach and touch all of the child's inner components. This contrasts with Western therapeutic approaches, which seek to diagnose and isolate undesirable phenomena and eliminate them, either by overcoming or suppressing them. The reliance on medication to suppress attention and hyperactivity disorders, which, in some cases, does indeed match the needs of certain children, more often creates an illusion of resolution. However, children and adults with congenital difficulties with attention and hyperactivity know that this experience is at the base, (or foundation) of who they are, and will accompany them throughout their life.

The essence of the therapeutic approach *Talking ADHD*

The foundation of the *Talking ADHD* therapeutic approach is to remember that true mental health comes from understanding our inner selves, and the gaps between our inner and external environments. Herman Wouk once wrote something I find particularly relevant: "What one doesn't understand in ordinary mental health is that daily life is a *show*. You have to put on the right costume, to improvise right speeches, to undertake the right actions, and all this is not automatic; it takes attention and concentration and work and an amazing degree of control."

These insights are the basis of the therapeutic approach I developed. This approach is based on talks with the child that are focused, so that they can learn how to precisely identify the phenomenon and the components of its expression, which are uniquely theirs.

Such conversations can be incorporated into any encounter with a child diagnosed with ADHD, as well as be used as part of emotional therapy for the child. This should occur in parallel to the assistance and guidance of her parents in how to cope with the manifestations of her hyperactivity and difficulties with attention.

The uniqueness of the *Talking ADHD* approach is that it is thoroughly and specifically adaptable to the wide variety of attention and hyperactivity disorders, and explains the varied and complex issues to parents and other adults in a simple and illustrative language, **enabling them to communicate with their child on equal terms**.

Using this approach, they can raise the child's awareness of the issue and enable them to understand their unique subjective and emotional experience. I developed this language over my 40 years of work with children with ADHD in order to create more open, intimate communication with them. This language enables parents to improve their relationships with their children by giving the child the feeling that their parent finally understands them and that they, therefore, can learn about themselves from their parent. This learning process improves the child's motivation to make a change in their life and behavior. The change the child generates on their own, and with the help of the adult environment, or via the assistance and aid of a professional, can occur in all fields of life: in the family, the school and their peer group. The purpose of the treatment, which is essentially an emotional therapy, is to improve the child's functioning in several ways: the gradual development of her self-awareness and identity, and hence a healthy feeling of self-worth; and the improvement of her ability to transmit communications and explain herself, freeing her up for growth and advancement, so that she can fulfill herself.

10 Principles of the *Talking ADHD* Therapeutic Approach

Principle #1: Accepting the child, seeing her as a whole and providing holistic therapy

What is first necessary, as previously outlined, is an understanding, accepting approach. Only after this is achieved comes the explanations, clarifications and therapeutic methods. We must always look upon your child as valid and complete unto herself, as she is, and not in comparison with some supposedly perfect template. The purpose of the therapy is not to fight or "solve" the "problem," but to help the child understand herself.

The parent of an ADHD child is often plagued by guilt, confusion, anger and frustration. Understanding the complexity of attention and hyperactivity disorders will help converting these difficult feelings into understanding and acceptance of their child. That is also how we help the child recognize her special strengths, which accompany her difficulties in attention and uncontrollable energies, channeling them and using them to her advantage, and finding the most efficient way for her to cope with them herself, as an individual.

Principle #2: The child becomes her own expert therapist

The *Talking ADHD* approach focuses on developing precise communication with the child to provide her with the help she needs in order to understand and accept herself. As the child develops her self-awareness, she will learn how to recognize the undesirable situations she gravitates towards. In this way, she also learns to recognize her abilities, and the triggers for her actions and responses. This is a continuous process of repetitive guidance and practice, during which the child will improve her ability to control her impulses and difficulties with attention.

Principle #3: The parent is the primary therapist

While the purpose of the treatment is to transform the child into her own expert therapist, at a young age she lacks the tools to understand human complexity, in general, and the complexity of difficulties specifically deriving from ADHD. For that, she requires the aid of the parent, the teacher or the responsible adult, who understands her and aims to help her understand, until she can understand herself and treat herself.

In other words, **according to this approach, the significant figures in the child's life become her primary therapists.** For the most part, it is her parents who are the most significant and stable figures throughout the child's life. The parent is there, accompanies her throughout childhood and maturation, and has the greatest willingness to help their child. This is why the parents must become the primary therapists of their child—they must learn about the subject, become an expert and then teach the teachers of their child, in order to rein them in to help in the task. The professional, who is the expert in the field, will be the guide and background escort; their job is to help the parent understand, internalize, be mindful, embrace, and accept non judgmentally, the manifestations of the child's attention and hyperactivity disorder.

Principle #4: Assembling the 'puzzle'—explaining things to the child

It is often difficult for children to understand the many shortfalls in their own ability to function and the lack of correlation between their intentions, actions and outcomes. They feel as if they are made up of pieces of a puzzle, which fail to come together into a coherent whole. Much like their parents, children also suffer from guilt, confusion, anger and frustration. The more intelligent the child, the greater the gaps between what they understand and their ability to translate thought into action—and the greater the frustration they may provoke. This frustration generates anger, avoidance, denial and sometimes also violence towards her surroundings.

It is the role of adults to understand the different pieces of the puzzle and interpret them to their children. They must explain to the children why a gap exists between what they intend to do and their failure to perform; why they can focus on an interesting game but cannot concentrate when performing a routine task; why they know what they want to say but cannot get the right words out; and why they cannot control their impulses.

Until the child learns to feel good about herself and disregard external judgements from the environment, she will not be able to assume full responsibility for herself. It is the role of the parents to help her reach self-sufficiency and – until then – to be there for her. Their job is to protect, mediate between the child and the environment, accompany, show, guide, teach and, as they do so, also deepen their connection with their child. Their role is to help the child understand their experiences by developing a discourse, which enables precise identification of their experiences.

Children with ADHD usually have good intuition and are extremely sensitive to dishonesty, lack of authenticity and inaccuracy. That is why it is important to precisely explain their experience to them, else they will lose their trust in us—parents, teachers and other caregivers. In my case, the pretext for sending me as an adolescent to a Catholic convent school in North Wales – to prevent me from marrying a non-Jew – made no sense to me, and hence damaged my trust of the grownups in my environment.

Principle #5: Explaining things to children as equals, using imagery and metaphors

The central purpose of therapy is to develop a common, constructive language between the child and the important adults in her life. This is how the child gets the chance to learn about herself and change her behavior with greater ease. This can be done through use of colorful imagery and metaphors from the child's world. Metaphors are a simple and readily accessible tool. They have a significant role in psychological therapy as they bridge between different worlds: play and reality, the internal and external world.

They are a sort of colorful, exciting mirror in which the child can create, and gradually observe, herself and connect to her difficulties without feeling threatened by them. This is a tool which helps the child achieve cognitive and emotional understanding of her abilities, responses and behavior. Later on, the imagery and metaphors will also connect her to her experiences and emotional world.

Principle #6: Developing a clear framework, providing boundaries and meaning

In an ideal inner world, the parents, the school and society provide a feeling of belonging, stability, enjoyment, motivation and discipline. These are translated into learning, accomplishment and self-confidence.

For children dealing with an attention and hyperactivity disorder, this equation does not exist. They often lack a sense of belonging and feel like outsiders. Society contributes to the formation of this feeling by criticizing, judging, labeling and not accepting these children. Furthermore, these children intrinsically lack self-discipline and impulse control. They therefore require a clear external framework with well-defined and unambiguous borders.

Principle #7: A general diagnosis of ADHD is insufficient

The diagnosis of ADHD is critical, for it dictates the method of therapy. However, each child is unique, and this is particularly true for children with ADHD, since the expressions of attention and hyperactivity disorders vary from child to child. Therefore, although the general diagnosis is indeed the first step towards making a change, it is insufficient and fails to provide a precise approach to individual children. Besides, the term "attention disorder" is often misunderstood by parents and adults, let alone the children themselves. They use it as a blanket term or excuse, without understanding its significance. That is why, following (or after) the initial diagnosis, it is necessary to break down the term "attention disorder" into precise components and characteristics unique to each child. This is the beginning of a suitable, adaptive treatment.

Principle #8: Emotions, understandings, insights

At the basis of the treatment is the emotional infrastructure of the child and the self-image it supports.

We must bear in mind that these emotional problems began due to objective difficulties with attention, hyperactivity and impulsivity, and in fact, were amplified by them. Significant emotional relief can, therefore, only be achieved once self-awareness and the ability to cope with the basic difficulties in these areas is achieved: This will lead to improvement of the child's ability to handle herself and the ability to function that is required of her. Strengthening the child's abilities will bring about a strengthening of her self-esteem. In my case, had the difficulties with attention and executive functions underlying my failure in exams been addressed by the relevant adults, rather than them focusing on the symptom – my fear of exams – I think I would have done much better.

I qualify this statement by noting that sometimes there are emotional difficulties which do not derive from hyperactivity, impulsivity or attention disorders. Such difficulties require a different therapeutic approach. However, in many cases where the child has been diagnosed with ADHD, and the primary cause of the emotional difficulties remains unidentified, the root cause of the emotional difficulties is unsuccessful coping of the child and her parents with the attention hyperactivity and impulsivity disorder. The child is provided, therefore, with insufficiently effective treatments, which, at best, relieve the symptoms without addressing root causes.

Principle #9: Medication—in moderation

Medications are a sort of protective lens, which enable the child to view the world somewhat more attentively while soothing her impulses. A correct dosage of the right medication can improve the child's attentiveness and regulate her impulse rhythm. As a result, her functioning will improve, and her capabilities will be able to be expressed. Nonetheless, ADHD is not a disease, and hence, medications cannot cure it—but only help relieve its expression. A healthy sense of "self" can only develop through explanations leading to understanding and insight. That is why the condition for the success of the medical treatment **is combining it** with conversations which expand the mindful awareness, connect the cognitive and emotional world, develop insight, and build up functional and behavioral self-control. Medications are not always required, and caretakers should be cautious of "trigger happiness" in prescribing them as a panacea. Precise diagnosis and therapy will indicate the direction most suitable for the child's needs.

Principle #10: ADHD is not a free pass

Often, parents and children tend to view an ADHD diagnosis as a confirmation of special privileges—sort of a free pass, which relieves the child of obligations imposed on other children. Some parents see the diagnosis as an "exemption" of parental responsibility for taking a significant role in the treatment of their child. After all, now she is accompanied by professionals who know what they are doing, right?

My view is: absolutely not! A core principle of the *Talking ADHD* approach is that difficulties result in obligations, more than rights—and certainly not in special privileges.

The *Talking ADHD* approach is easy to understand, but its implementation requires persistence and focused, exact discernment of the unique expression of the condition in each particular individual.

It is aimed at transforming the child into her own expert, enabling her to learn and understand herself in a full and precise manner, so she can believe in herself and succeed.

The expertise will enable her to deal with the challenges of life more effectively, explain herself well, deal with accusations and criticisms, and be her own defendant—in an affable and understandable manner.

As her own expert, she will have the tools to take responsibility for her actions, and acclimate both herself and her surroundings to the fact that she might occasionally be unpredictable, even volatile.

To promote the successful management of ADHD, we adults are required to be emissaries of good will in spreading knowledge and information. I hope that in the various existing treatments, we can **combine** the proposed principles of treatment, and "Talk ADHD" in every encounter with a child or adult dealing with the diagnosis.

OTHER CHILDREN

Suzanna sits right next to me;
She gets great grades, as you can see.
Across from me is my friend Jake,
He never makes a math mistake.
Anne answers all questions from the front row;
Her hand shoots up each time, you know.
It's uncanny how Danny, who sits by the door,
Is the first one to finish then ready for more.
Dianne is just great in writing and spelling,
Always writes the words right in the stories she's telling.

Why does it always seem to be
That school's so, so frustrating for me?
For everyone else, it goes like a snap,
But I must just struggle to bridge every gap!
How come for all of them, things are tidy and clear,
And my head's such a mess, though I still persevere?

Sometimes I just want to scream and to yell,
It's not fair it's so hard for me to do well!
Dad tells me I'm special, I'm his special kid,
That he's proud that I always aim to succeed,
When I try and I try, and I try one time more.
But when things don't get better, I just want to roar!

With his eyes toward the window sits my good friend Jim.
Deep in my heart I am always with him.
Such a space cadet, dreamer, glides along really slow,
Reminds me of me, don't you know? I think so!

CHAPTER 2

The Development of the *Talking ADHD* Approach

Talking ADHD stems from holistic non-judgmental understanding and informed observation.

Attention Deficit Hyperactivity Disorder – ADHD – has arisen in the public consciousness over the past few decades and has become a familiar and frequently discussed subject in almost every home. However, this is not a new phenomenon. Attention Deficit Hyperactivity Disorder is an innate genetic syndrome which has been recognized for many generations now, and which has been shaped by the environment. The gene causing it cannot be changed, but the environment can serve as a mediator to help one understand oneself.

This genetic variance represents a trait that survived over the ages, because it provided advantages as well as disadvantages, to those with the trait. For example, in prehistoric times, one may assume that a tendency to constantly shift position and walk around, rather than sitting down quietly by the fire, would be helpful in identifying approaching assailants—definitely a survival trait.

Similarly, one may assume that in times of tumult and revolution, including the American Revolution, creative, hyperactive, resourceful people with intense drives and improvisational abilities, capable of multitasking (though not always perfectly), enjoyed an advantage over focused individuals and, no doubt, contributed to the success of the American experiment.

The ambivalent attitude to this phenomenon is known from the dawn of history. Some described Esau as the first man described by biblical sources with ADHD"The babies jostled each other within her" (Genesis 25, 22). That is, even during pregnancy one could sense the excessive energies and movements of the fetus. Esau, the impulsive redhead, was first to emerge from the belly of his mother, to become a hunter. Jacob, on the other hand, was a tent dweller, and was more favored by his mother, who preferred the quiet child who walked the path set out before him. He was also more favored by society, who favored the conformist, adaptable individual over the "troublemaker". In contrast, Esau was his father's favorite, and he formed a stronger connection with the active, outdoors-loving child.

History in Short

As early as the mid-19th century, the German physician Heinrich Hoffmann wrote a poem "Shockheaded Peter"[1]—the hyperactive kid who can't sit still. This implies that this was already a well-known, if not accepted, phenomenon.

In 1902, the British doctor Sir George Still identified a small group of children, who had difficulties with impulse control, whom he described as children afflicted with chronic diseases, who suffer from an impairment in moral control.[2]

In 1917, the United States was afflicted with an encephalitis plague, which resulted in problems with attention, hyperactivity and impulsivity, leading, for the first time, to widespread, popular interest in these impairments.

By the 1950s, many studies on hyperactivity were published,[3] that utilized the term "Hyperkinetic Impulse Control" to describe it. In the 1960s and 1970s, the term changed to "minimal brain damage."[4]

In my opinion, these tags were hurtful to children and adults suffering from these difficulties. Worse, they did not encourage them to understand what was really happening to them. All these definitions focused on part of the phenomenon, not all of it; and all referred to a mental impairment that could not be overcome, but whose expression could be suppressed, perhaps even obliterated, via medication.

The Canadian psychologist Virginia Douglas expanded her approach to the different levels of attention,[5] when she compared the ongoing attentiveness capacity of hyperactive and non-hyperactive children, and coined the term ADD—Attention Deficit Disorder. The letter **"H"** was later added to the term to highlight the hyperactivity component which often accompanies the disorder of attention, which had been the focus of the discussion over the years. That is how the term ADHD – **Attention Deficit Hyperactivity Disorder** – was born.

In 1994, two American psychiatrists, Drs. Hallowell and Ratey, published the bestseller *Driven to Distraction*.[6] They claimed that the diagnosis of ADHD is not clear and, in fact, that the central characteristic of individuals suffering from ADHD is that they are insufficiently understood, by themselves or by the environment. Not only is the phenomenon itself not readily understandable, even the name of the condition is misunderstood.

Hallowell and Ratey explained that this goes far beyond semantics. If we look at what happens to a child suffering from Attention Deficit Hyperactivity Disorder, we will see, in fact, not a **deficit** but a **surfeit** of attention and impulses. As a result, their thoughts and impulses are all over the place. The child is in many places at the same time and, therefore, cannot perform actions in an organized, sequential manner, from beginning to end. The two rightfully claimed that the name should have been "driven to distraction" and, indeed, that is what they named their book. Hallowell and Ratey's book *Driven to Distraction* had a profound impact on me. At the time, I was also delving deeply into books about the narrative approach and the theories of "the self," trying to pinpoint the source of the difficulties of ADHD individuals have in forming a robust sense of "self."

Synthesizing different approaches, I reached insights regarding the role of the scientific misunderstanding of ADHD in empathic failures. I personally felt misunderstood by an environment which was accusatory and critical towards me. These failures left me, as well as others dealing with ADHD, misunderstood vis-à-vis the environment—and ourselves. I sought ways that would help me and others tell our life stories anew. During that period, I frequently traveled to India and participated in meditation and mindfulness workshops. The merger of the Eastern approach, according to which I had been raised in my formative years, and the contrasting influences of the Western societies where I was educated is what guides my approach. This is also the principle of this book—to try to deal with a neuropsychological syndrome through scientific understanding, mindfulness and a holistic perception—to understand the ADHD individual and to help her understand herself rather than treating a single symptom.

Talking ADHD is based on Holistic understanding

The holistic approach does not preclude medication (Ritalin and the like), or any other treatment. Sometimes such treatments are vital. However, it is critical to use them **together** with deep understanding and learning about the neuropsychological syndrome—both in the realm of familiarization with existing medical knowledge and in the realm of inner emotional observation. Mindful holistic understanding leads to insights; it has the power of helping the adult to link together the various components of the child's condition while understanding her inner world.

It also enables the adult to understand what she must do to help herself and help her child formulate her self-confidence and sense of self. The first component, therefore, in the *Talking ADHD* therapeutic approach is **holistic understanding.**

This approach is based on a perception according to which man should be seen holistically, as a complete individual—as a whole is greater than the sum of its parts. In this respect, the purpose of the therapeutic process is for the individual to experience herself as a whole and, therefore, to feel complete within herself. Only when the patient feels that the therapist is treating her as a complete individual will she be able to experience herself as a whole person.

It is important to emphasize this precisely because the ADHD syndrome has become so "fashionable" that few therapeutic professionals do not deal with it: neurologists, psychiatrists, psychologists, neuropsychologists, social workers, teachers, counselors, principles, kindergarten teachers, special education and adaptive learning teachers, classroom aids, occupational therapists, speech therapists, special education teachers, emotional therapists and various alternative therapists. Each of these professionals offers treatment of ADHD but, all too often, only to a single, narrow aspect of the syndrome.

They therefore cannot see the child as a whole, and the parents are thus bewildered before the myriad therapists, lacking any guidance in how to integrate their treatments or to treat the child as a whole. Likewise, the child also feels as if the therapist is only treating part of her, which makes it difficult for her to feel complete within herself.

Informed Observation

Another aspect of the therapeutic approach is **informed observation**. Throughout my career, I persevered in learning the evolving scientific foundation for the phenomena, studying it deeply and translating it into simple, mindful language that my patients and their parents can understand, based on a holistic perspective.

This deep, informed observation, in my opinion, is essential and necessary in all fields of life, but it is particularly vital when dealing with ADHD. Only by close observation of a person and understanding what she has experienced can we release ourselves from stigmatic and cliché thinking. Only then can we help, as parents or as professionals, by describing and reflecting rather than criticizing, interpreting, punishing and judging. Only then can we help an ADHD individual route her neurological syndrome toward serving her desires and interests. When the individual recognizes and understands her difficulties, she can improve her connection with herself and her environment. This is, in fact, the greatest contribution of this informed understanding. Let me demonstrate holistic understanding and informed observation of the hyperactivity characteristic of ADHD, a component which has received considerable attention over the years. What would we find should we seek to understand hyperactivity holistically, not just through a child's frenetic behavior but also by understanding how she thinks? We would realize that the brain of an ADHD individual operates differently than that of a neurotypical individual. The brain of an ADHD individual might operate hyperactively—but it might also be operating hypoactively!

These are two separate types of difficulties with attention and impulse control. Both derive from underactivity in the frontal lobes of the brain:

When the brain is hypoactive, thoughts simply fail to connect with one another. In order to help them connect, the child seeks stimuli, often in ways unsuitable to her environment.

In contrast, when the brain is hyperactive, the mind races and the individual with ADHD cannot control her thoughts or maintain a sequence (of attention).

The mechanism underlying hyper-and hypo-active brains is different, but the behavioral compensation is quite similar.

This description enables us to better understand the child who repeatedly says she is bored or has "thoughts racing through her head," when what is actually happening to her is that her thoughts are failing to connect or are heading off-tangent **unpredictably**. We can also better understand a child who finds it difficult to sit still for a long time—she feels a constant urge to be in motion or to be elsewhere, to do something else or to think about something else. If we understand that children and people diagnosed with ADHD are unpredictable to themselves and do not control their attentiveness or impulses, we will understand that sometimes they **do not choose** to act the way they do. To help our children free themselves of this undesirable behavioral pattern, we need to accept that their attention fluctuations are genuine, representing difficulties with regulation on all levels. We can also delve deeper into understanding the many consequences of regulatory difficulties and of the loss of a sense of time (characteristics which will be detailed later in the book).

The informed observation I am speaking of is, in fact, …

Meditative observation

As I was developing and implementing the holistic approach of informed observation, I was delighted to read Hallowell and Ratey's new book.[7] In their book, they refer to meditative observation, which is important both to therapists in understanding their patient, and to the patient, within the process by which she observes herself, learns to understand herself and develops better control of her life.

This book strengthened the meditative approach I had intuitively reached and encouraged me to continue to develop it.

Meditative observation in the context of ADHD is, in fact, observing all aspects of the syndrome in a manner that enables "becoming friendly" with, or embracing, the phenomenon—talking about it openly and discussing the feelings it arouses in and around the child within different situations. Furthermore, it enables highlighting the great confusion deriving from differences between her and her environment in relation to these very same phenomena. This is a type of observation which enables reaching agreements on how to cooperate. Through it, we can help the child identify and isolate specific aspects of ADHD, identifying them in real time curbing them and gradually learning to control them.

The goal of meditative observation is to arrive at a broad, deep and precise-as-possible understanding of the expressions of the syndrome and their consequences, so that we can keep them in check within us. It is why I reject the sentence "She (or I) has attention, hyperactivity, impulsiveness or attentiveness disorders."

I agree with Hallowell and Ratey and claim that "an attention hyperactivity disorder is much more than a neuropsychological syndrome, *it is much more than a list of symptoms*—**it is, in fact, a way of life.**"[7] This is the way of life for an individual, her family and her environment; and should it not be treated correctly, it will remain misunderstood even by the people dealing with it, and its emotional, social and behavioral impact will only grow, like a snowball rolling down a slope.

Studying the individual, her environment and the various characteristics of her syndrome, while emphasizing that while this is a genetic syndrome it can be both understood and molded through the environment, is the optimal method of therapy, as far as I am concerned. This is why I focused first on breaking down the general terms into more specific terms, so that we can examine and accommodate them. This accommodation means a full understanding that will not threaten us or trigger an emotional response. If we can accept these insights without judgment, criticism or a subjective response, our outlook will be more objective. Under these conditions, we can act to route the syndrome in the direction we desire. It is important to understand that the emotional and behavioral expressions of ADHD are a natural objective derivation of the condition, and any interpretation we make of these expressions is a subjective point of view which can lead the individual to feel misunderstood by the environment—and herself. For example, if we know that our child is impulsive, then we can know objectively that the source of the impulsiveness is in difficulties with impulse control, or neurological regulation, preventing her from delaying her responses. In other words, stimulation results in an immediate response. This enables us to understand that when the child bursts into a conversation, she does so because she finds it difficult to delay her response, not because she is an ill-mannered child. Indeed, looking at a child as ill-mannered or badly raised is a subjective point of view. It results in the child feeling misunderstood by the environment. If we internalize this understanding and are moved to view the impulsive behavior in this case as stemming from innate difficulties in regulating actions, rather than behavioral or emotional difficulties, we can avoid misunderstandings and empathic failures. This will allow us to focus on helping the child **understand, observe and identify** the different situations in which she responds impulsively. The child will gradually learn how to activate her brakes in order **to halt** her response and to achieve self-control and a sense of achievement. In other words, the emphasis in this process is in changing the experience of the child rather than the external symptoms of inattentiveness and hyperactivity. Due to her young age, a child cannot understand the complex array of ADHD, and so my approach incorporates individual and group parental instruction -- that has repeatedly proven itself over the years to my satisfaction.

Parental Instrtuction

The purpose of parental instruction is to teach the topic of ADHD in all of its expressions **to change the way parents, teachers and therapists look at the child, and to enable her to change how she perceives herself.**[8] Instruction helps the parent understand and accept ADHD, and so too, makes her an expert.

Over time, gradually, the parent can help the child transform herself into an expert who understands the source of her difficulties and learns how to control and improve her function. This will enable her to succeed and feel better about herself. This is the informed-observation approach, which enables the consolidation of the personality and self-management. I have implemented this approach both individually and in groups, and I have received very positive feedback. Many parents have told me that this approach "put things into order" for them, and this precise understanding has helped them accept their children's behavior without criticism, anger or judgment, although they were not always able to act accordingly.

In practicing precise observation over time, many parents were able to talk to their children eye to eye. Children reported that their parents were more understanding and less angry, and that the atmosphere at home was "more fun." Most children really loved the user-friendly illustrative imagery which is used, which they were easily able to connect to. These images constitute a foundation of the therapeutic language and work with both children and parents, individually or in groups, and really helped them.

Albert Einstein

If we return to the beginning of this chapter, we will recall those instances in which ADHD was beneficial to the individual coping with it. Delve into the biography of Albert Einstein and you will find an example of a man alleged to be born with ADHD who discovered how to harness it to his own benefit. It is not a coincidence that he coined the phrases:

"Out of clutter, find simplicity."
"From discord, find harmony."
"In the midst of difficulty lies opportunity."

In the *Talking ADHD* approach, such sentences are therapeutic and precisely describe the informed-observation approach—out of the mess, the essence needs to be understood; within the chaos, the underlying logic needs to be found; out of the observation of the chaos lies an opportunity to connect to the human spirit, to be there for them and to insist on helping them to feel good about themselves, to succeed and to develop in the desired direction. There are many creative and famous people with ADHD who have been able to route their syndrome in a desirable direction and use it in a way that benefited themselves (and the world). But there are many others who were unable to do so and who degenerated into crime, alcohol and drug use. Success is dependent on the ability of the individual to **understand, accept and observe** the syndrome, transforming the "defect" into an "effect." Those who have successfully done so did so thanks to their emotional intelligence, mental fortitude, determination and the people who believed in them. In contrast, those who failed were left with a sense of missing out, because they were unable to understand and overcome the difficulty, and break through into the desired direction.

ADHD – a misunderstood phenomena

It seems that research in ADHD has broken new ground in the past decades, and various therapeutic methods and treatment philosophies have developed in parallel. Nonetheless, it is important to remember that ADHD remains an often-misunderstood phenomenon that leads ADHD individuals to feel like "outsiders" and misunderstood, both by themselves and by their environments.

Society must understand that the ADHD individual is different, but not aberrant. When the people surrounding the ADHD individual show insufficient understanding, disruptions develop in the connections the individual forms with her environment, and this can deteriorate into a long-term rupture. In contrast, deep understanding by the environment results in acceptance. The decision to **accept or reject** the ADHD individual is critical and determines whether mutual understanding and respect-based relations can be formed. Lack of respect and acceptance will eventually also influence the attitude of the individual toward herself and her ability to accept who she is. That is why I aspire to spread the *Talking ADHD* approach—so that holistic understanding and informed observation become the normative life experience of ADHD individuals.

GIFTS

I always take note of the smallest detail,
All changes so slight grab my eyes without fail;
I'm the first to observe my teacher's new skirt,
Or a change in her hairstyle or color of shirt.
It is not that fashion I like to inspect;
It's just that small details I always detect.

I'm the one with the drive that is just like a rocket,
Or electric hand mixer plugged into its socket;
Nothing can stop me when I start to engage
In an exciting challenge, or project, or page.
I can move mountains, if that's what I intend,
For my energy's boundless, my pep has no end.

I get what you're feeling when you have no words,
Know you could use a friend before having heard
That you've had a hard day and just want to groan;
I'll reach out to you, so you won't feel alone.

Count on me to think up the most daring plan,
Not afraid to take risks, to imagine, and then,
Dreaming in color, I come up with a trick
That's outside the box and really quite slick!

We're the ones who know how to fall and to rise,
To take in our stride every irksome surprise.
To conquer the world, forge ahead, and break free,
To face down tough problems and never to flee.
With encouraging words from the ones whom we love,
We can face every challenge, with your help, hand, and glove.

CHAPTER 3

Talking ADHD – Who is the Child With ADHD?

All of us are born with the ability to pay attention. All of us develop and refine this ability with age and experience. Attention is a crucial ability which provides us a time window in which we can, listen, focus, divide our attention between different tasks or zero in on a single issue.

This is true for individuals with ADHD, as well, but they have a less efficient ability to control their attention and drive. That is why ADHD, which is often also accompanied by difficulties with executive functions, is considered a developmental deviation. The ability of people and children with ADHD to self-regulate themselves, that is, to control their fluctuations of attention and energy levels, and to actively focus and concentrate, is erratic—neither consistent nor stable. ADHD exists in various degrees of severity.

The executive functions represent a higher order system, which enables us to hold information in the brain for a given time, to self-regulate (both attention and behavior) and to perform higher level functions flexibly. Such high-level functions include organization and planning, categorizing relevant and irrelevant issues, reaching conclusions, solving problems and making decisions. Executive-attention difficulties can be seen (or understood as difficulties in self-management, decision-making, initiating, organizing information, using feedback and implementing effective strategies).

A more extensive and detailed explanation will be provided regarding each component of ADHD (including the executive functions) later in the book.

In this chapter, I will try to describe what ADHD looks like in day-to-day life.

The best way to describe a child with ADHD is through familiar examples close to our hearts—parables, fairy tales, songs and so forth. Later, when we discuss how the child can be brought to a closer understanding of her ADHD, we will see that every parent must find the example closest to the world of her child, to help her describe, from within her world, her personal ADHD experience. When I think about ADHD, there are two moving songs, close to my heart, which very illustratively describe the experience of an individual coping with ADHD, together with the difficulties experienced by those in their environment.

As a young girl who was frequently suspended from school, I empathized deeply with the figure of Maria, a young and vibrant woman, the heroine of the musical *The Sound of Music*—and not only just because she was a novice, and I was educated in a convent school! This lively and musical woman was about to take her vows and become a nun; after repeatedly being delayed in the mountains to watch the sunset, the Mother Superior decides to send her off to become a governess to a family with seven children, who had lost their mother.

One of the songs in the musical "How Do You Solve a Problem Like Maria" accurately depicts a case of ADHD, and well illustrates the dilemma imbued in this condition. Although Maria functions well, and is vivacious and energetic, she is also "Unpredictable as weather, as flighty as a feather." She confuses the nuns and triggers conflicting emotions within them. A few of the nuns plead her case, whereas others view her as a "wild child." The nuns complain that Maria leaves them "out of focus and bemused, and I never know exactly where I am." They do not know how to interpret or understand her—she is a riddle to them. Eventually they realize that she is "a moonbeam" in their lives, and wonder how they can best assist and understand her and "hold a moonbeam in your hand."

In my youth, I too sought out people who would help me understand what was different about my behavior and what I must do to fit in. The words of the song "Many a thing you know you'd like to tell her. Many a thing she ought to understand" echoed in my mind.

"Yossi, Yeled Sheli Mutzlach" or, in English, "Yossi, my Little Champion" is another example of a classic, old-time favorite Hebrew poem (by Ayin Hillel) that has been translated into several languages. It describes the experience of what it is like to have ADHD. Yossi is an example of a boy in whom attention difficulties (rather than just hyperactivity) predominate. In spite of his good intentions, he is constantly distracted by various environmental stimuli. He has no sense of time and repeatedly finds himself in situations where he does not fulfill his obligations—so his mother simply cannot rely on him. In spite of all these difficulties, he fills the home with joy and spontaneity.

Maria and Yossi are very different characters—but both illustrate the experience of a person with ADHD. As in these songs, children with ADHD present an extremely complex diagnostic picture; and each child is a world unto herself—special and uniquely different. In my search for a term that would clearly explain the condition of ADHD, I found that the most comprehensive explanation is that of Barkley,[1] and Hallowell and Ratey.[2] Both see ADHD as a disorder in which there is a difficulty in relating to **time**: For most people, time is divided into moments, and not everything occurs at once—but for people with ADHD, everything **does** occur at once, and linear time is a meaningless concept.

Since the mind is distracted by everything the ADHD child finds herself dealing with many things simultaneously and, furthermore, **cannot maintain order, sequences or continuity in her thinking.** The child feels like everything is happening at the same time, and to those around her, the child's thinking seems confused and associative.

ADHD is a condition composed of three components—attention, hyperactivity and impulsivity. In neurologically variant individuals with ADHD, these components are dysregulated. Later in the book, I will expand on the neurological basis of this dysregulation and its relation to the concept of time, but for now, let me emphasize that **the neurological basis dictates behavioral expression.** To reiterate, ADHD stems from neurologically based dysregulation, and is expressed in difficulties in regulating attention and drive. This is the reason that a child with ADHD finds it difficult to control his attention and **impulses** and, **as a result**, finds it difficult to curb or control himself. His functioning is inconsistent and unpredictable. This is why he sometimes lacks the ability to stop and exercise judgment.

These children find it difficult to act consistently and are unable to regulate themselves—that is, control their attention, thoughts, distractions and responses. They feel confused and are unpredictable, primarily to themselves. This is also the reason why they confuse the people around them. The children do not, of course, *choose* not to control themselves or to act the way they act.

In order to illustrate the essential difference between sequential, continuous thinking and simultaneous thinking about many things at once, we will describe the difference between a farmer and a hunter: A farmer who wishes to grow wheat must think about it in advance, plan how he will do it—what he does first and what later. He must then perform all that he had planned according to this sequence, and finally, once the wheat has grown, he must harvest his crop. The hunter, on the other hand, must simultaneously think about where he should fire his arrow, the direction of the wind, possible assailants and other dangers around him, and various other factors, and then, in a single instant, make the fateful decision that will enable him to survive. An ADHD person thinks like a hunter—he innately considers many things at once and makes rapid decisions accordingly.

I explain to the children that they have a **surplus of attention and attentiveness – not a lack of attentiveness**. They actually pay too much attention—to everything and all at once. As a result, they find it difficult to pay attention to things according to a logical sequence. Through this, every child can accept the explanation and even desires to understand what is happening to him. That is why I prefer to use description and explanation rather than a label such as "disability" or "attention disorder"—terms perceived as negative, and which mean nothing to children (or even adults).

The ability to think simultaneously about many different things at once has advantages. For example, managers, agents, negotiators, people in marketing, military commanders or people who work in creative or dynamic settings that demand multitasking are required to deal with many decisions and stimuli simultaneously. Their ADHD enables them to think of, and perform, several tasks simultaneously in a flexible, rapid and purposeful manner.

However, these people sometimes appear confused, since the ability to think simultaneously about many things is associated with the difficulty with maintaining sequence and continuity, to the point where they sometimes cannot recall a sequence of words which fit together in a sentence, or the sequence of actions which led them, only a few minutes ago, to leave their diary, or glasses, or coffee mug in a place they can no longer recall.

This same nonsequential thinking which seems confused is, in fact, another way of thinking which can be intuitive, creative and advantageous. The **way** people with ADHD think enables them to reach different results than other people, since they think and act spontaneously, with split-second decisions. Things seem to "happen to them unintentionally or by chance, and in a seemingly coincidental manner, because they do not plan their steps ahead, and when they encounter difficulties, they improvise.

Their difficulty is not in **what** they know, but **how** they learn and act upon their knowledge. Their way of learning and acting seems confused to those in their environment, who, on this count, often disqualify and discount them and their opinions.

The difficulty in maintaining sequential continuity leads individuals coping with ADHD to be very **associative**. They find it difficult to start and finish anything without losing track of their thoughts in the middle. The difficulty in planning their actions consecutively often leads them to live by putting out one fire after the next, without looking ahead and considering what the potential consequences of every action might be. However, the result of living a spontaneous and carefree life, without planning, is not necessarily negative. An individual who can deal with whatever comes up develops excellent improvisational capabilities, which will serve her well in every aspect of her life. Such an individual will not get stuck when preparing a dish just because she is missing an ingredient in the recipe but will throw something in the pot that seems appropriate. Still, even if this original concoction proves delicious, she will find it difficult to repeat her success and recreate the exact same product every time she cooks the same dish.

These people may find it difficult to maintain a sequence and organize things in their minds efficiently, but they can think up a huge project and carry it out the very next day. An ADHD child might calculate a complex mathematical formula in her mind but prove unable to describe the steps she undertook to reach the solution. In the exam, she will have points deducted because she did not write down her path to the solution. These **gaps** generate confusion and frustration, especially for intelligent children. In fact, in contrast to the prevailing opinion, ADHD is a problem of intelligent children, though it is not directly related to intelligence. The more intelligent the child, the more extreme the gaps in her functioning, and the more confusing and frustrating they are to her. Such a child tends to be tormented by the "What is wrong with me?" question more than less intelligent children, who may accept these gaps more easily—both because the gaps are smaller and because their ability to notice them is smaller.

In addition to nonsequential thinking and constant distraction, a child with ADHD is constantly driven by **uncontrollable urges.** The child responds immediately to every stimulus, without stopping to consider an appropriate response. Such children can be perceived as tactless, extremely aggressive and even violent, because they do not stop to choose their words carefully or consider the proper response to the behavior of their friends. Their behavior does not derive from a lack of knowledge of right and wrong, but from not being able to stop, think and exercise self-restraint. Their thinking and behavior are not characterized by shades of gray, but solely by extreme black and white hues leading to immediate outcomes. The strong urge can be positive, because it leads them to go "all the way" with their thoughts and desires, but often also leads to rash and thoughtless behavior which may lead to more negative outcomes.

An ADHD child often **lacks the attention and organizational capabilities required to persist in an idea or a task and see them through.** She may start preparing to do homework and go several times to the refrigerator as she does so, and then suddenly call a friend who will distract her and invite her over to play. That is how she finds herself arguing with her mother for failing to complete her homework. The child lacks the attention and impulse-control powers required to persist at her homework and, only afterwards, make a playdate with a friend. The child does not behave that way because she is reluctant to work on her homework or does not understand the tasks given to her in class, but because her attention was distracted and because she is driven by unpredictable and uncontrollable impulses. Similar conduct might also typify morning preparations to leave the home—many parents to ADHD children are familiar with the "nightmare" of leaving the house in the morning during the rush to work. That is why they prepare their child the evening before and explain to him why and how she should organize herself in the morning. But, the next morning, they find the child sitting in her bed and staring into the air, clothes strewn around her. When she finally rouses herself from bed, she plays with the dog instead of brushing her teeth and eating breakfast.

The limited capacity for attention and uncontrollable impulses can also be expressed in an ADHD child when she is at play with her friends, and suddenly decides she has had enough, and gets up and goes away.

As an adolescent, she can suddenly stand up from her chair and leave, slamming the door, without telling anyone where she is going. This feeling that "I've had enough" is actually her way to say that she has run out of the ability to direct her attention and urges. She loses patience, and feels overwhelmed and unable to restrain herself any more. This child or adolescent can initiate a given activity enthusiastically, but when her attention and her ability to control her impulses are exhausted, she experiences an overload of stimuli. Many things attract her attention at once, until she feels she can do nothing, decides she has "had enough" and leaves.

Children with ADHD also frequently have difficulties with learning habits. Intelligent children often do badly at school because they find it hard to do what they know how to do. Oftentimes they express themselves well verbally but find it hard to express themselves coherently in writing. This hardship does not stem from linguistic difficulty and is not in the content of **what** they know but in **how** they process language; they cannot organize an idea in their head in order to put it on paper in the most organized, continuous and coherent manner. So it seems that they often do not know what to write, whereas, in fact, they do know, but require frequent help in the process of **organizing** their writing. This description illustrates and demonstrates the frustrating dissonance between the level of their capabilities and knowledge, and their level of performance—which is all too often below the requirements of the school.

Academic difficulties also stem from the fact that children and adults with ADHD generally tend to generalize and find it difficult to recognize nuances and subtleties, as they often lack the requisite resources—sufficient resources of attention and capabilities of control to restrain their impulses. Fluctuations in attention and unpredictable impulses lead them to "hop" from one topic to another and, as a result, they find it difficult to maintain focus, and what they learn does not linger long enough to be internalized or for the information to be directed to the memory. Therefore, their learning remains superficial and unsatisfying. In addition, the spontaneity associated with ADHD, which derives from everything happening at once, leads some of these children to chatter endlessly. This occurs since they are experiencing a sense of overload and are finding it difficult to control the impulse to speak, leading them to interrupt the classroom and to wear out their teachers and classmates, who find it difficult to tolerate so much talking.

The basic experience of a child with ADHD in school is "**I'm bored.**" This experience is the result of the child "zoning out" for a moment or lacking the attention resources required to enlist themselves in the learning process. The child cannot explain that he finds it difficult to listen in class, is not even aware of zoning out and may not even realize that he has run out of attention. It is important to explain to such a child that he is bored because he finds it hard to listen, especially when the teacher or the material are not fascinating. He must be told that he loses attention when he loses interest, or else, when he perceives things as repetitive or routine; and should be helped to develop awareness of this hardship so that he can recapture his attention by seeking out something of interest within the activity. The basic state of boredom typifies more than the learning experience—this is the basic experience of the child. It is generated by the disruption of his attention capabilities and his impulses. The difficulty for a child to control his fluctuations in attention and the intensity of his impulses does not enable him to concentrate on anything and, as a result, he feels bored. He can sit quietly and then suddenly feel an impulse to begin moving in his chair, tap his fingers on the table or feel an uncontrollable need to rise from the chair, and begin pacing back and forth with no purpose. Suddenly, he might flip over the table, blame his siblings for it and go looking for a fight. He will make a big deal out of nothing and start talking about it with everyone around him—all to amplify the experience and, by so doing, to correct the disrupted balance. The child feels the lack of balance in his attention capabilities in these situations and intuitively feels that a powerful or interesting stimulus will restore the balance. The stimulus might be chattering, being a pest, watching TV, playing on the computer, occupying himself with extreme sports or constantly looking for some new project, something to thrill and stimulate them out of boredom. They need something to restore order and regulate their impulses. A child who acts this way does so intuitively. He feels the underactivity in his body or mind, and thus, activates himself, searches out subjects of interest or pushes the pedal to the metal to balance himself. Even if this behavior may seem destructive in daily life, the adults in his environment must realize that the child is acting this way because he has no alternative or choice. I will later explain how we can help him realize this and help him find ways through which he can route him to a path that won't hurt anyone—and even help. This is precisely the reason this hyperactive child can sit in front of the television or computer for days on end. These provide him with the interest and thrill he requires for stimuli, enabling him to maintain his attention over time. Those in the child's environment, who see him stare at screens for hours, may make the mistake of assuming that "he can when he wants to," and that he is simply "a lazy child who refuses to do his homework." However, his attraction to the screens actually provides the interest that helps a child restore the balance of attention that has been disrupted. As mentioned, children with ADHD are **lost in time.** They suffer from a very real difficulty to assess and feel the passage of time, and this difficulty has many implications. The absence of a sense of time makes it difficult to distinguish between past and present—it all gets mixed up. What happened in the past becomes the present, and vice versa. The child can confuse "morning" with "evening" and "yesterday" with "tomorrow" because the times get mixed up and are experienced simultaneously. Sometimes he also finds it hard to distinguish between thoughts and facts; and academic subjects based on a continuum, like history, become an especially tough task. The absence of the sense of time also leads the child to be in many places at once—and hence, he ends up getting distracted. The result is tardiness, not meeting obligations and commitments, and failing to show up to appointments. The child becomes chronically unpunctual and is perceived by those in the environment as disrespectful or disorganized.

Due to her difficulty with sensing time, a child with ADHD is not aware of her pace, and does not know if it is too slow or too fast. Furthermore, she does not know if she has done too little or too much. As a result, during a test, she cannot properly allocate the time meant to be devoted to the various questions and may end up taking too long on the first question without feeling that time is running out—and, hence, will fail to complete the test on time. These children do not **stop** in the middle of their activities to think, to contemplate, to decide, to study or to internalize, and instead, end up swept into activity. So it is, for example, that a child with ADHD can see something that triggers a given association and is swept away by it to fabulous provinces of the imagination, very distant from where she set off. Sometimes, they sail away in their imagination so far beyond the horizon that they fail to distinguish between fantasy and reality. Though this can also be viewed as a form of creativity, it is not always appropriate to the situation. Since the child often does not stop to think, this can generate situations that can be interpreted as bad judgment, when in fact there was **no** judgment, bad or otherwise. Thoughts and impulses arise, motivate and change so quickly that the child finds it hard to regulate and slow herself down to make the right call. When she can be brought to slow down, she can function optimally. If we realize that the problem is in her inability to regulate herself, stop and think, we need to help her do so!

Some children are not just lost in time but lost in **space** as well. They find it difficult to orient themselves in space and suffer from academic difficulties, as well (see Appendix A: "Differential development"). Due to a combination of attention difficulties and spatial difficulties, they cannot control concepts such as up and down, right and left, before and after, above and below, in and out, together and separately. When a child is given an instruction containing these concepts, she does not know what to do and needs to think a great deal about it. She has difficulties in gym class, because when the teacher says to lift the right hand, she lifts the left hand instead and is reprimanded. Another child finds it difficult to sort out pictures according to a logical sequence, since she does not know what the beginning is and what the end is, or confuses cause and effect. Some children can enjoy a movie but cannot say what they had seen when they are asked to recount the sequence. Some find it difficult to find their key, even though it is right in front of them, and some cannot recall the sequence of a given route and feel very confused in their experiences. On the other hand, since a child with ADHD is not aware of time or sequence, and does not stop to think, she is very **spontaneous, intuitive, primal, sincere, and honest**. She is blessed with many gifts—the gifts of surplus attention and energy. She brings considerable joy wherever she goes. She is easily excited, casual, spontaneously and authentically expresses emotions, is bursting with humor, delights with witty repartee, expresses herself naturally and freshly, and lives in the moment, perhaps precisely because she finds it so hard to stop and see the big picture. For example, when an individual with ADHD enters her friend's new house, she will immediately notice even the smallest new items in the house, get excited and express her earnest opinion about them, without noticing all of the building's construction problems. A child with ADHD can return home from a friend's birthday party and excitedly recount her experiences—the clown, the balloons and the general excitement at the event.

She did not notice that the cake was a bit squished, that many children failed to arrive and that, most of the time, the children discussed the absence of their friends. Similarly, an individual with ADHD directs our attention to details we take for granted—in the midst of a deep, weighty conversation, her attention is distracted suddenly as she notices a beautiful flower, an interesting piece of jewelry or the freshness of the grass, putting everything in perspective and filling our hearts with joy. These people usually have **powerful intuition** and sharp senses. Where most people use logic, they think with their hearts—their intuition. They also usually act according to this intuition; and it forms the basis for their abilities in various fields such as music, art, cooking, crafts, design and so forth. It is important to respect and develop this intuitive talent and not disqualify it, even if we don't always understand the logic behind a particular action or ability.

It is important to emphasize that although I am attempting to describe children with ADHD, this condition is not expressed in a single uniform way—it is expressed in very different ways for different children and adults, and no child or adult has the same ADHD expression as another—just as no two individuals are exactly identical. **ADHD is also expressed differently over the course of life.** That is another reason why I refuse to accept the catch-all categorization of ADHD "Attention Deficit Hyperactivity Disorder." Instead, I require both children and parents to describe the specific symptoms. For some children, the attention deficit is accompanied by hyperactivity; these children can't stop moving their head and body, and find it difficult to stop to think.

Some impulsive children say the first thing that comes to their mind and then regret it, but they don't stop to draw lessons from the experience.

Some children are very rigid and inflexible, finding it difficult to transition from one given situation to another, and require much preparation before making any change or transition.

Some children, on the other hand, have an attention deficit without hyperactivity. These children often seem "zoned out" and are frequently undiagnosed. These children may sit quietly in class like "good children," but they, in fact, learn nothing, because their mind wanders off into distant arenas, or cuts itself off from the immediate environment. For some children, the emotional component predominates. They lack security and fear what they are experiencing. In contrast, other children have no problem living with their condition and intuitively route it in a direction advantageous to them.

Other children find it very hard to make decisions, to choose between options, to set priorities, to apply feedback and to self-manage. Some children are demanding, requiring immediate responses constantly, without any concern for what is happening around them. These children demand constant recognition of their existence, and they truly require more time and care from adults, and for a longer period in comparison to other children.

There are also shy and withdrawn kids, whose ADHD prevents them from comprehending what is happening around them, who fail to understand the context, can't follow a joke, and find it hard to understand subtleties and social codes. They usually prefer to stay silent in order to avoid exposing their vulnerabilities. Other children deal with the insecurity generated by the difficulty of understanding what is happening around them by playing the clown—in order to cover up their misunderstanding. They would rather be thought of as naughty clowns than stupid, and prefer negative attention to being ignored—they look like they are "looking for trouble" just to secure the attention they crave.

There are also opinionated children who are extremely stubborn and defiant, and respond immediately and disproportionately to anything, especially when they feel they are the victims of injustice—even the slightest. There are those who insist on doing things their own way; this is an exhaustive list. We can see that children coping with ADHD are very different from one another, sometimes even completely the opposite in their expression of the condition. And yet, at the core of this great variance is ADHD—and its nature is what generates this great variety. In a generalized perspective, one can characterize the child with ADHD as an individual who is easily distracted or disconnected from the environment, who is motivated by uncontrollable urges, who sometimes finds school difficult. **She is a confused**

and confusing child, misinterpreted and misunderstood. This is a child who is adrift in time, and sometimes in space as well, who thinks intuitively, and who frequently surprises us by her creative thinking and free spirit.

Nonetheless, the child's main characteristic is that **she is misunderstood** to herself and to those in her environment. The great variance in the disorder's expression may lead us to conclude that ADHD is a universal phenomenon, which is valid for the entire population. This would, of course, cast doubt on its very distinction as a unique diagnosis, for any individual may well identify traces of the phenomenon in herself. This is particularly true today, when ubiquitous screens have led us to occupy ourselves constantly with numerous topics, all at once. We naturally find it difficult to listen, and our attention is scattered between multiple tasks and topics. It seems that we are all fearful of missing out on something from within this variety of stimuli, and become easily irritated. Nonetheless, most of us can function without undue distress to either ourselves or the environment, so we cannot all be said to have ADHD. It can only be classified as a disorder, after all, if its expression interferes with the function of an individual or with her environment. If we review the clinical definition of the disorder (see Appendix B: "ADHD Diagnosis"), we will realize that this is a well-defined and specific phenomenon, with many implications for all fields of life. The diagnosis is extremely important, as it alleviates the burden of the individuals coping with ADHD, as it helps them understand and direct themselves—and, thereby, liberates them. Understanding the phenomenon and its expression within a person frees her from dealing with the countless questions which habitually trouble her, and from investing too much energy in self-flagellation in an attempt to understand what she is experiencing. The diagnosis enables her to understand, identify, be aware and focus on improving her function in day-to-day life.

ZIG-ZAG CHILD

I'm a zig-zag child, so very contrary!
Sure, I look just like all the others my age,
But I'm one-of-a-kind, and so truly unruly
That so often I feel I'm just on the wrong page!

In a flash I'm alert and full of suggestions,
Then I find myself dreaming on soft dewy clouds.
Suddenly sharp and asking good questions,
The next instant so scattered, I'm lost in the crowds.

I can start out so happy, bouncy, and merry,
Then, next thing I know, I'm driving Mom crazy!
Wake up in the morning energetic and cheery,
Then grind to a halt, all unfocused and hazy.

Within seconds so smiley, excited I soar,
Then swiftly start sinking right down to the pits.
I can be really sensitive, wise, and what's more,
I love to give love, but you'll have to take hits.

I'm misunderstood, upside-down, inconsistent;
Surprise, shocks, and jolts make me stumble and reel.
Rain, sun, snow, and heat — all in one instant!
Like weather that's changing — it's all so unreal!

To be with me sometimes is the most fun you'll see,
Even though I can get on your nerves, heaven knows!
If surprise and adventure are your cup of tea,
Stick with me, and I'll keep you right up on your toes!

CHAPTER 4

Talking ADHD With the CHAMP Model

Children with varied expressions of ADHD were described in the previous chapter. As mentioned, the characteristics of the phenomenon are not yet sufficiently understood, and their interaction with the environment often creates various difficulties that prevent the diagnosed from fully expressing their abilities and positive qualities. ADHD is much more than a collection of symptoms. It becomes a way of life. In order to help children with oscillations in their attention to optimize how they live an appropriate life infrastructure must be set up. The child's environment must learn to know and understand her; so she can learn about herself. Only then can she fulfill her full potential and face life's challenges with greater ease.

In this chapter, I will detail the steps involved in the therapeutic process and emphasize a few vital details that are essential to understanding and implementing the process. The purpose of the learning-therapeutic approach *Talking ADHD* is to adopt the mindset of informed observation and develop a new language – the language of CHAMP – utilizing imagery. This language is meant to help the child be mindful, identify, understand and verbalize what she experiences. This language, which is based on a solid scientific infrastructure, is highly accessible and enables explaining complex topics in down-to-earth terms. It is meant to serve as a daily language that is incorporated in every conversation and interaction with the child. The CHAMP language was developed in order to assist children and their parents to engage in an open discussion, the goal of which is to help the children feel that they are finally understood. This feeling of being understood is the precious turning point which enables the process of change to take place. Difficulties in understanding the experience of the child and in developing a dialogue about it stem from two main reasons: First, we usually are talking "about" the child and not "to" the child; second, the phenomenon of ADHD is not sufficiently understood, and we tend to interpret, instruct, get angry, criticize, punish and judge, rather than aim to learn and understand it in depth. **The CHAMP model, on which the *Talking ADHD* therapeutic approach is based, was developed in order to speak WITH the child about her experience, as an emotional therapy (see, later in this chapter: The CHAMP Therapeutic Model)**

I have been treating children with ADHD for many years now in my role as a clinical and educational psychologist. My first target is their parents—parents seeking direction and guidance who are frequently frustrated, confused and at their wit's end.

Some parents do understand and are able to manage their children, intuitively directing them in desirable and beneficial directions. Some are untroubled that the child is not realizing her potential and merely wish her to be happy. Often, I encounter low expectations of parents from their children, and of the children from themselves. This is often a sign of a child's low self-esteem, which largely stems from the attitude of the environment towards them. The influence of childhood environments can leave an enduring mark on our soul. We must keep this in mind, particularly given the frequent problematic branding of ADHD. We must not brand the child and file him away in the pessimistic realm of generalizations that depict disorders and handicaps defined by a lack of capability. Pain and joy repeatedly fill me whenever I meet a child with ADHD for the first time, together with her parents. This pain stems from empathy for the parents, who must cope with a very difficult experience, and from the frustration of the child over being misunderstood—his difficulties misunderstood.

Nonetheless, I also feel joy, because I know that there is another way, by using an instructional process which is based on scientific knowledge—the psychological and physiological research of ADHD. This is a process that involves a comprehensive educational-therapeutic intervention in the child's life, which is intended to assist her in dealing with her capabilities and condition in an optimal manner. The therapy is based on understanding mental, emotional and behavioral patterns, and their effect on the "self" and the individual experience. Using it, the child gradually becomes better equipped with the tools necessary to cope, becomes aware of her strength and optimizes her potential. Throughout the process the child's awareness about her difficulties, their consequences and their influence on her emotions and behaviors grows. She will learn to cope, with greater success, with complex situations and challenges. This is a long learning process requiring considerable patience, the ability to non-judgmentally genuinely understand and embrace the child and much practice, but truly anyone can learn it. As it proceeds, the perspective broadens, interpretations of the complexities become more precise, and the awareness that develops directly influences the emotional experience and self-control of the child. The desire to improve day-to-day functional coping capabilities also strengthens.

It is important to note that this is not a traditional psychological clinical therapy but an extensive learning process, which incorporates various aspects of the child's life. Therefore, the psychological education is also aimed toward the siblings and other family members, the teachers, instructors and all the other professionals involved in the child's life. This psychological educational process, adapted to ADHD, underlies the **Talking ADHD** approach.

Parents take center stage throughout the learning process and in the therapeutic model, as well. Some parents understand this and seek guidance that will help them help their child. They are glad to take upon themselves the role of the child's primary therapist and they do well at it. In contrast, there are parents who believe that their child's ADHD means that only the child need therapy. In these cases, I believe the child should be treated only after the parents undergo extensive parental guidance in accordance with the approach outlined here. This counseling will enable the parents to understand the significance and the complexities of ADHD. In this manner, the parent will be able to understand her role and continue to take care of her child in parallel with the professional therapy. It is important for the parent, as the central character in the child's life, to learn the topic and adopt an active approach in treating the child. Parents who do not understand ADHD in depth and are not aware of its specific manifestations and ramifications cannot be aware of the important role they can fill in the lives of their ADHD child and are not aware of their incredible ability to help her.

In this chapter I will propose a means of talking with the child based on understanding and precise observation. These conversations will take place **gradually, in small doses** and in accordance with the circumstances. It is best to mention only one component of the model in any single conversation. Try to find a calm period to talk with the child, not when she is distraught or inattentive. It is important to normalize the conversation—to explain that there are many types of people and, in order to succeed, that it is important for every individual to know herself. Already in this initial stage, imagery should be used. One of them is smartphone imagery— *"You are smarter than the smartest phone—but you don't know all your applications. Just as we need to get to know the various applications to make the most out of our device, so must we get to know ourselves and all of our strengths and struggles, in order to manage ourselves most effectively."*

The role of the parents of children with ADHD, according to the CHAMP model, is based on the following principles:

1. ADHD stems from inborn qualities, **and absolutely does not develop due to bad parenting.**
2. The purpose of parental guidance is not to fix parenthood but to **study and deepen our knowledge of ADHD.** The parents must learn the topic and understand **how** to talk with the child with empathy and understanding to help her realize precisely what she is experiencing.
3. The ability of the parent to successfully manage the child grows as her **understanding** of ADHD deepens. We must remember the obvious—the less the child **is genuinely and sincerely, nonjudgmentally**

understood by the parent, the more **their relationship suffers** and, with time, may be severely impaired. A self-aware parent enables himself to hold a broad and exact perspective, as well as considerable knowledge about the matter. That is how she can become the **active therapist** who can accompany the child day to day and hour to hour, until the child is prepared to accept responsibility for herself. The goal is to create a better interaction with the child.

4. Parenting can be exhausting. But it's not very easy for the child either, especially for one who faces considerable ADHD-associated difficulties and frustrations. The earlier and better the parent studies and understands ADHD, the better **the parent's ability to empathically address her child's difficulties and ease her coping with them.**

5. To truly understand and experience any phenomenon, as is, it must be accepted **without judgment, anger or criticism.** This is why a central goal of parental guidance **is first** to teach the parent, so that she will be able to embrace the child and understand her, and only later speak to her about what she is experiencing.

6. **Developing consciousness** and understanding each of the various characteristics of ADHD will improve the understanding of the complexities and difficulties experienced by the child. This will make it easier for the parent to identify their manifestations – such as forgetfulness, difficulty organizing, outbursts, argumentativeness and so forth – and deal with them.

7. When the parents understand the child and "connect" to her way of thinking and behavior, she will find it easy to "**advocate**" for the child, protect her from the criticism-infused environment and "explain" her to the various professionals and the environment, in general. She will do so until the child learns how to identify and control her difficulties on her own.

8. **The child cannot walk this path on her own.** She requires close daily guidance and companionship. The parent must be there for her until the child becomes her own expert and assumes responsibility for herself.

9. Some parents tend to see the ADHD diagnosis as a permission slip granting their child extra rights, sort of as a **"discount coupon"** which relieves him of certain duties. This attitude should be absolutely rejected in order to avoid impairing the functioning of the child. The guiding principle must be that difficulty results in more obligations, not more rights!

10. In any event, boundaries are mandatory—our children lack internal boundaries, so they need external boundaries!

And from the perspective of the child...

"I am just a soul whose intentions are good;
Oh Lord, please don't let me be misunderstood"

(Bennie Benjamin, Gloria Caldwell and Sol Marcus)

The Champ Therapeutic Model

It is important to explain to both the parents and the children: Individuals must understand themselves to feel good about themselves. When we understand ourselves, we can help others understand us, as well, and can prevent misunderstandings towards us. If I don't like to go to the beach because I am sensitive to the grains of sand, then I had better explain this to my friends. That way, they won't think I don't want their company or cannot swim, and we can go to the pool instead. In other words, when we can explain ourselves, we defend ourselves. Each one of us should pay attention to ourselves and know when we integrate and "flow" with the environment, and when we resist it. Without this awareness, we can cause "accidents" and pay the, often high, price for them, without meaning to. I did not listen in class and did not know I was supposed to bring the equipment for the graduation party. This spoiled the event, and everyone thought, once again, that I was inconsiderate and unreliable. Therefore, it follows that everyone must learn to rely on themselves and take responsibility for themselves. That way, we can act independently, in a pleasant and reliable manner. So, if I know I tend to forget things, I will have to write myself notes and reminders. Likewise, each of us should be aware of their own pace and constantly check to see whether it has been adapted to and is compatible with society around them. As we do not live on desert islands, on our own, we must adapt ourselves to society. If we respond too rapidly, then we must be aware of this, and know that we need to stop for a second and think before we do something, in order to avoid harming others. If we are slow in how we conduct ourselves, we should explain this to society, so that it does not misinterpret our behavior and think us to be lazy, stupid or challenging of authority.

Everyone should pay attention to themselves and identify when a given behavior is appropriate and when it is not. It should be exploited when it is appropriate, and an effort should be made to stop it when it is not. Chattering in class, for example, is inappropriate since it is disruptive. During a break, or an in-class party, on the other hand, it is an excellent icebreaker.

Each of us has strengths and weaknesses, but perseverance and practice are required to achieve awareness of them. The process can be long, but it pays off. Awareness enables us to leverage our strengths to secure the things we want, while at the same time enabling us to consider whether we want to invest in weaknesses instead. We will likely invest in things that bother us and that we want to change. But there are things we will choose in advance not to invest in. The choice should only be performed with awareness. If I am no good at sports, then I will not insist on participating in sports activities—unless I want to because I like the company.

The *Talking ADHD* therapeutic approach is meant to create a new, focused conversation, derived from the basic need we all have to understand ourselves. It is also born from the great difficulty of many parents to start a conversation with a child with ADHD and to help her realize she needs to join the process of developing self-awareness. These parents fear a confrontation with their child or think the ADHD will vanish and difficulties will fade away on their own. A few seek professional help or insist that a professional will talk to the child. I wish to emphasize—the discussion with the child is the job of the parent, and the parent alone. A professional can help in the background, but the parent is the one who lives with the child and "talks with the child on a daily basis." Children, particularly children with ADHD, need their parents in order to develop their own awareness of themselves and their ADHD, and to study the consequences of their behavior. A child with ADHD is confused and finds it difficult to understand herself by herself. She needs a good, caring and supportive instructor—she needs her parent. This is why I see it fitting to teach how to *Talk ADHD* through the CHAMP model. **The therapeutic model – the CHAMP model – is composed of five steps. Their order of application, following the initial learning process, is not hierarchical or serial,** but they are incorporated within one another in order to help the child understand herself. Use of the model is meant to create a new language with the child; to raise her awareness of the characteristics of attention deficit, hyperactivity or impulsiveness; to help her understand herself and to learn how to protect herself. This is a gradual process which takes time.

C	Choose One Specific Component
H	Help (with the "How") via Reflecting, Redefining, Rehearsing and Responsibility
A	Active Adult Involvement in Raising Awareness
M	Mindful Metaphors
P	Practice Makes Perfect

CHAMP: Choose One Specific Component

Separate the specific ADHD Phenomenon from the Child

It is so easy to lump all children with ADHD together into a single category."
The child has ADHD". What could be easier? But what can the parent actually
do with this diagnosis? More importantly, what does the child do with this
information? The general diagnosis does nothing to explain to the child what
she is experiencing. Every child with ADHD has different and unique expressions of the phenomenon, which are mentioned throughout the various
chapters of this book. The great variance is why I am not satisfied with the
general category "ADHD." Rather, I treat it as an umbrella concept—a title
that needs to be broken up into its constituent components and analyzed.
For the diagnosis to be a precise, detailed observation requires learning the
unique characteristics of the child from the variety of different phenomena
expressed by children with ADHD. Only by breaking up the whole into the
characteristics unique to each child, and identifying them through deep insight and precise understanding, can parents and other responsible adults
help children make the necessary changes.

To start the CHAMP discussion, I suggest starting at the beginning—
seeing if the child is ready or able to talk, or whether he feels hostility and
criticism, and is unwilling to start a dialogue.

If the child does not feel ready, then the connection needs to be nurtured
to give him the feeling of safety he requires in order to open up. It is worth-
while talking about variance in general, as a source of color and interest
in life—there are so many types of flowers, birds, fish and people, and the
diversity enriches us! It is important to "normalize" the phenomenon, which
means talking about it as part of a spectrum of human behaviors and to absolutely avoid highbrow, condescending language, or resorting to medical and/
or professional terms. It is important to explain to the child that there are
many other children like her. We must bear in mind that the child requires
considerable time to recognize within herself the oscillations of attention
and energy, and to learn that her attention abilities, and also her ability to
remain still, are not like those of other children.

Another important principle – **don't teach the child how to swim in stormy water** – we tend to talk to the child while she is hyperactive, impulsive and inattentive. This is precisely the wrong time to do so! The child is not available and cannot be attentive in such a condition. We should select one specific manifestation of the child's condition and explain things to her when she is calm and ready to hear us. We should gradually arrive at an understanding with her that in real time, we will use a "code" – an agreed upon signal – as a reminder to help her understand. Of course, if she is about to put herself at risk, she needs to be stopped at once.

The moment we choose to talk about restlessness, for example, and start the CHAMP talks, we need to be able to separate the expression from the child and look at it with mindfulness, *"You are a very positive child—who tends to be restless. I want to talk for a moment about restlessness as a characteristic of yours."* This is how we will help the child develop self-reflection free of burdensome feelings. The parent must repeatedly emphasize the positive qualities of this characteristic: *"Restlessness can be great and is the source of much strength, which motivates you to get stuff done."* But that same quality can also sometimes be disruptive: *"Sometimes, when you are restless, you have a hard time stopping to think."* Another positive quality: *"Your thoughts leap between different associations, and this is a source of imagination and creative thinking."* But, sometimes, this quality can also be disruptive: *"Your thoughts race and you speak of many things at once, and it is hard to follow you."* It is also desirable to help her link between similar situations: *"Thoughts race through your mind at night, as well, and make it hard for you to fall asleep."*

From the beginning of the process, and throughout, we must strengthen the child, emphasize the positive and explain to her that she is not at fault in any of this. Just as any individual is born with her own characteristics, the same applies to ADHD. Sometimes, ADHD is beneficial, and sometimes it is disruptive. It is important to remember that prior to the CHAMP model being implemented, most children were not aware of their ADHD characteristics, since they were born this way and know no other way of life. This is why time and patience are so important in the process of identification.

This is a stage which can last for quite some time, until we help the child raise awareness about these matters. There is no point in pressing the child or trying to push the identification phase along. As I said, the "blanket diagnosis" of ADHD is very broad. This is a generalized diagnosis, and it cannot clarify every individual case precisely. The implementation of the principle, to choose one specific component via precise observation, will lead us to analyze which manifestations of oscillations in attention and energy are relevant in the specific case.

This principle will enable us to perform a precise identification of the phenomena, characterizing special difficulties differentiating our child. In fact, what we are doing is a process of focusing and identifying specific aspects of the general phenomenon known as ADHD. Thus, in the learning-therapeutic process, we can set down practical and feasible goals, rather than battle a generalized stigma, which might just make things worse.

Sheila's Case

Sheila is a five-year-old girl with ADHD. In the "**Choosing One Component**" stage, we will define which of the many components of ADHD Sheila expresses. In her specific case, her two dominant expressions are hyperactivity and impulsiveness. She also has difficulties with attention, but since her most dominant expressions of ADHD are hyperactivity and impulsivity, these are what we will choose to focus on. Sheila's hyperactivity is expressed in her behavior and reactions, as well as in her sequence of thoughts. Sheila is an energetic, bubbly and happy child, who is constantly in motion. She is very restless, and it is difficult for her to listen. Her mind is easily distracted, and she tends to skip from one game to another, as well as from one topic of conversation to another. She knows no other way to conduct herself; this is her internal rhythm.

In accordance with the **"Choose One Component"** stage, Sheila should have it explained to her what restlessness is. We should talk to her about rhythm in general, and she should be helped to realize that everyone, and everything, has their own rhythm—weather has a rhythm, sea has a rhythm, and music has a rhythm. We should help her dance according to the rhythm of music and to notice that music is made up of different types of rhythms. We should help her observe other people and notice their rhythms, and finally we should help her to assess her own rhythm in order to arrive at the realization that her rhythm is faster than that of other people.

At this point we will explain to Sheila the advantages of the fast rhythm and describe to her the cases in which she benefits from her swiftness—she thinks quickly, runs quickly, acts quickly.

Throughout the process, Sheila will learn about her rapid rhythm and will gradually learn to notice when operating in this rhythm helps her, and when it hurts her and is disruptive.

As in Sheila's case, once a child is prepared to speak about the phenomenon, the stage of developing awareness will begin. To help both the child and the parents to **separate one specific component** from the child and treat it distinctly, **it is best we give it a friendly name**—such as "coil-spring" in Sheila's case, and in other ways, as will later be detailed. In order to enable the child to perform an educational distinguishing process, which will be accompanied by greater understanding, we can play games that will help distinguish ADHD expressions such as:

> *"Every time you notice your coil spring, you will get three points."*
> *"Every time I notice your coil spring, I get one point."*

cHAMP – Help (with the "How") via Reflecting, Redefining, Rehearsing and Responsibility

The parent is required to provide the child with considerable attention so that she identify the deregulatory components of the ADHD as they occur, reflect them to the child, and be able to refer to the behavior of the child, her reactions and her emotions. The reflection only happens once the child is willing to cooperate and "make friends" with the specific imagery, and is prepared to talk about it. At this stage, we will summarize with her that, in real time, we will help her to pause for a moment and look at herself from the side, using the imagery we have selected together with her (upon which we will expand in the fourth component of the CHAMP model). This **reflection** will enable the child to pause for a moment, identify and familiarize herself with the phenomenon, recognize its existence and learn how to see it as it occurs. Later, the child will learn to recognize it on her own. The reflection stage is, in my opinion, the most difficult one. The parent needs to "be there" with the child, repeatedly, as the ADHD expression takes place, in order to observe it and reflect it to her accurately—but only after she has confirmed that the child is familiar with the imagery and is prepared to cooperate. This task is incredibly challenging because the reflection must be free of criticism, interpretation or judgment. That is why, in real time, when the children are so challenging (and challenged), my recommendation is for parents to adopt a short, descriptive explanation "eye to eye." Such an explanation, which will also help secure the cooperation of the child, will be based on the precise use of metaphors and imagery (as we will review later). These images will be selected together with the child, in order to help her see herself as others see her and develop her ability to observe herself.

Frequently, it will be necessary to **redefine** the language we use and the terms through which the child perceives her behavior. Since the child soaks up how the environment thinks about and defines her, she may be used to thinking of herself as incompetent, unintelligent, lazy, ill-mannered or violent. In these situations, the distinction, separation and redefinition are important. For example, in cases when hyperactivity results in behavior that is disruptive or disturbing to the environment, some people will think that the child is ill-mannered. We must make clear to the child that we know that she is a good child, with an abundance of energy-*"You are noticing that the 'spring' in your head got loose, and you aren't being attentive to me. I know you aren't ignoring me on purpose, but the result is that I cannot talk with you, and the people around us think you have no manners."*

Another example from the field of emotional regulation is emphasizing the difference between not listening and not understanding. The child did not understand because she was not available to listen—not because she was unintelligent. She needs to be told this repeatedly, because inwardly she thinks that she is not intelligent. *"You are an intelligent child who sometimes finds it hard to listen. Anyone, no matter how intelligent, who does not listen, cannot understand;"*

"Please notice that you did not understand what I said because you were not paying attention. As soon as you were able to focus, I repeated the instructions. This time, you noticed what I said and immediately understood what you had to do."

Likewise, difficulties in writing can be redefined: *"You are not lazy. You are a very curious and intelligent child. You begin to write with great enthusiasm, but notice how you 'run out of fuel' quickly, and then lack the patience to sit down and write what you already know. The result is that you cannot complete your homework. Let's take a break and then continue;"* or

"You have good ideas, but your thought wandered off somewhere else, and so you forgot what you wanted to write."

We must make a clear distinction between the child and her behavior:

"I know that you are a good child and that you did not mean to disrupt, but you were restless, and this influenced the environment."

In fact, we should redefine how we view the child and how the child views herself. Since the child is so used to hearing criticism, she begins to believe it and begins to believe that she is a bad child, that she understands nothing, that she is lazy and so forth. The goal is to help her observe, and to develop her abilities to explain herself to herself—and only afterwards to the environment.

As previously mentioned, the child does not know that she was born different; she does not understand that she acts somewhat differently than others. She needs time to identify her attention and hyperactive characteristics and understand that they are different than those of other children. This is complex and difficult since these qualities are an integral part of her, and she is often not even aware of them. In addition, the dysregulation of attention and energy are not predictable—they are not continuous or constant. Sometimes the oscillations are mild, and at other times they are intense. Via the reflection of the parents, the child will slowly develop the ability to pause and identify the specific phenomena that define her, and will develop the realization that these occurrences are not by her choice—or her fault. This realization will make her coping and functioning in life much easier. Many parents find themselves grappling with the dilemma of who, if at all, will explain to the child, and fear that their words will seem like a criticism or an accusation. I believe wholeheartedly that the phenomenon should be explained to her—without, of course, any criticism and accusation, but solely from understanding and believing that even recognizing the phenomenon will ease her ability to function and cope in her day-to-day life. Understanding each characteristic will help her gradually understand the different components and aspects, and enable her to accept and feel at ease with herself, as she is. When the child recognizes the moment in which inattention or hyperactivity occurs, she should be praised.

"It's so great that you just noticed that thoughts are racing through your head", and she should be encouraged to direct her attention at the phenomenon via positive reinforcement. What she says should be reflected back to her, and her experiences should be legitimized. Such a response by the parent will help the child relax, feel understood and seek to learn more about herself. In contrast, seeking to "hush" the child will generate stress, denial, anger and a general worsening of the situation.

Reflection will help our little Sheila observe and recognize the coil spring within her to confront it. Utilizing reflection such as, *"Notice how you are accelerating and might soon whirl out of control like a thunderstorm!"* she will begin to confront her behavior and responses. When we reflect with her, she will be able to recognize that her hyperactivity was aroused and will be able to respond in a specific manner: *"Please notice that when you feel you need to occupy yourself with something – a* need to move *your rubber ball or some other object – this is a sign that you need to move your body in order to feel good or soothe your restlessness."*

Her parents can tell her: *"We will remind you or show every time this happens to you so that you will finally learn to recognize this phenomenon in yourself and control it."*

Sheila must understand that hyperactivity is an integral part of her. She will learn where she can let go and act freely, and in what situations she should try harder to control herself. Through a gradual process, via reflection, she will learn about herself, expand her consciousness, identify and connect situations, and be able to choose how to behave. Throughout, she will accumulate knowledge, acquire understanding and become her own expert.

> **We need to remember that emotional well-being comes from self-awareness.**

Additional reflective sentences:

- *"Pay attention to your body and thoughts when you are calm."*
- *"You just spaced out of the conversation—did you notice?"*
- *"You seem to be restless. Notice how you move your body."*
- *"Let's play a game in which you need to respond quickly. See if your spring* helps you respond rapidly."
- "Now let's play the 'statues game.' Show me how you moment and control *your 'spring.' You will notice that your abilities improve the more you practi*ce and manage to pause for a *second."*

Once the child learns these reflective sentences, we should continue speaking with them, seeing when the phenomena occur and what triggers them, and ask the child to identify them and report about them; for example: lack of interest, boredom, routine, the child being filled with energy at a given moment, noise and so forth. Do this until the child learns to identify and control or explain herself.

Internal restlessness does not need any reason to occur. Nonetheless, an environmental event can trigger escalation.

chAmp — Active Adult Involvement

This involves active analysis of the central patterns of the child's function-ing and their characteristics, along with thinking about helpful solutions.

Once we have identified a specific way in which the child expresses her ADHD, the parent must actively help the child to notice this aspect and iden-tify it in real time. For example, we might notice if the child is more energetic or "wound up" when she is bored or when we go to dinner at grandma's, or if the spring is less wound up when she is on the phone. It is important to help her notice when the "released spring" is appropriate and effective, such as in physical education class or in recess, but less effective and even disruptive, as when the child chatters in class. It should gradually be explained to the child that if one identifies the cases in which the released spring is disruptive, then one can prepare in advance for them. Once children understand that a given aspect of ADHD does not serve them, we should play games with them in order to help them practice control of this aspect. Adapted games have helped me illustrate to my patients how they could in fact control their own "coil spring." When I have asked them what helped them control it (in order to raise their consciousness), their response was invariably: "Because this is a game."

I explained that, just as in a game, when they are interested in something, they could exert effort and try to control the "coil spring." Later, we spoke a great deal about "how" and "why" the "spring" should be controlled. With greater explanation and proactivity came a greater possibility of their being able to control the aspect of restlessness or inattention that they had learned to recognize.

When they do succeed, they should be praised, and recognition should be given for the great effort they have made to control themselves. It is im-portant to help them release the oscillations of their attention and energy at home, or in other situations when it is less disruptive, and gradually help them learn to limit their expressions of hyperactivity or inattention to these situations and only these situations.

> In Sheila's case, she can be bouncy and run or dance outside to release pent up energy, but she is not allowed to hop on the couch or pester her family about watching television when she is restless.

From the very beginning of the process, the parent or the adult therapist must be actively involved. As mentioned, the awareness of the child about what is happening to her is extremely low, and the parent must realize that this is her own job to explain it to her. Her duty is to acquire significant knowledge of the phenomena, to develop a broader observation-conducive awareness. Knowledge and awareness will lead the parent to help the child accurately identify expressions of the phenomena. The central part of this process is, in fact, for the parent to adopt an active role and assist the child in developing awareness in the analytical process.

The mission of the parent is to understand and "connect the dots," as well as to see the strengths, alongside the specific complexities and difficulties, of their child—all this, in accordance with the knowledge they have acquired about ADHD. They must develop conversations, which include the child, to analyze and find, together with her, ways to improve how she copes with situations she finds difficult. Of course, every analysis and explanation must be adapted to the child's age and ability to understand. Nonetheless, it is very important that analysis of the particular component be comprehensive and include central points that will be comprehensively explained later, such as offering a reference to the element of time:

> *"Do you notice that your thoughts right now are springlike? They are hopping from one topic to another, and you are drifting away from completing the task before you on time."*
>
> *"Your thoughts break off when you stare or daydream, and then you forget yourself."*

These can also reference their regulation abilities –
"Your thoughts race, your impulses take over, and you end up drift-ing away and goofing around",

their relationship with the environment –
"When you hop from one place to another, you also disturb your sister"

and difficulties specific to school –
"Your thoughts race even when there is noise in the class".

The child should be given help to realize that different people treat the same phenomenon in different ways, which makes it even more confusing. The sports educator is very encouraging of great energy and hyperactivity, but the teacher asks the child to calm down; one grandmother insists on the entire family sitting around the table, but the other grandmother has no problem eating while standing. Later we can think up solutions together, such as agreed-upon reminders and other solutions adapted to the needs, abilities and desires of the child.

Back to Sheila: **The active approach** enables dealing with the unique expressions of her ADHD – impulsivity and hyperactivity – while prioritizing. We decided to start with the "spring" (hyperactivity) rather than impulsivity, out of the realization that it would be easier to help her deal with the "spring" and that we should, at first, focus only on it. Success in dealing with it would increase her motivation to continue to learn about herself. Mapping out the phenomenon will help us to prioritize the foci of the therapy, and to devote the required professionalism and precision to learning and coping. The parent should direct Sheila's attention every time this specific aspect of hyperactive behavior springs up, expanding her awareness about which situations this behavior serves her, and in which situations this behavior is disruptive. It is also important to refer to her reactions and to her stream of thoughts, and to **connect between them** for her:

"It is so great that you are beginning to recognize the 'spring' in your body and are even trying to control it. I now want to explain to you that there is also a 'spring' in your head, and that your thoughts hop around from place to place, as well. This can be a great thing, because it means you are full of ideas, but sometimes it can also be disruptive."

We already know that Sheila's main difficulties are with regulation, and so we need to help her pause.

The more the process progresses, the more the parent must **pause** and explain to Sheila the significance and consequences of the coiled spring when she finds herself in hyperactive situations—in her personal functioning, her social environment, her emotional experiences, and other fields relevant to her personality and character.

We must bear in mind that she requires simple, matter-of-fact guidance. Examples and situations from Sheila's life should be used – situations occurring in the home, the playground, classes and so forth – and the main aspects of this phenomenon should be explained by utilizing these examples from her day-to-day reality. The outcome of her hyperactivity, which causes her to hop around for much of the time, should be shown and described to her, to enable her to identify when the "spring" helps her, and when it spoils things for her. She needs to be helped to realize that her difficulty is with pausing, and so, her parents will help her pause, even if it is contrary to her nature. So, for example, when she is helped to realize that the "spring" is also in her thoughts, one can add that if she wants to notice or remember something, she needs to **pause** for a moment. You can practice the pause with her, focus her and ask for her understanding. Afterwards, you can confirm with her that she did indeed listen by asking: "Now tell me what it is that I said." She should be helped to realize that she is capable of listening—when she pauses to listen and is motivated to cooperate.

CHA**M**P – **M**indful Metaphors and Images: Finding Metaphors and Images for the Various Expressions of ADHD

Colorful images and significant and meaningful metaphors from the child's world enable us to link the child's abilities, responses and behaviors to her cognitive understanding. They may also connect the child to her experiences and emotional world. The metaphor is a very simple and accessible tool, and it plays a major role in therapy as it connects between worlds – play with reality, the internal and the external – and thus enables the raising of awareness. It arouses emotions, while seemingly "pushing back" difficulties and limitations. It is a simple aide, which enables connection to complexities from a non-threatening place. Thus, the child's awareness of what is happening to her can gradually be raised, and her thinking about the difficulties she encounters can be deepened and broadened; the reactions, consequences and immediate outcomes can be examined together with her.

The metaphor also connects between cognition and emotion and can be likened to a colorful mirror which the child can both create and observe, develop and gradually see herself within. **It is this connection that develops the insights enabling growth and understanding.**

Some children prefer not to use metaphors. They need a direct and flowing conversation, which will be conducted in a permissive manner free of anger, criticism or judgment. These children do not require metaphors. There are also children who deny their difficulties or are reluctant to accept their difficulties. They too will not enjoy the use of metaphors. Some children won't even be willing to talk, given various complexities and complications such as their denial and refusal to cooperate, language difficulties, introversion or insecurity in their relationship with their parents. Having said that, most children use metaphors wonderfully. Use of metaphors with children has considerable power as a therapeutic tool, but much like other tools, it must be used in accordance with the ability of the child—according to her age and specific needs.

In introducing the use of metaphors as part of a positive discourse, it is always preferable for the child to select the code name—imagery or metaphor. This will make it easier to "connect" to the selected imagery. However, it is desirable that we, the adults involved in the child's life, also come up with imagery that can describe the manifestations of the child's lack of control of their attention and restlessness. In this way, we will formulate a more positive and distinctive mode of thinking and will be able to help the child generate her own metaphors. For example, one of the fathers who participated in a parent's workshop I facilitated chose the name "fun bomb" to describe a situation of dysregulation, because he thought this was a moment which was both explosive and fun! Another mother talked about "popsicle time," which is a moment to take a time-out and chill out with a popsicle she had prepared in advance in the freezer.

Expressions which can describe an energy surplus include **"spring," "turbo"** or **"energizer."** Others include: "You are like **a spinning top;"** "You are as **stormy** as waves in a stormy sea;" "You came into the room swirling like a **tornado**;" "You feel the need to make everyone laugh, like a **clown**."

Expressions which can describe spacing out: "You broke off from the conversation like a **balloon** flying out the window;" "Notice that you are like an **off-the-air radio**."

Metaphors can also be used to reflect assuming control: "Now you are like a **calm sea**, without any waves. The **storminess is gone**."

A future conversation which will include such metaphors will not be accusatory or confrontational and will not include sentences such as *"Stop running around!"*

Such a sentence will be replaced with *"Do you notice that you are still like a turbo engine?"*

Remember, understanding the physiology is important but not as significant when talking with a child. There is no need to discuss with her the chemical activity in her head, and thus, there is also no need to come up with metaphors or imagery for it. There is considerable importance in observing and understanding the distinct characteristics of the child, so that we will be able to describe them for her in simple but precise words that she will be able to see, understand and connect to. In the next few chapters I will detail several manifestations of ADHD, accompanied by additional examples of metaphors and imagery that can be used for each such expression.

Up 'til now, Sheila's behavior "won" her such reprimands as:

- *"Will you stop running around?"*
- *"Are you ready to finally listen to me and stop hopping in front me?!"*
- *"You can't finish even one game from beginning to end."*

Sheila and her parents are all too familiar with the dominant manifestations of her surplus energy and that they are accompanied with many complex emotions. Nonetheless, a real and conscious *pause* has never taken place. Now Sheila and her parents need to find imagery which will describe this "thing" that is aroused within her, which leads her to behave as she behaves. Something that will describe her behavior non accusingly and without any complaints. This imagery should be one that Sheila "connects" to.

Sheila, together with her parents, chose the "spring" imagery. She really connected to the feeling and experience ...

"It's as if there is a coiled spring within me," she said.

Now, Sheila's parents will need to practice communicating new sentences when speaking with Sheila—to begin, explaining to her that her "spring" is extremely vital and full of fun. It is a source of motility, strength and energy, which lead her into action and to do great and wonderful things. At the same time, they also need to show her those situations in which the "spring" is disruptive to her and the environment:

- *"Did you notice that the spring uncoiled again within you, and you find it hard to sit still?"*
- *"I see that your 'spring' is making it hard for you to be patient right now."*
- *"The spring is bouncing right now from topic to topic at lightning speed. You have so many creative ideas! Let's try to help you pause and focus on one of them."*

Our intention is not to use these sentences in order to open up deep conversations about ADHD with the child. Rather, our aim is to trigger certain significant processes which will gradually enable the child to be more mindful. Sheila is learning that she is seen and accepted as is, and that the reactions to her actions distinguish between her and the "spring" within her.

Most importantly, she is learning to identify the moments in which the "spring" within her awakens.

The child learns to gradually identify the shifting day-to-day moments in which the spring within her is awakened. The changes in daily interactions with the child are key to changing her self-perception and they help build better parent-child communication.

CHAM**P** – **P**ractice Makes Perfect Training and Practice for Efficient Therapy

Though I am listing this as the final stage, practice is an integral part of the process and can be used in all stages. Indeed, it **must** be used in all stages. I feel I must emphasize this point because it flies in the face of societal expectations—we live, after all, in a world where the pace of life is much more hectic than in the past. Many parents come to me seeking tools for instant, magic solutions. But those expecting such tools are in for disappointment. The process of developing consciousness by precise observation is slow, ongoing, often exhausting and leads to changes in perception only on the basis of deep understanding and internalization. This is a gradual process that requires much time. Furthermore, the incorporation of the CHAMP language is required in every framework the child is in, and in every therapy she might receive. **It is the constant practice** and implementation of **every** stage over time which triggers the change, developing mindfulness and awareness in the child, and helping the child improve her capabilities with successfully managing day-to-day life. The practice enables the child to understand herself and navigate her impulses:

"You noticed that you were bored, were looking for something to do and started pestering your sister—it's a good thing you noticed that the "turbo engine" switched on. Let's see how you can use the engine to find interest in something else more constructive—like teaching your sister how to play a game, for instance."

This will enable her to take responsibility for her actions, her activities and her reactions. The earlier the process is performed, the more the child's ability to learn and acquire new habits is empowered.

The claim that, with age, ADHD diminishes or disappears is essentially false. ADHD remains, and the requirements of the environment change and develop, becoming more complex and demanding. Without study, practice and accepting personal responsibility, the yearned-for change will not occur, and the child will find it difficult to face the great challenges of life.

PRACTICE PRACTICE PRACTICE

In many cases, the accompaniment of a psychologist or professional in the field is necessary to help generate the required change in perception. Whenever parents feel they have difficulties in managing their child or recognize a difficulty in any specific field, they should consider appropriate psychological counseling. Regarding medication—there is, today, a plentiful selection of medications adapted to ADHD. For some children, medication is necessary; and for others, it may certainly prove helpful. Since attention, concentration and impulse control are required throughout the day and in all life's tasks, we are obligated to provide the child with tools that will serve her effectively and comprehensively. That is why, when we choose to utilize ADHD medication, we should consider the attention and control functions required from the child throughout the day and adapt the medication regime to the needs of the child. Nonetheless, we need to recall that there are no magical solutions. The medications may help the child function, but they won't explain to the child who she really is, what the things are that she does. **External medications do not help us understand ourselves.** Therefore, medications cannot be the exclusive solution to ADHD. In contrast, the more we learn about the characteristics that are unique to our child, and the more we use the CHAMP language to explain specific and objective difficulties to her – learning to "Talk ADHD" in conversations with her – the more she will learn about herself.

In summary—practical principles in the CHAMP process:

- **Connect to the child from a positive premise** — For the most part, the child is bombarded with criticism of her behavior. The parent should not belong to the group doing this. What we need to do is construct a positive premise from which to "normalize" the various phenomena, soothe the child and connect to her. We must first help her see her strengths, advantages and capabilities. This is how we help the child have faith in her abilities and how we can instill in her the faith that we, her parents, are absolutely on her side. Many parents need to study the topic and undergo a process of change on their own in order to reach out to their child with an authentically positive attitude. This is a long, complex process, and it is **strongly recommended that both parents participate in it**.

- **Small successes should be bolstered** — It is important to bolster the functioning of the child by noticing her small successes and emphasizing them. These baby steps are the product of a significant effort by the child. No matter how small they are, we should not take these baby steps for granted or frame them as being obvious.

- **"Don't teach someone to swim in stormy water"** — You should talk to the child when she is calm. It is important **not** to develop a conversation while the child is acting or reacting and is not free to listen to the parent or consider her conduct and actions. We can try to use imagery and metaphors she is familiar with, as a reminder. Nevertheless, don't give up! When the child calms down, we will have to talk about what has occurred. The more conversations you have, the greater the child's understanding, and the greater her potential to learn lessons for the future.

- **Duties, not special privileges** — Often, both the parents and the child tend to see the ADHD diagnosis as a license granting the child extra rights, or a discount coupon absolving her from duties other children are obligated to fulfill. Let me re-emphasize—this is absolutely not the case! A central tenet of my approach is that the difficulties children with ADHD face means they have **more** duties, and certainly no special privileges. Only when the parent accepts the responsibility implied by this approach does the success rate of the learning/therapy rise.

- **Understanding the central cause of the behavior** — It is not easy for the parent or teacher to cope with the difficulties stemming from dysregulation of attention and energy by children with ADHD. Difficulties with regulation lead to extremism, exaggeration and a tendency to dramatize. The child tends to perceive things as polarized-"black and white." There is a clear tendency to drift, difficulties in halting a reaction, and also a general difficulty with the sense of time and functioning according to it. **We must recall that the difficulty with regulation is the primary cause for these reactions, and we must therefore focus on the difficulty and explain it. We need to accomodate, understand, not be angry, not interpret, not criticize, not punish and not judge—as much as possible.**

- **Therapeutic layers** — Different and subtle therapeutic layers are vital in the life of a child coping with ADHD, beyond referring to specific difficulties. Layers such as diagnosis, medical intervention, mindfulness, parental awareness, improvement of social skills, school intervention, educational therapy, technological aids or any adapted intervention to the unique needs of the child should all be incorporated in an informed and guided manner.

- **Group activity** which is specifically focused on learning ADHD helps the child understand what is going on with her. I recommend group therapy for children that is based on a structured process and enables initiating play, or activities that focus on the relevant issues on which we have chosen to work. In the process of play, itself, and in the discussion thereafter, situations and specific difficulties that have occurred can be illustrated. The children see each other as if images in a mirror. It is easy for them to see one another and recognize objective difficulties once these have been separated from their personal emotional context. Furthermore, having a group whose members all experience similar difficulties associated with ADHD encourages openness, which enables participants to reveal feelings of frustration or low self-esteem. This sharing forms a source of support and reinforcement when it comes to dealing with failure and with attempts to learn how to improve functioning.

The therapeutic discourse – **the CHAMP terminology – does not replace any other therapy**, and it is desirable that the therapy of the child be as holistic and comprehensive as possible. Nonetheless, the language of CHAMP is necessary in every therapy and in every encounter with the child in order to connect to her inner world and help her understand that ADHD is a complex affair. Without this discourse, the child will not be able to explain her ADHD on her own and will not actually be able to understand herself. Understanding ADHD is the basis for more comprehensive self-understanding and is what contributes to personality development. This is your chance to start *Talking ADHD*.

THE COIL SPRING

To you folks I must seem like some sort of coil spring:
I jump without warning from thing to thing,
I've got oodles of energy, don't seem to rest,
I twitch and switch poses — with the jitters, I'm "blessed."
On the table I'm drumming — drives you nuts, I don't doubt,
But that's me – I'm a coil spring, 'til I get to stretch out.

I pop up from my seat during school or a meal,
From one foot to the other I spring, toe and heel;
Too wired up to sleep, not a wink, not a fraction,
As I seek out some risk, tempting bait, or attraction;
Chatter and yak all the time without limit,
'Til the coil spring loosens up or gets stuck with me in it.

I know that my springing drives folks up a tree,
But did you know that to focus it really helps me?
When it seems that I scatter and flutter around,
In my head things sort out. I can pin some stuff down.

If when home with my family, there's less need to fight,
I can let the coil spring *spring* and not hold it so tight.
Then I can save strength, when it wants to go bump,
To control it, when needed, and not let it jump.

CHAPTER 5

Talking ADHD — Hyperactivity:

When Everything Happens at Once

This chapter, in my opinion, is fundamental to understanding the various complex phenomena of ADHD and so should be read by all parents of children with ADHD, even if their child is not physically hyperactive.

PART ONE
THE PHENOMENON AND ITS RAMIFICATIONS

Try to imagine that you are participating in a prize-winning television game show: Before you and the other contestants, there is a large, split television screen. You need to carefully observe the screen for five minutes. After five minutes of observation, you and the other contestants will be asked in-depth questions about one of the programs that have been broadcast on the channels shown to you. The clock starts ticking down five minutes. You peer at all the channels, since you have no idea which channel you will be questioned about. You focus first on one channel and then on the other, trying to take in everything and remember as best as you can.

Obviously, there is no chance you will be able to explain the convoluted web of family relationships in the telenovela channel, or the gameplay on the sports channel, let alone spot the turnaround in its second half. Perhaps you will be able to digress on the car accident covered on the news channel, or the touchdown in the football game on the sports channel when the entire crowd rose and cheered, and on several other events that, while perhaps less dramatic, still caught your eye because you were sensitive to a certain story being broadcast.

Oddly and inexplicably, the contestants beside you, who watched the exact same screen you were watching, knew how to answer most of the questions asked by the host. These questions all dealt with the news report on a specific channel. They knew that two news stories were being broadcast while they were watching; they knew the topic of each news story; they knew the gender of each broadcaster; and they even knew that the program following the news program was a thriller.

You are stunned, and don't understand how this is possible. Your self-esteem is knocked down a peg or three. You yearn for it all to be over, to vanish from the sight of the audience and be teleported somewhere, anywhere, else.

You missed out on one tiny detail: You don't know that a moment before the contest began, the gameshow host hinted to the other contestants that the questions that would follow would be focused exclusively on a particular channel.

Now imagine your child. Consider that in her daily life, she has run into countless similar situations. Just imagine how she feels when those around her know what "channel" they should watch, and can stay focused on it, while she does not know what to focus on, or how to do so.

Hyperactivity

We each have our own pace, sort of an internal rhythm that motivates us in our life—much like Vivaldi's well-known *The Four Seasons*, a composition in which each season has a different character expressed by different musical elements, and throughout which there is movement between rapid and slower sections. No section (season) is better than the other, and each has its own distinctiveness, its own character. Hyperactive children are characterized by a rapid pace. They have an overabundance of impulses and simultaneous thoughts that are expressed via hyperactivity. They are inundated in both body and mind with the feeling that "everything is happening at once," and every development pulls them in different directions simultaneously. In hyperactivity, a sense of time is lost, and people act according to what is happening to them "here and now"—no past and no future. The individual does not **stop**, even for a moment, to learn from the past or to plan for the future.

Consider for a moment the primary differences in the personality traits of a shepherd compared to a hunter. The shepherd, patient and forethoughtful, works according to a long-term yearly plan. In contrast, the hunter must respond immediately to a fluid environment. All his senses are tense, and he acts rapidly, lest his hunting expedition fail. Hyperactive children are like the hunter: sensitive to the environment and changes therein; they respond to it rapidly, and rapidly shift position and location. In the past, the hyperactivity phenomenon was perceived primarily as manifesting in excessive physical activity. Today, it is understood that this hyperactivity, which is seen by the outside world as physical, also occurs in the minds of children and adults with ADHD. A rapid sequence of associations and thoughts instantly crosses their minds when they focus, even for a moment, on one particular thing. The child thinks about one thing and … wham! She is already thinking about something else.

Excess of attention and energy instead of ADHD

Hyperactivity, which the "H" in ADHD stands for, represents the excess activity characterizing the phenomenon. **This hyperactivity underlies the diagnosis** and is represented with increased distractedness, and physical and cognitive restlessness. **ADHD is a syndrome which is based on difficulties with regulation**—**excess** attention and vigor in the body and mind, and difficulty in regulating them, as well as carrying **excess** baggage of thoughts and impulses, which generate disquiet. The manifestation of this is copious activity, difficulties in delaying responses, increased distractedness and other attention difficulties. As a consequence of understanding the experience and observing it precisely, I have chosen to use the expression "excess attention and energy" when I speak to children and parents. This is a term which describes the phenomena precisely and positively. "Excess attention"—for the child notices everything and finds it difficult to focus on any one thing or to follow the words of others by listening continuously. I believe that child therapy requires maximum caution, which makes even the name we give a condition highly significant, particularly when we are talking to them.

What are regulation difficulties?

When an individual regulates herself, she can **control** her attention and impulses, and **choose** to act consciously. The ability to regulate ourselves, and control our immediate impulses, gives us the chance to pause before acting, or to think about a given event after it has passed, comparing, analyzing things and learning from them. We learn from past experience how to direct ourselves in the present and towards the future. Regulation enables us to talk to ourselves to control our behavior; it helps us break down the data we receive and reconstruct it into messages or responses—in other words, to perform analysis and synthesis. It enables us to separate reality and imagination. With it, we can expand our imagination, or persist in a given game, class or other, task. Our regulation ability enables us to separate facts from emotions, when we assess a given situation or before we act. We can also understand past events in order to predict the future. We are not born with the ability to regulate ourselves—rather, this is a developmental ability that is achieved over time.

In people diagnosed with ADHD, the frontal lobes, responsible for regulation functions, display low activity or underdevelopment. As a result, functions associated with attention and impulse control are impaired—resulting in hyperactivity, impulsivity and frequent distractedness. Paradoxically, hyperactivity is the result of hypoactivity (underactivity) of the frontal lobes of the brain. The brain accelerates, increasing its tempo to a state of hyperactivity, which is why the child fidgets or chatters. This is actually self-stimulation meant to compensate for hypoactivity in the brain, in an attempt to reach a balance. In fact, the mind oscillates from hypoactivity to hyperactivity. Outwardly, the phenomenon is apparent in situations when the child "spaces out" or daydreams, as well as in situations in which she is restless or overactive and constantly chattering. There are also situations in which the child is quiet, and others in which she gets carried away, exaggerates and takes things to the extreme, and she tends to see situations in polarized, "black and white" terms. She finds it difficult to fine-tune her activity and find an intermediate stage—or even to **describe** "gray" situations. Furthermore, this lack of self-regulation is expressed in the difficulty to distinguish between facts and emotions. Many parents of hyperactive children are frustrated when their children don't learn or internalize what they are told:

"They don't learn from mistakes and don't improve, even when they are repeatedly explained things!"

"They can't successfully make plans and keep promises, because in a moment, everything changes."

At the basis of all of these difficulties lie the child's regulation difficulties. Those, and an erroneous sense of time.

Difficulties in the time dimension are the reason for impatience and restlessness. When these children feel bored, they seek interest and excitement. The difficulty to stop for a moment in the continuum of time explains the inability to refer to the future, and also results in difficulties in delaying gratification and difficulties in persistence in routine. This is accompanied by a lack of awareness of future consequences of their actions in the present, as well as by risk-taking in order to find subjects of interest in their surroundings. Unfortunately, the potential consequence of this behavior is often failing to consider risks, especially when the child is excited. These children find it hard to **stop**, to activate inhibitions or **to choose** between activities, and their behavior **is unpredictable.**

This important information dictates to us the therapeutic approach we need. We must understand that although their behavior is unpredictable, these children are intelligent and capable of coping. They know very well **"what"** they need to do but find the **"how"** difficult to implement. That is why we need to help them in their manner of performance, in the "how", rather than repeatedly teaching them the "what". **We need to explain to them that their difficulty is with regulation and an erroneous sense of time, which is why they need to upgrade their brakes!** We need to rely on the scientific understanding of their difficulties and, when talking to these children, we should focus on **breaks and pauses**, rather than interpret, criticize or judge. We must help them understand this during a "quiet time", rather than amid hyperactive thoughts or behaviors. For this reason, we must reach an agreement with them about a **"code"** that will help them see what is happening in real time, that will remind them and help them understand precisely, so that they can identify these situations and gradually come to control them.

Hyperactivity is the essence of ADHD and must be studied thoroughly—even in children not manifesting hyperactivity.

This reality, of uncontrolled oscillation and difficulties with regulation, can occasionally bring the child to a state of impatience—scurrying about and behaving as if she is being driven by an internal engine. Let us consider, for example, the course of a conversation. As soon as the child thinks she understands the words of her interlocutor, even if they had only started speaking, she will be impatient and find it very difficult to wait patiently until the end of the sentence. As far as she is concerned, she has already heard everything and must now move on—whether by disengaging from listening, or by transitioning to performing some other activity, breaking off contact from her interlocutor or transitioning to some other topic of conversation. This behavior can be perceived mistakenly as rude and impolite, when, in fact, this is not the case at all. It is hyperactivity which triggers this behavior, and we must understand and explain it to those in the child's environment and to the child herself, until she is able to understand it on her own. Hyperactivity is the constant companion of the child throughout the day, from the moment she hops out of bed in the morning to the moment she goes to sleep. She does not stop moving from morning to night, or doing things rapidly, and finds it hard to slow down and regulate herself—mostly not stopping at all. Not stopping to listen to the end, not stopping to consider the consequences of her actions. Without help, chances are low that she will internalize the consequences of her actions without paying a hard price along the way. Her interaction with the outside world is performed frenziedly, with sharp transitions from one thing to another, with impatience and disquiet, which accompany her from morning 'til evening.

Nonetheless, hyperactivity is not permanent and continuous, so difficulties with regulation cause the phenomenon to be both uncontrollable and **unpredictable**, which confuses us and the child even more. Sometimes we will find the child relaxed, more available and focused. For the most part, she will be able to focus on the activities that challenge or interest her extraordinarily (interest and challenge lead to the secretion of the neurotransmitter dopamine, which enables stability and neurocognitive continuity). In contrast, at other times, the child won't be able to hold still for even a moment. The ups and down in her functioning confuse her and those in her environment greatly, and we must internalize that the most expected thing with these children is the unexpected! Life with hyperactive children is like a roller coaster ride.

Does This Sound Familiar?

The moment when our child wants to share thoughts with us about something she went through—but even as she turns to us, her mind gets distracted, and we won't get to hear what she had to say to us. Sometimes, she will come to us and speak her mind, but if we failed to hear or understand her the first time, or if our response did not match her expectations, we will likely hear her mutter something like "Never mind" as she runs to play with a toy that catches her eye.

The positive side — the qualities we tend to forget

When we speak of hyperactivity, we tend to forget all the good things about it: The child has an abundance of energy—energy which leads her, which makes her want to know more, to think outside the box, to take initiative. This is an inexhaustible font of energy, which can serve as a source of strength that spurs us onwards to do and keep on doing. Disquiet and discomfort can interfere, but also can result in a need to change things and create new situations; this is the quality of leaders—and a wonderful energy for life exists at the basis of this child's personality. We need to explain this to the child; **hyperactivity should only be defined as a disturbance when it disturbs the individual or those around her.**

Rapid reactions, energetic activity, improvisation, initiative, willingness to take risks, spontaneity, bluntness—all these are qualities that can be very positive and advantageous if you learn how to channel them in a beneficial direction. This intense mental associativity is a source of original thinking and much creativity. Alongside jumping from one topic to another via endless ramblings, hyperactive children and adults also manage to focus and understand things thoroughly and deeply! If hyperactive children can learn how to use these wonderful qualities, and navigate them to their own benefit and the benefit of those in their environment, they will possess a significant source of strength. There are many additional qualities which characterize hyperactive children, including sharp intuition, curiosity, creativity, sensitivity, charisma, courage, stamina, imagination, initiative and entrepreneurship, humor and wit, purposefulness, activeness, alertness, adventurousness, the ability to persuade and an additional, very important quality—the ability to live in the moment. Every child, of course, has her own unique personality and characteristics, but let us not forget, even for a single moment, the positive side—qualities which are usually perceived as flaws can be positive and beneficial, both to herself and to those in her environment. Let us not underestimate the enormous strength and capabilities of our children.

As a clinical therapist, I am delighted to see hyperactivity! It is indicative of drive and power—qualities that will impel the child or adult to progress in her life, to strive and to fight for what she wants. The hyperactive child is well-suited to coping with the challenges of life, but frequently pays a heavy price along the way because she is not understood by either herself or those in her environment. The good news is that she and they can be spared a difficult, exhausting path—the advantages of her hyperactivity celebrated!

Genetic and Environmental Influences

ADHD is a genetic phenomenon, which is why many children with ADHD are sons and daughters of parents with ADHD. In the past, the scientific tools for diagnosing and treating the phenomenon were lacking, and hence, many parents were not diagnosed in their childhood. However, when their own child is diagnosed, they understand many things about themselves—given the traits they share with their children.

Tales From the Clinic

I was once approached by a mother of a hyperactive child, who had her own symptoms of hyperactivity. Before she even sat down, she began telling me that, when she was an infant, her parents took turns holding her in their arms at night as she screamed herself senseless.

"These were stories which always made us laugh. But when I was pregnant with my son, I felt, even when he was still in the womb, that he wouldn't stop moving. When he was born, we no longer laughed ..."

She continued speaking rapidly and with great excitement, and said the following: *"My son was born with an 'internal altimeter', a very sophisticated altitude meter."*

"Before putting him to sleep we would hold him in our arms to keep him from weeping. The second we put him down, he would burst into screaming, as if the change in altitude was an alarm clock which had immediately woken him up and triggered a screaming fit. It was an hours-long struggle every night to get him to fall asleep. Today, when he is big and understands things, these stories are much funnier to him than to me..."

The genetics of an individual cannot be changed over the course of her life. Nonetheless, we need to keep in mind that the genes responsible for hyperactivity were shaped by the environment—and that the trait **survived.** The trait survived **because it was beneficial**. For example, the more people were alert, vigorous and active in previous eras of history, the fighters who acted swiftly were better able to protect themselves and their loved ones. Endless energy is undoubtedly a survival characteristic. The people who discovered continents and invented great inventions for mankind did so using these powers!

In the modern world, good managers, marketing people, high-tech entrepreneurs and even professional combat soldiers need these hyperactive qualities. These are the people who need and can do many things at once, the witty people who don't stop to think and plan but always surprise others with original ideas. They include the vigorous salesperson, the hilarious stand-up artist, the thrill-seeking adventurer, the tour guide who has an affinity for the great outdoors, the person who searches constantly for a purposeful occupation, and is impatient when sitting in on an interminable meeting, and so forth. These are the people who things seemingly "just happen to"— coincidentally, and repeatedly. They just can't plan things out. Frequently, extraordinary and beneficial things "just happen" to them.

Hyperactivity generates "a different mind" but definitely not an aberrant mind.

So, back to genetics—genetics simply means that a **hyperactive child is born this way**. She does not know anything else; she is not **aware** of the difficulties deriving from hyperactivity. She naturally has a **tendency** to be restless and horse around, to exhaust her interest in things quickly, and to be in constant physical motion. Despite the genetic origins of the phenomenon, it springs up in radically different environments, families and cultures. The same gene can be expressed quite differently. Some cultures and environments can curb or channel hyperactivity in directions which are beneficial to the child. That is probably why the prevalence of diagnosed ADHD is so varied across different cultures.

Sometimes, we can see differences even in the behavior of the same child when she is in different environments. She will express her hyperactivity in a certain way at home, whereas in an unfamiliar environment or in a foreign culture, she will manifest it completely differently. Therefore, **different interactions** of the child with the environment will lead to different behavioral expressions, despite the identity of the specific ADHD associated gene.

The gene cannot be changed, **but its expression can be shaped,** and the child's development can be facilitated. This is the reason there is great importance in how the environment treats the hyperactive child. Our aspiration is to understand the scientific basis of hyperactivity, to study it and to develop an informed awareness of it. The implementation of these tools will enable us to shape an understanding and environmental framework which eventually will be successful in moderating and regulating some of the behavioral expressions of the phenomenon, to explain and improve them for the sake of those in the environment of the child. This requires teaching everyone around the child to exhibit patience and tolerance, and to adjust themselves to the child and her genetic expression. I believe that the parent has the primary responsibility of advocating for their child, studying the topic and becoming the primary therapist of their own children.

Cognitive, emotional, and behavioral expressions of hyperactivity

It is very easy to recognize the expressions of classic hyperactivity. If your child is hyperactive, you probably know some of them closely: The child has incredible strength! They are rambunctious, bubbly, bright-eyed, curious, sharp as a whip and communicative. They are always in motion, restless, quick on the uptake, sharp-thinking, witty, rash and very physically active. Some children speak rapidly, chatter, are extroverted, and tend toward drama and extremism. Some find it difficult to fall asleep, for thoughts constantly race in their head, constantly regurgitating the day that has gone by. For the most part, they can successfully route hyperactivity to areas which suit them, such as sports or outdoors activities. Below are the characteristics of the hyperactive child which are most important to be familiar with:

- Mental excitability — excess mental activity;
- Physical restlessness — the child shifts and finds it difficult to sit without moving;
- His behavior seems to be driven by an inexhaustible motor;
- Many strengths;
- Considerable rambunctiousness;
- Endless chatter;

- Difficulty falling asleep at night due to racing thoughts;
- A stormy temperament;
- Shifting moods — quick to tears, quick to get overexcited and stimulated;
- Impatience and restlessness — short-tempered and often dissatisfied;
- A tendency to exhaust one's interest and move on very quickly;
- A high level of distractedness;
- Thoughts that race and jump from one topic to another in an associative manner;
- Mental tiredness and a feeling of being overwhelmed, with a need for many breaks when preparing homework or doing mundane tasks;
- Constant striving to do things quickly, via shortcuts;
- Thrill-seeking, constantly pursuing challenges, interests and danger, as well!
- Significant difficulty with time management. Experiencing the feeling that "everything is happening at once," which pulls them in different directions;
- Difficulties with regulation — a tendency to bubble over, or to transition rapidly between reality and fantasy, between past and present;
- Difficulty in maintaining sequences of thought and action;
- Immature speech, with a tendency for drama, going to extremes, being swept up into things, generalizations and very harsh comments—all with no ill intent!
- Giving proofs or descriptions of everything in terms of "black and white," with no shades of gray.

Attitude of Society

What hyperactivity and impulsivity have in common is an overload and an unpredictable regulation of impulses alongside the difficulty in dealing with the time dimension. In hyperactivity, everything happens at once, and in impulsivity, the child does not pause before she responds. But in contrast to impulsivity, which constitutes a bad "calling card," the attitude of society towards hyperactivity is far more forgiving and tolerant. These children are captivating. Although the initial interpretation of their behavior is that they are ill-mannered, they mostly do not challenge society with violent outbursts or offensive behavior, and thus are treated with greater tolerance. It is not for nothing that they were once called "rambunctious." Today they might be given nicknames like "energizer" or "turbo engine." Though the use of the professional term *hyperactive* is very common today, most people still do not fully understand the phenomenon. Nor can they distinguish between children who have rambunctious character traits and hyperactive children who have genuine difficulties with the **regulation** that shapes their behavior.

When the behavior of hyperactive children is insufficiently understood, it can result in social difficulties, exclusion from their peer group, and sometimes even social hostility, punishment, rejection and finally, loss, of friendships. Hyperactive children frequently display impatience, generate a lot of "buzz" around them, speak a great deal, exaggerate and take things to the extreme. They speak incessantly, but their speech is often confused and hard to understand. They find it difficult to play according to the rules, exhaust their interest in games all too quickly, and get up and leave—and thus are perceived as insulting their friends. Sometimes, they do things their own way and find it difficult to compromise, to heed social codes and to accept social conventions. Many **misunderstandings** are formed between them and their environment, which is why these children find it difficult to establish social relationships and preserve them. Sometimes, they pester others in order to forestall boredom, not out of any malice. Nevertheless, they can be perceived as bothersome or lacking emotional maturity. This is a sensitive and painful issue which needs to be kept in mind as we monitor the social situation of the child. We will delve deeper into this issue in Chapter 10.

PART TWO
THE CHAMP MODEL FOR MINDFULNESS

For most of us, inner speech enables us to ruminate over, study and learn from past events and mistakes. It helps us think continuously and without confusion. It helps us organize information and directs us in life. It enables us to organize our thoughts to generate a uniform, continuous language (rather than chatter and excessive speech). It helps us resolve problems and conflicts. It also helps us control our behavior and act according to specific rules.

Hyperactive children find it difficult to maintain a continual train of thought, due to their erroneous sense of time and difficulties with regulating attention and energy. They do not pause to organize and develop their inner speech, and thus, their expressed speech often sounds confused, sparse and superficial.

Their inability to translate their thoughts into clear sentences confuses them, as well, and can even embarrass and stress them out.

Their difficulty with developing inner speech negatively impacts the conduct of these children in day-to-day life.

If we understand this and internalize the many significant consequences of this difficulty, we will be able to contain them, rather than being angry or judgmental. We can begin to free up space to try to help them understand what is happening to them and to provide them with focused treatment, which aims at teaching them how to pause and develop mindfulness in relation to their specific difficulties. We must help them understand the consequences of their behavior and aid them in reflecting and developing an inner speech, which will help them soothe and regulate themselves.

The Therapeutic Model: How to Implement the CHAMP Model?

I reiterate: the CHAMP model can be implemented by changing the order of its components, or else, by operating them in parallel—all in accordance with your understanding and reflections.

CHAMP — Choose One Component and Explain it to the Child

As we have seen, a hyperactive child is not aware of what is happening to her, and even if she does sense it, it will be easier for her if we describe the phenomena directly and precisely. That way, she can feel seen and understood for who she is. When she feels understood and not under attack, she will continue to wish to learn from us. Remember that she feels like a "jumbled-up puzzle," and every time her environment is keen enough to regard her with discernment and to explain what is happening to her, she manages to put together another piece of the puzzle and learn more about herself. This self-learning, which connects understanding to emotion, leads to insights. It is thanks to this awareness that she learns to identify and control her thoughts and behavior, that her personality forms accordingly, that she is more self-assured and that her self-image gets stronger. This is why the highest priority should be given to explain the phenomenon to the child, according to guidelines provided in Chapter 4—where focused conversation using the CHAMP model is first introduced, with an example of a restless child to illustrate how the model should be used. We adults must understand that hyperactivity has many diverse expressions, and we are obligated to learn to discover our child's unique expressions of it, so that we can explain to her what she is experiencing.. It is best to begin with normalizing the phenomenon and talking about the concept of **rhythm** in general. As I described in Chapter 4, we need to help the child notice that music has rhythm; that weather, nature, and everything around her has rhythm. We need to help her notice the changes in her own rhythm, as well. She should be told that sometimes she switches in seconds from a slow to a rapid rhythm and that, in other cases, she can regulate her own rhythm. From understanding the differences in rhythm, and to lighten the burden on her and on us, we need to focus on specific phenomena. The manifestations of hyperactivity must first be divided into four specific subtypes. Each will be given a codename specific to the child and to how she manifests her hyperactivity; and we will discuss them with the child one at a time:

1. Everything seems to **be happening at once** and I cannot control the "racing" in my body and mind. Possible code names: "sprinting"; "flooding"; "everything happening at once"; "coiled spring".

2. I feel thoughts racing through my head, or in my body, and find it hard **to pause**, even for a moment. Possible code words: "non-stop radio"; "stop".

3. It is hard for me to **regulate my responses**, and I oscillate between extremes. Possible code names: "surfing", "getting carried away"; "black and white"; "all or nothing"; "my way".

4. I **feel bored** and am looking for something to pique my interest. Code name: "bored now".

If we learn to **distinguish** between these four, distinct hyperactivity manifestation subtypes, we can use them precisely, in accordance with their different expressions. We should always choose only one expression to focus on, until the child learns how to gradually identify and internalize it and can perceive herself as others see her. It is best to begin with the behavior that is easiest to recognize and control, and to bear in mind that motivation is a function of success. I will reiterate—in order to speak with children, we must reach an accord with them by using metaphors.

I explain to them that their head is the most sophisticated phone in the world, and they simply are not familiar with all its applications. If they knew how to operate the applications, they would be able to operate themselves with greater success and efficiency. One can, of course, describe any aspect of this phenomenon utilizing different metaphors that are more suitable to the individual child.

cHAMP – Help (with the "How") via Reflecting, Redefining, Rehearsing and Responsibility

Type 1: When Everything is Happening at Once

We can start a conversation with the child with sentences such as:

"You are an intelligent and curious child, and you have many thoughts constantly racing through your head, as if it were constantly at work without a moment's rest. Do you notice this? I will help you recognize when this happens. What code name can we give this?"

"Have you ever noticed that you are better at chattering than writing? Do you want to understand why?"

"You are moving around and jumping about, opening the refrigerator to see what is in it and moving objects all over the place, as if your body is in several places at once. Everything is happening at once with you."

Type 2: When the Mind, or Body, are 'Racing'

We can start a conversation with a child using reflection sentences like those presented below. **Only later**, once the child has come to recognize these metaphors, can we proceed with focused conversation.

Metaphor: Coil spring

"*Sometimes, you are restless and boisterous, go into overdrive, touch everything and make a lot of noise.*"

Focused conversation: "*We understand that you need to act in this way, but it is disruptive to everyone else. So perhaps we should find a suitable place where you can be restless.*"

"*I notice that you find it difficult to organize your thoughts and to write down what is on your mind.*"

Later: "*I can help you pause and think about how to organize your thoughts and write down what you know.*"

Metaphor: "Race car without brakes"

Focused conversation: "*When you lose control of your brakes, it is difficult for you to think about what was, and you cannot learn for the future. Let's start noticing this together.*"

"*I will teach you to pause for a moment and think about the consequences.*"

Metaphor: Horsing around

"*Notice that you are pushing the pedal to the metal and are starting to horse around.*"

Later: "*If you don't pause, you are at risk of doing things that endanger yourself or your environment.*"

Alternatively: "*In this mode, you can also do things that might jeopardize yourself and the environment.*"

Type 3: When the Reaction is Difficult to Regulate

We can start a conversation with our child using sentences such as:

"Thanks to your super quick thinking, you are sharp and immediately grasp the issues; and, sometimes, you are also impatient to listen to the end. For example, sometimes you already understand what it is all about, even before the person you are talking to finishes speaking."

"We need to pay attention to the 'racing'—such as, for example, when you feel you have already exhausted your interest in something, or that you already know all that is to be taught in the class you are going to and that there is no point in continuing."

Or else, *"for example, when you immediately express your opinion, or go your own way with total disregard for other considerations."*

"Sometimes you tend to get very excited and get carried away in exaggerating your descriptions."

"Sometimes you describe what has occurred in "black and white," because it is all racing through your mind, and you can't center your thoughts."

Later: *"If we notice this together, then I can help you to pause and use shades of gray, as well."*

Type 4: When Feeling Bored and Seeking Stimulation

We can initiate a conversation with the child using sentences such as:

"... let's pause for a moment, notice what's around us and think."

"You are bored and "I think you played the class clown today because you lost interest in the class. When you grow bored, you immediately seek out something else to occupy your interest. I will help you notice whenever this happens."

"You are thrill-seeking now. Pay attention."

Later: *"You are looking for stimulation, something to catch your interest. But you are likely to get in over your head and endanger looking for stimulation—that is why you are pestering your sister."*

Later: *"The next time this happens, I will help you occupy your interest in some other way—whether playing with her, or taking some space and occupying yourself with something else."*

This breaking down of hyperactivity into subtypes is new to you, parents, and it may be difficult for you, at first, to describe to your child what is happening to her without providing her with the "solution." Nonetheless, it is very important to delve into the differentiation process and dwell upon identification and reflection! Remember that this stage is difficult for the child, as well, since she knows no alternative to her habitual reactions! This is how she was born, and this is how she manages herself in the world. You can play a game or encourage the child to tell you or point it out every time she recognizes a hyperactive behavior. In this manner, one can collect various examples of each of the different expressions. She should be emboldened every time she identifies them manifesting:

"Oops, I just noticed I need to take a pause!"
or *"I am looking for something to occupy my interest"*
or *"I am getting swept away or inundated."*

CH**A**MP — **A**ctive Adult Approach: Helping the Child With Taking a Pause

Hyperactive children do not pause to internalize what has just happened. They jump from one thing to the next, sometimes even before the previous event has ended. This is the reason they often reach no conclusions about what has just happened, draw no lessons from it for the future, and identify no outcomes, let alone plan ahead in accordance with these conclusions. They do not pause to internalize yesterday's conversation, or to understand why their friend was injured during the game, or to understand why they got a low grade on the test they spent so much time preparing for, or to reflect on how their friend was insulted by what they told them. They charge forward into the next thing, and do not understand the need to pause and reflect on what was to be learned from it. The mere **performance** of this pausing is difficult for them. They do not "waste" energy on something so difficult for them, whose importance they do not even recognize.

When we know that the difficulty is in the brakes, **we must help them take a pause** at every opportunity—pausing, so that the child can ask herself where she is going, what she wants, what was said, what she is looking for, what her friend meant, and so forth. The process of understanding hyperactive behavior, and the internalization that it is necessary to learn how to pause and think prior to a response or following an incident, is a long, and ongoing, process. The role of the adults surrounding the children – the parent, the teacher, the guide, the instructor or the therapist – is to repeatedly reiterate for them the new way of operating, which generates pauses in the continuum of self-management. This should be done via non-critical explanations, in a way that lets them know and feel that we want to help them.

Without external assistance, the children will find it very difficult to learn a new way of behavior that includes pausing and internal speech, and without pauses, they will find it difficult to learn from their mistakes. In every explanation, the principles of the CHAMP model should be used, and depending on the stage the children are in, the different issues should be linked, while emphasizing their strengths, their positive behavior and their every success.

We can *use sentences such as:*

- *"Well done! I am very proud of you for pausing for a moment and listening to me. I know this took a great deal of strength out of you."*
- *"I feel we are on the right track, that you are managing to stop and think about what has happened."*
- *"You have learned well, and learned your lesson, even if it was difficult for you. We will slowly learn to pause in order to generate a change in the future."*
- *"You identified the 'racing' and were even able to pause, think for a moment and separate between what happened and how you felt. You were able to perform an accurate assessment of the situation."*

Later, we will help her connect between the various situations in which she is able to pause:

- *"I see you are managing to notice the 'coiled spring' situation—you noticed the released 'coil spring' and were able to stop it in time, just as you identified your racing thoughts and were able to slow down and think in a continuous, uninterrupted manner."*
- *"You paused and marked the important sentences in the text. Now you can summarize them and prepare for the exam properly."*
- *"You are beginning to notice your rhythm, control your impulses and talk to yourself—this is wonderful!"*

- *"You keep on asking when we are going to visit grandma and find it difficult to stop talking about the visit. The thought of this visit clearly excites you … Try to quietly think and talk to yourself about it … You can think about what you will do there, and try to guess what surprises she has prepared for you …"*
- *"Did you notice that you precisely identified the moment you felt inundated? You paused, took a deep breath and even asked to take a moment to think … When you were calm, you were able to think anew and perform a correct evaluation of the situation. I am so proud of you!"*
- *"I felt you were restless; you took a break, walked to the garden, ran, released your tension, and returned."*

It is quite likely that the children will soon tell us:

"Enough with this tedious pestering already!" or something similar. I, too, during my meetings with the children feel that I am "tedious," but I know that this is a very powerful tool, which can help them acquire and internalize the strength that is imbued in pausing, and which will enable them to respond differently—this is why this should be practiced repeatedly whenever they encounter a situation that requires pausing before responding. This task is difficult for parents to perform. Their tendency to be purposeful and say something "educational" or judgmental, or to speak out of anger, is perfectly natural and understandable. But now they must learn how to respond differently. One must bear in mind that the things that are so understood by most of the population are not clear to these children, because they are not aware of them! They should be helped to develop awareness by us repeatedly reiterating the basics: Their behavior is uncontrolled, unpredictable and not functioning of their own choice. Should we expect them to act in accordance with the rules without developing their awareness of this area of difficulty, then we will not be able to reach them effectively.

CHA**M**P – **M**indful Metaphors: Using Metaphors to Raise Awareness

Once we explain hyperactivity to the child to raise his awareness of it, it is important to develop her self-identification capabilities. Again, we need to remember that **she is not aware that she is hyperactive**—this is her usual pace. This is the reason she needs to be helped to identify situations within herself in which this impulse is raging within her. When the child's awareness about the phenomena is raised, it is best to give it a friendly name the child can connect to and accept.

I like to use metaphors, because they facilitate communication and lead to insight, but some prefer to speak eye to eye.

After we secure the child's cooperation and manage to find, together, with much humor and patience, a name for the specific phenomena she deals with, there is a greater chance that she will be willing to hear what we have to say—in other words, for her to be prepared to learn about her difficulty. We know our child, and we must select, together with her, a friendly metaphor. This way, we can use it as a "code name" in real time. In-depth explanations should be provided to the child when she is calm and attentive and should be adapted to her age and ability to understand. When I worked with young infants, I used concrete reflection—I found myself running with them and speaking rapidly, and saying "fast," and then walking and speaking slowly, and saying "slow," so I believe one can work with every age.

The metaphor used must be associated with the behavior being expressed through distractedness, hyperactivity or jumping from one topic to another. Below are several examples of imagery which can be used:

Split-Screen Television

Remember the game show at the beginning of the chapter? One can use this simile, but slightly differently:

"Your head is like a new, highly advanced split-screen television. You are a curious and intelligent child, and constantly switch between the channels. You enjoy being in several places at once, and are able to enjoy many programs at once, but you haven't watched any of them from beginning to end. Should you be asked what was on a given program, you will not know how to answer, not because you do not know, but because you did not watch the program continuously. On the other hand, I noticed that when you are really interested in a given program, your curiosity enables you to persist and watch it from beginning to end."

When we want to reflect, we can say something like:

"Notice now how you are jumping from topic to topic, like flipping across different channels on TV."
"Notice now that you are immersed in the book and forgetting to perform your tasks."

You can also ask the child to enumerate or write up all of the examples she is familiar with that are associated with the "split-screen television" and expand upon them—when the "television" helped her and when it did not.

Coil Spring

We see the child doing everything hectically, not remaining long in one place, and almost running from one thing to another, as if her body contained a faulty coiled spring which has suddenly and unpredictably released.

It is this "coil spring" which leads her instantaneously to abandon what lies before her and to jump to another place or thing. "Coil spring" is a cute metaphor which most children easily connect with. There is nothing negative about it, and its energy is powerful:

"Sometimes you are like a 'coil spring'. The coil spring is at its best when we play or mess around, but sometimes it can get loose, uncoil and bounce all over the place, in less appropriate situations. A coil spring is an excellent thing, but you need to identify when it serves you well and inspires you to act in the best way, and when it is not so good for you. Sometimes you leave everything and jump to the next thing before you are done. Often, you harm yourself because you cannot persevere or complete a task. People around you do not understand why you don't finish what you have started."

We can also show the child how things appear from the outside:

"Think about what would happen if, in the middle of preparing on omelet, I would suddenly start watching television, and forget the omelet on the frying pan ... What do you think would happen?"
"Every time I see you jumping from one thing to another, I will remind you of our codeword, 'coil spring', until eventually you learn to identify these situations in yourself, and to control them."

When we want to reflect, we can state a sentence such as:

"Today, you were very successful in controlling the 'coil spring' and now you can unleash it at home."

The child also can be asked to enumerate or write down all the times she noticed the "coil spring" and expand upon them—when the "coil spring" helped her and when it did not.

Race Car

"You are behaving like a powerful, cutting-edge race car, and you get everywhere at lightning speed. You have many strengths, but occasionally you have a hard time pausing or slowing down, and this is what sometimes results in difficulties. The car (you) is highly advanced, but I think you need to think about how to upgrade your brakes. What do you think?"

When we want to provide them a mirror, we can say a sentence such as:

"You are beginning to accelerate."

And one can, of course, enumerate other examples in which this occurs.

CHAM**P** – **P**ractice Makes Perfect

As we practice, we will repeat all the CHAMP components. I very much recommend making use of the reflection tool, which is one of the most powerful tools we have in pointing to the situation and demonstrating how the child conducts herself, so that she can recognize it on her own.

The child experiences hyperactivity but it is such an integral part of her that she does not know how to identify it "from the side" and explain to herself what she experiences. We need to reflect this for her repeatedly, until she is able to achieve awareness of the moments when she is driven by her excess of rampant impulses. The goal is to lead her to identify these impulses, understand them and verbally express them, and to learn how to regulate her behavior. It is advisable to help her focus precisely by dividing her hyperactive behavior into its four distinctive subtypes, without any judgment or criticism, while carrying out a positive, constructive dialogue.

Type 1: When Everything is Happening at Once

We can use sentences and metaphors such as:

> *"Your thoughts jump from one issue to another, and you have plenty of highly creative ideas."*
>
> *"You have hawk eyes, and I see thoughts running through your head when I look into your eyes. You immediately identify what is missing in the game."*

Type 2: When the Mind, or Body, are 'Racing'

We can use sentences such as:

> *"You immediately approach the task without stopping to plan ahead, so you have a hard time stopping to organize your thoughts or homework."*
>
> *"You think with lightning speed and reach conclusions all at once. It is better to pause now, take a break, and reexamine the issue later."*
> *"You've worked hard, you feel overwhelmed and you understand you need a break—well done!"*

Type 3: When the Reaction is Difficult to Regulate

We can use sentences such as:

> *"You are excited and are speaking about everything at once, and this confuses me. Let us try to think about what you want to say. Let's make some order out of things."*
>
> *"You are getting swept away and exaggerating—let's try to moderate your reaction. It wasn't 'a million'. What you want to say is 'a lot'."*

Type 4: When Feeling Bored and Seeking Stimulation

"You are bored again, and as a result, you are seeking stimulation and wandering restlessly around the house."

"You are bored now and endangering yourself. Let us try to find interest in something else."

Redefinition is important throughout the process and should be continued also during the practice stage, so that our children understand themselves and can protect themselves. To this end, we can use sentences such as:

- *"I know you are a very sociable child and that you meant to play by the rules, but suddenly you had a new idea and you immediately implemented it. It is hard for you to stop and postpone your thoughts and impulses when they suddenly emerge. This jumping between thoughts can sometimes be good for you, but on other occasions, it can be disruptive..."*
- *"Sometimes you unpredictably become restless, and that leads people around you to think you are being deliberately disruptive. We must explain to the environment that you need help in order to relax."*
- *"You understand perfectly but are making the wrong decisions due to thinking rashly."*

- *"You and the teacher need to understand that the endless chattering is the result of thoughts that need to be rapidly released, not bad manners. Only once you are both convinced of this can we find a solution together."*
- *"You are a smart girl, and I am confident in your abilities. You find it difficult to deal with the racing thoughts in your head and to organize the information coherently, and that is why you find preparing homework to be so difficult."*
- *"You don't mean to pester when you endlessly beat the same drum. You repeat yourself because repetition helps you focus on the topic. This way of thinking enables you to delve in depth into every topic you choose. Nonetheless, you need to learn how to realize when your repetition is disruptive to you and those around you."*

The Parental Role in Mediation

The Car Race

Imagine yourselves to be race car drivers in a major competition. Your red car is on the same track as the other competing cars. The winner is the first to complete 20 laps of the racetrack. Usually, over such a rapid and long drive, the tires wear out and need to be replaced. Every car must pass through the pit stop several times to ensure everything is sound, and to replace the tires, if necessary. The starting pistol is fired, and you launch forward together with the other cars. After a few laps, certain drivers start pausing at the pit stop in order to examine and replace their tires. Every driver chooses when to stop at the pit stop. There is no standard procedure to the pit stop and, obviously, the cars do not pull over at the same time. Every time you compete a lap and pass the starting line, you see other race cars continuing to circuit the track. You briefly consider pulling over at the pit stop. You are very excited, body pumped with adrenaline, and you imagine the signaler waving the flag, marking the final, decisive lap, at you. You are constantly tempted to proceed to another lap rather than pulling over and inspecting the vehicle. With every lap, you avoid pulling over, and the risk of the tire exploding, forcing you to leave the race, grows. Nonetheless, you keep on driving. Now let us consider the children:

In the first lap, your children didn't even know that the tires could explode if you don't stop to replace them. In the second lap, they knew but thought they would manage. In the third lap, they intended to slow down but continued because they could not withstand the temptation not to. And so it was—also in the fourth, fifth and sixth laps. They had yet to learn that without the strength to stop, they could never win.

They need your help.

A considerable portion of the child's difficulties is caused by lack of understanding and lack of acceptance by those around her. Though awareness about attention and hyperactivity difficulties has risen, true understanding of the phenomena, of the difficulties and hardships experienced by the child, remains far from optimal. Our task, as parents, is to deepen our own awareness and knowledge, as well as those of the professionals surrounding our child and of her peer group—especially broadening the knowledge regarding her specific needs. Where she still encounters difficulties, we must be her advocates—to understand and help her to ask for what she needs. Sometimes, precise guidance and understanding will do much to improve her achievements and will greatly ease her path and protect her. For example, it is not enough to inform the teacher that our child is hyperactive. She must have it explained to her what specifically happens to the child:

"You know it is difficult for her to keep to her seat. Maybe you can decide on a break in the middle of the lesson? Can she perhaps be permitted to go to the back of the class and stand there when it is hard for her to concentrate, without disturbing the rest of the class when she feels the need to move?"

During the bus ride on the class trip, the teacher can be asked to permit your child to squeeze a rubber ball, to scribble in her notebook or to play, so that the long ride will be easier for her. A project with the child can also be initiated—a project on a topic she is interested in, and which she can present in class. This helps make the classroom more interesting and challenging for her, enabling her to mobilize herself to the task. Please note that these explanations are not a request to give your child a free pass. All they are meant to do is to help those in her environment understand her and adapt to the challenges she is confronted with. But, at the same time, the child must also be made aware of her hyperactivity and directed to channel it into desirable and productive channels. Our children oscillate between extremes and are unfamiliar with the middle ground. They rapidly move from hypoactivity to hyperactivity. Due to difficulties with regulation, it is very hard for them to find the middle ground. They will stand motionless in a single location and then suddenly run elsewhere. We must reflect to them what is happening to them and what they are doing, and teach them that there is another way of doing things—matching their activities to the requirement of the situation, and teach them how to regulate themselves through activities without going to extremes. To use "bicycle riding" as a metaphor, the child with ADHD is always in only one of two conditions: Either she is standing in place, or she is racing uncontrollably down the bicycle path, on the verge of careening out of control. We need to teach them that it is also possible to ride sedately, adapting their pace to the conditions of the path and to the needs of the passenger.

To reiterate yet again—the hyperactive child is born this way. Since she knows nothing else, it is very hard for her to understand that she can conduct herself at a different pace, and that other people have a different pace. This is why the challenge facing parents is so great. Only working over a period of time – which will include reflection, explanation and support – will teach the child about herself, grow her awareness, help her achieve self-control and moderate her outbursts of behavior. We must help her understand that she has great strengths and that she can, by utilizing the proper pathways, express these abilities to their full potential. These pathways include sports, preparing for events, initiating projects, developing drama and acting skills, and so on.

Difficulties with regulation and a false perception of time can have many ramifications. If we develop awareness about these ramifications, we will understand how important it is to develop a framework with clear rules for the child. We must insist on the child learning how to pause, think and develop an internal dialogue.

Impact on the environment

The behavior of hyperactive children may disturb their surroundings. Although the children do not mean to be disruptive, their behavior certainly can be. This situation can worsen if their environment includes people who tend to interpret their behavior in an incorrect manner and see them as ill-mannered children. In order to help our children, we must identify the elements of their behavior which are disruptive to their environments—and teach the children how to recognize them.

Examples:

- One can say to a child who endlessly plays with her ball:

"You constantly play with the ball because you need to release energy and the playing soothes you. That is excellent. You can do that as long as this does not disturb anyone else."
"It is great that this helps you cope, but you must not disturb other people, so it is best for you to play in your room."

- To a child who cannot stay in her seat for the entire class, you can explain and recommend the following:

"Perhaps you should find the proper time to explain your difficulty to the teacher and ask for permission to stand in the back of your class when it is very hard for you to sit down. Perhaps she herself will suggest that you leave for five minutes in the middle of the class."
"In any case, you must find a good time to find a solution together with your teacher. She will tell you what is possible and acceptable for her. It needs to be something that does not disturb the other students, and which is not disruptive to the class."
"I have an idea! Maybe we can prepare a presentation for the class and explain to them about the 'coil spring'?"

All too often, hyperactive children do not "see" those in their environment. They are so excited and occupied with what they see in the moment, that they don't even notice the person standing next to them. It sometimes seems that they are egocentric, self-centered or uncaring of the people around them.

On the contrary—they are extremely sensitive, but their hyperactivity leads them to occasionally overlook those next to them. It is important that we explain and demonstrate to them that their behavior can disturb those around them and be misinterpreted. It is important that we guide them to find non-disruptive solutions, and to do so, if possible, in cooperation with other children and adults.

Social Difficulties

Earlier in this chapter we detailed the social consequences of regulation difficulties. Now, knowing that social difficulties are the result of regulation difficulties, we need to explain to the child that she is sociable and loved, and that we know one other thing that other people are not aware of—her difficulty with pausing. Here is our chance to help the child understand this specific point, redefine it and connect it to her social conduct.

If the child does not stop for a moment to separate reality from emotion and insists that whatever she felt is what actually occurred, she is perceived as "unreliable," though deception was not her intent. By the same measure, should she decide on different rules in the middle of a game, due to a combination of creativity and lack of focus, other children won't want to play with her. If she expresses impatience or restlessness because she already came to understand the topic long before, they do not understand that she is getting bored. We must repeat, remind her and help her develop awareness of her specific regulation-associated difficulties, her inaccurate sense of time and her need to repair or upgrade her brakes. We need to help her pause and internalize their consequences, while keeping in mind that nothing is obvious.

"What is so hard for you to understand?" parents repeatedly ask and wonder. No, it is not obvious, and even when it does begin to become clear to the child, it takes time for her to internalize it.

- *"Thoughts are racing through your head just like your legs move when you run, and your friends are finding them hard to follow."*
- *"You should notice when you begin to get bored, impatient or restless—for example, when you move around in a way that is disruptive to the environment, when you get up in the middle of a meal or when you suddenly disappear."*
- *"Sometimes I can see your thoughts racing around in your eyes. Your friends might think that you are confused or that your mind is elsewhere."*
- *"When your thoughts race away, it is hard for you to listen or remember. Perhaps you should explain this to your friends."*
- *"Your friend just raised an idea and you immediately leapt in headfirst and treated it as a fact. This was very off-putting for her, and she is afraid to suggest any other ideas to you."*
- *"Pestering people is all about looking for stimulation, just like working on the project you love provides you with stimulation and interest."*
- *"You understood what your friend said very quickly, and now you are displaying impatience towards her. She feels like you are pressuring her."*
- *"Notice that you are bored now, seeking stimulation, and pestering the dog. Let's think about how you can occupy yourself with something positive. Maybe you can take the dog for a walk outside?"*
- *"I noticed that you paused and learned from your past experience with your friends. Well done!"*
- *"I noticed that you ran out of patience to play and politely asked to take a break and return later."*
- *"You now feel as if you have exhausted your interest in the class and do not want to continue with it. We will talk about this when you are calmer, and then I will detail to you the purposes of the class. We will not end it."*

Difficulties With Falling Asleep

For the hyperactive child, falling asleep at night is not a simple task. Her head continues to "work" at a rapid pace. She reconstructs the events of the day, looks at the room and the walls, hears the voices within the house and outside, and plays with her teddy bear. She pulls her covers off and on, turns from side to side and cannot fall asleep.

Tales From the Clinic

A mother who visited my clinic described her son with the following words:

"He begins to run as soon as he gets up in the morning. Throughout the day, he scampers from place to place. He watches television standing up, runs from the living room to the kitchen to grab a snack, jumps to his room to get his teddy bear. When night falls, and it is time to go to sleep, he restlessly shifts in his bed, not stopping for a moment. He sits up, he lies down, he turns around, he moves the teddy bear here and there, and then turns around again—until, suddenly, as if a string is being pulled or an electric switch pressed, he falls asleep. Just like that, in an instant."

Due to their difficulties with falling asleep, it is highly recommended that a regular routine be maintained for hyperactive children. It is very important to keep them to a regular bedtime, deliberately plan out their sleep, and help them understand the need to calm down before they go to bed. This is why it is desirable to begin toning down activity around the house an hour or two before bedtime. The child should be told that screens stimulate their minds and prevent them from falling asleep. This is the reason it is best they get used to going to sleep without watching television or some other screen. It is best to ensure there is no loud music when the evening preparations are underway, and it is also recommended to "let off steam" in the late afternoon by walking, running or doing other sports. During bedtime preparations, it is recommended to dim the lighting in the house. This improves chances that the child will reach her bed in a calmer state. One can make use of reading a story, meditation, guided imagination, massage or any other method of relaxation. This will make falling asleep much easier. Some children ask their parents to stay with them until they fall asleep, sometimes until a very late age. Since each child is a world unto her own, a special and unique case, I won't go into such sweeping recommendations. Rather, I will merely emphasize that the child's request derives from a genuine difficulty with falling asleep. This difficulty obligates us, the parents, to be attentive, and to help the child settle down in any beneficial way, treating her requests with respect.

Hyperactivity and Learning

Hyperactive children have no patience for words, for sequences, for continuity or for processes. They have no patience to stop in order to elaborate on a verbal message or to break down and reassemble information. They lack the patience required to hear out explanations, to consider their responses or to write out the long solution to the arithmetic assignment. They rush through the exam, run out of the classroom as soon as the bell rings, write with excessive conciseness, make no entries in their diary, read quickly, do not dig in and, so, achieve only superficial understanding, and so on. It is important to help them form associations and understand the importance of pausing to reflect, regulate themselves and persevere with a process until it is completed. Most hyperactive children do well in their studies in the short term but do not develop long-term learning habits, since most are rash and find it difficult to slow down or stop their hyperactive behavior. Their achievements will therefore probably be impaired at some point in their studies. Most people, neurotypicals included, do not derive much pleasure from things that require much effort on their part—and this is truer still for hyperactive children. One may expect them to make efforts to avoid such activities or else refuse to make any effort at all. They should be encouraged, therefore, to acquire learning habits as early as possible and to appreciate the efforts they have undertaken and should be helped to understand the payoff of coping, perseverance and putting in the effort of overcoming adversity. Given their lack of patience and difficulties with perseverance, the school years are a very challenging period for hyperactive children and their parents. Take reading, for instance. This is a basic activity required for almost every field of study in school. This is a relatively simple activity that requires little effort for a child without any learning difficulties, who does not suffer from hyperactivity. In contrast, for many hyperactive children, this is a difficult, sometimes impossible task, and therefore they try to avoid it. It is important that we keep in mind that the challenge is in the performance of the reading activity—not in their reading ability. The difficulties associated with hyperactivity deny the children the patience, focus and persistent attention required for the reading task.

As I noted, most hyperactive children face a little difficulty in school. But let us not be deceived—this does not mean they are anywhere near realizing their full learning potential. Hyperactivity can impair their academic habits and achievements, even without any apparent struggles or learning difficulties; it mostly creates a dissonance in function. There will be fields in which the child excels, and others in which she does poorly—even very poorly. Both the child and those around her have a hard time understanding and accepting this dissonance. For example, the child may not understand and be troubled by the fact she is so very successful in mathematics but finds it so difficult to answer a question in history. She should be told that solving mathematical formulas is easy for her because she instantly makes the calculations in her head, whereas history is more difficult, because it requires her to listen to many words and details in a sequence. Sometimes, the gaps will be apparent even within the same field. In mathematics, for example, she may find it easy to solve formulas but find it more difficult to solve word problems. Once again, we can help her understand and connect between things by explaining to her that she is good in arithmetic and solves formulas superbly, but she has no patience to follow the text or make links between the data in the word questions, which is why she has a hard time. The greater the gaps in her self-functioning, and the greater her intelligence, the greater her frustration. The more we explain to her, the more she will understand herself—we will be able to encourage her to cope and avoid getting stressed. We, the adults, need to understand that the specific gaps are a result of hyperactivity, which is expressed in different and specific ways. We need to highlight her abilities and the fields where she is strong, and explain to her where her difficulties lie and what they derive from:

- *"I am very proud of how rapidly you pick up arithmetic. This very same rapid intake and thinking is what makes it difficult for you to write down the answer in social studies … It is obvious to both me and you that you know the answer well, but you lack the patience to pause, organize your thoughts and put them down in writing."*
- *"This same difficulty with the concept of time interferes with history, when you need to remember dates and sequences of events."*
- *"You have no patience to think in **sequences** or remember countless details in an organized fashion, such as dates or long descriptions. However, if you care about succeeding, I will help you adopt learning habits that will enable you to overcome this."*

Note that a precise explanation of the issues is required for the child to understand and mobilize herself to make a change. This reflection, and a precise and empathic explanation have great significance. They are what helps the child feel understood. If we reach her soul, her pain, and are able to explain to her specific difficulty, if we are sufficiently precise in our understanding of her experience, then, and only then, will she understand that the process we are promoting is in her best interest. Then, and only then, will she seek to learn from us, to cooperate with us, and revere and respect us.

The problems hyperactive kids have with studying do not derive from difficulties with understanding and cognition but from their varied manifestations of hyperactivity. Since hyperactivity is expressed in all fields of life, every opportunity (not necessarily academic) should be exploited to explain the essence of the difficulty. We must show the children how this difficulty is expressed and offer suitable solutions. When the difficulties are related to their studies, we must teach the child how to learn, instilling them with learning habits and effective learning strategies, as we explain to them the essence of their hyperactivity-derived difficulties. For example, hyperactivity leads to distractedness, and this can lead to forgetfulness and disorganization. We must reflect the distractedness as it occurs and point out the difficulty in maintaining a functional sequence, which is at the root of the difficulty with organization. To make things easier, we can identify, together with the child, technical aids, which can help her organize and handle the required activity. It is very important for us to notice every success of the child, both large and small. From the side, it may be difficult for us to notice how much effort the child is investing to slow down, stop and think.

Even if all she remembered to do is check her bag before going to school and ensure she has everything she needs, this is a significant success. We must remind ourselves that sometimes the effort required from our child to perform small actions is quite significant. We must not sell her efforts short, and that is why it is so important for us to stop and praise her for any success.

Using Games

Games are the best! They are an incredible tool for reflecting and deliberately demonstrating hyperactivity-associated behaviors. Games create situations enabling the development of awareness and the practice of pausing before responding. Games help the child maintain control over her impulses. They prove to her that the task is, in fact, possible if she would only make the conscious effort to "order" herself to stop. You can see expressions of hyperactivity in almost every game. It is important that we adults learn to take advantage of the opportunity to pause, talk, reflect and highlight situations where hyperactivity serves the child, and work on improving this function when it is disruptive. Below are several examples for games that can be played at home, in the classroom and in children's groups.

- **A point-scoring game** (to develop awareness and recognition):
  As a continuation of the metaphors mentioned throughout the chapter, we can play or invent a game in which the child tries to identify when she is in a "bouncing coil spring" state, or when her head is in a "split-screen television" mode, when she cannot focus on any single thing.
  Every time the child identifies these states and points them out, she wins three points. Every time the adult identifies and calls them out, she wins a single point.

- **'Here comes the Tsunami!'** (to demonstrate the advantage of hyperactivity):
  Define two zones.
  The first is the land zone, where the game starts.
  The second is a mountain by the beach, which must be reached at top speed when the tsunami hits.
  Once the signal (a whistle, a ringing bell, or a hand wave) is given, everyone must run from the beach to the mountain.
  "The fast responders" win, thanks to hyperactivity—but, if they jump the gun, then they are disqualified.

- **'Stoplight'** (the importance of pausing):
  The children wander the room and play freely. When they reach a condition in which they start rampaging and causing "accidents," call for a break and have a discussion:
  "Just imagine a day in which there are no stoplights on the road ... sounds

like fun, right? Now think of all the downsides."
The children need to be helped to understand the importance of the stoplight and of the traffic regulations—they protect us and ensure order.

- **'Statues'** (developing self-control and the ability to stop):
The participants wander the room. They must move with exaggerated motions, such as hand waving, raised knees, sitting, lying down and so forth. They must remain in motion until the moderator says the word "statue." At that moment, they must freeze in place, motionless. Those who move are disqualified. The moderator decides how long the "statue" status lasts. After a while, she instructs the participants to resume movement. Occasionally, of course, the moderator can be switched.
When I moderate groups of children, I play against the entire team and never beat them. I ask them why they are so successful in the game. They respond that their success derives from the game being a contest. At this point, I explain to them that the contest brings interest into the game and helps them focus and pause. That is why, if one injects interest into different tasks in life, those too can be done successfully.
Games illustrate how, the more the child is interested in an activity, the more capable she is of stopping it.

- **'Mouse'** (the importance of pausing and paying attention):
Place a mouse doll (or any other), in the middle of the room. The children line up in two identical rows. Every child in each row gets a number, so that pairs of children with the same number form (each in a different row). When the moderator announces a given number, the two children with the same number, and they alone, run to catch the mouse. Whoever gets it wins. This game is meant to illustrate what happens when you begin running and playing without listening to the number being called out.

There is an infinite number of games that can be used to illustrate the advantages of hyperactivity and rapid responsiveness, and the importance of being able to hold back and restrain oneself. These advantages should be highlighted in the discussion, as well as when formulating self-control strategies, upon every possible opportunity.

It is important to pair these games with reflection processes, questions regarding the outcome, the identification of environmental influences and redefinition. The moments of the game which are pleasant and relaxed can also be used to initiate focused conversations:

"Tell me how you manage to control yourself and keep from horsing around in class, while going wild at home?"

If the child does not know how to answer, she can be helped:

"You really put in a lot of effort at school, and that is excellent! This is a sign that you are very intelligent—and we know that. But this is also a sign that you are capable of restraint ... At home, you allow yourself more freedom, because you know that we will always love you and accept you ... Let us see if you can show a bit more self-control at home, as well."

Extracurricular Activities

Channeling the surplus energy of hyperactive children and helping them find interest and joy in hobbies and extracurricular activities are very important. Any extracurricular activity the children might enjoy is good. Martial arts, track, soccer, horse-riding, drums, swimming, dancing, drama and, for some, yoga, meditation or any other activity which channels the child's energy productively, teaches them self-control and discipline, and builds up their self-image and belief in their abilities. Arts and crafts can also channel energy, provided the children find them to be of interest. I frequently recommend an activity the child clicks with and is motivated to attend over emotional therapy. Once an activity is selected with a child, a pre-agreement must be reached regarding persisting in it. It is best to decide on a given period of time for which he commits to persisting at the activity, however it is important to remember that one should start by agreeing to short periods which the child can endure successfully, and indeed experience the endurance itself as a form of success.

℘ Meditation

A small meditation exercise may well contribute to the ability of hyperactive children to calm down. Below is an example of one such suitable exercise:

℘ Close your eyes.

℘ Notice the contact of your feet with the floor.

℘ Place your right hand on your heart and try to feel it beating.

℘ Pay attention to the rhythm of the heart.

℘ Place your hands, palms up, on your knees.

℘ Notice your breath—is it quiet or fast?

℘ Notice your body—is it calm or stormy?

℘ Notice your inner rhythm.

℘ Notice your thoughts.

℘ Help your body and thoughts relax.

℘ Take a deep breath and soothe your body and mind.

℘ Try to stay in this condition of relaxation for several minutes.

℘ Open your eyes.

Summary

- The hyperactivity condition represents a surplus of urges that is expressed in excess activity in the body and mind. This is the "**H**" in ADHD. The significance of hyperactivity and its many ramifications should be understood.
- When hyperactivity is part of the ADHD diagnosis, its basis is neurological. It dictates behavior, underlies personality and is expressed in all fields of life, becoming part of the individual's way of life.

- Difficulties are apparent in both behavior and thought. Both body and mind race and everything seems to happen at once.
- At the basis of hyperactivity lie difficulties with regulation and an erroneous sense of time.
- The child is not aware of the fact that she is hyperactive. This is simply how she was born. This it is why it is the parent's responsibility to learn the topic and help the child develop awareness about it.
- We must never forget the positive aspects of hyperactivity: strength, endurance and the many other abilities and advantages of hyperactivity.
- Hyperactivity enables original, spontaneous thinking, as well as multi-tasking. But it makes it difficult to engage in planned, methodical and sequential organized activities.
- Children dealing with hyperactivity find it difficult to pause and maintain continuity. Any action which helps them halt and develop awareness about the importance of pausing is positive.
- Given the difficulties with regulation, everything tends towards polarization, getting swept from one extreme to another. The child finds it difficult to find his way towards the serene path of the center "mean".
- Impatience or limited powers of attention result in verbal expression that can become generalizing, extreme, dramatic, confused, spontaneous and sometimes superficial and limited.
- Hyperactive children do not stop to reflect on and internalize what has just occurred. The ability to pause is one of the most important elements the child must learn to be mindful of, to identify and internalize.
- The hyperactivity level is not constant, predictable or continuous. We will sometimes find the child relaxed and at rest, and at other times, she will be constantly in motion.
- Sometimes, there is considerable difficulty falling asleep at night. The mind continues working at a hectic pace.
- Hyperactivity sometimes leads children to overlook other people. In such cases their behavior can be misperceived as disruptive to their environment.

- The attitude of society towards the child is forgiving—as long as her hyperactivity level is not too high. However, society does not show any real understanding of her condition and difficulties.
- The academic challenge of the hyperactive child is in her difficulty to persevere and manage an organized learning process, not in understanding the material.
- It is very important that we notice and praise every success of the child, large or small.
- What to do:
  ▷ Explain the hyperactivity phenomena to the child.
  ▷ Divide it into four main types, in order to help the child focus on specific observation.
  ▷ Select one **specific behavior or manifestation of hyperactivity**, associate it with one of the subtypes and provide a precise explanation to help it be understood.
  ▷ Focused, consistent and gradual work:
  ▷ Implement the CHAMP principles—raise the child's awareness and ability to gradually identify phenomena, while using appropriate metaphors and images.
  ▷ Repeatedly use reflection and explanations regarding the influence of the environment—when the behavior is disruptive.
  ▷ Emphasize the importance of pausing. Any way by which we can help the child pause, if only for a moment, is a blessing.
  ▷ Emphasize the importance of safeguarding boundaries in the child's turbulent world. Guarding via learning and emphasizing, not reprimanding and punishing.
  ▷ Provide a new, advocative definition for the disruptive behavior: The parent must be the child's advocate and explain her behavior to society until the child is prepared to explain, advocate for and defend herself.
  ▷ The same CHAMP principles are also to be used by the parent to help teachers, instructors, grandparents, uncles and aunts to understand the phenomena—and the child.

▷ It is important to direct the child to appropriate extracurricular activities.

▷ Hyperactivity is not a "discount coupon"! We must understand and bear in mind that the surplus of drive is a source of strength for the child. These drives need to be directed to productive channels which are beneficial to the child.

THE TELEVISION

My head's a TV filled with thousands of shows,
You can flip back and forth, here and there you can go.
Every choice is so thrilling, flashy, splashy, and then,
It's no wonder no show do I watch to the end!
I taste, and I nibble, just a bit and a bite,
And now the mess in my head is one perfect fright!

The same thing in school—there's so much going on,
The chatter of friends, a bird on the lawn,
A creaking chair here, a torn paper there,
Rat-tat-tat on the blackboard, some gum in my hair,
John's really cool lunchbox with its broken latch—
And the words of my teacher you expect me catch!?!

But sometimes it happens, as I frantically flip
From channel to channel, my attention will grip
And I STOP at a show that's so grand and so fine
That it draws me in fully, captures all of my mind.
You can't drag me away when that happens, oh no!
For then to the bathroom, I won't even go!
So it seems I can focus, concentrate and zoom in
On the things that excite me, get under my skin.

CHAPTER 6

Talking ADHD – Impulsivity

When You Respond Immediately or Find It Hard to Stop

PART ONE
THE PHENOMENON AND ITS RAMIFICATIONS

Impulsivity: an overwhelming urge to act

Much like hyperactivity, impulsivity is also an urge. In both, a neurologically based, uncontrollable surplus of intensity and energy occur.

In hyperactivity, this is expressed in restlessness and considerable movement. Impulsivity, in contrast, represents an inability of the child to contain and regulate the excessively charged compulsion within her. This excess charge bursts forth, and she responds immediately, without exercising judgment. It is common to think of the behavioral expression of the outburst of this urge as harmful and negative, and we forget the positive aspects of impulsivity—creativity, spontaneity, improvisational ability and resourcefulness, powerful intuition, capacity for rapid decision making, joyfulness, authenticity, flow. Impulsive people are constrained to responding practically to issues as they arise, and to speaking truth, however bluntly, to their interlocutors; and, if they are also hyperactive, they will not bear a grudge, for they do not dwell on what is done and over with.

It is very important to keep the positive qualities of impulsivity in mind;

later in this chapter, I will expand on how they should be explained to the child and her environment at every opportunity. This must be done to enable her to direct her impulsivity in a positive direction. Nonetheless, we will dedicate our review to the less positive aspects of impulsivity – the many instances in which the child generates an unfavorable impression – and the ways in which its manifestation tends to be misinterpreted.

Impulsivity is one of the most prominent and socially significant characteristics of ADHD. It is what makes it hardest for the child to fit in. It all too soon becomes a lousy social "calling card," which the child's environment finds unacceptable. In the previous chapter, we saw that hyperactivity, in contrast, can be perceived by the environment as rambunctiousness—and its behavioral expressions can be treated in a forgiving manner, with forbearance. This is also true regarding the attention difficulties that will be outlined in the following chapters. A daydreaming child is not disruptive, she is sequestered in her own mind, and reality proceeds apace around her. In contrast, impulsivity is disruptive to the environment, and even harmful to it, and so it is often perceived as a significant problem. There is very little tolerance or forbearance for it from the environment. Impulsive children generally will be considered as acting up or behaving wildly due to bad upbringing or a lack of boundaries, and their behavior will be misunderstood and misinterpreted as ill-mannered, tactless or violent.

The child will rapidly be categorized as "problematic." Their impulsive behavior will generally not be understood as a problem of excess energy or urges, but will be explained within the context of the occasion, such as:

"She hates the teacher, and that is why she behaved that way;"

"She has held a grudge against that child for a long time now, and that is why she struck him;"

"My son needs to be kept away from that violent child."

In contrast to the hyperactive child, who is constantly active, like the Energizer Bunny, the impulsive child is a "fireball" that can roll all over the place and wreak havoc without ever intending to do so. She cannot contain the excess charge within her, and the environment views her as disruptive or else interprets her difficulties as stemming from a deep emotional difficulty. She **is misunderstood**, is subject to completely wrong interpretations by her environment and does not know how to defend herself.

It is very important to realize that there is no **deep underlying context** behind her impulses manifesting into action. The reason for her behavior is not emotional, **though it is interpreted as such**. Physiologically, the body contains an excess impulse which the child finds difficult to contain and which she seeks to discharge.

She can be compared to a truck stacked with an excess load, which is straining its engine, and which she must unload. Sometimes, for her, ordinary thoughts (which pass through the minds of other children, as well,) instantly become actions. For example, a non-impulsive child can be angry at another child and think to herself:

I really want to shove her."

Using her emotion-regulation mechanism and calling upon her ability to exercise restraint, she contains herself. She succeeds to avoid shoving or otherwise harming the child. An impulsive child, in contrast, cannot contain the rampaging urges within her or regulate herself, but immediately shoves the child who angered her.

For the child with excess urges, ordinary thoughts are transformed rapidly into actions that are aberrant in normative society. Many impulsive children can explain the urge well, the urgent need to respond or get something:

"I simply must have it."

Nonetheless, in spite of their understanding and general ability to explain what they are experiencing, they still cannot control the behavior bursting out of them or explain it to themselves. The excess urge is integrated into their lives, and they know no other way to live. This is why considerable resources should be invested in explaining the specific phenomenon of impulsivity to the child so that, with time, it will be possible to help her develop mindfulness, recognize the brewing impulsivity of her actions and take back control of herself.

The process is slow and gradual and must be focused and directed.

Understanding helps the environment to frame the phenomenon, to accept it without judgment or criticism, and to explain it to the child. It is very important to carefully observe the child and provide her with specific explanations, rather than speaking in generalities. Therefore, much like the description of hyperactivity, I have divided the term impulsivity into three typical expressions.

Three Typical Expressions of Impulsivity:

1. Flooding

Like a massive, sudden tsunami, the impulse rampages through the child's internal systems. The child cannot keep it contained or control it. These urges erupt with great power and without any discernible reason, and are very difficult to stop. They can be expressed by powerful screaming, laughter or sudden hysterical weeping, uncontrollable outbursts of anger, or harsh and sudden irritability, cursing and stubborn sulking. We must remember not to react critically or to attempt to explain when this happens but to be compassionate, hold the child and accept that she is overwhelmed and not in control.

An emotional flood can appear without any warning, following various types of triggers. It can be a happy event, such as a birthday, or a sad event, such as the household pet getting hurt. The trigger can be commonplace, such as the child being denied something she wants or things not working out as she expected. It can also occur when the child experiences significant changes. If we can identify the triggers of the tsunami, it will become easier to help the child, prepare her in advance, develop her awareness about her vulnerabilities and help her learn how to control both this urge and the emotional flood.

When this happens, all you need to do is hold the child and understand that she has been inundated.

2. **Excess-Charge Containment Failure**

All the strength, attention and energy of the child revolves around a single need—to release the excess charge within her, to soothe the flooding. The child will use words typical of an inability to restrain herself or shift her focus elsewhere. This inability is expressed in the difficulty to postpone gratification, even for a single instant. The child can see or think of nothing beyond what she "needs right now."

For example:

- *"I have to … right now;" "I can't wait … come on, already;" "pleaseeeeeee!"*
- *"When do we get there? Why aren't we there yet?"*
- *The child won't let go of something she wants right now:*
- *"I want an ice-cream cone; I want an ice-cream cone. I wish we would buy ice cream right now…."*
- The child feels she must call her mother three times in rapid succession; even when her mother does not answer, the child persists and immediately calls her father several times *("I simply must call him now!")*
- The child feels she needs to hit someone as a response to some real or imagined provocation.

At the moment of the emotional tsunami, the child seems unable to overcome this urge. Repeated conversations with her when things calm down, identifying and focusing on the emotional flooding, **without referring to it directly or interpreting it emotionally**, are very useful:

"In that moment you feel you simply must, and it is bigger than you, but you can overcome and control it if you understand the fierce need that takes control of you;" "You think you can't, but I am sure you understand that while you feel you are unable to overcome it, you are capable of overcoming it."

3. **Uncontrollable Reactions**

The flooding experienced by the child and her inability to contain the "excess charge" burden her greatly, and she discharges the excess, responding in an uncontrolled manner. Behavioral manifestations of this uncontrolled discharge can be nervousness, impatience, rudeness, stubbornness, getting extremely annoyed and irritated, outbursts of anger, physical or verbal "violence" directed at those around her, throwing objects, recalcitrance, argumentativeness, tactlessness, difficulty with standing in line, difficulty with losing a game, bursting into a conversation, a tendency to blame others, slamming doors, lying, cursing, petty theft, getting locked out or in, tactlessness, endless repetitive pestering and so forth. Below are two events to illustrate this:

- A slice of cake is on the plate that belongs to the child's brother. Without a second thought, the child will grab it and stuff it into her mouth.
- The child feels she must say the first thing that pops into her mind—she spits out a curse, reveals a "secret," lies or responds tactlessly in order to release the excess charge she feels in that moment. But afterwards, she feels humiliated.

The strength of her response is not proportionate or matched to the event, which is to say, it does not match the trigger which caused it to occur. Just as the child could suddenly burst out laughing, she could also grow irritated, begin to tear up or even burst into tears without any early warning. Such unmatched responses are sudden and surprising. They can be frightening and be perceived as odd. The unpredictable and uncontrolled response, meant to "discharge the excess charge," wreaks havoc on the child's environment. For example, the child sees something she wants and simply takes it. As far as she is concerned, this is no big deal; she may not even have noticed it isn't hers. The child can walk away with an item that does not belong to her (appearing as "petty theft" to those in the environment), even **when she has no need of it**.

As hard as these situations are for the environment, they are immeasurably more difficult, even terrifying, for the child. When she is told that what she casually took, out of a momentary need, is considered theft, she is very regretful and feels humiliated, for she did not understand the gravity of her actions. Or she might insist she did not take the item ... even in the face of irrefutable evidence to the contrary. Genuine and compassionate understanding by the environment that her action was uncontrollable, rather than judging her or being angry in real time, helps the child to feel genuinely understood. When we speak with the child, it is important to remember not to address the **content** of the action, but rather the **intensity** of the emotions flooding her, helping her calm down, recognizing the tsunami overwhelming her and helping her to regulate herself and to find a way to moderate her response or to speak about what she felt. It is important we remember the child can say the first thing that pops into her mind, physically lash out or grab the first thing she sees, regardless of the trigger for her outburst. A given trigger activated her impulsive reaction, and the thoughts racing through her mind at the time immediately manifested in unpredictable speech or behavior—unplanned, uncontrolled and unconstrained. There is no deep purpose behind this manifestation, no planning and no manipulation. The child simply says the first thing that pops into her mind to discharge her excess energy. Her frustration threshold is low, and she responds impatiently. She does not stop to ask herself if it is appropriate. After the fact, if a confrontation develops or a negative response occurs, she understands it was wrong, and she feels humiliation and regret. But in that moment, she was venting out whatever had surfaced, without filtering or deferring her response.

When she is calm, and her urges are not quite so powerful, **the same child** responds differently. She can express dissatisfaction and pause her response. The irregularity of her behavior, which derives from difficulties with regulation, is very confusing to us, and we need to understand that when the child is "supercharged," the odds are high that responses that do not match the situation will occur.

It is important to keep in mind that **uncontrollable** outbursts of rage, violent responses (such as hitting others) and nervousness are the hallmark of impulsivity, even though their expression is **emotional**.

For all three expressions of impulsivity, the particular difficulty is unpredictable and stems from the inability to contain, moderate, regulate and **stop** one's behavioral responses.

Metaphors to Illustrate Impulsive Behavior

Understanding impulsivity and changing our perception, as responsible adults, enable us to contain these uncontrollable and unpredictable behaviors. Our ability to understand genuinely and compassionately is critical, for that is what enables the child to feel understood even when we say nothing. When we desire to explain the child's impulsivity to her in words, it is best to use metaphors, as they enable us to communicate the issue to the child in a noncritical or nonjudgmental manner.

> *This is how I feel*

Try to imagine your child on rollerblades. She has learned how to maintain stability and can already skate forward at great speed. Although she is very confident, however, she remains unaware that her ability to turn and maneuver remains undeveloped. More importantly, her ability to **stop** is very weak. So long as she is riding in an open plaza, with no obstacles in her way, then all is well. But as soon as she steps up to the sidewalk, she will encounter dramatic difficulties with maintaining control. She will run into people and hurt them. She will crash into signposts, trash cans and bus stops. As far as she is concerned these are impassable obstacles. Obviously, she will fall and injure herself, and may cause injury to others.

As far as she is concerned, as she is unaware of her difficulties, the people she ran into suddenly appeared in her path, standing in her way—some, perhaps, even on purpose. They are really intolerable, and they even dared to be angry with **her**. Imagine her saying: "Who came up with the stupid idea of putting a trash can right in the middle of my path? And why is this fancy lady blocking my way, just when I wanted to pass?"

These are my brakes

I like to explain to these children that they are like a fast and powerful race car, shiny and bright. The car is incredible – amazing – but it has a problem—its brakes aren't great. Not yet. When they drive it too quickly, they can't bring it to a stop. So it is with the children—they are good children, and they have many great capabilities, but when they suddenly arrive at a turn, they cannot stop, and inadvertently cause an accident.

Look what happened

And another metaphor I like—

An impulsive reaction is like opening a well-shaken soda bottle.

As soon as the bottle has been opened, the liquid sprays out in every direction and soaks everyone in its path.

The cumulative pressure within the bottle is what leads the liquid to spray out every which way. I help the child imagine that she too has a container within her. Every time the child faces a difficulty, frustration or unexpected situation, the container fills up a little and is shaken up, leading the level of liquid, and the pressure within the container, to rise. Every such stressful, irritating or uncomfortable event just keeps increasing the pressure in the container.

Eventually, the bottle is so full, and the pressure so great, that any loosening of the top (any response by the child) will be uncontrolled, unregulated and will spray out of the child in all directions. This result would not occur if the bottle were not full.

The bottle metaphor helps me illustrate impulsivity to the children. Their response will most likely harm someone or something in their immediate environment. Once the child figures out how to measure how full her container is – **to feel when it is filling up** – she will be able to **drain** the container, and prevent the outburst and resultant harm. In other words, she will discover how to minimize the behavioral expression of her impulsivity. Simple actions can help drain the container—throwing a pillow, walking the dog, taking a deliberate break, music, screen time, a ball game, a massage, or any other method the child selects.

The Moment After

The moment after the impulsive outburst, the child feels badly about herself. She suffers regret and feels humiliated. She feels helpless and lonely. Sometimes, the child feels like everyone is looking at her scornfully, and she has no idea why. The difficulty of stopping should be illustrated and clarified to her. She should be told that while she did not mean any harm, it is not possible to return the carbonated drink to the bottle after she has sprayed it over her surroundings. This is the precise moment she needs someone compassionate and understanding, who can rein her in rather than being alarmed, critical and judgmental.

Tales From the Clinic

Several years ago, a couple came to me for an introductory conversation. They brought with them a letter written by their 10-year-old daughter after she had exploded at her mother in an extreme fashion.

Dear Mother
Mom,
I want you to know—I really love you!
I didn't really mean what I did and what I said!
I love you more than anything in the world and hope you can forgive me, even when it is difficult to be with me.
Sometimes, when I am angry, I am out of control.
I don't want to be angry, and I don't want us to get to such terrible rages, and I don't want everything to explode!
When I am angry, I can't control myself and my words and actions.
I don't want to live if you don't forgive me.
Please forgive me.

I don't want to fight, and I promise not to fight,
But sometimes I am very angry and don't know how to stop.
You are my mother and I love you!
And you help me and support me too!
I don't want things to continue this way. I want them to change.

The parents were deeply troubled by this letter. The overcharged cry expressed therein is what made them seek professional help. Reviewing the letter, I identified several different elements that might stem from impulsivity—and even characterize it. The letter presents a high level of awareness, but there is clearly a problem for the child with a lack of control. It expresses her genuine remorse at her outbursts and a particular distress she feels regarding the knowledge that her outbursts harm her relationship with her mother.

After gathering more information, I explained to the child's parents about impulsivity and the difficulty the child seemed to have with coping with the excess urges that periodically overtake her behavior. They were concerned primarily with her emotional tumultuousness .I explained to them that the extreme words and behavior, which they interpreted as a manifestation of emotional distress were actually, simply, a need to vent the excess associated with her impulsivity being triggered.

I said that I believed the best response they could provide their daughter is to focus on the impulsivity, and discuss it, for it is what triggered both her outburst and her writing of the letter. Even if their child was not diagnosed with ADHD, she must be helped to recognize and understand impulsivity, because her reactions were clearly uncontrolled.

The parents understood this and joined a parental counseling group. They explained impulsivity to their child and worked with her to improve her ability to control her reactions.

Gradually, their relationship with the child underwent remarkable improvement, and their child did not require any therapy.

The Attitude of the Environment—Intolerant Interpretation

It is readily apparent that impulsivity might lead a child to harm those around her. As far as the witnesses are concerned, the child is behaving unacceptably and "crossing the line."

Having acted impulsively and harmfully, she will not be treated with tolerance. Moreover, the child's actions will result usually in a wrong interpretation. Below are several examples, to illustrate:

- If the child sees something she likes and takes it without a second thought, because "she had to," she will be labeled a thief.
- If she tends to manipulate her environment, fan the flames during a quarrel and say the first thing that pops into her head in order to protect herself or shift blame, she will be labeled a liar.
- If she hits a child passing by, she will be labeled a violent child.
- If she erupts into screams in the middle of the shopping mall, it likely will be concluded that her parents did not raise her properly.
- And if our five-year-old child pulls down the pants of another child, all the alarm bells and defense systems of the environment will sound. It is likely that the parents will be urgently summoned for grave discussions on the lack of boundaries and sexual implications, and we will be admonished to send the child for immediate treatment.

PART TWO
CHAMP MODEL OPERATIONAL APPROACHES

Before I detail the operational approaches, I wish to re-emphasize—the child's behavior is **uncontrolled.** We need to internalize that, in her moments of impulsivity, she is experiencing a neurologically based lack of control. This is a condition in which the child cannot contain the impulses that are flooding her and cannot regulate the behaviors bursting out of her.

Interpretation versus acceptance

The initial tendency in the Western World is to interpret situations. This contrasts with the East, where the common approach is deep holistic observation, understanding, mindfulness, and acceptance of all things. I believe that this approach is especially pertinent with regard to ADHD—we need to try to learn, observe and accept things as they are. Make no mistake, acceptance does not mean disregard. Simultaneously to the acceptance, we must take charge of the impulsivity. Understanding does preclude setting boundaries. We – parents, teachers and therapists – must understand, embrace, and remember that the child does not control her responses. At the same time, we must explain and set clear boundaries meant to assist her externally. The child herself well understands this, even though she sometimes has a hard time accepting boundaries and authority.

The Importance of Addressing the Impulsive Reaction, Not the Content of the Outburst

As we have seen throughout this chapter, when we parents respond, it is very important for us to focus on the impulsivity that led to the behavior, and treat only it, rather than responding to the **content** expressed by the child. We must define the struggle that led to this behavior—emotional flooding, a need requiring immediate satisfaction or an uncontrollable response.

Referring to the specific content that led to the outburst is of secondary importance. When a child wants ice cream **now**, or wants to play with Lego **now,** or if there is anything else she needs **right now** ... the content of all of these is less important. If the child becomes very angry, then it is her conduct and behavior that are significant. At the moment of her outburst, it is hard to remember this. Almost automatically, **our response becomes pedagogical**

or emotional, referring to the content of our child's words (or screams). We must learn to change our responses. For example, a practical and more accurate response to the impulsive response might be:

> *"You feel you absolutely 'must' talk to Mother right now, and you are breaking into a conversation. Try to pause for a moment, write down for yourself what you want to talk to her about or think about it, and wait for a proper time."*

In contrast, the pedagogical or emotional response might sound like:

> *"When will you learn to wait for us to finish speaking?"* or *"You are rude."*

We need to focus on the child's impulsive behavior, her difficulty to hold back what is bursting out of her. We need to reflect on her inability to deal with the "must" and the "right now." We need to show and explain to her what she is doing and feeling. Only then can we find the appropriate way to relate to the contents of her request.

> *"This is precisely another example of this 'have to' ... I understand you feel you have to right now – you have to continue playing or really feel like an ice cream cone – but I must teach you how to stop, to think about this 'have to' and to ask yourself if you really do have to. You must learn to do this before you act, because your response was very unpleasant and even embarrassing... It resulted in an 'accident'."*

Sometimes the child does not even realize that she responded in this way, because it is so natural for her. This is why our **job** is to **pause** and illustrate this to her.

Since impulsive children feel constantly under attack, misunderstood and guilty, it is always best to start with the positive side of impulsivity—we should help them understand the advantages of excess urges and rapid response time.

Sentences we can say in favor of the power of these urges, a rapid response time or the inability to pause:

- ✓ *"Thanks to your ability to think rapidly, you understand things immediately and respond intelligently."*
- ✓ *"Thanks to your rapid response time, you right away created a beautiful container* for *the object that you saw."*
- ✓ *"You are brave and are not afraid to take action."*
- ✓ *"You usually follow your sharp intuition, and it is right for you. Learn to trust it."*
- ✓ *"Your lack of inhibitions makes your thinking very creative."*
- ✓ *"You have the ability to think 'outside the box'."*
- ✓ *"When you run into an obstacle, you immediately find a way to improvise and deal with it in a very impressive fashion."*
- ✓ *"Your friends rely on your intuition in difficult situations."*
- ✓ *"You are fun and spontaneous, with a great sense of humor, creative, and you 'go with the flow'."*
- ✓ *"You are opinionated and know what is right for you."*
- ✓ *"You are strongly motivated, don't quit, and can move mountains and motivate others to follow you when you so choose."*
- ✓ *"You have many strengths, and you fight for your opinions and principles."*
- ✓ *"If you have faith in your intuition, stick to your opinions and express yourself with chutzpah, you can achieve great things and progress quickly on your chosen path."*

✓ *"Impulsivity has many advantages, and I want us to learn how to channel them in productive, rather than disruptive, ways. I will help you identify the different expressions of impulsivity (or the situations where you find it hard to contain your urges) and understand how they can be channeled into advantages."*

The Therapeutic Model—How to Implement the CHAMP Model?

As described in previous chapters, the components of the model can be implemented in the order you see is best in accordance with what best suits your child.

CHAMP – Choose One Specific Component

Select one impulsive expression or behavior and slowly help the child notice it.

It is important to remember that the CHAMP dialogue should only be started after we have secured the agreement of the child to participate and to cooperate. Furthermore, we should hold discussions with the child when she is calm. There is no point in discussing things with her in "real time" when she is not attentive or in control of her responses. Once these basic conditions are met, we should choose one particular behavior or form of expression from the above list and focus solely on it.

For example:

"You tend to think very fast and respond immediately."

To raise her odds of success, it is best to begin with a behavior that the child can easily recognize. This will bolster her motivation to persist onwards, to more difficult challenges. This behavior should be isolated and given a single code name, to be used repeatedly until the child can identify the specific phenomenon and "make friends" with it. It is important to keep in mind that impulsivity is an inseparable part of the child, and she must learn to observe herself from the outside. This is a gradual process, which takes time. The **requisite time should be devoted to it, without any attempt to skip steps on the way to a resolution**!

CH**A**MP — **A**ctive Adult Involvement

The adult making use of the CHAMP method should assume active responsibility and repeatedly show the child that impulsivity occurs in different situations: She should be helped to understand the consequences and outcomes.

- *"Your thoughts are fast—you have reached a very creative and fitting solution."*
- *"You understood what they said very quickly and burst into the conversation, just like you burst into games without waiting your turn. People think you are rude. This is why we need to talk about this."*
- *"I know that you know what the answer is straight away. But we will learn to stop and think about how, when and if you should say it."*

Later, we should explain to the child that when she is having a fit or playing the clown, is argumentative, obsessive, repetitive or gets angry—she is, in fact, manifesting the same issue: an inability to halt the urges she feels within. This link will help the child increase her awareness and sharpen her understanding regarding impulsive behavior.

> • *"You play the clown as a way of dealing with embarrassment, and attract negative attention. This is just like having a fit or getting angry or even hitting someone."*

The same things should also be explained to those in her environment, and the child should be protected until she learns how to protect herself.

cHAMP – Help via Reflecting, Redefining, Rehearsing and Responsibility

We will seek to help the child observe what is happening to her, and learn about herself, via reflection. We will then reflect, redefine and rehearse, encouraging her to take *responsibility for her actions.*

> • *"Your emotions are overwhelming you and you are weeping. Let's try moderating your response."*
> • *"You were really excited just now and almost erupted, but I saw how you recognized the situation and tried to stop, raising your hand. Good work! A few more times and you will be a champion!"*
> • *"You are not tactless, and you are certainly not a liar or a thief, but if you say the first thing that pops into your head, exaggerate to escape an uncomfortable situation, or take whatever catches your eye, then what results looks to others like tactlessness, theft or lying. You can't pick up coins just because they are lying about at home. It becomes a bad habit."*

CHA**M**P – **M**indful Metaphors

Let us reiterate that the CHAMP dialogue can also be started by using metaphors, for the components of the model need not be applied in a linear order. Just as with the treatment of hyperactivity, here too, it is desirable to find time with the child while she is calm, to devise a code name and to use it in real scenarios to help the child see what is happening within her. Code words will represent what **she experiences** during her impulsive responses. It is important to understand that everyone experiences something that is specific to them. If the child is not interested in using a code name, a metaphor or imagery, then you should talk to them plainly—withholding all judgment! Below are several examples of useful metaphors and images that illustrate impulsivity:

> **Soda bottle – measuring cup/pressure gauge** – to measure the pressure welling up 'inside':
> *"Your bottle is filling up ...." "I will help you notice every time it fills up."*
> **Race car – stop sign** – representing the need to press the brakes or pause:
> *"Oops, there's a stop sign!" "You better step on the brakes."*
> **Volcano** or **fireball** – to indicate spontaneous eruption:
> *"The lava is beginning to erupt!"*

Any metaphor which can represent, for the child, the situation in which impulsivity surges within her is a useful one.

In real scenarios, when the child is acting impulsively, I strongly recommend you simply hold them in your arms and tell them everything is all right. The goal at this point is to help the child develop awareness of what is happening to her while reducing anger, judgment and criticism towards her. Developing awareness will gradually enable her to watch herself from the outside, perceive how others see her and link between different manifestations of the same phenomenon:

"The tsunami is flooding you with tears right now, just as yesterday it flooded you with laughter. It is the same flooding, and it has nothing to do with what has happened—just with the intensity of your own strengths. It rages, and I will help you overcome it."

CHAMP – Practice Makes Perfect

Only after the child develops awareness can she begin to practice self-help. The components of identification and awareness development are by no means obvious. Considerable effort must be invested in securing the child's agreement to cooperate, and only then can we really help her develop awareness. Only once the child is truly aware of what is happening to her, can connect between different examples or expressions of her impulsivity, and understands consequences is she able to find on her own, independently, the solutions that fit her best. If she cannot identify these solutions independently, we must actively help her. For example, if the child still cannot identify her rising anxiety levels, we can help her via the "inner soda bottle pressure gauge"—using the soda bottle metaphor mentioned above. Every time she feels frustration, the pressure in the bottle rises. The child should be helped to understand when this happens and how charged up she is. She can write on a real bottle, or a drawing of a bottle, and verbally report the pressure levels she feels. It is best to draw a bottle with volume markers, so that the child can easily mark them and describe to us and to herself her rising pressure level. The child should also be instructed to notice what the specific events are that fill the bottle. When the child notices her bottle filling up, then we can perhaps assist her in taking remedial action to drain it in a more controlled manner. Every child will find her own way to drain the bottle and reduce her impulsivity-driven actions. For example: taking a break or performing comforting actions, such as taking a shower; listening to music; taking some alone time and so forth. We can also teach the child to imagine she contains a more flexible bottle—a bottle that can expand and contain more.

Through this, she can be helped to practice her ability to take in and handle events and control her responses. The bottle metaphor lets us talk about an outburst which arrives in "stages," whereas the tsunami metaphor better describes a sudden outburst that has no early warning. It follows that the metaphor we select together with the child will only serve her well if it precisely matches the behavior we want to emphasize, the one we want the child to learn to control.

The child must eventually realize that the impulsivity which erupts from her – her inability to halt her response – puts her in inconvenient, and sometimes irreversible, situations.

She must learn to identify her tendency to obsess over things, dig her heels in, erupt, get irritated, argue, fight, lie and take items that don't belong to her. These behaviors come with the "have to" and the "right now." She must slowly learn to identify moments of emotional flooding, and the quick response that erupts from her without delay or regulation. Slowly, she will learn to see the impulsive reactiveness rising within her and will learn to actively resist these instinctive reactions. We will help her link "events" and phenomena that derive from imbalance or difficulties with regulating urges. Many parents repeatedly ask me for tips and practical tools—and I repeatedly explain that our goal is to teach the child how to fish, not to hand her a fish every time anew.

It is very important to prepare the child in advance for the CHAMP dialogue we want to have with her:

"I want to tell you something that might be hard for you to accept. I ask that you remember our stop sign and avoid responding immediately."

Some children instantly respond with nervousness and a lack of control. Nothing can be done in this situation beyond genuinely understanding that this reaction is greater than her—she is not in control. The child should be held tightly, with great love, compassion and full faith that she is not in control of her behavior. Love, compassion, understanding, genuine empathy and honesty are required to rein her in. Only later, once she calms down, should we start discussing the event with her. Of course, she should be restrained forcibly if she is about to endanger herself!

We must remind ourselves that as much as the child's outburst confuses and sometimes frightens us adults, the child is far more confused and scared. We must also remember that she is only a child. **She cannot learn this on her own**. The process is gradual and slow, and our job throughout is to rein in, understand and teach.

Even when various professionals understand or are persuaded that the child has a behavioral or emotional problem, if the child was diagnosed with impulsivity and is acting or behaving according to the mentioned descriptions, it is quite possible that impulsivity is the factor underlying her behavior or difficulties, and it needs to be addressed.

From Personal Advocacy to Self-Advocacy

Given the tendency of the child's environment to interpret (usually misinterpret) her actions, our job, as parents, is to explain, focus and direct attention toward the real problem, which is the problem of control, or lack thereof—impulsivity. Sometimes, we will have to face environmental pressure, like the teacher who calls us in for a talk after our child threw a chair in the classroom; the neighbor who complains about screaming or the incessant banging of the ball against the wall; and, perhaps, our friends, after our son has punched their daughter. The job of the parents is to be the advocates of the child and explain, understanding that two things will eventually happen:

The first—Our child will be able to identify the various situations where she has difficulties composing herself and controlling her impulsivity. Gradually, she will **learn** to moderate it and the behaviors it triggers.

The second—We will, in this manner, show her and teach her how to be her own advocate. As she grows up, she will learn to explain both to herself and to the environment what she is going through and feeling.

Impulsivity and 'Emotional Difficulties'

It is difficult, in between the impulsivity and emotional hardship, to keep the child's impulsivity in mind, especially when she is directing harsh or extreme impulsivity our way. Her behavior can startle, bewilder or shock us when she expresses such sentiments as:

- *"You are my number one enemy."*
- *"What will you do to me?"*
- *"I feel like smashing you to pieces."*
- *"I wish you weren't my mother/father!"*
- *"I wish I had never been born."*
- *"I don't want to live here anymore."*
- *"Is there a knife around here?"*
- *"It's not worth living like this. I would be better off if I died."*

Impulsive children can repeat these sentences quite frequently. They can also be spiced up with foul language and insults, and lead you to question the emotional stability of the children and to fear that they might put themselves at risk. These are very difficult moments, when our feelings can be deeply hurt. These are moments in which we feel shaken, frightened, concerned and upset. This is especially the case when the environment interprets these behaviors as violent, depressive or indicative of "emotional» difficulties. In such situations, many parents are themselves prone to reacting impulsively, which imposes a burden on their relationship with the child and interferes with their ability to teach the child about herself. In such cases, I help the parents to stop, and to choose not to respond at all. Later, the more they learn about impulsivity and internalize its sources and expressions, the more they will be able to identify it in real scenarios and rein in the child. These are the very same cases in which one must pay attention and remember—**if the child has been diagnosed as dealing with ADHD, these behaviors derive from difficulties with regulation and from the impulsivity** that erupts from her. They are the underlying cause of her tendency to extremism, of seeing only "black or white," and from her "excess charge," which she cannot contain. These difficulties result in polarized speech, which the child cannot stop and whose contents she cannot reflect upon. "I find this a little difficult" is transformed by her into,

"This is impossible. There is no way I can do this."

A slightly depressed mood is translated verbally into,

"It's not worth living this way;"

"It's better off to die;"

"This life is pointless."

And should we intervene, trying to help, we might well be greeted with such expressions as:

"So just kill me, all right?"

The (usually educational) system will seek intervention and a professional opinion. Many professionals who do not understand the field in-depth, or who feel that the severity of the incident is beyond their authority, might direct increasing pressure at the parents to send the child to therapy. What we must do in such a situation is ensure that our child is treated by a professional who is ADHD-conversant. Such a professional knows how to calm things down and will explain that this is not a case of a violent child who is at risk, suicidal or sexually deviant; and that the child has no desire to harm others or to die. Often, the child does not fully understand the word "death" or the finality of death. Her expressions merely derive from her tendency to exaggeration and polarization.

Only when we understand and are convinced that the deviant behavior is neurologically based will we find it easier to respond accordingly and to treat it correctly. An adapted response, derived from reining in impulsivity-driven behavior, very much helps the child to feel better about herself. At the same time, the parent also feels an improvement in their relationship with the child. This is why, as part of a professional treatment of impulsive and hyperactive children, and their families, we must explain to the parents about difficulties with regulation—and discuss this with the child as well.

It is necessary to help her understand that her restlessness, tendency to get swept away, chattering, screaming and aggressiveness are all a result of difficulties with **pausing** and halting her urges and thoughts. We must also help her link her harsh statements to this tendency to race forward and be carried away when she has a hard time pausing. She does not stop to explain to herself what she is going through. She does not stop to organize her thoughts, to think of the significance and consequences of her words. It is obligatory to explain to her the significance and consequences of what she says. It is obligatory to explain to her that, in her experience, **everything** is polarized into "black and white," but reality is composed of shades of gray.

Impulsivity is an extremely complex phenomenon, with many consequences which need to be considered. We, the parents, are therefore obligated, together with all adults in the environment, to understand the issue in depth, in order to tie together all the loose ends, and combine them into a tapestry that is clear and understandable for the child.

Nonetheless, when we speak with the child, we need to be cautious and pay careful attention. If there is emotional content, such as jealousy, dissatisfaction, anger, depression or an intent to harm herself or others, we must consider the possibility that the child may put herself in harm's way, when she is gripped by impulsivity—regardless of her intentions. When we are unsure of the child's judgment, and feel we cannot trust her, we must immediately turn to a professional to conduct a diagnosis.

Between Impulsivity and Lack of Boundaries

A distinction must be drawn between impulsivity and the absence of boundaries, between

"cannot" ... or perhaps ... **"do not want to?."**

We must distinguish between a genuine struggle the child may suffer from, due to her inability to stand up and take charge of the outbursts generated by the surfacing of her urges, and any **informed and conscious choice** the child makes to engage in a given behavior. Sometimes, this distinction is not easy; and should any doubt exist, we should treat the behavior as a defiance of boundaries and take appropriate educational steps emphasizing boundaries. But the line between the two is quite thin. In some cases, children use their impulsive experiences as a "defense," and we will find them "exploiting" their difficulties—as if testing their boundaries, boundaries which they are very well familiar with. In this case, we must understand that this can also be an emotional defense that they have built for themselves along the way. In fact, they have learned how to use their experience as a defense mechanism. They can say things such as:

"You know it is difficult for me to stop ... and that is why ...."

I repeatedly emphasize that impulsivity, like any other symptom, including the symptoms of ADHD, is not a "free lunch" coupon. There is a genuine struggle, and that struggle obligates the child and her parents to take responsibility and put in the hard work, for the consequences of failing to do so are very grave, indeed. We, the parents, must not give our children a free pass due to their struggles, and we must not forgive transgressions of their boundaries that they have learned, which do not derive from impulsivity.

The issues of boundaries and parental authority in raising children are an issue unto itself—this is not the space to discuss it at length, but I will refer to it briefly in the context of ADHD. In this case, we have a responsibility to rein in, understand and take care of our child. We must help the child understand that she tends to get carried away, racing forward without stopping to think. She must be taught that, within a split second, her behavior can become defiance—after erupting or getting stuck in a loop she might dig in and refuse to budge.. These are moments we must learn to identify, taking the opportunity to explain to the child compassionately that she is experiencing difficulties with regulating herself. Otherwise, she won't open up and won't learn anything about herself. She will not be able to develop mechanisms that will help her change her behavior and will also refuse to take responsibility for her behavior, which sometimes harms the people around her. If the child is opinionated, then she likely has an inner truth—and feels that we are wrong or dishonest. She tends to reply rudely, defying us, disparaging us, rejecting what we tell her, arguing and insisting on doing things in her own way.

When this difficulty derives from ADHD, and we are able to rein the child in and explain it to her, she will feel that she is learning from us, and her inclination to rebel will lessen.

However, if the behavior of a child with ADHD also stems from deliberate defiance of educational boundaries, then we must insist on their enforcement. We must insist on these boundaries remaining solid and stable. A child with issues of excessive attention and intensity needs clearer external boundaries, precisely because she finds it difficult to identify those boundaries on her own. If we cannot exercise authority in this way, then it is recommended that we seek the help of a professional who has specialized in the field.

> We must not give our child a free pass, and we must not teach her that she can give herself a free pass.

Behavioral Changes

Behavioral changes will only begin when the child can recognize her impulsivity, pay attention to it and reflect on her responses. She will reach this stage as a consequence of our ability to reflect her behavior to her—when we show her, in real scenarios and in a practical manner, what is happening to her; and when we teach her to identify and understand her regulation difficulties. We must help her understand how her behavior affects other people, and how each individual can respond differently to the same phenomenon. The phenomenon should be redefined

"You are not violent, but your response is perceived as violent by others",

and we must insist that she learns to know herself so that she can accept responsibility for herself. **For the most part, once she understands and internalizes these things, she** will find ways to manage. If she does not, we must offer her alternate ways to deal with it and take responsibility for herself. I believe that education should be positive and affirming. Negative responses and punishment, usually, can stop a given behavior, but they won't change them in the long run.

In contrast, positive reinforcement can certainly bring about behavioral changes, and that is our ambition as parents – for the child to learn and undergo internal transformation that comes from understanding and internalization. Nonetheless, we must avoid bribe-like incentives, such as –

"If you behave well, you will get …."

Such incentives can help for a while, but the child will not derive any real understanding about her condition, and her behavioral changes will not be internalized or real, but rather, reward-dependent. The actual reward is her improvement in functioning, and that is what brings about her continuation on the voyage of self-discovery.

Examples of a Child's Impulsive Behaviors, and Their Requisite Reflection and Instruction:

Behavior in social gatherings:

"Our children find it very difficult to play with their peers and understand social codes."

This is a sentence which many parents repeat. Our children are very social children and understand social codes well, **they just don't understand the meaning of impulsivity.** This is the reason we need to focus on the child's struggle with impulsivity, which results in social difficulties. There is no point in telling them,

"Go on—go with the flow,"

when the child digs her heels in. Rather, we should explain to her that she tends to cling to her positions.

Harmful behavior: some impulsive children tend to curse, lash out verbally, hit or destroy.

It is important to remember—they are not violent children; they simply find it hard to control themselves. They find it difficult to stop and suspend their reactions. In these cases, as well, we need to focus on the child's difficulties with impulsivity, which are leading to the harmful behavior.

We must explain to the child that cursing does not suit her, and that others are offended by it. She curses because that is the first thing that comes to mind. Sometimes, she does not even understand the meaning of the word she is using. In such situations, together with her, we can, for example, find a gibberish word which will help her vent what she is feeling—a word she can use and blurt out in impulsive moments.

"You said the first thing that popped into your mind, and I know you did not mean to hurt anyone. Let's think of something you can say in such situations. Maybe 'cheplulu'?"

A seeming lack of tact would be addressed slightly differently.

"You said the first thing that came to your mind when you saw your friend after a long time – 'You don't look good!' – and he was insulted!"

In cases where other parents pigeonhole the child and do not want to invite her to their homes because of her behavior, we should try to figure out the reason and explain it to the child.

"You played at your friend's and really wanted his new toy, so you put it in your backpack. You did not stop to think that this was, in fact, thought of as theft—and we both know that you are no thief. Let's explain this and apologize."

In the middle of a family board game, the child gets up after losing the game. She leaves the room in a depression and slams the door shut behind her. Once she calms down, or before we play together again, we should tell her:

"It is hard for you to lose the game—everything inside you erupts, your container fills up, you grow furious and you slam the door. Next time we play, try to notice how full your bottle is. When it is half full, take a break, drain it, and maybe also remember the 'stop' sign, and don't respond immediately. Not if you win, and not if you lose."

Only after we explain this to her, can we conclude with a pedagogical instruction.:

"You know that every game has a winner and a loser. Sometimes you win, and sometimes you lose."
During a game between two teams, in which each participant is only permitted to play when it is her own team's turn, our child was unable to wait for her turn, and her team was disqualified. This is a great opportunity to redefine the situation:

"I know you did not mean to spoil the game or get your team disqualified, but when you were playing, you got excited, forgot to pause, went when it wasn't your turn, and your team lost."

Things should be reflected as they are, free of criticism and complaints. When meeting a friend: The child enters the room like a storm, and "gets right down to business"—choosing a game and beginning to play. We need to stop her and direct her in proper conduct:

"You stormed into the room and forgot to stop. Come here—hold on for a moment, say hello. Ask your friend how she is feeling. Ask what she feels like playing; then, choose a game together, which will suit you both."

Part of the reward for a behavioral change is the resultant quality family time. No fighting, no yelling—and you can enjoy it together. We should emphasize what you feel when the child is able to identify, or avoids, making uncontrolled responses, when she is able to channel the energy which suddenly floods her. The child should be praised every time she consciously tries, and certainly when she is able to delay her response. Both this deferred response and the great effort invested in achieving it should be praised:

"I know that took a lot of effort, and you still managed to defer your response! Well done!"

As time goes by, the child will receive the true reward for her efforts as her own personal success. Therefore, we should celebrate every success, big and small. We should notice and praise the child every time she sets her mind to help herself, and tries; and every time she succeeds, however much:

"I saw that you really tried to restrain your response, and you nearly did it. Next time, you will do even better;" "Well done! It is so pleasant now; everything was so much fun."

Tales From the Clinic

An 11-year-old boy arrived at a youth group I was guiding and proudly reported that he identified the **"I have to"** impulse **on his own** and did not make a fuss when he felt that *"I had to buy something on the family trip."*

When we praised him and pointed out his progress, he expressed disappointment at how his parents did not notice and did not praise his success but treated it as obvious.

Later, this boy, who had been suspended from school, reported that he had hit a child, and that he had felt an injustice was committed against him. It later turned out that the other child had hit him first, and that he only struck back in order to defend himself, but the teacher had only seen **his** actions and was angry at him. At that moment, he reacted angrily towards the teacher, making her even angrier, and so she had insisted he be suspended.

We talked about how he was able to identify the "I have to" impulse, but still found it hard to not react the moment he felt injustice. His angry response towards the teacher led her to make his punishment more severe. She referred to how he responded (the "how"), yet he was, in fact, unable to explain to her during the course of the event the "what," as he explained it to us—that his reaction stemmed from self-defense.

We re-emphasized the gap between the "how" and the "what"—we know "what" we need to say or do but find it difficult to deal with the "how" because of objective difficulties—in this case, a child, who is sensitive to dishonesty, found it difficult to stop his reaction once he felt an injustice had been perpetrated against him.

In my session with the parents, I suggested they meet to discuss this incident with his teachers. During the conversation, the father asked impatiently if, in fact, his son is undeserving of a punishment. I replied that I was very happy that he was stopping to ask my opinion rather than exacting a punishment immediately, on his own. I explained that this was progress. The child was succeeding to identify within himself his moments of impulsivity, and control them, and he should be shown appreciation for this. I went on to explain that I thought the incident should be discussed with the teacher. However, as we were discussing this, the boy said:

"I will talk to the teacher tomorrow, and you will see that she won't suspend me." And so it happened!

Using Games to Develop Awareness

Many games can serve as excellent tools to learn and practice "pausing" before a behavioral response. The purpose of these games is to help the child develop a process of identifying, pausing and then responding. The game enables us to see the outcome of the behavior and understand it. In every game we play with the child, we should reflect with, guide and focus him, while emphasizing the word "**brakes**." Every game has its own rules, and the specific choice of a given game is not significant. The important thing during the game is noticing and developing awareness with regard to conduct, which means developing awareness about specific activities. This is the purpose of the game. So, for example, in the game

"**Visible Object,**" which kids particularly like, our goal is to identify what attention is and what impulsivity is.

The game can be played with one child or with a group: One can decide on a given item with which you will be playing. All of the children are to be told that the object to be spotted is "visible." The child or children will leave the room. One should place the chosen object in a visible location in the room. The object must be visible, and not concealed. The child must enter the room and walk around. She needs to be reminded that the object is visible and to sweep the room, "listening with her eyes," and to look for the object without pointing it out.

When the child sees the object, she should sit down quietly for a minute or two and make no indication that she has found the object—not verbally, and not through any physically expressed enthusiasm—just sitting down.

If the child sees the object and is able to **not** reveal it by the end of the allotted time—she wins. An hourglass or a watch showing seconds can help keep the child aware of the remaining time she must be still without revealing anything.

Sitting silently after finding the object confronts the child with her tendency to be impulsive. She really wants to show us that she has found the object, but if she does, she loses the game. If the child reveals that she has found the object, we need to reflect this back to her:

"You did not mean to show us, but you 'had' to show us that you had found the object ...."

One can also play a game in which we decide to challenge the child, with the aim of teaching her to control herself even in the face of us pestering her. She will realize that when she is **aware** of these comments, she can disregard the disturbances shifting her off-course.

From the moment the child manages to hold back in the game and wins, we should praise him, while explaining that she is capable of holding herself back. Parents need to understand that the central issue is not tactlessness, but her natural tendency to erupt and say whatever comes to her mind, particularly when she feels overburdened. They need to tell this to the child, explaining to her that she can be taught to consciously control her responses if she is aware of the situation. This requires instruction and effort, but she has proven to us that she is capable of it. The child should be empowered and praised for succeeding in developing her ability to control her behavior. The next step is to help her identify and transfer the ability she has developed in the game to other activities in her life, and to report them to her family and her peer group.

Impulsivity and Learning Strategies

Every student develops learning strategies during her school years. These are important to the learning process and aid both in learning the material and in developing learning habits for the future. For an impulsive child, they are particularly important, because it is all too easy for her to "get lost" in the learning environment. A child without ADHD will pick up various learning strategies on her own, throughout her years in school. An impulsive child will usually not stop to consider the advantages of using learning strategies, will not try them and, hence, will not adopt them independently. This is why there is great significance to **how** learning strategies are instilled within an impulsive child. We must explain to her that these are tools that will help her manage her functioning during learning, reading, answering questions or taking tests. When teaching learning strategies, it is extremely important to reflect and explain the child's impulsive behavior back to her. We need to remember and remind her about the differences between what she knows and her lower "operational" skills, which means explaining to **her** about the gap between **what** she knows and **how** she does things. The **ability** of our child to function **challenges** her far more than the difficulty of the studied **material**.

This first example needs to be underlined:

▶ *"You completed the assignment quickly and immediately wanted to hand it in. You don't have the patience to examine it. Let's take a break, after which you can recheck it and, only then, hand in the work."*

▶ *"You answered according to the first thing that caught your attention. Stop. Look over the entire exercise. Make sure that it does not continue to the other side of the page. Read everything first, and only then begin to answer."*

▶ *"You copied the exercise at lightning speed and got confused between plus and minus. After you copy the exercise, you had better stop and examine it again, read it out loud and make sure you copied it correctly. You should do this before you begin solving it."*

▶ *"It is better to go to sleep now and check the assignment again tomorrow. Pressing the 'send' button now is not a good idea, even though I know you want to get it over with."*

We need to explain to the child that she is "racing ahead," that she needs to slow down and stop before she starts with a new assignment. It is important to examine everything before starting to solve the problem.

The child should stop again once the assignment is done, take a break and then reinspect the final product.

We need to explain repeatedly to her that she needs to deal with her natural tendency to do things quickly and complete them without delving into it deeply or double-checking it. This will take many repetitions, but we must not give up hope. The true learning of the child will occur when she understands her tendency for impulsiveness and learns how to deal with it.

Eventually, these learning processes will be relevant to us outside schooling, as well. We often regret sending an overhasty email without reflecting on it or rechecking it. We find ourselves rushing out of the house to reach a lecture—jump into the car, start driving and, only after five minutes, realize we have driven in the opposite direction and that we will be late for the lecture. Planning before doing, stopping before acting, thinking before responding, rechecking—all these are indeed much more significant and important than the actual process of learning in school is for children, and are highly necessary where impulsivity is concerned. We need to gradually explain to the child the significance of impulsivity and help her develop self-awareness and the effective way to use these tools!

⌘ A Brief Meditation Exercise

A meditation exercise can do a lot for impulsive children. In order to do it, you should sit cross-legged on the ground with your feet on the ground. Your back is straight; the palms of your hands are on your knees, facing upwards. Let us direct the child:

- ⌘ Close your eyes.
- ⌘ Notice your feet touching the ground.
- ⌘ Take five deep, slow breaths.
- ⌘ Place your right hand on your heart. Try to feel it beating.
- ⌘ Now, place your hands back on your knees, palms facing upwards.
- ⌘ Notice how you inhale, with the air entering and filling your chest.
- ⌘ Notice your breathing rate—is it fast or slow? Try to reach a calm respiration rate.
- ⌘ Pay attention to how your exhalation pushes the air slowly out of your chest.

- Now try to pay attention to your private internal bottle. How is it? Is it beginning to fill up? What is filling it up?
- Try to notice whether the bottle is bubbling.
- Take a deep breath and calm your body down.
- It is all right if you have many thoughts racing around in your head, if you recall things you have gone through during the day, if you are troubled by something you want or need to do. Just take note of all these things.
- Slowly return to yourself.
- Take a deep breath and let your body relax. Take another three deep breaths and open your eyes.

After reading this chapter, I hope we can recognize the hotheaded child or adult who can, in a single instant, forget all about consequences, and whose actions are unpredictable.

I hope we can realize that the most predictable thing about her is that she is unpredictable, and that she can decide, in an instant, to buy half the store, because she saw a special sale and "it is worth it." This is an individual who gets in trouble, is tagged as problematic, jumps between jobs, is "tactless" and has a hard time maintaining her family ties. She is unaware of her environment, and we often cannot accurately and properly explain to her what happens to her.

We often feel guilt for we know that we have hurt her. The more we are disappointed in her, the more she is disappointed in herself. She wants to respond, to lash out and to hurt those who have hurt her, but she mostly does not discover the way to do this, and harms and disappoints herself first and foremost. She does not fight anyone but herself, hurling down the slope of the hill; at best, she tries to learn from her mistakes. The most frustrating thing is that such people are usually essentially good. They will be the first to leap to help or volunteer; their hearts are pure; and all they want is to be loved and for us to be proud of them.

With understanding, boundaries, the right word in the right place, unconditional love and increased awareness, they can turn their lives around.

To summarize:

- **When there is an ADHD diagnosis, the source of the impulsivity is neurological, and it dictates the personality and way of life of the individual.** The source of the problem is not a bad upbringing, a lack of boundaries, emotional or behavioral difficulties, or any other similar reasons, and so we must not respond by discussing content .

- Impulsivity and hyperactivity can, but will not necessarily, show up together. One of them may be more dominant.

- Impulsivity is like hyperactivity but is not identical to it: In both cases, there is a surplus of rampaging urges. But in impulsivity the child feels overwhelmed, cannot contain the excess "charge" and sometimes can respond **by discharging it in a harmful manner.**

- Children with impulsivity have difficulty with regulating and reining in the impulses which rampage unexpectedly and uncontrollably.

- Impulsivity is expressed in three main ways: sudden "flooding" and being swept away, an inability to contain an excess "charge" and uncontrollable responses deriving from a difficulty with deferring reactions.

- Impulsive outbursts usually stem from a spontaneous trigger.

- The response is to something which has just happened. It is important to remember to separate the impulsivity from the trigger. We should be aware about what triggers our child, but our focus should be on the impulsive response, not on the context which triggered it.

- Sometimes impulsivity appears without warning or any perceivable trigger, and it can be very confusing and frightening.

- Impulsivity can result in damage or harm to objects, people around the child or the child herself.

- Following an outburst of impulsivity, the child can be disappointed in herself and feel bad about herself. She may feel regret, humiliation and anger at herself, and will often feel inferiority to those in her immediate vicinity.

- Impulsivity makes it very difficult for the child to function in society, quickly becoming an odious social and behavioral "calling card," unacceptable to society.

- Nonetheless, impulsivity is also a source of spontaneity, creative thinking, humor and other positive qualities.

- The parent should focus on the child's inability to defer her response and treating this particular hardship, helping the child to learn how to identify it and control it.

- During the learning process, it is very important to **first rein in the child** and her impulsive behaviors, **without responding to them.** In the next stage, we should talk to the child. It is important to find, together with her, metaphors that will help her "connect" to what she is going through, to develop awareness, identify the impulsivity phenomenon and internalize it.

- We must learn to distinguish between impulsive behavior which requires reining in and explaining, and transgression of learned boundaries. We need to identify when the child **cannot** control the impulse bursting from her and when she does not **want** to behave as expected of her. In both cases, boundaries should be set down, and the excess impulse should not be permitted to benefit the child like a "free lunch" coupon. This should be explained to the child; she should have help provided to her in developing awareness, and we must insist that she learns to be mindful, identify, and improve her impulsive behavior.

- Should we give the child a free pass and fail to teach her to deal with her excess impulses, she will learn to give up on herself and get into trouble. This is the reason parents need to assume responsibility over this impulsivity.

- The child cannot change the impulses accumulating within her, but she can learn to identify them. This identification will also enable her to find a way to drain her inner "bottle" before it fills up and sprays in every direction.

- Time and effort should be put into the stage of identification and awareness-development, rather than in seeking solutions or strategies. Solutions will only come after the identification.

Just as there are many types of fish in the sea, so too are there many types of people, and this variation is precisely what makes our life so rich and interesting. In the same manner, every child is born different: One is a quick thinker, the other is meticulous, some are slower and some are more orderly. Each has her own natural tendency. The impulsive child has a natural tendency to act immediately, a natural tendency which is very hard to change. We need to show her the advantages of this tendency but also explain to her when it poses problems for her. We can help her ease her way by teaching her to identify, and to improve her coping with, this tendency.

We need to help the child identify her natural tendency to respond quickly, **to help her improve her brakes when they have caused accidents, and to develop her awareness about the advantages of her excess impulses!** We need to study them in a respectful manner—observing them, identifying them and investing the time necessary. We must therefore continually reiterate, focus, emphasize, explain and show—until they do manage to identify this tendency. The identification stage is the most difficult, for **the child was born this way and knows nothing** else. In fact, we are teaching her to observe herself and resist an inseparable part of who she is. This process takes a long time and requires considerable work both by us and by the child. We parents and adults are responsible for this therapeutic work—we need to be there for her, push the brakes with her or for her, and never give up.

This is difficult and exhausting, but no one else will do the job for us. You can and should make use of the services of a specialized expert who will explain and instruct, but I truly believe that the real job is ours—the parents. Our children's successes are our successes!

> The greater our ability to observe, study and understand our child, the more we can help her in more varied and suitable ways, and the more she will have faith in us. The relationship will improve, she will learn from us, she will love us – and the most important thing – she will understand herself and have faith in herself!

In my opinion, **there is no substitute to the power of observation and mindfulness**. An individual who learns to observe herself and her environment can adapt, cope and develop in the direction she desires. Any way to achieve this goal of developing awareness, in general, and self-awareness, in particular, is a blessing; and every individual will find the suitable path for herself and her child. This therapy must be focused and "free" of interpretation and criticism. The parent must teach the child about herself – **the advantages and the disadvantages** – about her tendency to react immediately – and provide assistance in any possible way, to identify and control, to distinguish and direct her tendencies in constructive directions.

RACE CAR

Sometimes I'm a race car, fancy and fine;
I vroom and I rumble, glitzy colors that shine;
I'm fast and I'm furious, the first on the scene,
But I miss most red lights … hard to stop … prefer green!
When I don't stop on time … oh no … accident!
Now I'm sorry, so sad, that's not what I meant.
Never wanted to hurt … now I'll do what it takes
To take things more in hand and pull up on my brakes!

So, if I cursed, interrupted, lashed out or cast blame,
If I hastily pouted, ran away from the game,
If I slammed the door shut or grabbed up what's not mine,
It's just 'cause I missed the word "STOP" on the sign!

THE SODA BOTTLE

Do you want to have fun that is jazzy and glitzy,
With bubbles so bursty and messy and spritzy?
Grab a bottle of soda and just shake, shake, shake;
Then open, and OH! What a mess you will make!
As bubbles and soda burst forth without stop
The second that stopper comes off with a pop!

What is fun when it's soda is less fun you see,
When the very same thing seems to happen to me!
My head gets like a bottle that's way over-jammed,
Not one tiny thing more can in it be crammed;
My body then rumbles and shivers and quakes,
With uncomfortable feelings I just cannot shake,
So, no matter the time or the day or the place,
I just boil over in everyone's face!
I joke and I clown, grab, or scream with a frown,
And though it's too late, it's still hard to calm down.

I'm told if my bottle, I could sort of make bigger,
Or drain it a bit, to ease up on the trigger,
I'd be more in control. I'd be calmer and stronger—
More sure that my stopper won't explode any longer.

CHAPTER 7

Talking ADHD – Wandering Attention

Leaps and breaks in attention, which make preserving continuity difficult

PART ONE
THE PHENOMENON AND ITS RAMIFICATIONS

While hyperactivity and impulsivity are clearly visible and disturb those in the environment, difficulties with attention, which I hereby title "wandering attention," are often less conspicuous. Difficulties with attention are relatively "quiet" and hard to quantify or measure. Indeed, many people doubt their existence, and even tend to disparage them and insist that the child *"can do it if he wants to—or if he puts his mind to it."* They also often assume it is intentional, or dismiss it as "schoolitis"—mere laziness. This is a very misleading and confusing subject, which is oftentimes interpreted as "unrealized potential" or "emotional" struggles.

1. The "wandering attention" phenomenon generates wide gaps in functioning and is expressed in fluctuations of attention. When the child is interested, challenged, excited or thrilled, she has no difficulties with attention. But when the child is supposed to be occupied with **routine** activities, she "suddenly" ceases to be attentive, or fails to maintain her

train of thought. The phenomenon is expressed in forgetfulness, staring, dreaminess, a tendency to "space out", distractedness and inconsistent associativity. Anyone can get distracted and be inattentive occasionally, but *Attention Deficit Disorder is a distinct, classified disorder, which can appear with or without hyperactivity and impulsivity.* I repeat that many parents are very confused and stress that the child can be attentive when she wants to be or is interested. This is precisely why we need to understand, identify and diagnose it as a disorder—that significantly interferes with the child's ability to function at the level of his ability. Attention difficulties are revealed during routine activities, in repetitive and monotonous situations—that is when one's attention "wanders" or train of thought breaks off or "stutters."

2. Fluctuations in attention are the result of **difficulties** with regulation. We must bear in mind that when a child is diagnosed with ADHD, their difficulty with attention is neurological and intrinsic. Attention is irregular, and its fluctuations are neither controlled nor predictable. The child cannot "choose" to be attentive and does not know when she is losing attention. This is why the phases of inattention are unpredictable, not only to those in her environment, but also to herself. One might say that, much like hyperactivity and impulsivity, the most consistent thing about attention deficit disorder is the lack of consistency. This inconsistency confuses and frustrates the individual and those in her environment, who respond with sentences such as, *"Oh, come on—you knew yesterday,"* or *"You just said …."* We need to realize that the lack of consistency is the hallmark of the condition, and not a reason for punishment.

3. The oscillations of attention generate an **enormous gap** between the ability to function well, when the child is interested or challenged, and the genuine difficulties he has in functioning, in routine and "boring" tasks. This gap misleads the parents, and sometimes teachers and professional therapists, as well. This mistake leads those in the child's environment to **interpret** their behavior as willfulness, a lack of motivation or insufficient cognitive abilities.

4. Oscillations of attention are unpredictable, and hence, confuse **the child, as well**, stressing her out. This stress further impairs her ability to function. This is why it is so important to learn about the topic, and to help the child understand and be aware of the situation. In most cases, the child simply isn't aware that she suddenly stopped listening or phased out for a few moments, and she often uses the terms "I'm bored" in situations in which she actually lost focus.

5. When the parent, teacher or any other individual around the child is unaware of her specific attention difficulties and does not focus on them, they tend to interpret, criticize, blame, judge or express harsh disappointment. As a result, the child will be even more confused.

The Neurological Basis of Wandering Attention

Instead of doubting the existence of the phenomenon, we need to understand and be convinced that difficulties with regulating attention are the genuine reason that children and adults cannot sustain attention. This is also why they cannot concentrate over time on various activities, such as, in their childhood – building puzzles or assembling Lego – and later, in their studies and in adulthood—activities demanded by the workplace.

Anybody can demonstrate difficulties with attention occasionally, but this is not necessarily indicative of ADHD, of the inattention variety.

Inattention disorder is a real, specific, clearly diagnosed disorder, and is distinct from other conditions. To ensure that one's attention is wandering due to ADHD, a professional diagnosis must be made—which includes a **differential diagnosis** between ADHD and other "silent" problems such as impaired hearing, speech impairment, depression, anxiety, difficulties with sensory regulation, autism or non-verbal difficulties. The differential diagnosis is what dictates the appropriate therapeutic approach, and it is particularly important when children with attention issues also have emotional issues—which can often mask their attention difficulties.

Inattentive ADHD has a physiological-neurological basis, with a firm scientific basis. Oscillations of attention are the result of a certain neurological irregularity. In simple words, difficulties with regulation range between under-activity and over-activity, with many intermediate moments of sound functioning. There are two conditions in which the disorder manifests itself:

1. When thoughts "wander," independent of any external stimuli, cognitive flooding occurs. Thoughts are not focused and do not connect together in a sequential manner. **Everything seems to be happening at once,** and it is very difficult to maintain trains of thought. The child seems restless but is not hyperactive—she does not horse around or shift from one spot to another. We might compare this to "traveling to many places at the same time" or a difficulty in sticking to a single itinerary over time.

2. When thoughts do not come together, a disconnect forms, like an "off broadcast" radio, and the child or the person experiences "under-activity." In these situations, they will feel distracted or disconnect from the task or thought they were occupied with, and they naturally seek stimulation or a subject of interest to increase their activity level. This is how they restore balance and become attentive again.

These oscillations of attention, between being flooded and being disconnected, enable associative or simultaneous functioning in many tasks. Therefore, people with an attention disorder tend to select certain professions such as marketing, high-tech or management, rather than professions that require sequential or regular work and study. They intuitively select these professions since they "feel" that their attention oscillations are **unpredictable** and do not enable them to function according to an ordered sequence.

Often, the oscillations of attention **cause a variety of difficulties** in the ability to function, for both adults and children. These difficulties are expressed in various life functions—behavioral, social, academic and emotional. Outside observers sometimes have a hard time believing that this struggle is real, but we need to understand and ponder upon this rather than responding in anger, criticism or judgment. **People with ADHD do not lose**

focus intentionally or in order to irritate—they are not being contrary! Here too, the neurological basis for the attention disorder is what dictates the function and life path of the individual. This is why we need to learn the subject, rein in the child and insist on **"talking ADHD"**—and discuss with her, each of the **various components** of dysregulation that we observe in her. These discussions should be held in accordance with the CHAMP model.

It is important to remember that children are born with fluctuations in attention, much like the inborn struggles with regulation that are expressed in hyperactivity and impulsivity, which we detailed in the previous chapters. Most children are not familiar with anything else, and they do not know they are losing attention.

When they are asked to describe how they succeed or fail to pay attention, some children can describe the phenomenon in part, whereas other children are more self-aware and can describe it precisely. In both cases they do not fully understand its many ramifications and consequences. We need to help them in various ways to understand and identify when they are attentive and when their mind is wandering.

In a certain sense, one can say that our children have their own attention framework. Their difficulties with regulation mean they cannot "choose" to be focused and attentive. Their attention independently wanders where it wills, not necessarily to where the child needs. This "wandering" attention tends to draw the child explicitly away from everyday, mundane activities which those in her environment are directing her towards and expecting her to function in—such as routine house chores or homework. A genuine irregularity in attention is one of the greatest challenges our children face. It is a relatively quiet difficulty, whose expression is sometimes internal – not outwardly apparent – and not disruptive to the environment. The child unpredictably phases out, finds it difficult to maintain continuity and is not attentive to what is happening around her. Often, these difficulties are disguised, and people do not notice their existence. Teachers in class prioritize outbursts and disruptive disturbances over addressing the inattentive child staring out the open window. This is particularly true when the child is intelligent and manages to compensate for her difficulties.

Sometimes, these difficulties are felt outside the classroom more than in it, and the people around the child can **misinterpret her behavior**. For example, if the child stays outside the classroom at the end of recess, the teacher might think she is being defiant and deliberately staying out of class, when in fact the child simply did not notice the bell ring. She was not able to pay attention, and so never heard it and did not return to class. Furthermore, intelligent and disciplined children, who function reasonably and earn no complaints, will also draw no attention. Hence, their attention disorder will not be noticed, and they will not be given the help they require to realize their potential. Alternatively, the child may be tagged as a daydreamer, but no one will understand why she behaves that way. Distractedness or associativeness, or jumping and linking of thoughts, on the other hand, are more apparent. A detailed distinction between these two conditions follows.

Manifestations of 'Wandering' Attention

Just as we have avoided speaking generally about hyperactivity and impulsivity, and instead have learned how to break down these concepts into their various expressions, it is equally important to break down and analyze the term "attention oscillations" or "inattention" according to its various components and expressions. We need to do this to fully understand the various manifestations and be precise when we talk with a child within the framework of the CHAMP model.

If your child presents conspicuous oscillations in her attentional abilities, you will no doubt recognize many of the behavioral expressions presented here.

Generally speaking, as we previously noted, oscillations of attention can be divided into two types—the **"jumping or leaping"** type, which is more visible, and the **"spacing out or disconnecting"** type, which is quieter. In each, one must distinguish between attention difficulties in connection to visual and audible stimuli.

Possible expressions in children of **"jumping or leaping"** attention:

- Thoughts constantly race in their mind, and the child "jumps" between them. The child reports that her head is filled with many thoughts all at once."
- Associativeness —thoughts jump from one topic to another in a nonsystematic manner, for no apparent reason;
- The surplus of jumping thoughts and high associativity enables wonderful imagination, creativity and improvisation;
- Difficulties with functioning due to spacing out or distractedness, and a difficulty with maintaining continuity of thought or action ;
- Difficulties regarding sequence and a sense of time—the child finds it difficult to follow or perform a sequence of actions or thoughts, or finds it difficult to keep track of time, dates and so forth;
- A high level of distractedness—the child is distracted by every stimulus around him, even the slightest;
- Eyes that wander every way, all the time;
- Great difficulty with getting back on track and paying attention to something after being distracted;
- Forgetfulness and a lack of mental focus, due to mental overload;
- Racing thoughts, rapid reading and impatience, leading to a superficial reading or referral of what has been said or asked—understanding is, therefore, superficial and sometimes imprecise;
- Difficulty falling asleep due to racing thoughts;
- Considerable chatter, repetitiveness of a given issue, without always focusing on the main point;
- Behavior that is interpreted as impatience but stems from flooding or spacing out, with difficulty with following a sequence of ideas closely.

Possible expressions in children of "**spacing out**" or disconnected attention:

- Significant concentration limited to things that interest the child;
- Staring blankly, dreaminess, like an "astronaut" floating adrift in space;
- Unpredictable spacing out, in which the child "suddenly" loses interest

in the environment and dives into her own inner world;
- Rapid loss of interest, sense of boredom;
- Slow and sluggish progression of activity, due to an erroneous sense of time;
- Insufficient attention to details, or else excessive attention to **all** details;
- Many careless mistakes due to insufficient attention;
- Often forgetting about daily activities;
- Losing items or constantly searching for them;
- Difficulty with mobilizing attention on routine tasks, which is sometimes also expressed in yawning (which is not due to lack of sleep);
- Avoidance of activities which require continuous concentration of mental effort;
- Inconsistent functioning during the day

The difficulty is in the "how", not the "what":
"How do you manage to focus and understand the question?"
Not, "What do you understand about what you have read?"

Attention and Motivation

Many characteristics of attention difficulties can also be attributed to difficulties with motivation. This is one reason for the confusion. The following characteristics can also be **misinterpreted as a lack of motivation:**
- A genuine difficulty with perceiving time or referring to the concept of time.
- Difficulty with self-motivation.
- A tendency to procrastinate and postpone tasks, particularly routine tasks.

- Difficulty with staying focused in study or play.
- Slow and sluggish performance of tasks and a mode which seems "half-asleep."
- A feeling that the child is not trying hard enough or does not like to put in the effort.
- A description of the child as lazy in certain activities, in contrast to performing with boundless joy and merriment things that are of interest to her.
- Significant difficulties with preparing homework.
- A preference for singing and dancing or playing soccer rather than studying.
- Not realizing her full potential.

These oscillations of attention are particularly felt within the educational system. We will now detail the manifestations of the "wandering attention" of both types ("spacing out" and "jumping") **in school**. Some of these expressions can occasionally be observed already in kindergarten:

- The children find it difficult to start their school day and motivate. themselves, yawning and stretching throughout the entire morning.
- The children seem tired, apathetic and unmotivated.
- The children find it hard to mobilize their powers of attention toward the assignments.
- They frequently say, *"I don't understand,"* when, in fact, they didn't pay attention! It is really important to insist on repeatedly explaining that they cannot understand if they do not pay attention.
- They ask many *"What?"* questions due to getting distracted. Frequently, they ask for the question that was asked in class to be repeated.
- They find it difficult to persist over time and impatient when performing tasks requiring attention and concentration.
- Many of them find it difficult to manage time or to use a diary or calendar. They tend to procrastinate and run out of time before completing their tasks.

- Their assignments only get done at the last minute and only under pressure.
- They fixate on specific things and need help and intervention to move forward.
- Many of their answers are noticeably short, and only "sort of" the right answer. Sometimes they guess the answer, and sometimes the answer is completely unrelated to the topic. If a written response is required, they finish it too quickly due to difficulties sustaining attention. (due to impatience and not being able to delve into the problem) or too slowly (due to dreaminess and "getting lost").
- Their reading difficulties are sometimes apparent also due to the difficulties with attention – losing their place while reading, mixing up the letters in a word, adding or dropping letters or words, repetitive reading of words– **and not as a result of not being able to read or not understanding the text.**
- They tend to repetitively read paragraphs or pages because their mind wanders.
- Their difficulties are most apparent in highly verbal lectures, as they find it difficult to listen sequentially to long wordy descriptions or explanations and follow them.
- They exhibit impatience and reluctance to elaborate on a text, due to difficulties with sustaining attention and keeping to a sequence.
- They exhibit great difficulty with written work, and particularly in expanding on, and organizing a text.
- Their handwriting is sometimes illegible, and they find it difficult to maintain spacing, or the writing begins to "wander" all over the page. (the child got distracted exactly when the writing began to wander).
- Their notebooks are disorganized and messy. Alternatively, for children who find external organization to be a tool for focus, they cope by using many colors, headings and lines, in an attempt to compensate and be extremely organised.
- In math, their difficulties derive from inattention to details in **verbal** questions or formulas, as opposed to numeric exercises.

- They find it difficult to adapt correct and efficient learning habits.
- They space out momentarily and, as a result, find it difficult to connect and associate items and topics, or to perform transference from one topic to another.
- In response to the question *"How was school?"* the children will usually respond with a single, simple monosyllable word-*"boring"* or *"all right."*
- Listening will often take place during physical movement, such as walking or the rocking of feet. The physical movement helps circulate dopamine in the mind, regulation of attention returns, and it becomes easier to listen. The child is mostly unaware and does not connect his movements to attentiveness. Sometimes, listening to music, scribbling on a page, squeezing a rubber ball or playing with putty can also help.
- When they are approached and addressed, it sometimes seems that they are not listening, at all (do not look at you, gaze, or continue watching television and so on), when in fact they are listening.
- Their difficulties with regulation often make their inconsistencies in their ability to function unpredictable or conspicuous—sometimes their functioning is successful and their ability to cope with tasks is efficient; whereas, on other occasions, "everything goes wrong," and the outcome is bad.

Attention difficulties can also generate **social and behavioral difficulties**:

- Children with oscillations of attention are generally successful in forming social relationships. However, despite their desire for company, and in spite of being social, they cannot maintain their relationships due to attention difficulties.
- These children sometimes seem listless, inactive or daydream, and do not do well in taking in new information. They, therefore, tend to be ignored and others do not form social connections with them.
- The children find it difficult to follow a detailed sequence or a conversation between friends or to understand who is on what side of any issue.

- They do not notice body language and find it difficult to link cause with effect in social situations.
- They do not know how to fit into a conversation and find it difficult to follow a joke and, hence, do not get the punch line, or understand social nuances and codes.
- Things often coincidentally seem to "happen to them" without their planning them in advance, because of their attention disorder.

Identifying attention difficulties enables us to treat them rather than the social difficulties, which are secondary.

It is particularly important to understand that all these expressions can be directly translated to, or perceived as, an **emotional experience**—typical expressions of which include "flooding", "confusion" ("scatter-mindedness"), being an outsider, frustration and anger, or, alternately, shyness and introversion. Some children choose avoidance: They lack confidence and faith in themselves. Hence, they develop a low self-image and experience depression or loneliness. Some children are trapped in conflict and stress in connection with their feelings of capability "can" or "can't," "smart" or "stupid," "know" or "don't know." They busy themselves with self-flagellating. Many of them are disappointed with themselves, even if they don't know how to express it. They constantly compare themselves to other —" *Why are they more successful than I am?*" In this case, as well, children do not always express themselves openly. Some of them are sensitive to criticism and dishonesty by others. Others try to please. Some deny the situation or, alternately, tend to blame others or the situation. Some become clowns—children who would rather get a laugh than admit they are having difficulties. Some utter harsh statements such as *"I am stupid;" "I'm nothing."* Sometimes they fear losing control. Often, they do not want to go to school, and present physical symptoms there, as well—frequent head aches and stomach aches, especially before a significant assignment, such as a test, or even just from going to school. In adulthood, these symptoms will show up before a job interview or important deadlines.

Oscillations of attention create a constant struggle for the child. This is not expressed only in school, but in any situation in which they are required to be active. In basketball, for example, paying attention to the rules of the game and its progression is required. Going to the store requires attention in order to purchase the necessary groceries and pay for them correctly. Reading a menu in a restaurant also requires attention. Consider even listening to a joke—to understand it, you need to listen to it from beginning to end; you need to notice the tension building up while it is being relayed, wait for the punch line, and connect it to the beginning of the joke to understand what is funny. In fact, most actions in our life require paying attention. Paying attention is what enables us to notice all the details and to connect between them.

From the perspective of the child—she is adrift in a chaotic world. She feels that it is exceedingly difficult for her to pick up on developments in the world surrounding her. The child's distractedness leads her to notice many things around her and to be inundated by them—whereas, she fails to notice or maintain concentration on any single thing from beginning to end. As a result, she finds it difficult to maintain sequence and continuity. She is lacking the measure of attention that is required for any encounter with the world.

Mornings, Organization, and Mundane Chores and Preparations in General

One of the most common difficulties of children with "wandering" attention is getting ready in the morning. A morning routine requires effective organization, delineated by **time**, which illustrates the successful management of a **sequence** of activities. While the organization is associated with executive attention, and will be detailed in the next chapter, the characteristics of "wandering" attention also influence organizing, in general, and morning organization, in particular. Accordingly, it is important to refer to each of these characteristics separately, in order to understand which of the specific organizational difficulties of the child are a direct outcome of "wandering" attention. This is necessary for us to be able to speak to the child in accordance with the CHAMP model, and to address each of these characteristics separately:

Difficulty getting up — Many children find it hard to get up in the morning. This represents a combination of difficulties with wandering attention and with executive attention. They yawn, procrastinate in bed, go back to sleep and get up 10 minutes before they have to leave. They are restless, irritable when getting organized, and generally create tension and unease around them. Some will only arrive at school at the last minute, or late, and often are sloppily dressed or disorganized. Frequently, they insist that this is an effective way of doing things and refuse to change their habits.

Daydreaming and staring — Even after we manage to wake up children who have a hard time getting up in the morning, we can find them still sitting in bed, staring, for a good long while. Even when they are awake, they do not start to get ready for the day, and when they do get themselves started, everything is done very slowly.

Distractedness — The child is on the way to brush his teeth when his sister calls him to her room, and he immediately goes to her. Or he might meet the dog on the way to the bathroom and begin playing with him. Distractedness of this type leads him to forget brushing his teeth and impedes the morning routine. Or he might absent-mindedly put on sandals when his eyes catch them, as he sits on his bed, forgetting that he has a sports lesson that day.

Scatter-mindedness — Given her distractedness and listlessness, the child's behavior is scattered. Her life seems to unfold of its own accord, with the child managing what is happening to her moment by moment, with no sense of control or design. Often, it also seems that things "go missing" for these children, and they can't find the equipment they need to organize their bags. Other children, in contrast, will carry all their equipment in their bag, even what they do not need on a given day, just to avoid forgetting or the need to look for it. Some children will be obsessed with keeping everything orderly, but if we look, we will discover their "messy corner", where they accumulate things over time. In such cases, it is important to realize that the child has her own order in the chaos. We parents must heed this, and avoid touching or changing anything in the child's arrangement. This occupation with "order" and "mess" may sometimes seem domineering, even obsessive. But we must not make the mistake of misinterpreting it that way. That is merely the child's way of trying to generate some stability in her world and her belongings. We must keep in mind that the more the child experiences a lack of inner control, the more external control she requires. The more we help her improve her ability to function and control herself, the less the need for external control.

If we add to the morning factors such as:

- The time dimension, which generates pressure for the parents,
- Challenging outbursts of rage by the child,
- The knowledge that, although we woke up early, in spite of all our efforts, the child will be late for school,

… then our morning routine will be challenging, to put it mildly.

Realizing Potential: 'You can do it if you set your mind to it'

A child whose attention wanders significantly and dominantly, who presents almost no expressions of hyperactivity and impulsivity, will not disturb those in her environment too much, and will therefore, presumably, not receive much attention from those in her surroundings. Indeed, they may not even notice her difficulties, or in a worst-case scenario, they might interpret them as emotional difficulties.

Such children may not be diagnosed and, accordingly, may not be treated. They "fall between the cracks," get left behind or wander about, lost. These children will not get the attention and therapy they so badly need to connect with their strengths and progress on their optimal path, and hence, will not realize their potential.

What this means is that "wandering" attention harms the child's realization of their basic **innate potential.**

When we consider the realization of potential, it is important that we do so by comparing the child to **herself** rather than to her classmates. **This potential is not realized due to the oscillations in attention.** These fluctuations make it harder for the child to present the opinion she has acquired or to perform different tasks. The attention oscillations do not enable the child to efficiently access her knowledge, or even to organize her thoughts to express what she knows, let along expand upon verbal communication in a continuous and organized manner. They also make it difficult to maintain or sustain attention, and complete a task in an organized and systematic manner.

Presenting knowledge in an appropriate way demands another type of attention – **executive attention** – which we will discuss in detail in the next chapter. A child can experience difficulties with each of the attention types separately, or with both at once. Any difficulty with any one of the attention types is sufficient to prevent their potential from being realized.

Graphically, this can be presented as follows:

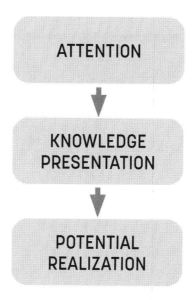

"Knowing and not saying" is the equivalent of not knowing.
"Being able and not doing" is the equivalent of not being able.

One cannot reach any conclusions about the child's realization of their potential based on a single grade in any exam or even subject. The realization of potential is expressed when the true ability of the child is realized, in practice, in most life tasks.

Sometimes one can "feel" the child's ability is higher than what she is expressing. For example, a child who easily scores an "A" in an exam, even though she didn't listen during classes and never prepared her homework, is probably far from realizing her potential. It seems that she has a great deal of unrealized capacity for learning and understanding that simply isn't being realized. To define this gap, we should compare the child's potential to her own basic ability—not compare her achievements to those of her classmates.

Non-realization of learning potential and the inability to mobilize oneself to learning derive from attention oscillations, which are unpredictable and unexpected. Thoughts can "escape" precisely when the child is required to respond—either by answering a question from the teacher in class, or when writing her answer to a question in an exam. Even when she knows the answer, she cannot express it; even when she knows how to do something, she cannot perform it at the right time. It is very difficult and frustrating to know something and to fail to express it correctly. It is particularly frustrating to realize that others do it so naturally, simply and quickly. Over time, frustrations accumulate, such a child will fear to raise her hand in class, even when she knows the answer, for fear of getting it wrong. She will feel frustrated and disappointed when another child raises her hand and utters the very same answer she had thought of. The child feels like she is driving a car which sometimes malfunctions with no warning. This is why she cannot fully trust it yet, and in order to avoid getting stuck in the middle of the road, she avoids driving it as much as she can. **This is the source of her constant lack of inner security.**

Given the above, it is easy to realize that a child with ADHD is in danger of becoming frustrated and developing a negative self-image. She will feel that other people have identified that she has a problem but fail to focus on it. She will feel incompetent and foolish, since she cannot realize her abilities and knowledge. The greater the gap between realization and potential, the more frustrated the child will become, and the more negative her self-image.

Some children manage to summon great powers of attention and overcome the difficulties they feel intuitively, in a reasonable fashion. However, the greater the demands and the greater their lack of attention reserves, the more their learning abilities are impaired. **It is important to identify the difficulties of these children as genuine difficulties with attention, and not to overlook them or treat them as if they are emotional difficulties.**

Some children feel difficulties but do not know how to define them or give them a verbal description. Often, they manage to compensate, cope and conceal their difficulties via wild guesses or clowning around. Indeed, they play the clown precisely to avoid attracting negative attention.

One can also find children with attention oscillations who are successful and avid readers. However, their reading will be focused primarily on specific topics which are of great interest to them. The fact that they manage to read "when they want to" greatly confuses us and leads us to doubt their objective difficulties once again.

It is important to recall that reading requires many different types of attention (continuous attention, focus and executive attention). Children with attention disorder tend to read texts several times. The first time they try to invest their attention reserves merely in paying attention as they decipher the words.

Only on the second or third reading will they begin to mobilize their powers of attention to concentrate on understanding the writing. This makes the task of reading require such great effort as to be almost unbearably difficult. Therefore, it is no wonder that many children with attention disorders tend to avoid reading.

When we read to a child, we spare her the first stage – the deciphering stage – and she is able to succeed in understanding better what she is reading. It is unnecessary to say that writing and arithmetic, and studies in general, also require the mobilization of powers of attention.

PART TWO
CHAMP MODEL OPERATIONAL APPROACHES

How should wandering attention be discussed according to the CHAMP model?

Our job, as adults, is to study the subject of attention oscillations, and to know how to separate the difficulty from the child. The child herself is not the difficulty, and the difficulty is not the child. This is an intelligent child who has genuine difficulty, which we must understand how to deal with and cope with. We must clarify, first to ourselves and then to her as well, that her difficulty is not with perception and understanding, but with her inability to regularly listen sequentially and in an ordered fashion. We must repeat this time and time again, so that this knowledge penetrates the child's awareness.

As we said, the concept of "attention" might be misleading and confusing to the teacher, the parent and especially the child. The child is used to hearing *"You aren't listening,"* a phrase which is associated for most of us with the sense of hearing. However, the sense of hearing is not a participant in the process of attentiveness. Attentiveness is the ability to focus on a given thing **after** it has been registered by the eye or the ear. It requires the operation of cognitive functions and continuous and consistent thought. In my interactions with children, I explain to them that "attentiveness" is the ability to pay sufficiently sustained attention regularly. You can see with your eyes; you can hear with your ears; you can feel and smell, and even touch, but to pick up information, we need to be attentive to it, which means being focused on it. This explanation helps the child understand that "attentiveness" is a broad concept that is not connected just to hearing or seeing and is not associated only with learning.

It is important to emphasize and explain the difference between attention and concentration. Attention is a more passive process; concentration is active. **Once we succeed in mobilizing ourselves to pay attention, we are able to concentrate.** This confuses us—and those in our environment even more!

It is also important to explain that each of us sometimes has trouble listening or paying attention, but children diagnosed with ADHD have more significant, or more frequently recurring, difficulties over a longer period of time. As in reference to hyperactivity and impulsivity, the same holds true for wandering attention.

We should start from the beginning and take nothing for granted. We must speak to the child about the concept of "attentiveness" more generally, to feel out what she understands and how aware she is about the subject.

Afterwards, we should go on to detail to the child **her** individual characteristics indicating fluctuations of attention.

I reiterate that implementing the CHAMP model does not require sticking to the order of the components that was presented in Chapter 4. These are not hierarchical stages, so they can be implemented in parallel with one another. This time, I will start off with the importance of metaphors as a basis for conversation and for raising mindfulness and awareness.

CHA**M**P – **M**indful Metaphors and Imagery

Choose one specific manifestation of attention difficulties, and decide upon a friendly code name to refer to it, using a metaphor or imagery.
I have previously stated that children find it easier to connect to and "understand" explanations when we use metaphors and humor. **"The scatterbrained professor"** metaphor is loved and often a favorite. It is much easier to accept that he is scatterbrained when one knows that he is a genius scientist. Beyond the smiles raised by this metaphor, it enables the child to link her abilities more easily to her behavior. It helps connect the child to her emotional world.

According to the CHAMP model, we should begin with one manifestation of attention fluctuations; it is best to choose an expression that is relatively easy to talk about and identify. Success will motivate the child to continue to learn about her difficulties. This is an expression for which it is highly recommended that we find an appropriate metaphor and perform the entire learning process with it: "Let us think about a code name or metaphor we can use every time we recognize a given phenomenon."

I often tell children that I too have attention difficulties in order to normalize the difficulty and to describe the metaphors that have helped me cope. I recommend to their parents to point out their own difficulties.

Over the years, my personal metaphor for wandering attention was the **"balloon."** I likened it to a big red balloon that I hold in my hand, controlling it and deciding when to release it.

Despite my best intentions, it sometimes happens, that this balloon has been swept away by the wind, beyond my control and, therefore, not my fault. When the balloon breaks loose, it is extremely frustrating. I might even panic, because I very much want to recover it immediately. But when I feel under pressure,

I find it hard to recapture this balloon. In contrast, it slips away even further.

Today, I realize and remember that my balloon (my attention) sometimes plays tricks on me and slips away. I try to internalize this, to understand and accept it, to not fight it or be pressured by it; because I understand that when I am under pressure, the balloon flies higher. When I manage to relax, I am usually able to recall quickly what I had forgotten, but that does not mean that what I remembered is here to stay. I must realize and understand that this ability to pay attention slips away from me occasionally, because **it is** rambunctious and unpredictable.

The code name in this case is **"the balloon"** or "the rambunctious balloon which must be caught by the tail."

Below, I provide several different metaphors, all suited for the "wandering attention" phenomenon. When we want to illustrate the **"spacing out"** – or **disconnecting** – phenomenon, we might use the **"off the air" radio or television** metaphor. The selected metaphor or code name can be "off the air"—in other words, the reception on the television is usually excellent, but it sometimes gets cut off or goes off the air. This is an irritating and frustrating situation, particularly when I am in the middle of an important program. Nonetheless, there is no point in getting irritated, because the interference is not the fault of the quality or capabilities of the device, but of the broadcast itself. The broadcast is the attentiveness, or intake, of the information. It is important to remember and reiterate to the child that this is a marvelous device. Any difficulty stems not from it but from the actual attentiveness beyond the antenna—from the reception of the broadcast, in other words, the way in which the information reaches the device—the child. Therefore, any disruption is unexpected, and we find it hard to understand why we sometimes see a sharp image and then "snow" suddenly appears onscreen.

We feel like bashing the screen into smithereens, but that won't help, because the disruption is not screen-dependent, but broadcast-dependent. It must be stressed that just as the disruption of the broadcast has nothing to do with the quality of the television, there is no flaw in the intelligence or capabilities of the child. The disruption is in the reception—the attentiveness. Without attentiveness, the child cannot listen or concentrate. Another example is the use of eyeglasses—without glasses, the individual who requires them cannot read.

In the hyperactivity chapter, the metaphor of the split-screen television was used to describe distractedness. To illustrate the **leaping or "jumping" thoughts associatively**, one can use imagery of the **"bee" or the "butterfly."** For example, the bee in your head sits in class and listens to a lesson on migrating birds. Suddenly, she sees a bird on the windowsill and she imagines it jumps over to her ...

The bird reminds the bee of Donald Duck, and she asks herself: *"Is Donald Duck a bird?"* Before the "bee" can complete the thought, Donald Duck reminds her of Walt Disney, who reminds her of the amusement park, which reminds her of summer vacation, and so forth. When the teacher asks a question about migrating birds, the "inner bee" immediately answers *"summer vacation!"* The whole class bursts into laughter, and you have no idea why ... This metaphor underlines how associative thinking can be a source of creativity—but one must be paying attention to notice when it is out of place and disruptive. Creativity, particularly that of children, enables them and us to create countless metaphors, which help connect understanding with emotion, leading to insightfulness. In actual time, all that is necessary is to remind child of the code name or metaphor for her to understand and connect to the phenomenon one wishes to relate to.

CHAMP — Choose One Specific Manifestation

We must study the various ways attention oscillations are manifested, being aware of them so we can actively help the child develop mindfulness and self-awareness. Until she does, we must pay attention on her behalf. We must **notice things** ourselves, and help her notice and distinguish between them. When, for example, she is acting scatterbrained or staring into the air, we need to reflect this back to her and help her refocus. This way, we will respond appropriately when she is distracted and jumps from one subject to the next and so on. We must do so without bitterness, complaining or criticizing, actively directing her to observe her attention-related behavior, as much as possible. All of this is to help her develop mindfulness and awareness of herself and her habits of attentiveness, slowly learning how to identify and control them. It is very important to **carefully distinguish** between the different components of attention, particularly between "wandering" attention characteristics, to understand them precisely and to help the child identify them precisely.

In order to increase the child's awareness about her attention-related difficulties, it is very important to first show her the situations in which she manages to be attentive, emphasizing them and point out to her the many times when she is attentive. For example:

- *"I've noticed that you are very focused and attentive right now. Please take note of the situations (and there are many) in which you stay focused."*
- *"Let's see what these situations are ... When you are extremely interested in something, you manage to maintain your attention. This does not mean that when you want to you can, but that **being interested** generally helps us concentrate, because it 'grabs our attention'."*
- *"If we are convinced that being interested helps us, what should we do? Seek after whatever generates our interest. This can be a small thing which helps restore our attention. Please notice what catches your interest and tell me what you discover."*

- *"When you manage to focus on a project you have undertaken or a fascinating book you are reading, you cannot be pulled away; the results are amazing, and your ability to concentrate is deep and extremely impressive."*

In the next stage, we should reflect to the child the situations of inattention or attention oscillations that we observe. For example:

- When the child spaces out and stares into the air:
  "Do you notice that you have just phased out and are staring into space? If you haven't, then I will help you notice; every time you space out, I will give you a sign, or we will use a code name. Do you want to pick a code name?"
- When he is distracted and his mind races
  "We began to talk about ... and you remembered or saw ... and you thought that ... It is wonderful and even funny, but we were not able to maintain continuity in the conversation, and we still haven't talked about what we meant to discuss."
  "When you create many associations and one thing reminds you of another, you might reach original ideas. This is the principle underlying stand-up comedy or startups. Did you know that?"
- When it is very hard for the child to get up in the morning and start the day:
  "I've noticed that it is very hard for you to get yourself moving, to mobilize the necessary attention to get busy and out of bed in the morning. Let me help you."

We should only talk to the child when she is calm. As we have said in previous chapters, "you don't teach someone to swim in stormy waters." When talking with the child, it is important not to use jargon, words with negative connotations or generalizations, which describe a broad phenomenon which would be unclear to her. "Dopamine deficiency," "attention disorder," "impairment," "disease," "brain dysfunction" or even "learning difficulties"-all these are concepts that will only push the child away from us and lead her to shut herself down. One can explain what attention is, and then say:

"I want to talk to you about the rambunctious balloon, or the off-the-wave radio, or the split-screen television, or the buzzing bee or whatever it is that is happening to you—to talk about how you notice everything ... or about how you space out ... or about how you tend to be forgetful ... or about the thoughts racing through your head."

We should choose the single factor we want the child to be mindful of, at that point in time. Aside from raising their awareness, their behavior should be normalized. This should be done to help the child identify those moments in which she phases out or loses continuity; and she should be gradually taught to learn how to direct her attention. There is nothing wrong with the child's regular, natural behavior. This message is incredibly important, since the feedback the child receives from the environment is mostly negative. For the child to open up and be prepared to learn about herself, we need to ensure she does not feel under attack, does not close herself off and does not experience criticism. Our role is to teach her about herself, and we can do so only once she is convinced that we are on her side. After she develops her own awareness about herself and her attention skills, she will be able to manage herself and behave in an optimal, more self-aware manner. An intelligent and sensitive child once told me,

"Do you know how many times I was told that I was not trying hard enough and that I could achieve something if I really wanted to?" He spoke positively, with a smile: *"I really want to know why this is happening to me."*

CH**A**MP – **A**ctive Adult Involvement

The parent or adult assisting the child with her attention oscillations acts as a guardian or intermediary. Like an anchor connecting the ship to the seabed, to keep it from drifting in the waves and the currents, the mediator connects the child with reality, and keeps her from drifting away in the currents of her thoughts, from sailing into her inner world, from appearing passive and from gradually withdrawing into her own world. Unlike a child with hyperactivity or impulsivity, a child with "wandering" attention who lacks impulsivity frequently does not initiate, or put up a fight. This is why we must assist her by fighting for her more and teaching her how to fight for herself. Some will need a lot of assistance; some will need less—each according to their own needs.

This support will include mediation and premeditated help that children lacking hyperactivity tend to require, since they lack the drive required to fight for themselves by themselves. Without specific intervention, the child will find it much more difficult to "connect" to her environment, understand the situation, and do whatever is required of her. The role of mediation is about more than anchoring the child to reality. Setting sail into the deep sea requires understanding many other things, such as the tides, the currents and the winds. A child with fluctuations of attention requires the way they are going to be sensitive to tasks requiring capable functioning within the sea of letters and words, in the sea of simultaneously occurring events surrounding her, and in many other complex situations. To develop this awareness, the child requires explicit reflection about what is happening to her and explanations which are suitable for her specific difficulty.

We must bear in mind that the child is constantly struggling to narrow the gap that has formed between her and others. She requires support, encouragement and positive feedback. How important, how wonderful it would be for her to receive this from the main adults in her life – her parents – who would provide her with the necessary encouragement and intervention. Verbal encouragement, such as *"Well done;" "How great it is that you noticed this;" "I can see how hard you try"* and so on, is very important, alongside non-verbal support.

'Sometimes, This Is What I Think'

The example provided below can help us understand to some extent how an intelligent, sensitive, confident and charming nine-year-old experiences attention oscillations following the help of an external anchor—a person who helped her focus and asked her about these attention oscillations. The child entered my room, and we began talking, and suddenly, during the discussion, she replied to one of my questions with an answer that was completely disconnected. I stopped and asked her:

"Can you describe to me what just happened?"

In her response, she wrote the following on a small note to me, indicating her high awareness and understanding of what happens to her attention.

> I first think,
> And then my thought connects,
> But then it splits in two,
> And in the middle, when I intend to say what I think,
> My thought collapses,
> And I say something without knowing why.

I praised her insightfulness and impressive powers of self-observation. I helped her come to recognize the phenomenon, to "make friends" with it, to not get stressed out and to explain herself as necessary. She was very reassured and encouraged to know that this was, in fact, a frequent, well-known phenomenon that many people experienced.

Mirroring, repetition and redefinition are intended to remind the child gradually, again and again, and encourage mindfulness so that she can assume responsibility and become part of the intervention process.

Initiating **intervention** that includes mirroring, repetition and redefinition is necessary since the child is not even aware of the fact that her attention has drifted and that she is not listening. This is particularly true if the child is not hyperactive or impulsive. Intelligent, hyperactive and impulsive children with attention disorders usually manage to cope with attention oscillations thanks to their basic intelligence **and intense drive, which help them fight and not give up**. Intervention by an adult makes the process much easier for these children. In contrast, children without hyperactivity or impulsivity, who "only" have attention disorder, find it more difficult to motivate themselves and **must** have active, close and supportive adult intervention. They may space out because routine bores them. Either way, since they do not disrupt the environment or erupt, it is very easy not to notice when their minds wander. They can spend an entire day at school without getting anything out of it.

Without mirroring and intervention they "fall," withdraw into themselves, avoid making decisions, give up and develop self-image problems. They continue by disconnecting from their environment. We need to remember that the dreamy children, who neither listen nor disrupt the class, are also the children who will not rally their strength to propel themselves forward; that is why we need to mobilize ourselves to encourage them to take action until they are able to identify their difficulties and assume responsibility for them. We need to be there for them, to ensure they don't give up and to find the most optimal method of intervention for them, which will connect them to what is happening around them—a method of intervention which will generate interest that will increase their motivation, and lead them to connect to the environment and to do what is required.

We adults, need to take the initiative to show the child when she slips away and loses focus, so that she can later identify it on her own. It is important she understands we want to help, not berate her. It is important to create a basis for a good relationship and ensure that the child understands and takes upon herself the goal of learning from us.

It must be explained to her that we will help her identify situations in which she is not paying attention by pointing them out. To maintain the child's motivation to make a change, it is very important to accompany this intervention method with honest reinforcement, support and encouragement, even regarding the smallest changes: *"I've noticed that you are beginning to pay attention and become aware of what you are experiencing. "Well done;" "Don't be afraid to ask for help"* and so on.

Examples for illustration:

- *"Notice every time you manage to 'listen with your eyes'."*
- *"Tell me how you were able to rekindle your interest and restore your attention."*
- *"The balloon blew away—that's all. We will get it back with no pressure." "Pay attention tomorrow and tell me when and how many times the balloon flew away."*
- *"Can you tell me in what situations the balloon flies away?"*
- *"The radio is off the air right now. How do you feel when that happens?"*
- *"The bee buzzed off to a very interesting thing, but we can see that it is not relevant to 'here and now', right?"*
- *"The multichannel television enables you to zap between channels and notice many different things but makes it difficult for you to maintain continuity of thought."*
- *"The balloon blew away again just now and you spaced out. Did you notice?"*
- *"Now tell me when you did not 'listen with your ears'."*
- *"There is also attentiveness in your sense of touch, smell and taste. Give me a few examples …."*
- *"Now stop and check to see if there is a third part to the question"* Or: *"You didn't notice just now that there are two additional questions on the other side of the page."*
- *"You have just lost the ability to listen. Let's take a break and then continue. Tell me when this happens throughout the day."*

- *"When you lose focus, you need to pay attention, take a break and try to find something of interest which will recapture your attention."*
- *"Daydreaming in class, especially when you feel that the teacher is repeating herself is all right. Tell me when this happens ... and tell me when you try being attentive again, when she starts to talk about a new subject."*
- *"Did you notice that you are daydreaming right now? I want you to start noticing when this happens and to tell me about it whenever it happens to you."*
- *"You had a sequence of associative thoughts which took your mind in different, interesting and creative directions, but you lost focus on the 'here and now'."*
- *"You began doing your homework, and the dog came into the room and distracted you."*

As I previously stated, you need a great deal of "attention energy" to start the day. Some children find it very difficult to generate this energy in the morning. Their energy is low, and they have great difficulty "breaking out" into a new, challenging day. When they are woken up and are helped to get organized in the morning, one can tell them, "I am forcing you awake for your own good. I am helping you get your day started" ... and then it is recommended that you direct the child to activities such as a light athletic exercise, breakfast or some other vigorous activity that will help her wake up. **It is important to provide explanations to increase her awareness, and only after, to propose a solution**. A solution without an explanation will not help the process of developing awareness. It may lead to an immediate, short-term change in external behavior, but not to a sustainable, long-term inner change.

It is important to help children link between different examples of the "wandering attention" phenomenon—when they make a mistake due to a lack of attention given to the small details, when associativity arises and thoughts "jump" between different topics, when discontinuity emerges. The link between different examples will expand the child's awareness and help her understand the phenomenon, since children with ADHD frequently do not make these connections on their own.

In parallel, to help the child to understand what she is going through and to not make errors of interpretation, it is very important to **redefine** the situation whenever she or another individual misunderstands and misinterprets or judges her. Throughout, we must repeatedly explain and emphasize to the child that she is intelligent. Her difficulty is in listening to things that don't interest her, or focusing on them. When, for example, the child describes her experiences in school and says she feels stupid and that she does not understand anything, it is very important to explain to her that if she was not able to listen, or her attention wandered from the teacher's explanation in class, she will not be able to respond to the question she is asked; this is not a function of stupidity but of failure to listen.

Albert Einstein also could not have understood if he had not listened. Children with "wandering" attentional abilities tend to repeatedly say, *"I do not understand" or "I do not know."* These sentences have a negative connotation that implies that these children are not intelligent. Usually, their difficulty is in losing focus, which effects their ability to listen—they have no difficulty with actually understanding. We need to redefine and emphasize attention and listening. We need to correct them:

"You did not know because you sailed away;"

"You cannot understand if you lost focus and didn't listen as a result."

We must explain to them repeatedly that without paying attention or listening there is no possibility of concentrating, knowing or understanding.

I find myself repeating such sentences as:

"You cannot answer this question—not because you are not smart, but because you were unable to pay sufficient attention or listen. Even Einstein needed to listen to understand."

A few more examples:

- ..."*There is no chance you will understand if you do not listen. You are a smart child and have no problem with understanding. But if you space out and daydream and don't follow explanations, then you will not be able to understand or answer questions. This has* nothing to do with intelligence."
- *"You know how to calculate, but now you have made a careless mistake because you have not paid sufficient attention—and, as a result, you got the exercise wrong—you wrote a plus rather than a minus. I will be happy for you to tell me, in the future, when this happens to you."*
- *"You were able to understand this tendency to suddenly dream, and I can see how hard you try to listen to your sister and explain to her, as well! She very much wants to listen to you, but sometimes she daydreams too! Let's all help her pay attention to this."*

Regarding Redefinition and Learning Strategies

Learning difficulties typical to children with attention oscillations are not cognitive difficulties within understanding material, so they are quite different from those typical of children with learning disabilities. These difficulties may manifest similarly, but they derive from difficulties with attention. This is why it is imperative that we help the child adopt learning strategies and habits in a focused way, which is adapted to her needs and attention difficulties. The goal is to develop her awareness of her specific difficulties, so that she can acquire learning habits which are adapted specifically to her and gradually learn to assume responsibility for her difficulties. Any individual who understands the child's difficulties and develops a good bond with her can instill in her appropriate habits or learning strategies. When parents feel they lack the time or skill, they should make use of instructors for adaptive teaching or occupational therapists who teach learning strategies. If a child proves unable to cooperate in the process and does not progress due to her attention difficulties, then medication, not psychological or any other alternative therapy, should be considered. Oftentimes medication enables a child to mobilize herself into learning and helps her indirectly by changing her self-perception. Medication can help children realize that they are smart, but that they have an attention difficulty which makes it hard for them to concentrate—and the pills can help them with that. I called the pills "Concentricks", and we likened them to eyeglasses which snap everything into focus. In this situation, when the child is more attentive and her self-image improves, she is also able to learn better and acquire effective learning strategies.

Mirroring and reflecting are an important part of developing awareness about specific difficulties, as well as adopting and instilling effective learning strategies.

- *"Have you noticed that after writing very well indeed, suddenly your handwriting started wandering all over the place? That is precisely the point when you lost your focus. In those moments, you should take a break, and only continue afterwards."*

- *"You knew the multiplication table excellently when we had break-fast. When the quiz began, you felt pressured, or were excited or weren't concentrating; and so, you were unable to solve the exercises. Note that it is your attention wandering—it is not that you don't know how to solve the multiplication table."*
- *"You were overwhelmed or confused just now, and you are finding it difficult to continue. Let's take a short break and then come back to this later."*
- *"This is another example of being flooded. You got stressed just now when you saw this page packed with words. It overwhelms you. Let's take a ruler, and read it line by line. It will help."*
- *"We can think together about a place where you can leave your glasses regularly. Choose a place—that way we won't have to look for them all over the house."*

It is best to reflect to the child her specific difficulty with time estimation, forgetfulness or organization, **and only then** help her make use of practical aids: an alarm clock, a timer, notes, calendars, diaries, colorful bags, boxes and various other objects which help impose order and give a sense of control. Sometimes we might witness excessive searching for various gadgets, until this tendency seems like an obsession. If the cause for this is an attempt to impose order, and if the individual has been diagnosed with attention disorder, we must understand that she is doing this in order to protect herself from the inundation she has experienced, and understands intuitively that it will serve her well. If the attention disorder becomes an excuse for shopping, on the other hand, it is best to reflect this to the child, and thereby gradually reduce her excessive occupation with gadgets and items. It is important to remember—reflecting, redefining, rehearsing and assuming responsibility will lead the child to increased self-awareness.

More on Developing Self-Awareness

There are many people who have been very successful in life despite their attention difficulties. These are the people who were self-aware, or who intuitively understood themselves, and were able to channel themselves onto their desired path in life. There are advantages to daydreaming, associativity, distractedness. Intuition, Imagination, originality and creativity are only three products of these characteristics. The people who know themselves and their attention capabilities intuitively understand that they think differently, and find creative ways of dealing with their difficulties and their life challenges, and thereby frequently contribute a lot to humanity. Others understand that they find it difficult to sit quietly and listen, and choose their professions and occupations accordingly, so that their attention difficulties will not pose a hindrance in their professional path.

Below is an example of a 14-year-old girl who understands full well what she is experiencing and can manage herself well as a result. All that was required was to speak with her about the phenomenon, present it as a known characteristic, and increase her knowledge on the subject in order to help her continue to identify, internalize and control its various components. In this way, she improved her performance, explained her difficulties and protected herself from her environment. This is how she describes herself:

"I often suddenly wake up and notice people talking around me. I find it very difficult to sit for a long time in class. I am very much offended when I am told that I do not listen, because I can't control it. Sometimes I scribble and draw while I am listening in class, and this helps, but sometimes I simply stop hearing what is being said. Even when I prepare homework—if there is noise around me, I stop hearing. I noticed that I think fast but write slowly."

I explained to the girl that she had an attention disorder that was innate. We get it from our parents. She was born this way, and it is good she is aware of it. She should learn a little about the issue and direct her life path in a way that her attention-disorder manifestations can serve her. Empathy, accompanied by genuine understanding, spiced up with knowledge and a few tools to manage her attention difficulties did a lot to help her. She was able to improve her ability to function, connect to her many strengths, and improve her self-image and confidence.

In contrast, some children **are not aware** of the fluctuations of their attention, and they will find it difficult to understand themselves and realize their potential. A few will get good grades but will still fall far short of realizing all their abilities. Others will function on a mediocre level, with those around them not even noticing their difficulties. Over the course of a slow, ongoing process, developmental, social and academic gaps between children with attention oscillations and their peers will in many cases develop. These gaps will only grow wider with time, leading to lower achievements; and, sometimes, these gaps will be so great that these children will be suspended or dismissed from their schools or workplaces. It is reasonable to assume that their academic difficulties, as well as difficulties in their social relationships, will also result in emotional difficulties, particularly concerning their self-image.

The more aware the child is of what she is experiencing and the processes going on within her, the easier it will be for her to identify her difficulties and to understand herself. Through this, she will be able to explain and defend herself, and find her ideal behavioral expression, to realize her abilities and be integrated in her environment. We, the adults – parents, teachers, therapists and instructors – must help the child increase her awareness, learn about herself and look at herself objectively, to identify the various situations in which she is not attentive, understand the exact reason for this and learn how to direct her attention. We can do this via reflection based on scientific knowledge, which we will use consistently and without criticism or judgment. We will also, redefine her specific difficulty. With increasing awareness, her ability to direct her attention will grow stronger, and her self-esteem will grow.

Tales From the Clinic

I will present here an example of an initial meeting with a 10-year-old child, which occurred several years ago. I met a very pleasant boy, bubbly and wild, with sparkling eyes. He explained to me that he was very curious about the conversation with me and was very excited.

"Tell me a little about yourself and about school."

"I really like school, my friends and the recesses, as well."

"What don't you like?"

"I don't like the classes."

"Why don't you like them?"

"Sometimes I don't understand the teacher's instructions."

"Are there any lessons you do like?"

"Sure—I like physical education, mathematics, language and computers."

"And reading and comprehension?"

"I don't like them, at all. I am often unfocused. Sometimes I try to participate, and then I get stickers for excellence."

"Tell me a little about your ability to concentrate—when do you manage to stay focused?"

"If it is easy for me, I am focused. But if it is even a little bit difficult and I need help, then I immediately start thinking about something else. And I, also, always forget if people interrupt."

"Are there any other occasions where you cannot concentrate?"

"Yes, it happens a lot with difficult homework, when the answers require explanations. I find it difficult to divide my attention. Also, when many things are asked in a single question."

"And how do you do in tests?"

"When I am in a test, if I hear voices outside, or if children are whispering next to me, then I forget what I wanted to write."

"Does this distract you?"

"Yes. And then the teacher tells me to concentrate. She does not want to insult me, or for me to be sad, and she isn't really angry at me."

"How do you get along with your friends?"

"Very well. I am popular and they always want to play with me. I visit my friends' homes a lot, and they ask me every day if I can visit them ...."

Suddenly he stopped talking, and continued after a long pause:

"... Sometimes I fight, but then I make up for it."

"Can you tell me what happened to you just now?"

"Yes, my thoughts sometimes race or run away."

"Really? How does this feel?"

"Annoying."

"Yes, this happens to many children, and to me as well."

"Sometimes I speak really quickly; sometimes I daydream. I daydream about other things in school, such as what will be in the next lesson; and if I know the answer, will I raise my hand; will I grow confused and, maybe, will I also fail. Very often, my answers are almost right, but only almost—not quite the correct answer."

This is an excellent example of an intelligent child, mature and emotionally sound, with a high emotional intelligence, and impressive – even unusual – self-awareness. In such a short conversation, he accurately described the various phenomena presented in this chapter. He is well aware of his attention oscillations and describes his difficulties accurately. His answers imply that he has a supportive environment, which embraces and accepts him, an environment which has helped him develop an impressive self-awareness. All that is necessary is to help him more precisely understand what attention is, and to explain to him why, for example, he has a hard time understanding instructions, why he is distracted, why he finds it hard to follow sequences and why it is difficult for him to elaborate when answering questions which require him to explain his reasoning. In other words, a focused discussion about attention needs to be continued.

Despite the high awareness of this child, he showed signs that he is beginning to question his capabilities.

Such unease about his abilities can rapidly result in the deterioration of his self-confidence. This is why this needs to be stopped in its tracks. Focused work is needed to help the child understand and internalize the genuine attention difficulties he has. This should be done even if he seems to be coping impressively with his difficulties already.

We need to *Talk ADHD* **to reach a child's heart and** help him develop self-awareness:

- *"I have no doubt that you understand instructions because you are a very smart child. However, sometimes it is difficult to follow a complicated or wordy text."*
- *"Note that you love physical education and other classes when you don't find it hard to listen attentively. Have you noticed that there are also differences within the same class? For example – in mathematics – is solving exercises easier than answering word questions, given that you need to follow instructions in the latter?"*
- *"Isn't this something! Reading comprehension is just like following instructions! You need to keep track of several things at once and sometimes you lose focus."*
- *"When you say that if this is easy for you then you are focused, you are actually saying that when the material is interesting, you manage to rally your powers of attention and are able to maintain concentration."*
- *"Let's talk about this 'explaining' for a moment. What does it require of you? It requires patience to elaborate on and verbalize your knowledge. You don't always have the necessary focus or patience to elaborate or express in words what you know, particularly when you already know that you know the material—so 'why bother elaborating?'"*

- *"Your thoughts race around and run away! What a precise description! You sometimes feel like everything is running around in your head, and it is hard for you to follow continuously and on time! Tell me about all the examples when this has happened, start connecting them and understand that this is the basic issue! Thoughts race around, run away, jump all over the place, get disconnected and make it difficult for you to listen, to follow or to maintain continuity. If you focus on this fact and don't stress yourself out (which is only natural), you will slowly learn to identify those times when you are distracted or space out, and learn to direct your attention."*
- *"You are a charming child—you have many friends and that is the most important thing in the world. You have a loving family and an understanding and supportive teacher; the sky is the limit!"*

I will re-emphasize several points which are the principles of focused discussion, given their great importance to this topic—and their great importance to the child.

- **Understanding:** Emphasize the child's ability to understand. She can understand what the teacher says, but if she does not listen to everything she has to say, she will not be able to respond. This has nothing to do with her capacity to understand. It's like a car passing by you on the road—if you don't look at it, you will not be able to say what color it is. This does not mean that you are color blind.
- **Attention, not concentration**: It is very common to use the word concentration rather than attention. It is important to help both children and adults understand that in order to concentrate you must first devote attention to the task.
- **Identification** It can be of great help practicing identifying situations or conditions in which the child's thoughts race, as well as those in which she is daydreaming. Another part of this exercise is for restoring and regulating attention.

More Tales From the Clinic

A seven-and-a-half-year-old child arrived for an initial meeting with me. I asked her to describe what she feels when she sits in class. She then dictated to me a song she had just invented, insisting I stick to her phrasing:

"Boom, Boom, out, out, my mind is large and wonderful, filled with ideas and beautiful thoughts.

"I have a brain which is as smart as a pointy peak;

"It is very large,

"As everyone knows."

She said she could not pay attention and listen to the teacher in the classroom, and when I asked her, "Why?" she replied:

"My brain took all sorts of things from friends in other countries, and that is not good, because my head has filled up, and it will eventually fall and get hurt. But don't worry; a doctor is coming to help."

I asked if she needed help with anything and she answered:

"The people are also angry at me for taking from them, and I didn't really take anything."

"What did you take?"

"A baguette from France, Pizza from Italy, an insect shish kebab from China, a camel from Egypt and a kibbutz from Israel."

"An entire kibbutz? How is that possible?"

"Well, then … What kind of food can I take from Israel? Falafel."

In accordance with the principles of the CHAMP model, I helped her understand that she the word kibbutz popped up whenever she thought of anything that reminded her of Israel but that it represented a deviation from the topic—food. The focusing I provided her helped her get back on topic, and then she immediately corrected herself and said falafel.

For the most part, children with attention oscillations, such as this child, are partially aware of their difficulties. The child we met here is partially aware of her "wandering" attention, the flooding of her thoughts and her associative inclination. She tries to demonstrate confidence by claiming her brain is huge but feels that something bad is going to happen. She needs help and is asking for it. This is an example of how I speak with children using the language of the CHAMP.

> *"Your head is really huge, creative and wonderful! Sometimes I feel that it is packed because you have many thoughts which flood it all at once. In such moments, with so much 'incoming mail', it is hard for you to keep track and your attention wanders. People even get angry at you, and you don't quite understand why. A surplus of thoughts is wonderful, but notice when they get in your way. Let me help you—perhaps we can write a book of poems and fill it with your beautiful thoughts. What do you think?"*

Children with partial self-awareness intuitively understand that they have difficulty with academics, something that may lead them to avoid learning. Sometimes, in a direct conversation, the child will be able to describe the "spacing out," the distractedness and the various other phenomena. However, since she does not fully understand her attention oscillations, she is extremely sensitive to criticism or feedback that is not authentic, and might perceive this as a general lack of capability. She will speak in general, often exaggerated terms, such as

"I will never get it right;" "I am a failure;" "Everyone is better than me;" "People think I am not smart" and so forth.

Difficulties with regulation make this even more problematic, as they lead the child to adopt an extreme "all or nothing" worldview. If the child fails at a given task in a given time, she will feel herself to be a "nothing" or "worthless." She will feel like a "total failure." Her emotional experience is an outcome of the consequences of her difficulties with attention, since they also generate difficulties in regulating her thoughts and emotions. It is very important for the adults around the child to be sensitive to her and to understand her explicitly, so as to be able to help her understand and practice awareness, enabling her to cope better with the phenomena.

About Mediation, Understanding and the Ability to Help

A child with an attention disorder is sitting in front of a question in an exam and does not solve it. The reason she does not solve the question is not that she does not know the solution but that she finds it hard to concentrate and focus on the test question. The question remains for her no more than a collection of words on the page before her.

The teacher approaches her. Intending to help, she gives her a hint, and points her to the answer. But this is not the help our child needs. Her attention difficulties do not result in a lack of knowledge but in an inability to focus on the question. Therefore, in order to accurately focus the child on the test, we need to help her focus on the question: One can try reading her the question or explaining it to her differently.

Without this external focus, a considerable gap remains between the child and the question. This is why any hint directing the child toward the answer will remain "hanging in the air" and will not bring the child closer to the solution. On the contrary—once the child has realized she is failing to understand in spite of the teacher's help she will become stressed out; the stress will increase her attention difficulties, and she will guess the answer. It may well be that the child's grade will be low even with the teacher's attempt to help. It is all too easy to imagine what would happen to the child's self-image. It is also all too easy to imagine what the teacher will think of the child's abilities. It is important to understand that the grade the child receives in such an exam is not a reflection of her knowledge, but of her difficulty on focusing and paying attention to the question.

Doubtless, understanding the specific manifestation of the attention difficulty, and the correct intervention to use, can help turn things around. In this example, the teacher was far from understanding the child's true difficulty. Despite her good intentions, she only made the situation worse. If, on the other hand, the teacher would have helped the child redirect their attention – by taking a short break, reading the question or rephrasing it – then her help would have been effective and would have matched the needs of the child. This is yet another example of the principle that

the difficulty is in the "how," not the "what."
*"**How** do you concentrate and understand the question?"*
And not *"**What** do you know about the question?"*

If it's Not Disruptive, Then Don't Impede It

If the child prepares homework effectively while rolling on the bed or lying on the floor, if her answers are correct and she completes her tasks in a satisfactory manner—then her method helps her direct her attention. Let her choose how to do her homework, while explaining that in class she would have to find some other method that does not disturb others. As long as her behavior does not disturb either her or those in the environment, the child should be permitted to do it, even if it is less acceptable, and is unique and special to her. Beyond affirming and backing her tendency to being in motion, it is very important to explain to the child that the movement helps her listen and concentrate, that this is her way to solve exercises or focus on an assignment, and that this is fine. She merely needs to make sure that she is not disturbing or harming someone else next to her. The child should be gradually helped to find alternate ways of action that do not disturb her surroundings. For example, if she makes use of a bouncing ball at home, she can be allowed to quietly mold a rubber ball in the classroom, without bouncing it. The teacher can be asked if it is all right with her for the child to stand and move a little during the class, at the back of the classroom, behind the desks, to recapture her attention without being disruptive—or if she can leave the classroom for brief breaks, delimited by time. All this is to be combined with an explanation/reminder to the class that every student is to be treated according to his or her unique needs.

CHAM**P** – **P**ractice Makes Perfect

As I repeatedly noted, encouraging mindfulness and increasing **awareness** require repetition and practice until the understanding and the awareness become automatic. For this to happen, we need to talk with the child, ask questions, link issues, and continually help her to remember and understand.

We must bear in mind that:

IMPROVED PERFOTMANCE → ACHIEVEMENT → INCREASED EXPERIENCE OF SUCCESS → INCREASED MOTIVATION → IMPROVES SELF-IMAGE

Below are several examples of practice sentences:

> • *"Tomorrow, in history class, count how many times the 'balloon blows away' and tell me about it."*
> • *"How do you retrieve the 'balloon' when it flies far away?"*
> • *"In what conditions is the 'bee' particularly disruptive, and when is it helpful?"*
> • *"When is it easy for you to concentrate on only one thing? Why?"*
> • *"How do you think it is possible to halt the racing of thoughts between separate subjects—when you want to?"*
> • *"How did you feel when the balloon blew away from you in the middle of a test?"*

- *"Did this embarrass you so much it paralyzed you?"*
- *"Were you able to explain this to the teacher?"*
- *"How do you feel now that your grades have risen so much?"*
- *"You managed to listen to jokes around the table, and we feel that you are completely with us. Do you feel a difference?"*
- *"We have divided the tasks into smaller parts, which is why you can perform them, and your anger level has declined."*
- *"You are going to school more happily now, because you feel that you understand yourself better, and you can explain and defend yourself better."*
- *"Does the fact that it is easier for you to listen to the teacher contribute to your feeling good about yourself?*
- *"You told me about your experiences today in recess, and you are actually saying that you are more part of things. That is wonderful, and it's happening because you were able to understand and overcome your attention difficulties. Well done!"*
- *"Understanding and overcoming help us feel better about ourselves, so we will continue practicing these skills until they become completely natural to you."*

In the children's groups I facilitated over many years I was repeatedly surprised that most children proudly reported an improvement in their ability to listen in class and in groups thanks to mindfulness and self-awareness! I was encouraged and thrilled to discover how important this was to them, and it increased my own motivation to persevere in this seemingly so-simple mission of "Talking ADHD!"

✒ Games to Increase Self-Awareness

Games can be an excellent aid for practice and training in situations of wandering attention, as well, a tool that helps identify and grow understanding of behavioral patterns. The game should be used as an aid to illustrate and encourage a discussion which will direct the child towards noticing her attention habits, in order to help her see and understand what happens when she loses focus and cannot listen. **Throughout the game we need to "Talk ADHD." To reflect, guide and focus the child.**

There are endless simple games with which we can emphasize the concept of attention and its characterizations, and to fine tune awareness about it. Every game has its own rules, and the choice of the game is not significant. I will present several examples of games:

⤜ The point-accumulation game:

The situations in which the child's attention is distracted or associative, due to excess thoughts in her head, in comparison to situations in which she spaces out, stares into the distance, daydreams and generally does not notice the world around her.

Every time the child identifies and points out these situations, she gets three points. Every time the adult identifies them, she gets one point.

⤜ Visible object game:

Mentioned in Chapter 6, here, "wandering attention" should be emphasized. For example,

"Notice the object with your wandering attention, and when you make out the object, go back to your seat without telling anyone."

⤜ Items in a row:

Line up several items and ask a group of children to try remember them. Explain that we need to listen with our eyes and "photograph" the order of the items in order to remember them.

One of the children should be asked to remove one item while the other participant(s) close their eyes. The other participants must then open their eyes and identify the missing item.

Alternatively, one item can be swapped with another, and the replaced item identified. Our explanation should refer to the fact that the child managed to remember her "photograph" splendidly—in other words, she directed her attention, with her eyes, to the order of the items. Non-success means that the photography needs to be improved or the lens of the camera cleaned!

⬤ Drawing on a page:

"What is missing in the picture?"; "Find the differences;" "Painting a shape by connecting the dots" ("Dot to Dot"). One can ask in advance:

"What do we need to do to succeed in these games?" "Use your eyes to notice the tiny details."

⬤ The Broken Telephone Game:

This is a group game, where the first participant invents a sentence and whispers it to the next person; and each person whispers the sentence he has heard to the next participant. Do this until you reach the final participant, who should say aloud what she has heard. Usually, an amusing gap has been formed between the sentence uttered by the first participant and that of the final participant. Through this, we can explain that you need to listen with your ears in order to accurately transmit the message.

⬤ "What starts with the letter …":

"Look around you for items which start with a given letter of the alphabet. "

We can also pay attention to all the objects that end with the selected letter. During the game, it is important to refer to the advantages of "wandering" attention:

"Now, I want to see how your attention 'wanders' and picks up all these items with your hawk-like eyes."

⬤ The drumming game:

One participant drums a given rhythmic sequence. The other participant must repeat it, drumming the same rhythm. Then they switch. The mediator can refer to the type of attention required:

"What kind of attention do you need? Attention with your eyes? With your ears? With your hands?"

● Feeling games:

The child's eyes are covered, and she needs to guess what she is being served—sugar, coffee, lemon, a bell, cloth and so forth. This should be done to illustrate attention with various senses.

● The Simon game:

This game starts when the console illuminate this or that button. The player must press the illuminated button. With every round, another button joins the sequence. The player must repeat the **entire sequence** accurately. This game is intended to develop the memory, but in order to remember the sequence of sounds and colors, focused attention is required—you need to notice which colors and sounds are emitted by the console in order to repeat them in the correct sequence.

▶ Meditation exercises:

Meditation exercises can greatly benefit children with attention oscillations, much as it aids hyperactive or impulsive children. This time, the exercise may help them focus.

You should sit cross legged on the ground, or else sit on a chair with your feet on the ground. Your back should be straight, palms spread out on your knees and facing upward. One exercise, for example:

- Sit up straight.
- Close your eyes.
- Take several deep breaths.
- Try to listen to yourself, to your breathing.
- If something bothers you (such as a noise), pay attention to it.
- Continue to listen to yourself, your breathing, your body.
- Now, when you manage to listen, focus on your breathing.
- Pay attention to your thoughts.

Focus on your thoughts about yourself, your body. Stay focused on the thoughts. If your thoughts wander or jump from place to place, simply take note of them.

Try to return to yourself, your body, your breathing.

Take a few more deep breaths, and open your eyes.

Parental Insight

I cannot end this chapter without briefly referring to the insight of the parents. Once they have studied the attention disorders of their children, many of them report themselves to possess attention disorders. Frequently they undergo a personal process in the group sessions.

In every parent workshop I have directed, the parents enjoyed, and were relieved to discover, that they or their partners were people with attention oscillations. They become preoccupied with their new self-revelation and feel a need to retell their life story.

The example below is of a greeting a teacher wrote to her student. This student later became a father of a child with ADHD, who participated, as a parent, in a parent workshop I moderated.

> *"You are an intelligent student who wants to study and cram,*
> *but if you want to achieve all that you can,*
> *you can't let social issues distract you from the plan.*
> *I know how hard it is when things happen drawing your attention to this and that,*
> *But it is important that you don't cut yourself any slack.*
> *You are a talented, intelligent and creative child,*
> *And even if soccer and friends are what grab your attention,*
> *Remember that order and proper work habits will help you present all you have to give."*

This man has an attention disorder which went undiagnosed as a child. For many years, he kept the teacher's words because he felt they were significant, but he did not fully understand their significance, because he was not fully aware of his attention difficulties. The teacher had described attention disorder symptoms, and the father only fully understood what she was talking about after he had participated in the parent workshop and learned what it meant to have an attention disorder. This direct intervention helped him understand the meaning of the words in depth. This father further explained that he did rather well in life, but he felt that he had "missed out." Following the new understanding regarding his son and himself, he managed to perform a significant turnaround in his own life!

This is a thrilling example of the importance of understanding and the precise observations of the teacher. Without any aspiration to perform a diagnosis of her student, she "got" him, and her words proved to be of great significance to him, both as a child, and as the father he became. Another example is that of the woman who wrote the post below. She too was a parent of children with attention disorders, who participated in the workshop. This post summarizes her words and illustrates just how much attention difficulties continue to influence us even as adults, and how much understanding and awareness enable us to perceive past experiences differently. They enable us, as adults, to understand the weight of the past, which would otherwise inexplicably burden us, and to retell our life story.

> *"Ever since I was a child, I could tell that there was something different about me. I could not point out what it was exactly. My friends were always focused, knew what was 'in,' who to hang out with, where to be and what to wear. I relied on a good friend and followed her blindly, because that is what my intuition told me I should do. The most common sentence back then was 'your daughter has potential,' a very frustrating sentence, particularly because I was raised by parents who always told me that 'you can be anything you want' and were disappointed I did not reach the heavens. They did not understand that what I achieved took much more out of me than it did from others, because I was really nothing like them.*

I blossomed in the army, of all places, because that is where my leadership skill was revealed. In basic training, I became the 'class queen' but, even there, my nickname was 'astro' (astronaut). During this time, I underwent a severe crisis which ruined the whole experience, and I just carried on with my life. I found it very hard to study, and I underwent a diagnosis just to make sure that I was not an idiot. That was when I discovered I had ADHD. I coped with it for years. Recently I began participating in a workshop for children with attention disorders. I've tried to find tools that would enable me to help my son. Throughout the workshop, I have learned about myself, my understanding and my continual awareness of the issue grows.

I find myself asking more, and relying more on external help and advice, but also feeling greater frustration at how the people around me manage themselves and their lives so easily while nothing comes naturally to me. One of the most difficult things for me is communication. I can express myself, but sometimes I say things in a way that seems to me natural and logical, but which is not understood by other people. I can apologize once, twice, but no more.

I am beginning to lose my confidence. Afraid to fight for what matters to me, to not be too aggressive, afraid of saying what I think in order to not be considered cynical. I am scared.

I would like to hear from others, if they too are familiar with this experience, and acquire any tips they might have for dealing with the situation. I don't always have someone available to edit my responses, especially when I need to respond immediately, and this is truly frustrating.

Thank you for those who managed to read this post to the end!"

To Summarize:

- Attention disorder can appear with or without hyperactivity and impulsivity.
- Attention disorder without hyperactivity and impulsivity is a congenital neurological disorder, referred to in the literature as ADHD—inattentive presentation.
- Attention disorder lacking hyperactivity is a "quiet" disorder which is not apparent; it should be noticed and diagnosed.
- When undiagnosed, it can be mistakenly interpreted as silent or lazy emotional disturbances, lack of motivation, underachievement, or even anxiety, depression or a tendency towards obsessiveness. This is why the diagnosis and differential diagnosis are so important.
- When the level of hyperactivity and impulsivity are low, inattention becomes the silent, dangerous enemy of our child.
- A combination of low motivation for action and non-disturbance of the environment may lead the child to withdraw into her own inner world. We adults, therefore, must be aware of this danger and fight for the child until she is able to manage on her own.
- The oscillations in attention are primarily expressed by jumping, association, discontinuity, distractedness, forgetfulness, and cases in which the child disconnects and is not aware of what is happening around her. Performance is inconsistent, unpredictable, and very confusing for the child and her environment.
- The difficulty is most conspicuous when the child is asked to perform routine or monotonous tasks. On the other hand, when the child is challenged or interested, no attention difficulty exists. This characteristic poses a significant portion of the diagnosis.
- Many emotional manifestations derive from these difficulties, including a tendency for procrastination, avoidance, lack of motivation, disappointment, frustration, anger, low self-esteem, constructing wisecracks and various "tricks" to camouflage, mask or bypass the difficulty. The primary inner conflict revolves around a feeling of incapability.

- Unlike hyperactive children, children without hyperactivity tend to give up or "get lost." They do not fight, and thus, the role of the adult as an active mediator is vital.

- Significant and correct intervention in the child's life will bring her closer to a better understanding of what she is experiencing both inside and out. The intervention will enable her to realize her potential to a greater extent.

- Attention oscillations pose a significant advantage for many types of tasks which require imagination, creative thinking and improvisation, but do not enable planning and continual activity in sequence. In other words, the neurological basis of the attention disorder dictates the personality basis and way of life of the individual.

- The initial difficulty is one with listening/paying attention—not with concentration. Once a child or adult successfully rallies their attention reserves, they do manage to concentrate. It is important to distinguish between attention and concentration.

- Attention oscillations result in great difficulties with getting organized and maintaining continuity of thought and action.

- Attention oscillations will often result in the child not realizing their basic potential.

- The child is immersed in a constant struggle in all her activities throughout the day. Every moment of distractedness, of unfocused attention, generates a gap between her and the environment.

- The greater the difficulties, and the higher the intelligence of the child, the greater the gaps between her potential and its realization—and the greater her frustration.

- Misinterpretation of the difficulty ("I am not smart") will lead to the child's self-image being harmed, and with it a decline in her feeling that she's capable. Her self-awareness needs to be strengthened, and she needs to be helped to distinguish between "don't understand" and "don't listen." This distinction will help her redefine herself.

- It is important to reflect to the child the situations in which her attention is sound, as well as the situations in which her attention oscillations are not disruptive, and even serve her well. So it is, for example, that daydreaming can serve as a source of creativity.
- The child should be helped to understand the consequences of attention oscillations on learning, and on life in general.
- The child should be helped to understand, develop awareness, and adopt appropriate strategies to deal with various situations in her life to help her assume responsibility for herself and her difficulties.
- The child will evolve and grow when she feels that we understand her, when she feels we are compassionate and empathetic to the complex experience she is undergoing.
- Every method of action which would encourage mindfulness and lead the child to learn about herself, to develop awareness about her attention capabilities and to improve her ability to function, is a blessing.
- We must insist on gradually teaching her to learn to identify and direct her behavior, and gradually to become her own expert. It will optimize her behavior and her conduct in the reality changing around her.
- If the child fails to implement the proposed approach due to attention difficulties, medical treatment should be considered.

THE PUZZLE

It's Monday morning—I can't move, I can't think,
Twenty minutes I lie here, in a daydream I sink;
Then for nearly an hour at the mirror I stand,
My thoughts all a-wander, my toothbrush in hand;
"Asleep on the toilet again?" my Dad growls.
"Go get dressed! Brush your hair!" he continues to howl.

In the morning I wake like a puzzle all broken,
My head's not connected, my mouth is unspoken.
To gather my pieces takes more than you think;
I have to make order, place myself back in synch.
It takes all my focus—there's none left for tasks,
And you, my dear Father, have so many "asks!"
With my shirt in my hand, and my head in the clouds,
As the time ticks away, I can tell you're not proud!

In the morning, remember, please give me a break,
Though my eyes may be open, I am not yet awake.
But from the minute I rev up, get into full gear,
You all want me to doze off again—that is clear.

CHAPTER 8

Talking ADHD – Executive Attention:

The Conductor of the Orchestra

In the children's groups I've facilitated, I also talked about the topic of executive attention.

In one of the workshops, when we first started to learn about and practice this idea, the children immediately invented a name "complicated attention."

"Hey," they told me, "You just explained to us about simple attention, and now this is complicated attention."

So here, before you, is the chapter about "complicated attention."

PART ONE
THE PHENOMENON AND ITS RAMIFICATIONS

Executive Function and Its Role

"Executive attention" or "executive functions" is a general title for an array of human, higher-level cognitive functions that develop over childhood and adolescence. This is an array of mechanisms which enable self-regulation and act in a conscious manner to process **new** information and secure a specific goal.

This network has access to our long-term memory storage. By extracting data from our long-term memory, the information fed to us from our senses can be processed and properly stored. Executive attention enables us to **handle new or changing situations** and is aimed at preventing an automatic or intuitive response, which is considered easier and more basic.

Executive functions facilitate human conduct in almost every area—regarding motivation, initiative, persistence, setbacks or changing situations, as well as in relation to maintaining sequences and an order of actions, understanding complex instructions and dealing with situations of conflict.

A sound function of executive attention enables delaying or overruling a response, as well as ignoring various other distractors, and allocating attention resources optimally. Without it, our sense of time is off the mark, and we have significant difficulties with understanding, organizing and managing a proper sequence of actions in the time continuum. **In fact, every complex activity requires executive attention.**

Executive attention can be likened to the conductor of an orchestra, whose role is essential to getting a group of musicians to play in harmony. A considerable portion of human higher function is dependent on this "complicated" attention resource.

The literature broadly agrees that at the core of executive attention are three primary components: **working memory, delayed response and mental flexibility.**

A successful combination of these three components enables the development of additional executive functions, such as the ability to plan, monitoring situations and taking initiative, which enable efficient decision making, problem solving and deduction of conclusions. Executive attention is essential to learning new information or new skills, but once these become familiar through training and practice, the activity or knowledge become automatic, and the involvement of executive attention declines.

So it is, for example, when we learn the multiplication table, the executive function is highly involved in the process of understanding and calculation, but once we master it, we extract the results of the multiplication exercises from memory without involvement of the executive attention.

Executive attention sorts the flood of information which has arrived in our consciousness through our sensory system, processes significant and important new stimuli with regard to what has happened up 'til now, and navigates the target of conscious thinking and action accordingly. It maps out the importance of stimuli and selects those stimulations which need to be noticed. This is how it manages to function according to need. This is a dynamic process which occurs anew at every moment.

- Take for example a **literature class**. The student needs to listen to the teacher speak, summarize the teacher's words in her notebook, copy text from the blackboard, and deal with the noises and behavior of the other children in the classroom. All this requires performance of many activities at the same time. A child with difficulties with executive management might manage to listen to the explanation but probably won't manage to also copy the text from the blackboard. The child sitting next to her has drawn her attention, and the teacher has already wiped the board clean and moved on to a new topic.

- **Driving**. Think about the number of resources required to simultaneously drive safely on the road—staying in the correct lane, and paying attention to the cars driving next to us, to the traffic signs and to the traffic lights. We must also take unexpected traffic jams into account and do all this without abandoning the route to our destination. We must find a rapid solution when we make a wrong turn or when we run into an unforeseen issue. Professional literature and research results indicate there is a higher incidence of young drivers with ADHD who drive dangerously and are more involved in traffic accidents, in comparison to drivers without ADHD.

Executive attention is embedded in our consciousness. It is fed by information arriving from our various channels of perception in situations where attention is regulated. The information can be visual (such as the traffic lights we see as we drive), audible (such as music or speech), tactile (brushing against a type of fabric, for example). Executive management is activated when we pick up a great deal of information and need to process it, when we need to manage several things simultaneously, or when we require complex, non-automatic thinking. But in situations when something is happening, but **there is no conscious pause** or focusing of attention at it, the information passes without executive attention being activated. In such a scenario, the current information will not be processed, no executive ability will develop, no internalization or passing on of the information towards long-term memory will take place, and of course, no learning process will occur. This situation, in which the executive attention goes unused, has many ramifications in all fields of life.

I will reiterate that executive difficulties are often the reason for non-internalization and non-learning. Therefore, there is no point in being angry or disappointed with the child or to judge her severely. **It is important to understand, pause and help the child take in the information, performing a conscious process of effective processing via the executive attention system.**

We will now discover the main components of executive attention.

Working Memory

Try to imagine calculating the payment of three friends who have just finished a meal at a restaurant. The first ordered only a drink and a dessert, the second—the appetizer and a drink, and the third—only the first course, without a drink. Think about what is necessary to calculate the payment of each of the three friends individually, and don't forget the tip....

As mentioned above, one of the three basic components of executive attention is working memory. This component, which also includes its own cognitive function, makes it possible to hold information and operate it for a short, limited period of time. Its role is to collect short-term data and process it on a very basic level, while relying on the ability to extract additional data, as required, from the long-term memory. Beyond preserving and processing the data, working memory also enables us to manipulate the information in order to perform required tasks. We make use of working memory in a broad variety of daily tasks. For example, when we have a conversation, we need to remember what our discussion partner has said and process the information in accordance with earlier information which has arisen from our long-term memory. All this should be done in order to respond properly and add new and relevant information to the conversation.

Working memory also plays a significant role in the learning process. In this process, we are exposed to new information and incorporate it into previous knowledge and skills which we have extracted from our long-term memory. All this information undergoes processing in the working memory and then is channeled into understanding and drawing conclusions, or into some manner of activity—or else transmitted on to the long-term memory for future use.

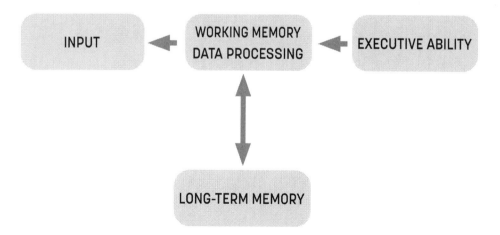

Working memory is like a surface upon which we are preparing a cake. To make the cake, we lay out all the ingredients we have purchased (this is the input) along with those we have stored in the cupboard (this is our long-term memory). We will use this surface to prepare the dough, the filling and the glaze. The size of the surface is limited, and its role ends when we put the cake in the oven and the remaining ingredients back in the cupboard.

As with a work surface, the capacity of working memory is limited. It is customary to attribute to the working memory of a grown man a capacity of seven to nine items. So, for example, a grown man can read a list containing that number of items, remember them and sort them into groups at the same time.

Analogy from the World of Computers

RAM — Random Access Memory

The influence of cognitive psychology introduced the term "working memory" into the field of computer science. This resulted in the development of temporary memory, which improves both the ability to use information on the computer and the speed of performing the required tasks. All the inputted data (such as the text typed into a typing program) enters the working memory, and is made accessible for performing tasks and initial manipulations of the data (such as erasing, correcting and adding text). The volume of the working memory (RAM) is limited, and its contents are replaced in accordance with the required task.

This memory is distinguished from the memory in the hard drive. When we keep the memory that we worked on, in the computer, it is transferred to storage on the hard drive (pictures, music, text files and more), and is extracted back to working memory as required, and according to our command. The hard drive is the equivalent, in its usage, to the long-term memory in our organic brains. Much like the distinction between RAM and hard disk memory on the computer, working memory is different from the long-term memory in the organic human brain.

Difficulties with working memory will prevent an individual from accurately remembering a number of instructions given to her in sequence—even if they are quite simple or common instructions; she will find it difficult to etch into her memory information which is supposed to become automatic (such as the multiplication table); she will find it very difficult to hold certain information in her mind in order to plan her desired path of action with this information, and so on.

Delayed Response:

Another component of the executive attention array is delayed response, which refers to the behavioral and cognitive capability of "delaying" a response. This is a system of executive-control processes that, among other roles, are responsible for delaying or actively suppressing irrelevant information, and include the ability to ignore distractions. The ability to activate a delayed response time is a vital prerequisite condition for delaying impulsive responses, as well as to plan ahead effectively.

Delaying the response is also involved in learning processes, because we need to suppress peripheral information or irrelevant thoughts in order to avoid overloading the working memory with irrelevant information, and preserve within it only the information necessary for continued effective processing.

When their response-delay capability is ineffective, the children cannot sift through the data to deal only with the primary, relevant information. Everything becomes "top priority." They also tend to respond before they think or plan, and are therefore often wrong or appear insulting, since they cannot stop and separate between their thoughts and what they say. We need to keep in mind that this is a very real difficulty. Children with response-delay difficulties do not choose not to stop. This difficulty was detailed extensively in Chapter 6, in which I provided many examples of the characteristics of impulsivity, as well as regarding how to practice the CHAMP model dialogue.

It is important to emphasize that the natural tendency of the environment is to interpret, explain, judge, criticize and punish. To avoid amplifying this tendency, we need to be aware of, understand and internalize that the child has a genuine objective difficulty with moderating their responses. This requires us to learn to observe, embrace and practice.

Mental Flexibility or the Ability to Transition:

A third component of the executive function system – mental flexibility – is based on the components of delayed response and working memory. This flexibility enables adapting to change, and transitioning between conditions and different tasks, deliberately selecting a goal to meet in the rapidly shifting reality surrounding us. Mental flexibility also enables us to examine a point of stimulus from different perspectives and shift our mental perspective regarding a given topic. Think, for example, about a situation in which several consecutive meetings were set up for you, but your schedule changes at the last moment. Flexible people will respond to the changes easily, and immediately fill up their time with activities other than those they had planned. In contrast, inflexible people might be ineffectual in coming to grips with the new situation.

Like a Television Remote

You have a big screen TV with a split screen. On the left side of the screen, you are watching the program you have chosen, and on the right side, all the other channels you could be watching at this moment appear. You are holding a remote control enabling rapid switching between the channels. You watch a program for as long as it interests you. As soon as you pick up something which attracts your attention in the small displays on the right, you can click and switch a channel.

But what if your remote control is broken? You press the button and press again… and again. Sometimes the remote responds and you switch channels. But sometimes it takes the remote many, many attempts to respond—and sometimes, it never does.

When there are difficulties with stopping a certain behavior and reinitiating – in other words, when the ability to transition between different focus states is damaged – a significant barrier is formed within the ability to adapt the required action to the changing scenario. Such a difficulty can, for example, be expressed in school, such as when the child transitions from one class to another (math to geography). The difficulty can also be expressed in everyday conduct at home. Imagine for a moment that dinner time has come. The child is watching television, and you call her in to eat. Regardless of how much you call her, she is simply incapable of tearing her eyes from the television screen. She finds it difficult to turn her head and listen to you, even for a second. Unless you lower the volume of the television or switch it off, you will not be able to direct her attention towards dinner.

A child experiencing difficulties with transitions will present considerable frustration when she realizes she is facing a circumstance she did not prepare for. Parents who spontaneously decide on Sunday morning to drive off to visit friends will find it very difficult indeed to secure the cooperation of their child if she finds "transitions" difficult. She had gotten up in the morning and had begun building with Lego; and the sudden change makes it very difficult for her to change her thinking and conduct.

The difficulties of transitions are very confusing and might be interpreted as emotional or communication difficulties when they are also expressed before enjoyable events, such as traveling abroad or moving to a new apartment. The difficulty can be expressed in deep anxiety, which is accompanied by excessive occupation with details. If we realize that there is considerable difficulty with transitions and explain this to the child in accordance with the CHAMP model, we will manage to reduce her anxiety level and help her deal with the objective difficulties—the transition and the need to rapidly adapt to change.

Functional Elements Comprising Executive Attention:

"Why does "1/2" = "0.5"? Does this seem simple to you? Why does "8/16" = "50/100", and what is a fraction anyway?"

Seemingly, this is simple math. However, each such problem requires the utilization of previous knowledge, breaking up the problem into specific factors, remembering all of them, processing the data, and presenting an answer or explanation. Only when full mastery of this knowledge has been achieved does it cease to demand complex mental efforts.

Reading a complex and varied menu in the restaurant or listening to a waiter who offers to us a variety of special dishes challenges our attention in general, and our executive attention in particular. Under such circumstances, we see many people find it very hard to make a decision. They deliberate a lot about "what they should do" until they end up leaving the decision up to their friends. It is often the case that they feel embarrassed, especially when those around them interpret their behavior as indecisiveness or ambivalence. The discovery and understanding that they are actually inundated by the excess stimuli, and find it difficult to choose among them, may help them and those in their environment draw new insights, which will empower them and enable them to function more effectively and calmly.

Executive attention develops over childhood and adolescence. In other words, this is a system which evolves over several years, even after the other attention systems have come into their own. This is why difficulties with executive attention appear relatively later than other attention difficulties—the oscillations of attention, impulsivity and hyperactivity. Sometimes they are more apparent in adolescence and adulthood, and often they are misperceived as difficulties stemming from emotional sources.

We will now detail various difficulties with executive attention, but it is important to stress that not **every** ADHD diagnosis necessarily implies executive-attention difficulties, as well.

Organization and Planning Abilities:

The title "executive attention" represents, as mentioned, how the system operates. It manages the data input, the stored data and the data that is undergoing processing. It enables reasoning and the ability to come to conclusions, sends the new insights to the long-term memory network and is responsible for many other activities. One of the basic roles of any executive is to generate order and organization in the systems she manages—a proper arrangement of data and activity. She is responsible for **prioritizing tasks**. The executive must answer such questions as: What data should be addressed first? How do we solve the problem? What is the required action? Furthermore, she must do so while taking in all the existing information and what has been done to date. In fact, any "decision" regarding generating priorities in the functional sequence is a planning and organizational process that also constitutes conflict resolution between competing stimuli and processes. The processes of planning and organization are required for any action in our day-to-day life. We need them in order to get organized in the morning, to prepare our schoolwork or workplace chores; we need to plan and organize our thoughts when we want to say something to a friend; we require efficient planning in order to shop for the groceries we need to prepare our meals, and we require efficient organization to follow a recipe—and, it stands to reason, we also require some basic organization in order to keep our homes and cupboards tidy.

In Chapter 7, we noted difficulties with getting organized in the morning due to difficulties with "wandering" attention—difficulty with getting up, staring into air, distractedness and forgetfulness. The simple process of getting organized in the morning requires "wandering" attention elements, together with executive management functions. Children with executive management difficulties do not manage to recall a sequence of simple actions and make them "automatic" and, as a result, find it difficult to perform routine tasks. Thus, routine organization tasks such as brushing teeth, getting dressed, making the bed, sorting a bag and having breakfast can become a very challenging task. The child does not properly recall this simple sequence of activities and can get confused and "stuck" in front of the closet or the mirror as she agonizes about what she should wear that day. If she somehow manages to learn this order and we change it, even in the slightest way – telling her, for example, that today is rainy and that she also needs to pack a raincoat – an explosion or tantrum is quite possible!

Tales From the Clinic
"What should I buy?"

A difficulty with resolving conflicts.

A woman who arrived at my clinic told me that she has terrible fights with her husband, because he believes that she has "shopping fever." I should note that, on that day, she entered my store with shopping bags for six separate dresses, identical save for their color. She confessed to me that, on most occasions, she returns from clothes shopping only after purchasing several identical items.

"My husband is right: I don't really need all the things I purchase. But I had to, because there was a sale I simply couldn't miss, and I simply don't know what to choose. It is easier for me to get it all. I think I really do need to treat my 'shopping fever'."

The woman was diagnosed with ADHD, which was expressed via vigorous hyperactivity, and she described herself as possessing a very impulsive character. It was clear that she also had a problem with executive attention, a problem that resulted in her "shopping fever", as her husband called it. But this does not explain her behavior in any way. In fact, every time she went shopping, her attention system was flooded with many different stimuli; she was faced with many items, and she could not choose between them—hence, the six identical dresses. She was unable to make a choice—which color dress she preferred, if she wanted black for the evening or yellow for an afternoon outing—but she loved white—but what if her husband disliked the color? She had better also take the red dress … just to be sure.

The executive attention system should have sifted out information from these points of stimulus, extracted information from her long-term memory—including information on the need which had spurred the shopping, information regarding preferences and perhaps also memories of the colors of the other similar dresses she already had in her wardrobe. In other words, a process of sorting, filtering, selecting and deciding had to be performed – and wasn't – because dealing with the process was too complex. Eventually, impulsivity would take over, and she would simply purchase all the dresses. This spared her the need to decide while in the store, and at home, she would be able to choose what dress to wear. As for her husband—he claims she is a shopaholic because he was not aware of her true difficulty.

Likewise, our child might stare at his wardrobe and ponder, and eventually turn to us to ask,

"What should I wear?" or, perhaps, *"What is better?"*; *"How should I choose?"*; *"Which option is better?"* and so on. These are questions which characterize executive difficulty—the difficulty with making an informed decision based on an entire mechanism of planning ability, organization and conflict resolution—generating priorities based on referral to prior knowledge, linkage to preexisting information, sorting, reaching conclusions and so forth. It is superfluous to note that this difficulty can be interpreted as ambivalence and an emotional difficulty with making decisions.

The Ability to Present Data:

When the computer has no ability to generate an output, it becomes a purposeless lump of metal. Likewise, our ability to present the data we take in and process is how we express ourselves in the world. If we cannot express what is within us, we will not be clear and understood by the environment we live in. Expression of the knowledge we have, the sort that is built up based on information and data that we have been able to process, is the ability that will help us advance and realize who we are.

Beyond this, presenting information, which is an ability which enables us to deepen our knowledge and internalize it better, is also a result of executive attention activity. Information (or data) that has been received, processed and understood is presented externally. During this presentation, an additional processing step occurs, and room is now "cleared" to receive and process additional data. One of the difficult problems that can derive from executive attention which operates incorrectly is impairment of the ability to present the data. Data presentation requires the organizing, sequencing and ordering of the data in our head. Memory activities are required in combination with data processes, accompanied by actions such as writing. Considerable effort is required to direct concentration and focus on this entire process. In addition, this is a revelatory process which exposes the weaknesses of the child—something a child who is intuitively aware of her limits might well shy away from.

Let us take, for example, the process of reading comprehension. This process requires, of course, continual and focused attention, knowledge necessary to decipher the written word, and linguistic knowledge. But it also requires executive attention. When we read a text, we are required to manage the reading—to initiate the beginning of the reading, to set a goal for the reading, to keep in our working memory the main details of the text, to organize the information arising from the text, and also to delay our responses, in other words, delaying impulsive thoughts in order to avoid reaching mistaken conclusions. When there are difficulties with executive management, there may also be difficulties with reading comprehension.

The reader will not understand what is read fully, or else will fail to properly convey what she has understood.

Likewise, solving verbal problems in math requires executive attention. We need to read the question, efficiently organize the data, bring into the working memory the mathematical procedures required for the solution, calculate and come to the solution. It is often the case that difficulties with executive management will not enable the student to adequately convey her knowledge, given the flooding of her working memory. She may also arrive at the correct solution without being able to show her calculation process. Under such circumstances we need to explain to the child that she knows arithmetic but finds it difficult to simultaneously hold all the data in her mind and recall the mathematical procedure she requires, or else finds it difficult to properly organize the data to be presented.

Sense of Time, Time Management:
The ability to prioritize functional sequences links the executive attention function with the time dimension. Every action needs to be performed in its proper time to ensure we function efficiently. As we discussed, children with ADHD have difficulties with regulating stimuli and impulses. Things seem to happen simultaneously, and the child experiences overload. This overload makes it difficult to conduct themselves properly on the time continuum, and the difficulty of coping with this is significant. When there are also executive difficulties, the child finds it difficult to utilize planning and organizational processes in their time management. Therefore, she has no way to "organize" the overload or to take control over it. This difficulty is expressed in her immediate functions, such as that which keeps her from forgetting whether there was homework and in which subjects; regarding which part of the problem one should solve first; and, regarding the perception of time, and relating to it with non-immediate functions. For example, "tomorrow" or "next week" are, for the child, in the distant, unknowable future, and due to her executive difficulties, she does not utilize strategic thinking in organizing her time and future tasks. This is why she won't start

work on time, and in the night, before submitting her assignment, she will find herself staring at an empty screen, having failed to write even a single word. Furthermore, her sense of time is limited. Her internal ability to assess time as it goes by is low in comparison to people without difficulties with regulating attention and energy levels. Performing a task which requires only a few moments may seem to her to be an eternity. Alternatively, when she sinks into something interesting, she does not feel time go by, even if she is required to transition to another task. If she is also dealing with executive difficulties, she will not be able to assess how long she needs to devote to doing her homework or to completing a puzzle, and will not know how to prepare herself effectively.

Difficulties with processing new information while using information in the long-term memory:

Jerry, who was supposed to drive his son to school, received a call from his boss one morning. The boss told him that his car had broken down and asked Jerry to leave early to pick him up on the way to work. Jerry responded immediately, and prepared to leave. He had forgotten that he had to take his son to school. The son was supposed to start his school day late, and the school was in the opposite direction to his boss's residence.

- If the father did not take his son to school, the son would be very insulted and might think his father cared about his work more than he cared about him.
- If he called his boss after he had already agreed to his request and explained the problem, the boss might think him irresponsible and disorganized.

What had happened was that during his phone conversation with his boss, Jerry's faulty attention management did not extract from his memory his earlier commitment—hence, he wrongfully assumed a new, conflicting commitment. In cases where there is a problem in the function of executive management, a difficulty also exists in the management of tasks according to timetables. Adding a new event to the schedule might go wrong due to difficulties with extracting preexisting data.

Monitoring – How many times have we heard children say, *"Enough already. I understand"* or *"I'm done; and I have no strength to double-check what I wrote"?*

Excessive information burdens the attention, and particularly the executive attention system. This is because dealing with an excess of information requires one's full attention, disallowing spacing out even momentarily. The information needs to be held within the working memory, tracked, internalized, used to arrive at conclusions, compared with preexisting information and so forth.

This is why children find everything related to multilingual professions, reading comprehension and verbal questions in arithmetic so difficult. This is also the reason for their difficulty with expanding upon a verbal message. Expanding upon a verbal message requires stopping, thinking and planning what one wishes to say. In other words, thoughts need to be organized, options need to be selected, the wheat needs to be separated from the chaff—and only then is it possible to write at length, convincingly, and even beautifully. Many children find it difficult to perform some of the mentioned stages, and when they do not understand the source of the difficulty, they give up in advance, saying such things as

"I don't like English;" "I don't like reading comprehension;" "I find it difficult to write;" "I don't know what they want from me" or *"I don't like school."*

For the same reasons, we will often find these children say – " *I am done – I have had enough of this and don't want to stop and correct my work.*"

An excess or overload of information challenges attention, and in particular, executive attention. Even if these children manage to put in the attention and executive resources required to fulfill a task, they likely lack the resources to continue to focus and invest the mental effort required to read it again and double-check it for the mistakes that require correction.

Effort – the ability to self-check, and **control** – the ability to perform the required corrections – require concentration in order to understand them in depth. The same is true for the ability to devote significant attention in order to check if the task was completed according to specifications. Considerable attention is also required in order to assess what is more important, and to distinguish between it and what is not important. After fulfilling the task, these children feel overwhelmed and are incapable of holding any more data in their minds; they find it difficult to compare between the results and the expected product—and, consequently, decide simultaneously about the changes required. They therefore adopt incorrect learning habits, and over time, gaps form between the "what" and "how"—between what they know and their inability to perform.

Paying attention and using executive attention are processes that require an investment of effort. This is a conscious process which requires pausing, focusing one's attention and concentrating. Anyone can experience executive difficulties, but they are more common in children with ADHD, and they are often expressed by them in a dramatic way. Therefore, the effort required to operate executive attention is considerably greater for children with attention difficulties. The greater the attention difficulties, the greater the required challenges, and the more effort is required.

Initiation

Difficulties with executive functions can also make it difficult for children to self-initiate and get started on a task. They find it difficult to mobilize their powers of attention and direct their efforts. This is why their ability to perform complex mental processes and, moreover, their ability to control themselves and function according to a day-to-day routine, in a consistent and efficient manner, is impaired. It is, therefore, very important for children with executive difficulties to develop their awareness about each of the executive functions that are relevant to them, and for them to learn about themselves. This will lead them to adopt learning strategies and make the most of themselves. The development of these skills and awareness is very necessary, even if it seems to them that they are successfully compensating, improvising and succeeding thanks to their high intelligence and mental strength. It is often the case that this compensatory ability is limited and will not be stable over time. As we mentioned in previous chapters, let me reiterate—when we want to help a child realize her potential, we must not compare her achievements to those of her classmates, but to her own abilities. If she fails to perform in accordance with her innate ability, she will develop frustration and gaps in learning. This situation requires understanding and appropriate care. Many parents doubt the very existence of executive difficulties, mostly because these are transparent and elusive difficulties. They often say: *"She is simply lazy—she can't motivate herself and would rather lie on the couch or play... but she doesn't have an attention disorder, because she is not hyperactive. It is only that her room is always a mess, and she cannot focus on her classes, and she finds it very difficult to deal with changes. When she wants to accomplish something, she succeeds."*

"She does very well at school or when she is staying over at a friend's. In the presence of her own peers, she is attentive and sensitive. But the moment she comes home, everything erupts. She simply can't recall two simple instructions in a row, and I still need to prepare her bag for school. When she decides to behave otherwise, she acts maturely."

This is the place to reiterate that attention difficulties have many diverse expressions, and executive-attention difficulties even more so. Since the executive attention is a complex system, it has many expressions. This is why, rather than looking for a single, uniform characteristic, it is important to "break up" the difficulties into their different expressions and understand the complexity. We will now enumerate some central difficulties; but there are many others, of course:

- A weakness in the function of working memory, which results in forgetfulness when many things need to be recalled at the same time.
- Slowness in processing new data, which demands mental effort.
- A limited sense of time and a low ability to estimate time, which is expressed in difficulties with planning and organizing. This is why, at any time, dependent actions can go wrong, and there is great difficulty with maintaining a sequence of actions and responses.
- A difficulty with pausing before responding in order to examine possible actions and their potential, future repercussions.
- A difficulty with stopping after responding in order to learn lessons, internalize and assess.
- A difficulty with initiating and persevering in tasks, hobbies and courses.
- A tendency to superficiality, which derives from the difficulty to plumb issues in depth when there is an overload of information.
- A limited ability to break down, process and reassemble.
- Difficulty with using feedback, tracking down errors and correcting them.
- A limited ability with delaying immediate gratification in order to fulfill long-term goals.
- Difficulty with getting motivated and taking initiative, and a tendency to procrastination. "Later" becomes both a common sentence and a way of doing things.
- Difficulty with making decisions. "I don't care" is a sentence that comes up every time a decision needs to be made, or an option needs to be selected. The data overwhelm the child or the individual, and she prefers to avoid making a decision (not due to ambivalence).

Executive attention is, as mentioned before, a mechanism which is activated in almost every higher cognitive function of human beings. It is one of the most essential challenges within the various expressions of ADHD. In order to help our child as much as possible, we need to identify and understand their specific difficulties, teach them how to use their strengths, and supply them with the most fitting tools to manage their difficulties. These tools are relatively simple in grade school, but become more complex as the child grows older, the learning material grows more complex, and the life tasks more varied. A deeper, more precise understanding for how to identify executive difficulties – genuine difficulties with initiating tasks, working memory, flexibility, delayed response time, processing and organizing complex information – will help us avoid mistaken interpretation. **Our child is not lazy!** This understanding helps us identify her objective difficulties, difficulties which can and should be recognized and overcome. We can help her with this, without expressing criticism. If our help is insufficient, we need to support the child with enlisting the help of a teacher who has the expertise in instilling learning strategies.

PART TWO
CHAMP MODEL OPERATIONAL APPROACHES

As mentioned, executive attention is an internal process that is hidden from the gaze of external observers. It is nothing like other ADHD phenomena. It is difficult not to notice impulsivity and hyperactivity, and expressions of daydreaming, forgetfulness, spacing out, distractedness and associativity are usually identifiable as well. But even in the days we are in, with awareness of ADHD having risen, parents, teachers and the other adults and professionals surrounding the children find it difficult to understand and accept their significant difficulties with executive attention. Parents and teachers can usually describe learning difficulties, but generally they will not identify and understand the specific difficulties and expressions of executive attention.

Increasing the Awareness of the Child

Since executive attention is a complex and not readily apparent system, it is also not easy to understand. This is why we need to learn the significance of the various executive functions in depth and understand that the process of intervention for the child will be a continual process of guidance and assistance. This is a process which we, the adults around the child, need to perform, so that the child can improve her functioning abilities. Like any phenomena we need to treat, increasing awareness is the first step that must be taken. For the child to grow familiar with each of the executive functions with which she has difficulty coping, it is necessary to help her identify the specific difficulties and grow aware of the processes occurring within her. Identifying and understanding these difficulties will make it easier for her to find inside and beyond herself methods and tools, and to discover the optimal method of behavior and the optimal conduct in the environment she finds herself. We adults need to be patient, we need to learn and repeatedly help the child recognize, whenever necessary, the precise expression of her difficulty with executive attention, to pause, and to gradually come to understand it. Only much later in the process will the child improve her ability to overcome her difficulties with executive attention. For example, if we wish to increase her awareness of her difficulties with working memory, using the CHAMP model, we can explain to the child that it is hard for her to hold two or more data points in her head and manipulate them at the same time. As a result, she grows confused, gets overwhelmed or gives up. We will help her by focusing on different occasions when she "gets lost", and we must show and convince her adamantly that it is not due to impaired understanding, but because she finds it difficult to handle several stimuli at the same time. We will help her pause, stay calm, recognize the specific difficulty she is facing, take a deep breath, and try to filter out the verbiage or thoughts associated with the task; we will remind her that she needs to take note of, highlight, and remember the main points, and to process them. If she does not do well, she should be encouraged to ask for help, and it should be explained to her that she was unable to follow the details of the task. If we understand that there is a genuine difficulty with performing simple daily instructions due to working memory difficulties, we will use the "Active Adult Involvement," according to the CHAMP model. We will try to break up the instructions into smaller units and say them one at a time. We can also explain to the child that she finds it difficult to follow new instructions or complex instructions in routine, day-to-day tasks; we can help her relax and understand that practicing will transform some of the information into becoming automatic, and this will make it much easier for her to function.

Tales From the Clinic
The 'All for a Dollar' Store

A father of one of my young patients recounted the following: Recently, he took his six-year-old son to The Dollar Store. The child wandered around the store, lingered by certain toys and then continued on. He stopped by other toys, picked them up and then put them back in their stands. It was not a large store, but the child went all around it half a dozen times as he studied and deliberated about what to take. The father did not hurry to leave the store and was curious to know how his child would deal with the need to choose the three toys he had been told he could purchase. After two more rounds throughout the store, the child approached his father and told him he did not know what to choose. The father who had observed that the child had repeatedly stopped six or seven items during his rounds, decided to make it easier for him. He suggested to his son that they go around the store together, and that he would hold the toys the child was interested in for him: He explained to the child that he did not need to make a final decision right now and assured him that they would make a final decision afterwards. During the joint circling of the store, the son selected only five toys. Once he was reassured that he could gather toys during his circling of the store and did not need to make a final decision about what to buy, it seemed like he was relieved of a great burden and could conduct himself without difficulty. At the end of the circuit, the five selected toys were placed on the counter, and the son was easily able to choose from among them which two toys he was willing to give up.

Infinite Toys = Infinite Decisions
In this particular example, the father was able to accurately identify and describe his son's specific difficulty with choosing toys in a situation in which he found himself overwhelmed with an excess of information.

After he succeeded in identifying the specific difficulty, he was able to describe the reductive process he carried out with his child. This reduction enabled the child to deal with less data, and eased the decision-making process. Most importantly, the child left the store feeling he had a positive decision-making experience.

I admired the father for the steps he took and told him that I was impressed with how he was able to help his son, and attempted to address and explain this example in the context of attention, in general, and executive attention, specifically. I talked with him about the flooding many children with oscillations of attention experience in situations in which they are excited and overwhelmed with information. I explained the difficulties that arise in dealing effectively with complex situations, such as this one, in which he was required to make a decision to choose one specific toy with so many other toys lying around.

In cases, such as this, when a child has a hard time making a choice due to information overload, she should be helped with an explanation, recommendation or instruction.

Morning Routine

We have discussed how children with executive-attention difficulties often have a hard time performing tasks requiring organization and planning, with morning organization being a particularly noticeable difficulty. The child should be made aware of these difficulties and gradually helped to link morning chores to planning and organization in general—both he and we need to understand that organization requires a sequence of actions, comparison, decision-making, prioritization and making use of environmental feedback and/or prior knowledge.

Within the CHAMP dialogue, it is highly recommended we explain to the children this specific Achilles' heel. They should be helped to defend themselves by learning to distinguish and separate between their objective difficulties and the emotional interpretations and criticisms of those in their environment. Only then should they be helped to prepare themselves accordingly, via various reminders—a user-friendly table outlining the order of activities, choosing their clothes the evening before and pre-organizing their school bag and pencil case. It is important to remember that, as useful and effective as these aides and tools are, they will only help the child after she understands and internalizes her specific difficulties. Once she is **aware** and understands, she will find her own creative and efficient solutions. I cannot emphasize enough that it is important for us to understand that the goal is to teach the child about herself so that she can manage more easily. We need to teach her to organize herself, not to organize things for her.

Daily Routine

Many parents contrast the polite behavior of the child throughout the day at school, or with friends, with the outburst that occurs the moment they enter their home.

I repeatedly explain to the parents that they must appreciate the effort the children have invested to function adequately in various capacities outside their home. This indicates that they have a good emotional intelligence—they intuitively sense their difficulties and invest a maximum effort in managing. They invest considerable effort in self-management and challenge their executive attention when they are mobilized to do so. Much more serious is the opposite condition—when the child makes an effort and behaves in accordance with expectations at home and erupts when not at home.

The ability to restrain herself outside her home is a sign that the child can learn to regulate herself via her executive attention and in accordance with socially accepted norms. Having an accurate understanding will help us explain to the child the precise characteristics of the executive-attention difficulties she experiences and increase her awareness of them. By understanding this difficulty and reinforcing every step of progress in identification and function, we will help her become more understanding of herself and her environment. We can also gradually demand the respect of limits in the household, as well. In other words, the child will put in the effort to cope in certain situations in the home, as well, and there will be accepted or agreed upon places where she can vent and release tension.

Executive Attention and Schoolwork

Many parents mistakenly define attention and executive-attention difficulties as learning difficulties or disabilities. There are indeed similarities between learning difficulties and attention difficulties. In both cases, students find it difficult to optimally express their ability to think and, thus, to succeed in the learning process. Nonetheless, it is important to emphasize that it is very important to distinguish between learning difficulties, and attention and executive-attention difficulties, even when the latter are expressed in the form of difficulties with learning, or negatively impact learning.

Primary language difficulties or learning disabilities are consistent difficulties that are expressed both in verbal expressions and throughout the learning process. In contrast, learning difficulties deriving from attention difficulties, in general, and difficulties with executive attention, in particular, are in no way consistent. A student with attention difficulties can understand a passage of English literature splendidly, if she happens to be focused or if she finds it of interest, but she will find it very difficult to understand a history lesson if she is distracted, or if she fails to follow the sequence of events. At the times in which she experiences difficulty rallying her general attention or her executive attention, her understanding will be impaired. Children with attention and executive-attention difficulties will display inconsistent behavior—sometimes they will know the material and sometimes they won't. Furthermore, children with attention and executive-attention difficulties will frequently find it difficult to transform knowledge or techniques into "automatic" skills—but will not find it difficult to understand the essentials. Take for example mathematics—a child with a learning disability in mathematics will present a genuine difficulty with the concept of numbers or the significance of quantity, or in understanding the essence of the counting sequence. She will find it difficult to understand the essence of arithmetic operations and when they are required. A child with executive difficulties will understand the significance of the sequence and the amount, and will be able to better understand the significance of the operations and be able to adapt arithmetic operations to a math word problem. Difficulties with working memory may not enable her to remember the multiplication table off by heart, or else fail to recall the rules governing the addition of simple fractions, and hence find it difficult to solve the problems. It may be that due to organizational difficulties, she will not manage to correctly arrange the verbal data into an organized solution but arrive at the answer without fully understanding how she arrived at it.

Given the similarities, overlap and differences between genuine primary-learning difficulties and disabilities, and difficulties with attention and executive attention, it is important to seek appropriate professional advice—adaptive teachers, occupational therapists and speech therapists. In the first stage, it is important to conduct a differential diagnosis to determine the source of the difficulty. Based on its results, an intervention plan should be prepared. For the most part, learning difficulties deriving from attention and executive-attention difficulties will require instructional methods designed to increase awareness of attention difficulties and ways to bypass it—in other words, assimilating learning strategies. Learning strategies are taught by an adaptive teacher. Treating executive-attention difficulties requires of the specialist, adaptive teacher considerable awareness and understanding regarding attention and management difficulties, as well as identification of the characteristics unique to every student. This specialty enables the teacher to devote their adaptive teaching lessons to identifying the source of the specific difficulty, while raising the student's awareness of her executive-attention difficulties. Through this, it will be possible to help her adopt appropriate learning strategies and supportive tools to ease her learning processes. A specialized adaptive learning teacher, who teaches specific learning strategies, can provide the child with learning habits, teaching her to function better, and these can certainly help her improve her academic achievement. The child will learn how to use tools which will help her deal with higher thinking processes, such as factorization and separating the essential from the superfluous. She will learn to use varied memory methods and external aides. As in other expressions of ADHD, here too, the teacher or mediator must strengthen the child throughout the process, isolate the difficulty from the other capabilities of the child and provide her with the specific tools appropriate for her needs. The strengths which define and distinguish the child should be pinpointed, and they should be used in order to identify the path easiest for her to study. This path will help her bypass her difficulties. For example, for some children, executive attention operates better when they deal with visual data than with audible data. These children should be taught methods of presenting data visually—using graphic tools, charts, underlining (with colorful pens or markers) and so forth, as these tools can be very beneficial for them. Children who find clearly defined rules to be of assistance in helping them get organized can use cards on which their rules are clearly written. These cards can serve as an aide in organizing themselves.

In addition to making use of the child's strengths, the foci of executive difficulties need to be **precisely** identified to help overcome them. For example, we should investigate whether the child needs help distinguishing the main issue from peripheral concerns, or whether she requires help factoring a problem, or perhaps whether her difficulty is in transitioning between situations or content, which require a change in the focus of her attention. Throughout this work, it is very important to make the child aware of the precise difficulty she is dealing with, and to find, together, appropriate tools and efficient management strategies. The combination of the child's strengths and the appropriate learning strategies is what will help the child better acquire and strengthen her learning material. For example, in order to help children develop the capability of transition between different focus states, their specific difficulty needs to be identified and defined and explained to them, and they need to be taught methods and techniques for dealing with specific situations in their own life. It must be noted that the specific difficulty at the source here is completely different from daydreaming or inattention, even though the external expression of these phenomena can be quite similar.

These, admittedly, are tools which will help all pupils, regardless of their difficulties. However, students without any difficulties will get along even if we don't teach them any specific tools, without external assistance.

In contrast, students with attention and executive-attention difficulties will not adopt efficient learning methods on their own. This is why diagnosing and identifying difficulties with executive attention is the cornerstone upon which the most appropriate help for the child, which will best help her realize her potential, should be built.

It is important for the child to gradually internalize, as the process progresses, that her difficulty is with attention and executive attention rather than with understanding. From self-perception defined by a sense of failure and incapability, she will transition to an experience of successful functioning and the adaptation of a relatively simple strategy which enables her to solve a defined problem. Every time we hear the sentence *"I don't understand,"* we must re-emphasize to the child that she is extremely intelligent, with excellent potential for understanding, but that without listening and effective management processes, true understanding cannot be achieved. We need to repeatedly tell her that her difficulty is with listening and management—not with understanding. When, during her studies, the child repeatedly complains of boredom, we need to remember that this can be indicative of attention difficulties, and we must therefore raise her awareness of this. She was not able to say, *"I spaced out and could not hear what the teacher said ..."* and, instead, she will think that her understanding is at fault; and as she is not interested in exposing her weaknesses, what she will actually say is that the lesson or teacher was boring. In such situations, we will explain to her that her difficulty with listening for a prolonged period of time or transitioning from one lesson to another, or separating the gist of the teacher's explanation from the finer details, led her to stop listening, and that was why she could not follow what was said. In these situations the lesson becomes *"boring."*

In every framework the child participates in, we can and should utilize the CHAMP model. In this chapter, we will refer to the implementation of the model in adaptive teaching. It is important to remember that pupils with attention and executive difficulties do not find it difficult to understand the learned material, but rather find it difficult to adequately absorb, process, organize and store it in their long-term memory. This is why there is no need for the adaptive learning process to focus on studying the material. The pupil does not need to study the material again and again—she needs to learn **how** to study the material in order to internalize it. The difference between learning the "what" and learning the "how" is essential; and learning the "how" is at the core of adaptive teaching—certainly when the pupil is a talented child with ADHD and executive difficulties.

As I noted in previous chapters, the CHAMP model is not hierarchical. It is generally recommended not to start at the end, but in this case, I chose to do so, as it summarizes what we have just said.

CHAM**P** – **P**ractice Makes Perfect

The adaptive teaching process is systematic and ongoing, aimed at generating a perceptual change in the child which stems from in-depth understanding of the methods of learning. This is a process aimed at reducing the dependence of the pupil on the teacher, and to help her accept responsibility for her learning processes, in order to make her into an independent learner. The process of adaptive teaching can be performed equally, in elementary school, middle school and high school (or even in college/university). During this process, the pupil experiences a variety of learning strategies, in accordance with her age and learning tasks, in order to choose those that are most suitable for her, given her strengths and her needs. When this is a pupil with attention disorders, in general, and executive attention disorders, in particular, the learning strategies need to be adapted to their distinct attention characteristics. Throughout this process, the pupil repeatedly practices the various strategies—first, with the intensive mediation of the adaptive teaching instructor, and then gradually, with a reduction of the intervention method, until she achieves independent and successful function. It is often the case that pupils with attention and executive-attention disorders find it difficult to deploy effective learning strategies and persevere in them. Accordingly, practice is incredibly important, and one must not make do with one-time learning of strategies or learning paths. Practice will take place over time until the learning strategies become a habit for the pupil and serve her consistently and efficiently.

CHAMp – Mindful Metaphors and Imagery

One of the most effective tools to raise the awareness of a child about her attention and executive difficulties is, as previously discussed, the use of metaphors and imagery. This tool is, therefore, extremely efficient also in adaptive teaching. The metaphors one can make use of are many and varied, especially given the creativity of many ADHD pupils. It is very important to match the metaphor to the pupil, so that it is significant for her, and thus, it is important to encourage her to identify it herself. I will introduce here, also, examples of metaphors relating to difficulties with delaying responses. We will use them only after the pupil understands and notices that this is the difficulty that defines her. Referring to the metaphor will help the pupil remember that she needs to invest herself into this component during the learning process.

Some pupils with reaction-delay difficulties utilize the **stoplight** metaphor, which reminds them to stop, prepare, and only then work. The stoplight can help us both in reading texts and in solving mathematical formulas.

The **reins** metaphor can also be efficient in reminding us of the importance of delaying responses. It enables the pupil to remember that the natural need to race forward without thinking must be restrained. This metaphor helps greatly in adaptive learning processes of young pupils, as well as in similar processes among teenagers. This is simple language, which is easy to "connect" to. Additional code names or metaphors for executive difficulties can be:

A starter that finds it difficult to ignite the engines and get us moving.

The user-friendly operations manual that enables us to present data in a pleasant manner.

The oversight and control department that reexamines our data.

The sieve, which is essential to separating the essential from the superfluous.

Confused when cannot manipulate concepts due to an overload of data.

A white blank board, for when data disappears momentarily and is not absorbed by the memory.

What should I do? When it is hard to reach a decision.

There are many other possible examples—each pupil should be encouraged to find the metaphor which speaks to her and helps her.

Champ — Choose One Specific Component

As mentioned before, in order to enable the reader to understand her executive difficulties and change them, we need to be precise in their definition, distinguish between them, and differentiate them from the pupil. For example:

A pupil with excellent mathematical thinking who finds it difficult to perform monitoring processes cannot manage to notice her calculation errors and, hence, cannot fix them. She knows the material well at every test, but gets low grades due to errors performed out of distraction, and because she does not check her work before she submits the test.

After each test she repeatedly says she must be very bad in math. The adaptive teacher must perform a process of differentiation and distinction:

*"Your mathematical thinking is excellent—here, in this formula you just solved, you suggested two different but equally correct ways to solve the equation. Now pay attention, we will solve five formulas in sequence, but once this is done, we will take a short break, and then you will activate the **personal guardian**—the one who examines the equations carefully, seeks out mistakes and corrects them. You should also use the personal guardian during the test."*

c**H**AMP — **H**elp (with the "How") via Reflecting, Redefining, Rehearsing and Responsibility

During the adaptive teaching lessons, the teacher must identify the characteristics of dysregulation, or the executive difficulties of the pupil, in order to reflect them to the pupil in the academic context.

For example:

During reading a text about horses, the reader halts and begins to recount in detail a horse-riding class she is participating in. Most of the details are associative and irrelevant.

The adaptive teacher must reflect the associations that might interfere with the *reading:*

"You are reading about horses and immediately recall your horse-riding class. The class is racing through your thoughts, and you feel you need to talk about it, but it is irrelevant. These thoughts do not contribute to understanding the text, because they are not relevant to its content. They can be confusing."

If the student can understand this, increase her awareness about her associative thoughts, and direct them—we will encourage her to do so as much as possible to optimize her process of reading comprehension.

If the pupil cannot control her associations, we will take a break with the reading, let her vent her thoughts, and then continue reading, so that the racing thoughts from the past will not interfere with picking up new information.

It is often the case that the adaptive teacher will redefine the characteristics that surface, so that the pupil will be able to redefine for herself how she treats herself and the learning process. For example:

After reading a section in a history book, a student is required to answer an accompanying question. The question is long and complex, and when she is done reading, she pauses and says, "*I don't understand.*" The adaptive teacher identifies the difficulty formed by the reader's working-memory difficulties and says,

*"Please note that the question is long and composed of several sections. We must have **overfilled the pool** (= the working memory). Let's try to break up the question into its components. Now you will see that the difficulty is not in understanding but in remembering and connecting the different parts."*

CH**A**MP — **A**ctive Adult Involvement

An active approach by the adult is a basic precondition to adaptive teaching. The adaptive teacher must be active throughout the classes and operate constant mediation processes—identifying difficulties with management, explaining them to the student in order to increase her awareness of them, analyzing and finding with her new management and control strategies and, particularly, praising her when she successfully utilizes such strategies and achieves good and effective results. Should the teacher suffice with finding a solution for the student's difficulty without utilizing the intervention processes of the CHAMP model, she will not provide her with any long-term benefit, for she will remain dependent on external assistance. For the students to arrive at self-awareness and be independent in their learning, it is necessary to use mediation that refers to the specific difficulty in each instance when such a difficulty arises. For example:

> A pupil tells an adaptive teacher repeatedly that she does not manage to hand in assignments she was given in school. The adaptive teacher must **link** the different events for her and reflect to her how she conducts herself:
>
> *"Last month, two weeks ago, and also today, you told me that you did not hand in your assignments in history, science and math. What do you think is the connection between the three cases?"*
> *"You seem to be postponing, to the last minute, doing the assignments, and then you don't have enough time to do them as you would like. Let's talk about procrastination and your difficulty with" the starter" and then think together of some way to help you start doing the assignments on time, without putting them off to the last moment."*

Basic Principles in Instilling Learning Strategies or Executive Strategies

> **Like an operational manual of a complex electronic device:**
>
> We require executive strategies in order to present our knowledge or act effectively.
> This can be illustrated to the child with a comparison to using the operational manual of a complex and very advanced electronic

device. This is the latest, and best, hit. However, it is so complex that it cannot be fully enjoyed or operated beyond the most basic level without the operations manual. It is the operations manual which enables a full understanding of the incredible, "magical" abilities of the advanced device, and their presentation to all.

The child's brain is the advanced device, and the operations manual is the executive abilities enabling the presentation of the knowledge. This metaphor separates between the child and her expression and ability to present knowledge, much like the difference between the device and the operations manual. The child is intelligent and talented, but she must learn to use her executive attention to present her knowledge.

- **Decomposition:**

It is important to teach the child to use the "decomposition" tool—breaking up knowledge into portions or stages, and then learning it stage by stage. Simplifying the problem or breaking down the information is less challenging to executive knowledge. A large, general mission that is broken down into many smaller missions, such that each small task is composed of fewer elements that need to be considered simultaneously, is why it can be more focused and easier to perform or learn.

The child can be told:

"You find it difficult when you need to listen or consider several things at once. It seems to you that you do not understand, that the material is too difficult for you—but this is not the case. I know that you aren't just saying it is difficult for you, but it is important that you understand what your difficulty is. I want you to know that you are a smart child, and that nothing is wrong with your understanding. Now, let us break the chapter down into several smaller chunks, and see if you will find it easier to pay attention to them, understand the information and remember it."

Some children are overloaded and give up as soon as they see a page filled with exercises. They can be told:

"The full page is driving you nuts, and you say you can't do it. Let's cover the entire page with a white sheet, and you will only expose one exercise at a time to solve it."

- **Essential and peripheral**

Separating what is essential from that which is peripheral requires executive attention. When there is difficulty with the executive functions, there is often also a difficulty with isolating the essence from the entire contents. We need to help children and adults focus on learning this skill, since following this differentiation it is much easier to deal only with the essence, and therefore also much easier to learn or to respond. This filtering action can reduce many data points that are not necessary and might confuse or overload our thinking and memory. Indeed, most data points might be excluded in this manner. The overall picture the child is required to deal with becomes simpler, cleared of distractions, doubts and the decisions needed to confront the chaos of the intermixed essential and peripheral.

I often use the sieve metaphor with these children.

Pasta for lunch:
"I am preparing pasta for lunch. I boil water, sprinkle salt and add pasta to the pot. A few minutes in the boiling water, and the pasta is soft and ready to eat. If I don't use a sieve to separate the pasta from the water, then all I can serve the children is a pot filled with water and pasta ... hardly an appetizing lunch.

Using the sieve to separate the pasta from the water is much like separating the essential from the peripheral. It enables us to get the results we are interested in. In this way, we can recognize the truly important things we want to focus on, and this is how others will understand us and listen to us when we say something."

Large marbles and small marbles:
Imagine you have before you a box filled with two sizes of marbles, all mixed up. You need to count the number of small marbles in the box. The first option is to count the marbles when they are inside the box. But you are not permitted to take them out of the box.

The second option—you have a sieve through which the smaller marbles can pass into a different box. This way, you can count only them without the confusion and distraction of the larger marbles. It is easy to see which option is preferable, and what is the complexity in the required action when no process of filtration takes place.

- **Order and organization**

Do any of these sentences sound familiar?

"I understand what the teacher said, so why do I need to take time to write it down?"

"… but I know, I don't feel like explaining."

"I don't have energy, so I will write briefly."

"Ugh … Why do I need to write?"

"It is hard for me to organize my thoughts to write them down—why do I need to do this?"

"What did you just say? You said two things and I lost you".

Do you remember the example of the operational manual? If I have the most advanced and complex device in the world but lack an operation manual for it, then I will not be able to utilize all of the opportunities it can offer me.

We need to keep in mind that the child has a very hard time arranging data and presenting it in an orderly and impressionable fashion. However, there is no doubt that the more order and organization, the more she will be able to draw from herself. She needs to understand this and to learn how to do this—with our help. We need to enable her to understand the value of writing things in a notebook or on a test—to understand, that if she only writes what she knows clearly will the teacher be able to know what she knows. Only then will her grade score truly reflect what she knows. Likewise, order and organization will enable her to manage to do everything she wants to do every day; with order and organization she will be able to do things on time and will not be stressed out from getting things done at the last moment. There are also various useful aides which can assist in the organizational process, and there are more of them every year in this digital age. Nonetheless, such tools can only truly benefit our child once she understands her executive difficulties and accepts the need for external organizational tools.

Here are a few examples of such tools:

▷ Use of a diary to track time and the sequence of events
▷ Use of reminders – a diary, notes, digital and other memos – to undertake all the tasks without forgetting them
▷ Use of color markers, Post-Its, and any other tool that will help us create separation and emphasis.
▷ Use of a tape recorder. Recording a lesson, for example, will enable the child to focus on what is said, write up only significant points without needing to write up everything the teacher says.
▷ Using a camera—for example, photographing the blackboard instead of copying it to the notebook.
▷ Using memorization techniques, such as acronyms of the subject matter, linking the information we are studying to known and familiar information, and so forth.
▷ Studying in pairs or groups; this enables the child to hear the subject matter anew and generate interest in the process via brainstorming. This enables the assimilation of the material in additional ways beyond reading and summarizing it.

- **The importance of adaptations in the learning process:**

Take, for example, a situation in which the same teacher consecutively teaches two lessons on two different topics. There is no break between them and not even a bell to mark the transition. The teacher finishes one lesson and immediately transitions to the next lesson. The only thing separating the two is her announcement:

"Close the grammar books now, put them in your bag, and take out your English literature books and notebooks."

For our child, these are three different instructions, provided consecutively. It is hard for her to remember all three, since this requires the ability to preserve information in the working memory, to differentiate and to create a sequence. Furthermore, it requires the ability to transfer the focus of attention from grammar exercises to the English literature subject matter … and, besides, the child may still be writing down the grammar homework.

Clearly, any adaptation, however slight, that the teacher might implement for our child at this point would be most beneficial. A brief break and appropriate guidance, broken into small pieces, which will help the child direct her attention from grammar to English literature, will enable her to track what is happening in class and be part of the class's learning process.

My Personal Experience

Throughout my years in school, I was repeatedly told:
"You have excellent mathematical understanding, so why do you keep on failing???"
Today, I know that solving mathematical equations requires executive attention. You need to hold in your head two or more data points, manipulate them, calculate the result, and transition thereby from one stage to another in order to solve the equation.
I recall that solving word problems in mathematics was particularly difficult for me. Time and distance problems, trains leaving from different destinations who pass by each other at some point or another—I blew them all up in my imagination. They never had a chance to pass each other by. This was a real nightmare for me.

Another word about strategies:
Since executive attention is expressed throughout life, it is very important to make use of the executive strategies which will be taught in adaptive teaching, and should also be implemented in day-to-day conduct. Therefore, there should be transference from the field of learning to the other fields of life. This should be done by a person with a close personal connection to the child, a connection based on trust. This person will be able to accompany the child, explain to her, and help her adopt thinking and behavioral strategies to find practical solutions in their daily life. This process can accompany the child throughout her maturation and development, much like the strategies used by the child during her studies.

Games

There are countless games that can be played to demonstrate various elements of the "complicated attention." I will provide one as an illustration, which is particularly beloved by both myself and the children. This is a game which helps children understand what action strategy is and how it should be used.

I love to play this game in my group sessions with children. I use it to demonstrate and explain to children the meaning of executive attention. Children also particularly enjoy and remember this game, and it initiates conversation and discussion.

I distribute play money in various denominations (20, 50, 100, 200) to the children. Each child gets a wad of bills. The purpose of the game is to collect as many bills as possible with the same value (not necessarily the highest value). I do not explain to the children how they should collect the bills, but rather let them choose their own action strategy.

It is very interesting to observe the various strategies implemented by the children—some do not understand the instruction, others get it immediately, some collect the highest valued bills, and others realize they are better off gathering the low-value bills, since they are less sought after. At some point, some children realize they should join others in order to win, and they ask if this is permitted. At the end of the exciting activity, I hold a discussion about the various strategies used to perform the task, based on the bills each child holds.

Summary

Executive attention is a complex cognitive system, and many, but not all, children with ADHD have difficulties with this system. Given this complexity, securing a diagnostic profile of the child, so we can understand her source of difficulty, is essential.

Once we precisely pinpoint the child's specific difficulty, we can explain it to her and reflect her behavior back to her. The precise explanation and reflection will assist in increasing her awareness, and thus, we can teach her to create linkages between tasks and the difficulties that prevent effectively dealing with them. Instead of providing the child with a solution for every instance of difficulty, we need to help her understand and identify the various and varied expressions of "complicated" attention, instill in her management strategies and teach her how to conduct herself independently.

Only in this manner can she make a change in her ability to function—and start to function independently and realize more of her abilities.

As mentioned, difficulties with executive attention are not visible, unlike other attention-oscillation difficulties, hyperactivity and impulsivity. Parents and teachers sometimes grow confused when they see a talented child, with many abilities, who cannot realize even a few of her abilities in school. Often, she remains an unsolved enigma to them. Frequently, they interpret her difficulties as emotional difficulties or learning disabilities, and the resultant treatment is maladapted to the needs of the child. Difficulties with executive functions will influence all aspects of the child's life. A significant expression of this difficulty will take place during her studies, leading to failure to realize her potential, an accumulation of learning gaps, frustration and increasing difficulties leading to dropping out from school. However, we must keep in mind that difficulties with executive attention are apparent in every complex situation. Understanding the specific difficulties with executive attention might solve a considerable portion of the puzzle which makes up our child. Self-control, goal-oriented behavior, and the development of the ability to consider future consequences will be influenced by operational abilities, which are focused on the executive attention funnel. In this process, the necessity for active, close adult involvement, which will provide the child with support, mediation and precise reflection to increase her awareness, becomes clear. This is how we provide our child with the help she requires and study her, so she can better understand herself, and so she can manage to find the ways that are suitable for her to improve her operational abilities, in school, the workplace and in life, more generally.

THE SIEVE

There's a bowl in our kitchen that's all full of holes,
And it's sort of strange — not like all other bowls;
When you pour hot soup in it, broth falls through, grains remain;
For this bowl is a sieve, and it knows how to strain.
Mom says a sieve is a most useful tool,
When we want to tell stories that sound really cool.

Alas, sometimes my sieve I forget when I speak,
And then I start talking just like a blue streak.
I pile details on details as high as the sky,
To my tale's main idea you can just say, "Good-bye!"
For nobody's listening when the point I do reach—
They can't stay in tune with my so lengthy speech!

"Be aware," my Mom tells me, "of where folks are at;
They can't always listen when you want to chat.
If the food starts to burn or the baby to cry,
You'll just have to wait, you really must try!"
So I'll try'n notice when people can pay me attention,
And then just the main details, I'll be sure to mention!

CHAPTER 9

Talking ADHD — Compensatory Attention

Whenever I face a task, such as reading, proofreading, writing, preparing a presentation or even preparing a meal for many guests, planning a trip to a new destination, or packing a suitcase for traveling abroad, I start to think about it many days in advance. I prepare my gear in advance, organize everything by categories, prepare mental and written lists, and get ready. These are tasks which demand many attentional resources from me, and I prepare myself for the moment that I feel that I am focused enough to do them, and wait for the moment where I can rally sufficient reserves to complete the task. In most cases I do indeed complete the task successfully, but people around me are never aware of just how much energy I invested, the preparation involved, and the mental resources I require to get it done. To the outside observer, my behavior may even seem somewhat obsessive. I usually choose not to explain, save on special occasions, when I feel I face an empathic individual who identifies with me and my condition.

PART ONE
THE PHENOMENON AND ITS RAMIFICATIONS

The compensatory attention phenomena, which is also one of the expressions of ADHD, is neither as common or as well-known as the other phenomena characterizing the dysregulation of attention and hyperactivity. Hyperactivity, impulsivity and wandering-attention difficulties have been extensively reviewed within the research literature. Over the past few years, considerable research has also been devoted to executive attention. The phenomenon of "compensatory attention," in contrast, has not benefited from nearly as much research and coverage. The externalized expressions of "compensatory attention" tend to be interpreted as superior ability, rather than as difficulty. However, the personal, emotional and mental price of this ability is very grave, indeed. The cognitive and behavioral expressions associated with the phenomenon seemingly stem from an emotional basis rather than a neurological one—ADHD.

I was first exposed to the phenomenon known as "overfocusing" when I was well into my professional career, in the 1990s. Although ADHD has been a familiar, treated phenomenon since the mid-1900s, overfocusing had never been linked to it. The understanding that overfocusing is a phenomenon which stems from ADHD developed among research and medical circles only several years later, and was documented by two neurologists, Dr. Marcel Kinsbourne[1] and Dr. Daniel Amen.[2] In describing the phenomenon in this chapter, I have adopted certain ideas of theirs, as well as the questionnaire composed by Dr. Amen to identify the phenomenon. However, since the term "overfocusing" has come to mean a hyper-focusing ability, achieved following external stimulation (a computer screen, a smartphone or a particularly challenging video game), I feel the phenomenon needs to be redefined in connection with ADHD. I define the phenomena and its attendant characteristics as "compensatory attention." This term refers to the ability to focus that is derived from the **inner motives and efforts** of the individual, unlike "overfocus" which is achieved, as mentioned, via external stimuli.

As I see it, **compensatory attention** is a **system of strategies** which an individual with ADHD generates for herself as a means of dealing with the flooding she experiences when confronted with an overload of information. She utilizes an array of these strategies to deal with and direct the inundation derived from the attention difficulties. This system is an inner-cognitive system which serves her and enables her to deal with the excess of information and data which floods her thoughts and consciousness. Via compensatory attention she gathers her forces, rallies herself for the task and performs it successfully, while disguising her attention difficulties. The disguise is so good that those around her don't even notice that she has a hard time—and are even astounded at her abilities.

However, her commitment to the process and its success sometimes demands so much effort that her strength is drained, and she becomes exhausted. As a result, she will therefore usually prove unable to sustain focus on long-term missions. In addition, the excessive effort might result in a heavy emotional price, both in the short-term and in the long-term. This way of coping serves human beings and enables them to mobilize their attentional abilities, but may also lead them to rigidity, difficulty with accepting changes, a compulsive need to maintain control, outbursts, argumentativeness, fixation, defiance, anxiety around issues of capability, negative thoughts and so forth. It is, therefore, **very difficult to diagnose.** In-depth understanding of the subject by professionals, and if possible, by those in the environment, alongside development of awareness by the individual herself, helps her identify her optimal place on the continuum—between the effectiveness of the compensatory-attention mechanism and the many downsides that can be generated by the incredible effort required to cope.

About Efforts to Focus and Maintain Attention

Imagine that you are put in the middle of a circle of people, each reading a section from a different book. You need to focus only on the words of the third guy standing behind you—hear, listen and understand what he has read out. The circle also includes another guy with a very grating voice, another fellow with a booming bass voice, a woman who reads very rapidly and with no regard for punctuation marks, and another woman who really yells out the text ... so everyone can hear her.

Amidst the din, you try to listen to what the third guy standing behind you is saying. Sometimes you do better and sometimes worse. In some moments you cannot hear him or focus on his voice, and then you need to fill in the blanks in your mind while still listening to him ...

Imagine how much energy you would have to invest in meeting this task, and how tired you would be at its end.

So ... Yes, it is likely you will meet this challenge. You can do it. So can your child, but the price is very high, and the ramifications, over time, will most likely be primarily emotional.

For the most part, people with compensatory attention will be those who are committed to those in their environment: positive people who rise to the challenge throughout their daily routine and throughout their entire lifetime. They intuitively understand themselves, but are not aware, or are only partially aware, of their objective difficulty with attention, and try to deal with it on their own. No one notices their incredible inner struggle. No one notices the incredible effort they invest in dealing with this difficulty. This coping leads most of them to be relatively closed and introverted people. I have worked with many patients over the years. I have met with adults, parents, children and adolescents, and each time I have explained the compensatory-attention phenomenon, I have perceived an incredible relief in the patients' responses.

I ask them—

"Is it true that you manage to perform the tasks, but that this costs you so much effort that it leaves you exhausted at the end?"

Their response is almost invariably, *"Finally someone gets me!"*

This sentence is usually accompanied by a deep sigh of relief and tears that overflow from their eyes. All too often, no one else in their environment has truly understood the very real difficulties which have accompanied them throughout their life. No one has appreciated the mental fortitude required by them to function successfully and to meet the expectation of those around them. No one has assumed that their emotional difficulties were in fact derived from ADHD. These difficulties characterize children and even adults who were not diagnosed, or who were diagnosed but remain unaware of the phenomena manifesting within them. Simply being diagnosed, and the diagnosis being explained to them, frees them of the deluge of questions, fears and concerns that have burdened them throughout their life. A deep genuine and empathic understanding, focused conversations and assistance with coping help them greatly in formulating insights that enable them to tell their life story anew. The more the awareness of the phenomena is developed, the more the burden of anxiety and and accompanying phenomena is reduced, and the greater the improvement of function.

Compensatory attention may result in extreme and inconsistent behaviors, such as cases of rapid transitioning from absolutely silent concentration to an impulsive outburst of rage or lockdown; or cases in which the child smiles and tries to please, but actually is feeling low—as she is most of the time. Sometimes we witness a room so messy that we cannot see the floor, but one drawer is meticulously organized, as if it belongs to someone else; in another case, the child or adult display an impressive ability to do research or demonstrate broad knowledge about a particular subject which is of great interest to them, but they are unable to rally their strength for simple and routine tasks.

Common Characteristics and the Typical Expression of the Compensatory Attention System

- **Seeking control to generate and preserve stability:**

Our lives are filled with situations of information overload, a continual state of uncertainty and frequent changes. These situations lead some of us to "take charge," to try and achieve maximum control to keep our function as focused as possible, despite the turmoil within our attentional systems. A person with a compensatory attention ability will have a tendency for "bossiness", which can steady and pin down the situation as she understands it. This spares her the need to change her method of operation, to reexamine conclusions and, above all else, to have to deal with being inundated. Such an individual tends to fixate or erupt when things do not develop according to their expectations or planning.

- **A need for order and quiet:**

The inundation of data, which usually results in distraction – a transition from one thing to another, both mentally and physically – will be expressed completely differently here. People who tend to use their compensatory attention system require extreme quiet around them. Sometimes we will see them stand away from the group. They will back off a bit, or sit with their backs to the group or to what is going on. They like to sit in front of the computer screen, and many of them like to read. There are quite a few bookworms among them, who read a whole lot. Sometimes, their over-occupation with certain things will seems to the outside observer to be nearly obsessive. But this is not the case—they are so inundated that their experience is as if they are drowning in endless data or the many tasks they must perform. The "chaos" experience in their head leads them to aspire to maximize the order around them, but they find it very difficult to do so. Sometimes, we will meet adults with compensatory attention in the hallway at work, so completely self-absorbed, that they don't even acknowledge their colleagues. One can easily interpret this behavior as unsocial.

- **Pace of activity:**

For some people, compensatory attention leads them to conduct themselves very slowly. They plough their way through mountains of stimuli, information and decisions, and constantly try to stick to the focused track they have selected.

They are so careful to not deviate from it even in the slightest, to avoid losing focus, that their progress slows down to a snail's pace.

- **Transition and change:**

By their very nature, require dealing with new information, making decisions, and letting go of what has already happened or is no longer relevant, in order to enable something new to arise. Adopting to deal with compensatory attention leads people to invest considerable effort and energy in focusing on their present activities, preserving a barrier which enables them to deal with "disruptive" stimuli from within and without. It is therefore extremely difficult to stop them in the middle of whatever activity they are engaged in. It doesn't matter whether they are reading, playing or building a 3-D model. Transition, adaptability and change are perceived as being very simple for most people, but for them, finishing one activity and transitioning to a new one is accompanied with much difficulty.

To the external observer, their response may seem rigid or stiff, or completely disproportionate to what is expected of them. If they are also impulsive, they will likely erupt with an angry and uncontrollable response toward everyone around them. Adopting compensatory attention leads people to immerse themselves in one specific activity to the exclusion of everything else, cutting themselves off from the environment. Compensatory attention can sometimes also lead to spacing out in situations when a change in the environment forces the child to redirect her attention to events around her.

It seems this can happen to all of us from time to time. A good book or television series can drag us in, not to mention the smartphone screen, which we are overly occupied with. But this is not what I am talking about. Compensatory attention defines certain people as a recurring pattern, a way to cope with information overload. **This is an inner mechanism which is not connected to the type of external stimuli.** Unlike "addiction" to a television series or a good book, where we do not invest any effort, the coping mechanism of compensatory attention is associated with the investment of **considerable effort**. It is often accompanied by anxiety, worrying, rigidity, excessive occupation with details and a need for control that can be interpreted as a condescending attitude. Such people are so immersed in themselves that they are sometimes perceived as inconsiderate of those in their environment. They can be immersed in activity or even thought, such that they are not attentive to a conversation taking place in the room, and do not participate in it. Such children can continue speaking to their mother when the phone rings and she is engaged in a conversation, or when she goes to deal with their younger brother. They can be occupied with a certain topic, and repeatedly return to it, even when the circumstances are in no way appropriate. They can even not notice the smell of a nearby fire if they are occupied with their own concerns.

This is like a man walking the tightrope until he reaches the midpoint, glistening with sweat and totally focused on maintaining his balance. Suppose at that moment you would ask him: "Hey, step down for a moment please. I want us to do something else. You can continue with what you are doing now later, after we are done."

Will he really be able to comply?

• **Conduct Supervision:**
Since people who cope by using strategies of the compensatory attention system are so "immersed" and focused, concentrating on a single thing, their ability to see the whole picture is impaired. Take, for instance, an individual

who goes shopping in the supermarket, who comes to the cereal shelf and who tries to choose one box out of the selection. She reads the small print, the ingredients and the calories, imagines the taste of it, compares prices, calculates the cost per 100 grams … and tries to reach a decision. The problem is that she has been standing there for over 10 minutes, it is late in the evening, the store will close soon, and her cart is still empty.

It is important to understand that this particular behavior does not stem from the executive-attention difficulties with decision-making that were discussed in the previous chapter. **The difficulty in the case of compensatory attention is not in reaching a decision, but in dealing with the overload of data required to make the decision.** When a person who utilizes compensatory attention successfully "takes control" of this mass of data, she can reach a rapid decision. In contrast, an individual suffering from executive-attention difficulties would continue to agonize over the decision even after all the data is known to her.

- **Tendency to worry:**

Usually, it is precisely the sensitive, intelligent and aware people who make use of the compensatory attention system. They invest all their energy in the issue facing them. They are partially aware of this and feel that "all of the eggs are in the same basket." This aphorism demonstrates why this should be a matter of some concern. Should any mishap befall the basket, there wouldn't be even a single egg left for dinner. This is the concern they experience. In more complex cases, this concern might develop into anxieties surrounding self-capability or stink into recurrent negative thoughts.

- **Emotional expression of insecurity, verging on anxiety:**

Experiencing inundation, intuitive awareness of complex operational abilities, fixation, outbursts, lockdown, a feeling of being misunderstood by one's surroundings, and all of the other difficulties present with the use of compensatory attention, may lead to routine daily behaviors that are plagued by insecurity, verging on episodes of extreme anxiety. (More on this in Chapter 10)

- **Argumentativeness and rejectionism:**

People who adopt these compensatory strategies in order to cope with attention overload can often be argumentative, oppositional and defiant.

These people feel that they are misunderstood, and this is often quite true. It is often the case that there is a vast gap between their capabilities in different fields, a gap that is the "beneficiary" of varied interpretations, but likely not the accurate explanation. Furthermore, none of the people around them truly understands the effort they invest into succeeding at their tasks, and this distances them even more from their surroundings. Beyond their experience of being misunderstood, from the moment they have selected a method of operations, a certain way of doing things or a given line of thought, they get fixated upon them. As far as they are concerned, they have found the correct path. They feel they must respond, express their position and explain their thinking. They don't give up, and repeatedly try to get themselves understood, even trying to repeatedly convince others to think as they do.

- **Rigidity:**

People who cope by adopting strategies of compensatory attention demand a lot from themselves. They understand that they need to "rally" considerable strength to cope and function. The massive amount of energy they invest into each target also results in a certain need for control, rigidity, intolerance and unwillingness to make a change. They need things to be done as they have planned, or as they have understood. This tendency leads them to get fixated and stuck on certain ideas and modes of action. After they make their minds up, it is very difficult for them to identify additional options or open themselves up to the opinions or suggestions of others.

The importance of diagnosis

As mentioned, compensatory attention is a system of strategies the individual adopts to deal with information overload and difficulties with regulating attention. People with a high degree of self-awareness will be able to partially explain their experience to themselves. Compensatory attention enables the individual to rally strength and disguise their difficulties, but they pay a high emotional toll, find it difficult to persist and wear themselves down over time. The gap between a seemingly high functioning ability, which is positively reinforced by the environment, and the massive effort invested by the individual is huge. The proven ability of the individual generates an expectation among the parents, teachers and therapists (or work colleagues and bosses for adults) that she will succeed equally well in all her tasks. The compensatory attention might therefore generate a misleading clinical picture that is completely different from the real difficulty. The emotional component of the compensatory attention system might be expressed in complexity and difficulties that are seemingly unrelated to the attention disorder, but rather to emotional and even personality complexities. The more extreme the emotional expression, the more difficult it will be to notice the attention difficulties and diagnose them. In such a case, a mistaken diagnosis might be made that will lead to a mistaken interpretation, and distance us from accurately understanding the experiences of the individual with compensatory attention. It will put us a long way away from the correct clinical image, and lead to empathic failures.

I see fit to emphasize this point, since the diagnosis is what determines the appropriate therapeutic approach and the active guidance required to improve the function and quality of life of the individual. Should the individual have an attention disorder which is camouflaged by compensatory attention, and we fail to identify it, this will lead her to situations and therapies which are neither necessary nor beneficial. Failing to identify the compensatory attention system, or misdiagnosis, might result in disappointment, frustration, anger and considerable pain for the people themselves and for those around them. Lacking a diagnosis, and interpreting the symptoms as emotional difficulties, can worsen the situation and threaten the therapeutic alliance. I recommend using Dr. Amen's[2] questionnaire to diagnose ADHD; the third subtype in this questionnaire refers to the type he termed "overfocus", and which I define here by the title "compensatory attention." The descriptions which appear in the questionnaire for this subtype deal with emotional symptoms and behavioral patterns characteristic of the phenomenon.

The questionnaire appears in full on the next page.

Dr. Amen states that **this questionnaire should only be used after an attention disorder is identified**.

Nonetheless, when people utilize compensatory attention, it may well be that their use of the compensation strategy is so effective that the environment does not notice all the criteria required to diagnose an attention disorder. This is why, even when only four to five attention disorder criteria are identified, rather than the six required to provide an unambiguous diagnosis, I recommend utilizing this questionnaire and further investigating whether an attention disorder is disguised by strategies of compensatory attention.

A positive mark next to six or more of the symptoms listed on the attached questionnaire will indicate use of the compensatory attention by the diagnosed child or adult.

1. Worries excessively or senselessly
2. Is oppositional and argumentative
3. Has a strong tendency to get locked into negative thoughts, having the same thought over and over
4. Has a tendency toward compulsive behaviors
5. Has a tendency to hold grudges
6. Has trouble shifting attention from subject to subject
7. Has difficulty seeing options in situations
8. Has a tendency to hold on to his or her own opinion and not listen to others

9. Has a tendency to get locked into a course of action, whether or not it is good for him or her
10. Needs to have things done a certain way or becomes very upset
11. Is criticized by others for worrying too much

Quite a few parents have arrived at my clinic to consult about the emotional symptoms of their son or daughter, and following their children—of them themselves. They were generally very much surprised to discover undiagnosed attention difficulties, difficulties that nourish and generate the emotional symptoms.

I emphasize that a diagnosis of compensatory attention must be made by **a professional in the field. As in every diagnosis, here too, a differential diagnosis must be performed between compensatory attention and pure emotional difficulties, or else symptoms linked to difficulties stemming from the autistic spectrum.**

Tales From the Clinic

A child who had successfully concealed his attention difficulties at elementary school by using strategies of compensatory attention, was referred to me. On the academic front, compensatory attention enabled him to stay under the radar. When he matriculated into middle school, the academic requirements suddenly rose sharply, his academic achievements declined and his parents noticed he had social difficulties, as well. The child frequently began to express anger at himself, and many frustrations, to the point of self-flagellation. The initial tendency is to understand or interpret the crisis as a phenomenon typical of adolescence and the new academic challenges. Indeed, there is no doubt that the demands of middle school are more challenging. It is, likewise, indisputable that adolescence brings with it new social tensions, that biological urges rise and that most adolescents display behavioral radicalization. However, if the child has attention difficulties, then it will be far more difficult for him to cope with all these challenges. **His tools** for the challenge are those requiring significant treatment. Though it seems that his difficulties arose due to changes in his life, these difficulties were aggravated by attention difficulties and reliance on compensatory attention.

Diagnosis by an experienced and trained professional is imperative in such situations. It must be remembered that, unlike hyperactivity or impulsivity, which are immediately linked to difficulty with attention regulation, **the compensatory attention phenomenon can be misleading and is harder to diagnose.** An accurate diagnosis provides the child and the parents with important, practical and relevant information for their daily routine—both the child's and her parents. For the most part, a correct diagnosis will lead the child to experience a very positive and liberating experience. Suddenly, she is understood, and most importantly, she now better understands herself and the intensity of the anxiety, and her concern decreases. **Psychological education** is necessary to understand the diagnosis, and that is what effectively dictates the therapeutic approach (see Chapter 4).

PART TWO
CHAMP MODEL OPERATIONAL APPROACHES

How should we discuss compensatory attention in accordance with the CHAMP model?

CHAMP — Help (with the "How") via Reflecting, Redefining, Rehearsing and Responsibility

We need to help the child by understanding and explaining the compensatory attention system, learning and teaching the topic according to the CHAMP model, which is based on the approach of psychological education. **Learning, internalizing and genuinely understanding this specific phenomenon will result in reduction of the emotional symptoms of anxiety, rigidity, disproportionate outbursts, argumentativeness, oppositional behavior, holding grudges and having a certain tendency towards a one-track approach, which can seem like verbal rumination or even "obsessive" behavior.**

According to the CHAMP model, the first step for all ADHD phenomena is to raise the awareness of the individual, through talking about and explaining the phenomena, while reflecting on the personal conduct of the individual with reference to them; expressing empathy and appreciation of the individual's effort, accompanied by expressing a genuine understanding of her difficulty; and emphasizing that this phenomenon is characteristic of other children and adults.

When we come to reflect on compensatory attention to the child or the individual, we must help her identify situations in which this strategy is used. For example:

"I've noticed your willingness to mobilize yourself to the task even though this is difficult for you, and very much appreciate you for it."

"I feel that you are making an effort to concentrate and act, in spite of feeling inundated."

"Can you notice cases when this happens and tell me about them?"

"Well done! I know how much of an effort you are making to succeed."

"How do you feel when you try to build a puzzle with 1000 pieces?"

If the child is having a hard time describe her feeling that she should be helped:

"This is tiring, isn't it?"

"Do you feel like you are making an effort, as if you were swimming against the current?"

It is likely that the child or individual will be aware of some of these characteristics. This is because, sometimes, their coping with the inundation of their attention takes place via compensatory attention, a conscious action which they have chosen. **Raising the awareness of the individual** will develop her ability to gradually identify situations in which she is inundated and tends to select a given way of coping. This understanding enables her to reduce anxiety, focus, concentrate and avoid distractions. Even when there is partial awareness about the compensatory attention system, considerable time must be invested at this stage of gradually identifying the phenomena. When this is for a child, the explanation must, of course, be adapted to her age and ability to understand.

CHA**M**P – **M**indful Metaphors

It is recommended that the phenomena be explained via **metaphors** the child will find easy to connect with, and that these be used to help her understand her behavior and actions.

For example:

> We can use the "**lock**" metaphor to describe to the child the state she will sometimes be in; after feeling flooded by the sounds surrounding her she will close herself off and seems to lock herself up. As far as she is concerned, there is no other option – there are no more maneuvers, the decisions which need to be made have been made, everything has been determined—by which the "noise" which inundates her can be greatly reduced. She gets locked in, or stuck on what is obvious, known or clear. This is the only way she is able to feel calmer and more focused.
>
> *"Anything which might add to this sense of burden, can lead you to grow irritated or to be 'locked up,' and it is hard for you to let it go."*
>
> The metaphor can be expanded, to use tools such as **"the key to the lock"** or **"the secret code"** that can help the child be freed from the **"locked"** condition, and assist her to move on from this mode which constrains her:
>
> *"You came back extremely tired from your test and from the great effort you exerted in studying for it. **The key to the lock** might be taking a break to calm down."*
>
> *"You activated your **secret code** and were able to release the tension and pressure which had plagued you prior to the soccer game."*

This explanation makes it much easier for children, as well as for adults, and helps them understand themselves and their lives.

CHAMP – Choose One Specific Component

The more we reflect to the child on the situations in which she conducts herself using the compensatory attention mechanisms, the more she will be able to develop her own self-awareness, as well as her awareness of the moments in which she is driven by the strategies she has developed to deal with information overload in her attention system. For example

---

"You are investing a great deal of effort in learning a given topic, and it is very difficult for you when the topic is explained to you in a slightly different manner." Only after the child understands and internalizes this particular characteristic of hers, we can help her make a further connection by adding, *"This is why you don't like changes and why you need things to be done your way,"* or, *"This is why you always try to be in control."*

Once we secure an agreement to cooperate, we can say:
"Let's pay attention to all of the examples where this occurs."
To explain to the child the social consequences of a tendency to seek order and silence we can say:
"Sometimes, you are so immersed in the attempt to organize your own thoughts that you cannot see what is happening around you. People can interpret this as a lack of interest in their company. You should notice this. Try to shut yourself off from thinking when you go on a break, so you can hang out with your friends. You can return to your thoughts when you go back home."

To raise the child's awareness of her progress, we can say:
"Please notice that your slowness derives from your need to focus in situations in which you are faced with many stimuli, and you are

distracted or overwhelmed by them. It is as if you are swimming against the current."

There are also many advantages to rallying one's strength for managing strategies, and it is important to acknowledge the children for the efforts they have exerted to do so:

"Well done! I truly appreciate your efforts. I absolutely understand how much effort you are investing to deal with the challenge of completing the puzzle."

We must always remember that these efforts take a high emotional toll on children as well as adults, who undertake them. Their awareness and understanding of this can help them learn how to relax and balance their investment of effort with the pressure, concern or anxiety accompanying the use of compensatory attention:

"I know you need to put in a lot of effort to sit and study for your literature exam, and you do so quite impressively, but you seem very concerned and anxious that you will not succeed, and your worry leads you to focus on the test incessantly. Your worry is a strategy you rally to focus yourself on preparing for the exam and mastering this task. I will help you to internalize this, and you will be able to somewhat reduce your anxiety and concern; then you will be more available to study for the test."

CH**A**MP – **A**ctive Adult Approach – Via Mediation

Mediation in this case has two main roles. The first is raising awareness in the child and mediating in situations where she tends to ruminate, ponder, repeat herself or get stuck; whereas, the other is explaining for the purpose of raising the awareness of those around the child. The importance of learning and mediation is especially great in relation to this phenomenon of compensatory attention, since it is not sufficiently familiar; and also, because, given the good performance of the child in certain fields, its characteristics are very confusing. The mediation process must also be performed slowly and gradually.

Only once the child is prepared to cooperate and learn about herself, and only once we identify the characteristics of her compensatory attention, should she be given additional help in understanding its consequences. I instruct parents not to be tempted to explain everything right off the bat "*because she is an intelligent child.*" I cannot underestimate the vital importance of the process of raising awareness, which strengthens the emotional process that the child is experiencing. Time is required to internalize and implement this process, and so it is important for the parent to teach the child gradually over time. Below are several examples of mediation:

> If we see the child place her hands on her ears, we should instruct her to step away from the noisy location or the activity, and take a break to reduce the load –
>
> "*It is hard for you with noises around you and that is why you shut your ears*" – and then help her connect this particular example to other situations, or understand consequences or possible misinterpretations.
>
> "*It is hard for you to handle noises, so you don't like going to birthday parties.*"
>
> Only after she has successfully internalized this, can we add:
>
> "*I understand that you shut your ears in order to help with your difficulty with noise, but it can be interpreted as impolite and inappropriate behavior. This is why you should explain it to your friends.*"

- **Pre-Preparation:**

Since the conduct of children, and adults, who use compensatory attention is intuitive and partially conscious, and they put a great deal of effort into it, they find changes, particularly sudden changes, difficult. Explaining and preparing in advance helps them get ready for the change, organize themselves for what is about to happen, and replan their activities.

> *"We know that you need to know in advance when plans change, and we will take that into account. We will go over all the stages, slowly, so that you will be ready to make the change."*
>
> *"Notice that this is true regarding any change—even a change for the better gets you stressed."*

It is important that both the parents and the child understand that this is a difficulty with **transitioning** from one thing to another, or making a **change**. This is not a difficulty with the **content** of the task. Therefore, we should not refer to the content, but to the very change or transition:

> *"We know you find changes difficult. This is why we will prepare you in advance, and there is no need to worry."*
> - This sort of sentence refers to a change, and therefore, it is welcomed.
>
> *"Your friends rang up 15 minutes ago to invite you on a hike. Why not join them? You enjoy hanging out with them—it will be fun." This sentence, unlike the previous one, refers to the content of the event and is therefore not efficient in mediating the compensatory attention."*

- **Precise Directing of Attention:**

Since children and adults who utilize compensatory attention tend to "sink" into a given issue and exclusively focus on it, with a lot of concern and rigidity, they especially need mediation and guidance. Very specific direction is meant to help them grow familiarized with the level of inundation and to notice it, to take multiple breaks, and to calm the associated emotional responses. It is true that following these breaks, they will need more time to complete the task, but they will "pay" a lower emotional price. Furthermore, we have learned that excessive occupation with a certain matter, rumination and brooding are disruptive to the environment, and tend to be misinterpreted as egocentric or "obsessive."

"You are really excited about your birthday party now, and can't stop thinking about it and planning every detail. Your thoughts are running around your head, and you are repeating them out loud. I understand how excited you are, and how this repetitive thinking and even excessive pondering helps you to focus, but this can be tiring for me, so let's try and stop the verbalization ...."

And not:

"I know—we have talked about this; stop pestering me and give me a chance to plan the event."

It follows that we also need to help those in the environment understand the phenomenon, rather than misinterpret and judge, or misdiagnose it as obsession, anxiety, rigidity, antisocial behavior, repetitiveness or bossiness. It is important to remember that what can seem like excessive focus on a specific issue usually serves children and adults by helping them to overcome attention difficulties and enabling them to delve deeper into themselves and discover things that others have yet to discover.

We can explain:

"She is excited and cannot stop thinking about her birthday party."

We can also explain, for example, that she tends to over-focus on reading a book deep into the night without noticing the clock, or to be occupied with building a Lego model to the point where she can forget to eat.

On the other hand, we can explain that she can sometimes be so deeply immersed that she "forgets time" and chooses to focus on things which brings her little benefit and are perhaps even disruptive to them.

In all of these situations, the parents or the responsible adult is required to display non-judgmental understanding of the child, as well as to provide the child and those in her immediate environment with the explanations and mediation that will help her focus her attention. This guidance will enable her to find the balance between using compensatory attention as an effective coping strategy and her attention difficulties with their high emotional toll. Mediation will also enable the child to notice social conventions, and to avoid being perceived as pestering, condescending or socially aberrant.

- **A Broad View of Things:**

Disproportionate outbursts or getting completely locked on a single line of thought or action, are one of the common expressions of compensatory attention. The child clings to this line of thought or action without opening herself to various other options. In other words, she has considerable difficulty with examining the range of possible actions. Furthermore, she has extreme difficulty with reexamining the choice that was recently made. On such occasions, mediation has considerable importance, as it can help with reexamining the focus of attention and redirecting it to another focus, if required.

Many children make a considerable effort in school and return home in an overloaded state. I witnessed many cases in which these children were badly "locked down" at the slightest frustration. All that was necessary to trigger this outburst or lockdown was to tell them that afternoon plans had changed, or that Grandmother would not arrive as they had thought, or that their room had been arranged without them being notified. I encourage parents to understand the pattern and to try to mediate these situations for their children precisely.

> *"I want to inform you of a change in plan, which you will not like. I know this will be difficult for you, but I ask you to listen for a moment before responding."*

I find myself suggesting and requesting once again not to interpret the situation as an emotional problem, or to try to explain the behavior. Many parents, as well as other adults, instructors and therapists, **confuse the objective difficulties with primary emotional difficulties.**

Imprecise mediation only amplifies the outburst or lockdown. An uncontrolled outburst or lockdown is an impulsive action stemming from being inundated and feeling a lack of control—**there is no hidden emotional content.** This is why considerable patience, precise empathic, genuine understanding are required to mediate properly. In the case of outbursts, one should act according to the principles of the CHAMP model, as discussed in the chapter on impulsivity; and understand that in case of compensatory attention, the intensity of the response could be much greater than it is with impulsivity, or that the response is amplified with time.

When the cases are more complex and it is harder to recognize or foresee the outburst, the parents should turn to mediation by a professional. This mediation will teach them how to identify the specific point at which the child erupts, or might erupt, and help them mediate for the child down the line.

Reflection and mediation sentences can be something like:

"You are beginning to get over-excited, and I am noticing you getting inundated … Let's try to release some excess energy by bouncing a ball outside …"

And when she accomplishes this:

"Well done; you succeeded to avoid a disaster! Let's work on how we can continue to notice this situation …"

"Take, for example, the math problem. Remember how hard you tried to solve it in a certain way? And then, your teacher came and showed you another way. You were very angry. It took you a great deal of time to learn a certain way of solving the problem; you had no strength left to invest in thinking about another, perhaps better, way. Please note that it is difficult for you to change things which you have grown used to. This could be a math problem, and it could be the arrangement of your room, which changed because I cleaned up and moved things around."

It is important, for us adults too, to repeatedly say,

"Tell me about all of the cases where adapting to change has been difficult for you,"

until the child internalizes it.

Tales From the Clinic

A couple came to me to treat their 10-year-old son after they had participated in the parents' workshop. They reported that their daughter simply refused to write in class. The school was anxious and was pressuring her, and the more the school pressured her, the more the child resisted. The teachers recommended occupational therapy and did not accept the parents' opinion that there was no problem with her fine motor skills, and that the child was even extremely skilled at sketching and painting. The parents also told me that they were not concerned, since their child was a smart girl who was very much in control of the studied material. They added that they had explained to the school that their daughter was very fond of the theater class she was participating in and was even pre-pared to write scripts for it. The school counselor recommended emotional therapy, and this was the reason they had come to me. The child arrived with her parents to our third meeting, a bit earlier than the time we had set for our appointment. I was in the middle of a telephone call. I heard her get excited and declare that it was fun coming here. When the time for the meeting arrived, I warmly invited her to come into the room, together with her parents (that is my usual custom, in order to transfer responsibility to the parents). Suddenly, the child turned her back to me, sat on her mother's lap and refused to speak.

The parents did not understand her unexpected behavior, especially given the fact that she had wanted to come. Many varied attempts to conciliate her did not work. The child continued to resist. I suggest-ed I read the poem "The Lock" from my book *My Mind Races*.[3] She refused that, as well. I read the poem to her parents, in her presence, and explained to them that I believed she was "locked down" and asked whether I was right. When I finished reading the poem, the parents nodded and affirmed that part of the poem described their daughter well, but that the final lines were nothing like her:

"You see, only when things are all anchored and clear,

Do I feel relaxed and with nothing to fear."

I explained that entire poems in the book cannot perfectly match each and every child, and I added that, nonetheless, I believe that hers was a pattern of "locking," which is very typical of children with ADHD, in general, and children with a display of compensatory attention, in particular.

It is important for me to note at this point that even if the child does not regularly utilize the compensatory attention system, patterns or expressions of compensatory attention should be identified and treated appropriately. Treatment with the CHAMP model is suitable where these patterns exist, even if there is no clear diagnosis for the existence of the compensatory attention system.

The parents and I continued to talk in the presence of the child, until she began to participate. Then, it turned out that she had heard my phone conversation before the meeting and understood from it that I was retiring. She erupted at me and said:

"You are retiring!" I told her that I had heard her say in the waiting room that she liked coming to me and must have been disappointed when she heard I was retiring. The child did not respond. I added that she had just begun to cooperate and even look forward to our meetings and she had suddenly heard that this might change soon. I assured her that I was not retiring any time soon, and that we could go on meeting. We discussed the fact that she has difficulty when things change and invited and encouraged her and her parents to talk about her reactions to change in general. I specified that she had locked down when she had overheard the telephone conversation. I explained to the parents that this pattern of sudden "lockdown" defines many children with "compensatory attention," and uncontrollable impulsivity, when something does not work out as they expected. We need to help them recognize this and control it. I connected "lockdown" with the issue of refusal to

write. I explained that the more the school pressured the child, the more she "locked down" and resisted, and that the educational staff needed to be helped to understand the mechanism and to stop pressuring the child. I believed that the child sometimes lacked the patience or necessary attentional capacity to write down what she knew and understood. The mother said that her daughter repeatedly said this: "Why should I write down something I know?" I asked the child to read, together with her parents, the poem "The Lock," to write her own script and to stage it in a play, or take a video that I could watch. I also offered to participate in the video clip so that I could use it to teach other children.

She asked if I could also put the video clip on YouTube, and I expressed my full consent, conditional to receiving her and her parents' approval. When I suggested setting up a meeting for the next week, the child announced that she would not be coming. I decided to try to help her transfer the focus of her "lockdown" and asked: *"How would I see the video clip?"*
She left the room after agreeing to come the following week.

The father did indeed read the poem with his daughter, and the child staged a very creative video, with the father asking mediating questions related to the breaking of locks, with the goal of helping his daughter look at herself from the outside:
"Are there children who lock up like a lock?"
"What happens to them when they lock up?"
"What can help them find the secret code and open the lock?"
"Is there a greater tendency to lock up when something doesn't go well?"
"What can you invent to help children in such moments?"

In this way, the father was able to get his daughter to look at herself from the outside and see how others see her. They arrived with the video clip to the next meeting, and I, of course, was excited, sang her praises, added a few emphases and suggested we put the movie online to help others learn about themselves. I repeatedly explained to the parents that they should repeat the mirroring and mediation process until it had been internalized. I also requested the school not insist that she write.

Several months later, the mother called me and said that she spoke with her daughter and attempted to link the "locking" with the refusal to write. She asked her casually if the refusal to write was also a type of "locking."

She smiled with understanding, conciliated, and began to write. The teacher responded to the change in wonder, and asked how this happened. The parents encouraged the child to bring the video clip to class to explain herself to her classmates and the teacher.

This story is an example of a complex case in which the emotional content and the objective condition coexist, side by side, and that is why it is so difficult to see the objective difficulty, which is, in fact, the primary difficulty. The emotional difficulty is driven by the objective difficulty.

The child reached me excited but "locked down" when she heard I was retiring. The very possibility of **change** (the fact I would cease working with her) sparked an impulsive, difficult "lockdown" response. It was necessary to identify the locking down without dwelling on the content (my supposed retirement) or working on my relationship with her. Such cases require the intervention of a trained professional. Once the pattern is recognized, the parents can continue to mediate to the child the cases in which the pattern recurs. Keep in mind that content can activate the "lockdown" or the outburst, **but it is imperative that we do not relate to the content but to the response to change, as a distinct pattern of the lockdown.**

- **Emotional help:**

The clinical expressions of compensatory attention are primarily emotional, which makes diagnosis extremely misleading. In addition to "lockdown," repetitive speech or outbursts, a tendency to sink into recurrent negative thoughts, rigidity, refusal, oppositional behavior, argumentativeness, difficulty with changes, transitions and so forth, is all possible. When there is a diagnosis of ADHD with a tendency to engage in ineffective use of compensatory attention, we need to reflect on these emotional expressions and explain them to the child. We need to persist in helping her to identify and connect to additional expressions, so that she will be able to recognize the pattern in various other situations. We need to reflect on and emphasize the efforts she is making to deal with the overloading of her attention and to express appreciation of her for it; to link, for her, the emotional difficulty with her specific method of coping and the way she chooses to make her way between the mountains of information and options.

Gradually and slowly but surely, the child can transition from a self-perception characterized by anxiousness about her ability to succeed to a healthy self-perception, the sort that will enable her to appreciate her talents, have faith in her abilities and not flinch at facing specific difficulties. I will dwell further on the treatment of the emotional aspects in detail in Chapter 10.

cHAMP — Help (with the "How") via Reflecting, Redefining, Rehearsing and Responsibility through positive reinforcement

A teenager can be told:

> *"I want you to know that many people have this ability to compensate for difficulties with attention. This is a well-known phenomenon, which some children and teenagers with attention oscillations have. This strategy you have adopted has many advantages, and well done for making use of it—you always get organized, persist and finish tasks despite the difficulties!!!"*

Smaller children can be told:

> *"You are a child who so much wants to succeed and that is super admirable! I notice that you exert a lot of effort into succeeding—you put in so much effort and end up so tired! You do this in order to overcome your attention difficulties. Many people succeed in this way."*
> Other possible statements are:
> *"It is very good that you are able to identify this and tell me about it. It is a good thing you don't keep this a secret! That way, I can help! You don't need to deal with this alone; I'm here with you."*
> *"You are a wise child who suddenly has realized that you are experiencing something and don't know how to explain it. It isn't easy and must be difficult when everyone around you interprets it inaccurately..."*
> *"Notice that the more you understand and internalize what it is that you are experiencing, the less anxious you are and the better you are able to go with the flow."*

The child or adult, must be helped to understand that compensatory attention is a defense mechanism, which serves her well. To her credit, she manages to rally attention resources for short periods of time, when she faces situations of data overload. However, she pays a heavy emotional toll for this—she finds it difficult to persist in tasks over time and exhausts herself. We can tell the child statements such as:

> *"You are a very positive person, you challenge yourself and you seek with all your willpower to succeed. You make a great deal of effort to rally your powers of attention to the task, and indeed you succeed at this, for brief intervals. However, you have a hard time sustaining your attention over time because you exhaust yourself with the effort."*

"You are looking for a way to control the flooding you experience in your head. You have learned to master organizing your backpack for school very well, and you are now also trying to manage all of your activities with your friends, and this sometimes leads you to be angry and erupt at them."

"I will continue to try to help you to understand and identify these things, so that you can try to cope better and explain yourself. It will help you not to erupt, not to argue and not to lock down or be oppositional. This way, you will also worry less, and perhaps manage to let go a little and make things easier for yourself."

"Let us reexamine why you are worried about taking a field trip with the Boy Scouts and sleeping away from home overnight? After all, you are a sociable child. Perhaps you are not used to sleeping somewhere else? Are you afraid that something unexpected or something out of your control might happen? Do you not like following the instructions of the counselor? Are you afraid of activities you will not be able to do? Or, are you afraid children might pester you? You must notice that many reasons might be possible. If we know what your fear comes from, we can make a wiser decision."

- We must encourage the child when she manages to rally the strength to deal with the inundation she is experiencing. We can tell him statements such as:

"Well done for managing to rally yourself in the face of the inundation (noise, humming, music, a complex task for school) that you experience. Well done for managing to focus, in spite of the difficulties.

- We must praise her for her desire to succeed, for the challenges she chooses to face and overcomes. We can say such things like:

> *"I notice you choose to set challenges for yourself, and this is very admirable! When you want something and try so hard, you succeed. But over time, this becomes very tiring. Perhaps you should learn to take a break and do something else for your enjoyment? Maybe let go a little? After all, you already know the material … You don't have to check yourself repeatedly—what you did so far is certainly good enough."*
>
> *"I noticed you were reading the book the teacher asked you to read. I see how you are diving into it and how you are enjoying the read. Well done!!"*

- We need to empathize with our child and repeatedly and sincerely tell her that we know that she is investing a great deal of energy and effort in what she does. Nonetheless, her rigidity and argumentativeness are not helping her. We need to encourage her to take a timeout, think and return when she is prepared to handle things. We can tell her things like:

> *"When you are interested in a book you are reading, assembling a puzzle or are deeply immersed in some other activity, you really manage to do it quite well. But you put in so much effort that you find it very disturbing when I call you to eat or take a shower. Sometimes you erupt in anger because you can't hold it inside you."*
>
> *"I know that it is hard for you and that is why you have a natural tendency to stress out. Well done for sharing your feelings with me. If this is important for you, anything can be overcome. I will help you—we will devote a short time to solve the math exercise, take a break and then return to it. This way you will not be stressed out by having a lot of homework."*

"Now, you can start to identify by yourself those moments when you are overwhelmed, and take multiple breaks. This may take you longer, but you will do it in the best possible way."

Statements such as those below, told to the child over a period of time (not all at once!), can be helpful:

"Those negative thoughts are back again! Let's think for a moment— does it make sense that she suddenly does not love you? After all, you are very good friends. Did something happen? Maybe she is simply busy right now with other things? Try to let it go."

"You are rejecting and arguing. If you feel that your position is not immediately accepted, you immediately respond, sometimes in an undesirable way. You feel that you are not always told everything that people are thinking."

"Since you are a very sensitive child, you detect even the smallest falseness. You are insulted when you are not understood and inter- pret it as if you are not loved."

"Sometimes, you can be very grumpy, respond in an exaggerated fashion and reject others, even cutting off contact with your closest friends. For this to happen less, you should try to explain that you want to 'flow' with your friends, but that you find it hard to be flex- ible and change your position. This is why it is so important to me that before anything else, you first understand yourself. Throughout your life, there will be many other people who will not understand you precisely—that is why your job is to explain things!"

- Compliments, compliments, and more compliments:

We need not be sparing in complimenting the genuine efforts and successes of our child. Her efforts cannot be taken for granted, and sincere compliments should be accompanied with a relevant and accurate explanation regarding her ability to deal with "flooding," or her ability to be more flexible and change the course of her thoughts or actions once she has set upon a given course. The same applies for the success of a child in persisting with a task. We can tell him something like:

> *"You are very sensitive and feel insulted when you are misunderstood. Do you remember that the teacher was angry and said she did not want to hear from you until the end of the day? At that moment, you were very insulted and locked down, but congratulations for identifying the lock—thanks to that, you were able to make an effort and avoid erupting."*
>
> *"I know how difficult this was for you but you were adamant, and it paid off! Hats off to you!"*

It is very important for us parents to **avoid "educational"** sentences which ignore the child's difficulties. You should **avoid** using such sentences as:

- *"It's no big deal; this will pass. You are still young. When you grow up, you will do better."*
- *"You always complain how hard it is for you, and then you manage to get an excellent grade."*
- *"Everyone needs to put in an effort to succeed!"*
- *"Don't say you don't have any friends: I know you have quite a few."*
- *When a child gets stuck or locks down, the last thing that will help her is a sentence such as "Come on; just go along with it. It's not that difficult."*

CHAM**P** – **P**ractice, Practice, Practice!

We will use the "H" of the CHAMP model again and again, and practice again and again, because the primary task we adults have is the reinforcement of the child and redefinition of the attention and compensatory attention characteristics which are unique to her. This should be done while using conscious dialogue, that is empathic and free of judgment. Below are several examples of a discourse meant to strengthen the child:

- We need to explain to the child that there is such a phenomenon—compensatory attention. She is not the first to have it, and many other children and adults deal with it.

Imagine that you need to arrive at a party on the ninth floor in a luxurious building. Your friends arrive 10 minutes before you do. Unfortunately, just when you arrive, the elevator breaks down. You end up climbing nine flights in a stairwell without any ventilation or air conditioning. It is hot, and you slowly make your way up, floor by floor. Your leg muscles are unused to such efforts, and you are panting and sweating. Finally you arrive at the ninth floor and enter the party. You feel that all eyes are on you; everyone is staring at your red, sweaty face.

And then a good friend passes by and says: *"Oh, you finally arrived …"*

We need to pay attention to the child or adult, notice their effort and the path they walk.
We will do them a great wrong if we only judge them on the basis of the outcomes or their successes.

The more we, the parents, understand deeply and precisely the phenomenon of ADHD in general, and compensatory attention in particular, the more we will be able to explain the child's conduct to her in a more empathic and successful manner, and the more we will be able to help her understand herself. Only our understanding can help us be genuinely compassionate and embrace, rather than be angry, which will help the child feel better. Later, with the relevant information which will gradually and slowly accumulate, we too will learn the best way to conduct ourselves. We will learn, for example, not to be rational and impatient –

"Come on. Grow up. You cannot just stay in your comfort zone and play on screens all day; you have to think of the consequences. Everyone needs a turn to play sometime."

We need to be careful about misinterpreting the child's behavior, such as *"You are just slacking off now; I already saw, beforehand, that you are capable."*

We will understand that every individual rallies strength in order to focus on a particular task, but children with ADHD who rely on the compensatory attention system, mobilize a huge amount of effort, which is not proportionate to the task they are facing. It seems that this effort leads the children to develop difficulties that they express emotionally, and it may levy a high tax on them which will appear, from the outside, to be emotional. This can be illustrated with the following diagram:

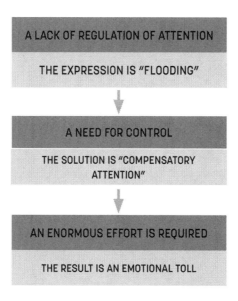

Tales From the Clinic

I was approached by a mother who wished to come to the clinic with her 12-year-old daughter. Already on the phone call, she told me that she was recommended to me as I was a clinical psychologist for children and that I was an expert in attention difficulties. However, she thought that her daughter had emotional difficulties, not any difficulty with attention and concentration.

The mother arrived with her daughter, a beautiful and impressive girl, the youngest of four. The family had been relocated and had traveled around the world, and each one in the family was fluent in several different languages. This was an educated and culture-consuming family. The mother started the conversation and told me that her daughter very much enjoyed reading and tended to read a lot. She was also a very good girl. But, occasionally, she would have moments in which she would decide that she did not know something, and then she would make all sorts of inattention-derived mistakes. When she had been alerted to this and was told to pay attention, she managed to fix these mistakes. The mother emphasized that this was proof that her daughter was capable and that she had no attention and concentration problems.

I turned to the child and asked her to tell me about her experience. She explained that she sometimes felt she had too many thoughts in her head, as if her head was about to explode from all these thoughts. When this happened, she was unable to do anything.

"Do you often feel like your head is overloaded?" I asked.

She smiled and answered:

"Sometimes I feel that I have so many thoughts in my head that I can't hold back; I need to answer and speak, even when I know that I am interrupting by bursting into the conversation and that this is impolite."

Then she continued.

"Even when I have something disorganized in my room, I can't restrain myself and have to put it in order right away."

I asked if she was generally an organized child?

"I have my own kind of order. Most of the room is organized, but I have a few piles of mess. Even when I go to sleep, I can't stand it when the sheet is not properly stretched out."

The child seemed very distressed. She explained that since the parent's day, she had found it very difficult with the classroom teacher. The classroom teacher had told her that she must avoid bursting into conversations or must interrupt politely when someone else is speaking. She went on to say that she had made a lot of effort and had some success. She even received an excellent citation in her report card. I asked her in astonishment how she did it, and she answered simply:

"The teacher insulted me badly; she shouted at me in front of everyone else, saying that she didn't want to hear me interrupt again. Since then, I have been frightened that she will yell again, and I really make an effort not to interrupt."

She felt that I understood her, and proceeded to tell me the following:

"I don't have many friends. I am actually quite popular, but I have high expectations from my friends. I expect our friendship to be total. I am prepared to do anything for my friends, and they should do the same. Often I am disappointed and very angry."

Later on, she told me about her experience at home, with her family:

"I play the violin. My brothers do, as well, but I feel that they are more successful than I am."

Her mother, with the best of intentions, had said that this wasn't terrible, because she was still young, and went on to say that the violin teacher said she was an excellent student. The mother did not understand that in this effort to help, she was actually ignoring the difficulties of the child, was not giving her a chance to bring them to the surface and was not even prepared to discuss them.

I asked the mother to fill a diagnostic questionnaire about her daughter. Her answers to the questionnaire were clearly positive for attention difficulties, such as hyperactivity, impulsivity and especially compensatory-attention issues.

I explained to the mother that she has an amazing and very talented daughter, who was describing a very real difficulty that she experiences: The child feels a huge gap between her potential, which she cannot see, and her ability in practice, which she does see. Furthermore, she experiences a huge data overload in her mind that she is trying to deal with, but is unable to filter out the excess. She rallies all her strength to direct her attention and deal with the overload. I explained how ineffective use of compensatory attention can lead to a need for control.

Suddenly, something changed in the mother's expression. She took a deep breath, as if she was internalizing a new insight. She then told me that her daughter has a daily chart in her room, where she lists all the struggles of all the family members. **Her** own columns always describe issues dealing with control.

"Today I was in control ... Today I was less in control ..."
"Today was terrible; I controlled nothing," and so forth.
I suggested to the mother to learn about the phenomenon and participate in a parental guidance workshop. Following the workshop,

she was able to internalize what had been taught and discussed it with her child, helping her.

The mother and the daughter arrived at the clinic to hold two individual sessions with me, spaced several months apart. In these sessions, I was happy to see that they were on the right track, and I encouraged them to continue in the same way, and not to turn to emotional therapy. The daughter was able to get in touch with her inner strengths and significantly decreased her anxiety level. She still had to direct the inundation she was experiencing in her head, by mobilizing her attention reserves for brief periods of time.

On a return visit, about three years later, the girl told me how understanding about attention difficulties and compensatory attention had changed her life. She had learned to deal with the information overload and even had learned to enjoy it. She manages to impose order in a manner that may seem to outsiders as excessive, almost "obsessive," but she is now convinced that it organizes the world for her. The mother told me that she enjoys seeing her daughter display her strengths, which enable her to do everything to their fullness.

I reinforced the mother's view, and encouraged her to continue to defend her daughter and encourage her to believe in herself. I also encouraged her daughter to try to explain herself to those in her environment, whenever and wherever possible.

A Thought Exercise: The Same Result with a Different Investment of Effort

The goal: You have to transfer a liter of water from the kitchen into the glasses of the guests in the living room. The first time, you take a pitcher and deliver the water within it. You come into the living room and pour the water into the guests' glasses. How simple.

The second time, you have no pitcher. The only option is to transfer the water in a large tray with low sides. The tray contains the same amount of water as the pitcher did. Now, you try to pour the water from the corner of the tray into the glasses of the guests. This is how you might understand the amount of effort required.

In both cases, you were polite and served your guests a glass of water. Seemingly, there was nothing complex or difficult about the task—just a glass of water for a guest. However, the second time required much more effort and concentration to get the job done.

There is no way of knowing if the guests will appreciate the effort you put into serving them with a tray, just as the teacher will not necessarily know how to appreciate the assignment the child was able to complete in spite of the ungodly din in the classroom, and the massive amounts of effort she invested.

It is important not to interpret the difficulty as "emotional" without understanding the objective difficulty, which is a difficulty with attention. The more we understand the specific difficulty with attention and help the child understand it, the more she will be able to rally her strength against being overloaded, and utilize the advantages of compensatory attention without paying an enormous emotional toll. She will also learn gradually to effectively channel this very same strategy into achieving, succeeding and surprising even herself!

Summary

This chapter was written based on my personal and clinical experience over many years. The information I have gathered is based on the overfocusing phenomenon, which was independently documented by Dr. Kinsbourne and Dr. Amen and remains insufficiently familiar to many. This foundation, along with a broad and somewhat special, holistic, clinical and dynamic perspective, led me to term the phenomenon "compensatory attention." This term refers to a system of strategies that the individual almost intuitively adopts to cope with an excess of data and with difficulties with attention.

It is important to stress that this method of coping with compensatory attention, serves the individual, and enables him to enlist attention, but, the tremendous effort involved can also cause him to be rigid and experience difficulty with transitions or changes, and even to lockdown.

It can also lead to an exaggerated or disproportionate need to control, outbursts, defiance, argumentativeness, and to considerable anxiety in regard to successfully coping in new situations, and in regard to feeling self – competent, in general. **These accompanying manifestations are infact side effects that can be all too easily be interpreted as emotional, or communication** difficulties, and this **makes it very challenging to diagnose the phenomenon of compensatory attention.**

In depth understanding of the subject by professionals, aimed at developing awareness in the child or adult, will assist them to find the balance between the advantages and the efficiency of adopting this strategy of compensatory attention, and the many disadvantages that can be caused as a result of the tremendous effort involved in order to compensate for difficulties with attention.

THE LOCK

I came home from school, very happy but tired—
Was fun. Learned a lot — but much focus required.
Then I suddenly heard they called off my ballgame;
Now my world's upside-down, and nothing's the same!
I just cannot calm down now that everything's changed;
All day I looked forward — it was so well-arranged!
I worked hard all day long with that game in my sight;
Now my base has collapsed, and it just is not right!

Sometimes I feel like I just cannot win,
Then my mind starts to freeze 'til I get all locked in.
I can't loosen up — it's so hard to break free;
I get captured in lockdown and can't find the key.
Dad says, "Try to relax and go with the flow.
Change is surprising — and frustrating, I know!"

If everything'd only remain the right way,
I'd sit back and unwind, send my worries away;
But when life gets messy, I can't break the code
For unlocking that lock and changing my mode.
You see, only when things are all anchored and clear
Do I feel relaxed and with nothing to fear.

CHAPTER 10

Talking ADHD – Emotional Therapy

Over the years, I have received very positive feedback from parents, children, teachers and educators. This feedback has been the fuel which has driven my mission, and which convinced me to write this book – and particularly this chapter – despite great objective difficulties I have in my writing. Here is an example:

> "After many years of participating in social groups, psychological therapy, art therapy, occupational therapy and more, we arrived at Esther Goldberg's clinic. Her condition for initiating treatment of a child was participation in parent group therapy. She explained to us that many children with ADHD do not require additional psychological treatments after their parents have participated in the parents' workshop. We didn't believe it, but it's true! The 10 weekly meetings at the parents' workshop turned things around. We really began to understand our son!"

My many years of educational and clinical practice together with my familiarity with my patients and with their parents has led me to understand and recognize the fact that treatment of ADHD is also an emotional therapy—even when it focuses on the neurodevelopmental and cognitive components.

Also, and perhaps especially, when it is performed by the parents and other important adults in the child's environment.

Conversely, my approach is that emotional therapy for a child with ADHD is not sufficiently effective if it does not involve the neurodevelopmental and cognitive components that are unique to every child and her specific ADHD manifestations.

This chapter serves to integrate all the chapters presented in this book. Here, I will refer to issues explained in the previous chapters and will link between them. I have deliberately elaborated on my approach and hope that this chapter will increase your understanding of how to conduct emotional therapy.

It took me years to understand, comprehend, internalize, learn, and apply the complex knowledge and implications that came with the diagnosis of Adhd that I was given.

The scientific understanding of the neurological base, together with a complete holistic understanding of its many ramifications, enabled me to tell my life story anew, to see and realise my many strengths, and to make a breakthrough in my life. This realization of my true potential, strengths, and abilities, was so significant that I was determined to choose to specialize in the subject of ADHD out of great passion and a deep sense of mission.

I graduated with distinction from the Hebrew University of Jerusalem in 1976. As a Clinical and educational psychologist, I repeatedly see, to my dismay, that we are still "wandering in the desert". The subject of Adhd is highly publicized, but is still grossly lacking in deep holistic understanding.

It is generally treated as a mostly meaningless list of symptoms . This, by fault of no one, leads to basic empathic failures. This lack of empathy and genuine understanding, leads to the feeling many people diagnosed with ADHD have," I first, do not understand myself, and then It must follow that I am not understood to others." It results in a sense of vulnerability and of the injured self. leads to much frustration, to repeated self disappointment, and to self flagellation and anger. It is translated into a lack of self confidence, and to a sense of low self esteem. In addition, when an individual feels a difficulty in regard to lack of ability to control himself, and is only partially understood to himself, or to others, he is proposed to develop anxiety. When he feels he is not understood, he feels alone, lacks self confidence, and is unable to love respect and value himself. He ceases to love himself, to feel self worth, and can develop depression.

Onyx Yogev, 12 (who requested to be named and credited), wrote a poem in Hebrew, when participating in one of my workshops. This poem precisely describes how children with ADHD feel regarding their inner sense of incompetence.

Little Bird
Little bird, quiet bird,
In everything except her spirit …
Flies, silently gliding,
In a low flight.
She cannot fly high, for the winds will knock her down.
Big birds, which stand up fearlessly to the wind,
Will descend to peck at her wings, pluck her feathers, snap at her tail.
She will want to show them that she can, as well.
But she will not be able to, for she cannot.

The role of every parent and teacher, guide, coach, instructor and therapist is to understand the child and teach her about herself. I am reminded repeatedly of the wise words of my dear mentor, Prof. Aleksandrowicz of blessed memory:

"Children love their parents and teachers, because they learn from them;
But children learn from their parents and teachers, because they love them."

This wise sentence is **destined** to fail in the face of this neurodevelopmental factor with so many consequences, about whose significance no one has taught parents and teachers. This is why our job, as responsible adults, who have encountered this unique population and its specific needs, is to study and teach this complex topic, so that our children can **stand** tall and proud, and know how to understand and explain themselves.

I had the honor of meeting again with Prof. Aleksandrowicz a year before he passed away.

I asked to quote this sentence, which he had shared with me as an oral saying. He smiled an embarrassed smile of contentment, considered it and said: "Yes, I remember saying this statement; and you, quite justly, want to emphasize that it is the responsibility of parents to teach their children. He then dictated the following to me, and suggested I add it to the previous sentence:

"Love grants the child the basic trust that the world is fundamentally good. Being frustrated, struggling and overcoming adversity build up self-esteem."

Children and adults who are diagnosed with ADHD have genuine difficulties with self-regulation and cannot control their attention or impulses. We will find more frustration in their life than success; they are like the protagonist of the poem "Little Bird." They feel less capable and less worthy since they cannot do what others around them do so easily. They are preoccupied with questions such as:

"Will I succeed?;" "Should I even try?"; "What if my attention vanishes and I embarrass myself?"; "Why can't I concentrate?"; "Why do others succeed, and I don't? What do they have that I don't?"

They think:

"I wish I could focus today until the end of the test …; maybe I should give up because I know in advance that I will not succeed."

They are so occupied with these thoughts that their concern sometimes seems like obsession or anxiety. But while these do indeed exist, one must remember that they revolve around the child's doubts regarding their ability or, more accurately, regarding their inability to regulate attention and drives or to cope with the tasks they need to do.

When they are not able to do what they know they want to do, they often tend to **need to control** their environment. This tendency is often perceived as obsessiveness or perfectionism. This tendency is so great that it becomes part of their lives. Some of them grow up to be people who constantly analyze themselves in order to successfully manage and reach the greatest achievements possible, and indeed they do succeed. **Sometimes, the anxiety about their lack of self-control is transformed into anxiety about their lack of control over their environment.** These children or adults experience a lack of control over themselves and fear that there is nowhere where they can experience total control. Therefore, they tend to fear anything and everything regarding control :

"What will happen if the elevator falls?"; "What will happen if the plane crashes?" Some children fear, for the same reason, walking alone up to their room on the second floor of the house; refuse to stay alone in a dark room; and won't stay alone at home during the evening or night, or ask to not close the restroom doors. When there is an ADHD diagnosis, we need to examine whether, in fact, their fears are derived from a genuine difficulty with control or from a need to control that stems from a low sense of capability or self-esteem, which is derived from difficulties regulating their attention and drive.

Some children will, due to their anxiety and doubts regarding their ability to cope adequately, avoid "doing" so as to avoid facing the conflict or conditions of failure. Such children, for example, are afraid to go to school, or avoid having to deal with what is associated with extracurricular activities after school.

In most cases, the more the children's ability to function improves, and the more they can successfully control themselves, the more the tendency for obsessiveness or anxiety lessens. We in the adult environment need to help our children overcome their objective difficulties so that they can strengthen their ability to function and, with it, their feeling of self-competence. This success will increase their motivation to continue to learn how to succeed in the future. Succeeding in one's ability to function is generated from developing one's awareness, understanding, and knowledge, and not only, or just, through practice. Knowledge enables us to develop awareness of the subject and to slowly learn to identify the specific difficulties associated with them, and control them. Even if the child, or adult, fails to fully control them, when they are aware of the source of their difficulties, and can explain them to themselves and those in their environment, they are able to focus on improving their ability to function and find alternative ways to cope, thereby reducing their frustration.

The *Talking ADHD* therapeutic approach is eclectic "a little of this and a little of that." Since the primary characterization of children with ADHD is that they are misunderstood, this approach is based on the need for precise and genuine empathic understanding on the part of those in the immediate environment— which is intended to prevent empathic failures towards the child with ADHD. Thus, we can come to understand the child with an emphasis on learning the scientific explanations along with developing our own psychological understanding. Along with the mindfulness approach, this enables deliberate and nonjudgmental observations of the child's present experiences. In addition, the *Talking ADHD* approach makes use of various techniques derived from several different psychological approaches. Principles from narrative therapy[1] are used, which seek to help individuals reconstruct the story of their lives. In this therapeutic process, referring to the individual's specific objective hardships and travails, while separating them from one another, enables understanding and the development of a new perspective, in order to build a new story, which makes dealing with them easier. In addition, I use principles of cognitive-behavioral therapy from the field of learning. This is based on the assumption that cognitive patterns of understanding influence behavior and need to be addressed by logical analysis. Beyond the principles of therapy and the therapeutic tools I use, the overall approach of the therapy is **clinical**—the therapy is aimed at understanding the behavioral, academic, social and **emotional** ramifications of this complex neurodevelopmental issue, **to understand the soul** of the person with ADHD and to **make her feel understood.** This understanding is what will help her realize and amplify her **"sense of self,"** and consolidate the feeling: "I am well." Mental health means being at peace with, and understanding, oneself as a whole, complete person. Hence, all the aspects of ADHD should be understood in a **holistic** manner, while understanding that the whole is more than the sum of its parts, and it is this wholeness that leads to healing. The emphasis in this approach is on **understanding the mental-emotional landscape of the child.** To do this, we need to address the mind, or soul, directly, so we cannot be content with using only medication or practical tools aimed to improve functioning abilities. The practical tools, the endless advice, even the medications which currently exist and are constantly updated, are very important, to be sure. However, they become truly effective only **after** the individual becomes **self-aware,** and only when those in the environment become aware of the topic and can understand her.

I hope that reading this book so far, has helped you to understand, in a general manner, the neurodevelopmental basis of ADHD and its many ramifications. Now let us take a moment to ask:

Have you acquired any new knowledge? What did working to understand the subject do for you? Has it "opened your mind"? Has this knowledge helped you, if only slightly, to comprehend the child and her difficulties, to stop for a moment and not immediately respond with criticism or anger? Has this information enabled you to gradually understand the behavioral, social and emotional ramifications of ADHD? Has this knowledge given way to empathy? Has it helped you to look at these children differently, out of a desire to make them realize who they are and believe in themselves?

Each of these insights is beneficial, and each constitutes an important step to understanding, and talking, ADHD.

This final chapter of the book is meant to explain, at length, **that the emotional difficulties of children dealing with ADHD are for the most part a direct product of an attention and hyperactivity disorder, and the approach of *Talking ADHD* with your child serves as emotional therapy for these children.** Of course, when there are other emotional difficulties which are **not** a direct outcome of difficulties with attention and impulsiveness, it is best to consult with a professional **and incorporate** treatment of those ADHD-related difficulties during the child's therapy. This integration is not the focus of this book, so I will only address it briefly. **Integration of these principles strengthens the therapeutic bond between the adult and the child**. When the child feels understood, she trusts and comes to rely on the adult – the instructor or the therapist – lowering her resistance and defenses, and her anxiety lessens. Later, coming to understand her precisely makes way to discussions of other emotional issues, sometimes more highly charged. In other words, because **the neurodevelopmental difficulties develop together with other emotional difficulties, they must be incorporated in the therapeutic response.**

PART ONE
CHOOSING THE ADHD THERAPY

The way to choose the best treatment starts with a precise diagnosis.

As mentioned, many parents find it difficult to accept their child's diagnosis and, even more so, find it difficult to accept the recommendation of medical treatment. Therefore, they often prefer to seek out other methods of treatment. I understand the difficulty with accepting this diagnosis, and very much understand the difficulty with accepting a medical treatment; for, after all, none of us is eager to use medications regularly. Nonetheless, the parents' difficulty also derives from a lack of knowledge and fear of facing the unknown. However, just as we treat our eyes when we have sight-related problems, we must treat our attention and impulses when we find it difficult to control them. It is important to note that when an individual does not see well, she requires eyeglasses throughout her life; whereas a child, or adult, with ADHD only takes medications when they are beneficial for her. If she understands her exact issues, and develops mindfulness, there is no need for her to take these medications throughout her life. Over time, she will learn when she should use it. Many children and adults who have made use of medical treatment have been convinced that their difficulty is with controlling attention and impulses, and not with their abilities or understanding. Thanks to this insight, they have decided to study this topic and deal with it without medical treatment. This holistic understanding enables them to make calculated decisions regarding this subject. There is no avoiding this simple fact—when there is a diagnosis of hyperactivity, impulsivity and difficulty with regulating attention, **one must first treat these specific difficulties, not anything else.** The child needs to develop an awareness about her difficulties and learn about them, and to identify the gaps in her functioning ability and understand them, in order to direct them and improve her functioning ability in these areas. Through this, she can develop a healthy and "whole" sense of self and personality.

By this stage, you must be aware of the most important point—**when we identify that those difficulties with school, behavior, social interactions or the family are a direct result of ADHD, we also understand that emotional distress is a side effect of the ADHD, and not the main problem.** That is why attention and hyperactivity must first be addressed, rather than focusing on the emotional distress as if it stands alone.

In my assessment, this understanding is associated with great optimism: We know that an emotional difficulty exists, and moreover, we understand what is causing it; hence, we know that relief and improvement of functioning abilities will come from developing awareness of this basic difficulty in the areas of hyperactivity, impulsivity and attention oscillations. **Emotional change** will come from focused treatment and the improvement of behavior and functioning ability, in relation to the varied, complex issues hat stem from ADHD. **Succeeding in developing the ability to function will result in the increased motivation of the child and the development of her ability to cope; these, in turn, will relieve her emotional distress. As we have seen throughout this book, we need to help children develop awareness of** their specific difficulties that stem from ADHD, so they can understand the gaps in their ability to function together with the emotional ramifications of these difficulties. **This awareness is a vital tool for them, so they can defend themselves from the insufficient understanding, misinterpretation and criticism that comes from their environment—alongside their own self-misunderstanding and self-criticism. This awareness will also enable them to gradually coalesce their personality and believe in themselves.**

Moreover, when a child is diagnosed with ADHD and the parents begin to learn about the subject via friends or frenzied online searches, they often think they "get the idea"—after all, they know the child cannot mediate her attention or impulses and has a hard time regulating them. They also know that her performance and behavior are influenced by this lack of control. But, often, they are still unaware of additional characteristics, such as that they are unpredictable both to themselves and to their environment, and that the **most consistent thing about their behavior is the inconsistency.** This inconsistency greatly confuses them, and often leads them to doubt their diagnosis. After all, *"she can, if she only puts her mind to it!"* When they doubt, they begin to interpret and seek other reasons to explain what is happening to them. Through no fault of their own, they respond angrily, punish, criticize, judge and make the wrong decisions, and then go back to asking themselves if the ADHD diagnosis is reliable or whether someone made it up:

"Perhaps the difficulty is actually emotional?;"

"Perhaps it is the child's nature and she is actually lazy?;"

"The diagnosis of the doctor was so quick; perhaps it isn't an attention disorder but something else?"

"How do we know if an emotional difficulty really does derive from ADHD and is not some other emotional difficulty?"

My answer is that the correct diagnosis is the final determinant; those who wish to delve deeper into the diagnosis are invited to read Appendix B at the end of this book—"Diagnosing ADHD".

A **formal diagnosis** by a professional is essential since it dictates the therapeutic approach. The diagnosis helps us focus on the three characteristics of ADHD – hyperactivity, impulsivity and attention oscillations – and their various and varied ramifications and intensities.

This diagnosis should only be done by a professional who specializes in the field, and it is very important to conduct a differential diagnosis to separate between attention disorders and other difficulties that may have symptoms similar to ADHD among children, teenagers and adults. Impairments such as a primary-language impairment, communication difficulties (on the autism spectrum), hearing impairments, learning difficulties or learning disabilities, an anxiety disorder or unusual fears, depression, oppositional defiant disorder or conduct disorder can all present similar symptoms to those of ADHD disorders.

These diagnoses are separate or distinct from ADHD and can also sometimes coexist together. The purpose of a **differential diagnosis** is to determine the existence of a given difficulty or several difficulties together. I will illustrate the commonalities and differences regarding the final two difficulties I mentioned: Oppositional Defiant Disorder (ODD) and Conduct Disorder (C.D.).

The differentiation between ADHD and ODD or C.D. is difficult, since these disorders include, like ADHD, a difficulty with control which leads to difficulties with accepting authority. First, we will briefly define these disorders. Oppositional Defiant Disorder, ODD, is a psychiatric diagnosis which is increasingly common, mostly in children who are under 10 years old. There are innate elements to it; it is expressed in rebellious, undisciplined and defiant behavior, usually towards authority figures. The disorder can often coexist with ADHD. Conduct Disorder, C.D., is often an escalation of ODD, and it is defined by antisocial, aggressive and rebellious behavior which violates the rights of others or else ignores the rules.

A child with C.D. is not sensitive to critiques by the environment and repeats destructive behaviors without learning from experience. **Children with ODD or C.D. can control their behavior and reactions**, unlike a child with ADHD, who experiences an innate difficulty with regulating and controlling attention and behavior, and must invest awareness and resources in improving, or successfully achieving control.

ODD and C.D. disorder are quite different from the rebelliousness or argumentativeness which are common among children with ADHD.

Children diagnosed with ADHD present irregularity of attention, hyperactivity and impulsivity, and react by arguing or rebelling when they intuitively feel misunderstood. The more intelligent and sensitive these children are, and the more misunderstood they feel, the more they tend to become opinionated and obstinate, deciding that they, and only they, know how things work. They can slam doors, shatter windows and decide to do things their own way. When there is a diagnosis of ADHD, and these children are understood, I see in the argumentativeness and rebelliousness, forces that can be routed in directions that will serve these children and help them express their opinions, be strong and assertive, put up a fight, believe in themselves, and successfully develop in a direction that will allow them to successfully develop in the direction they desire.

There are children with ADHD who use behavioral problems as a defense mechanism or strategy. In such cases, the child has a genuine problem with control, but "exploits" the difficulty with control, to disguise it even from herself. She can become the "class clown" to attract attention, emphasize the difference, argue, defy or provoke, and say things like: *"What will you do to me?, I don't care..."* and the like. Such situations are confusing, but when one manages to work with the child on her difficulties with attention, impulsivity and hyperactivity in accordance with the CHAMP model, the child feels better understood and reined in. Her behavior improves, and the tendency to argue, prove a point, rebel and defy abates.

If these behavioral difficulties mentioned above are not a spinoff of ADHD, they should be treated professionally and separately. If they exist alongside an attention disorder, they should be treated first, to get the child to cooperate. ODD and C.D. are severe disorders, whose dominant expressions do not enable treatment of an attention disorder or any other behavior.

With regard to the need for differential diagnosis between ADHD and other difficulties, we must also remember something else that we have already learned. When we seek to examine whether an attention or hyperactivity disorder exists, it is important to bear in mind that **ADHD is <u>not</u> the result of**:

- Bad parenthood or upbringing
- A given type of family (single parent, adopted child and so forth)
- Changes in the status of the family (the birth of a younger sibling, divorce, moving to a new apartment)
- Lack of boundaries and discipline
- The personality of the child
- A bad atmosphere at home or at school; or a teacher or important adult who does not like the child
- A given environment (a given extracurricular activity, certain friends)

Take for example the issue of boundaries in the context of ADHD. Many hyperactive and impulsive children are referred to specialists and diagnosed with ADHD, when the school or the parents are primarily concerned with issues regarding boundaries and discipline. In such cases, it may very well be that in addition to the diagnosis of ADHD, the environment in which the child is raised lacks discipline and does not set sufficient limits and boundaries, letting the child run wild. If this is indeed the case, then both subjects (areas, fields) need to be dealt with—both the ADHD and the boundaries. The ADHD should be treated with the CHAMP model, to build self-awareness and improve the child's ability to function; at the same time, it is important to bear in mind that a child with ADHD does not have internal boundaries and frequently tends to test her external boundaries. When these boundaries are lax or nonexistent, it is easy for her to breach them, defy, rebel, put herself at risk and engage in behavior which is antisocial and, in more extreme cases, even criminal.

Sometimes, experiencing a lack of control becomes a coping mechanism, and children and teenagers use it as a defense, "excuse" or "coupon".

"I don't pay attention to time; so I arrived late;" "I am disruptive because I can't sit still."

It is important to keep in mind that inconsistency with regulating their thoughts and behavior is what makes it so difficult for children diagnosed with ADHD to be disciplined. They lack the ability to regulate and control themselves, and they neither mean nor choose to act as they do!

They are forgetful, scatterbrained, distracted, frenzied, heedless, argumentative, change the rules, slam doors, do things their own way and often find it hard to obey boundaries. But rules, order and frameworks, the things they find so difficult, are precisely what they most need. It should also be noted that these children constantly test their boundaries.

Our job is **to set the boundaries** as early as possible and explain to the children that this is how we protect them until they can protect themselves.

Parents often make excuses for children diagnosed with ADHD and do not set limits. Hyperactive and impulsive children, and particularly those diagnosed with ADHD, need external boundaries, even if they resist them at first. Well-defined, known and clear rules and limits will help them get organized and function better. In this way, the children will feel reined in, understood, protected and in control, and their tendency to violate rules and limits will decrease.

An accurate and focused diagnosis of ADHD will help us refer to each of the three components of the phenomenon – hyperactivity, impulsivity and attention oscillations – as they are described in the previous chapters. The diagnosis enables us to understand how these phenomena are manifested or expressed in our child; in addition, we will understand the academic, functional, behavioral, emotional and social ramifications, and the coping mechanisms the child has adopted. We will also understand the influence of the characteristics of the attention, impulsivity and hyperactivity disorder on each stage of development. Above all, we will understand that it is not controlled, and this is what leads to their difficulty with the ability to function; as expected, this is also translated into a social, behavioral, educational or emotional difficulty. It is also important to conduct a differential diagnosis as described above or understand that a number of difficulties coexist.

Let us take, for example, a child of divorced parents, 13 years old, whom we will call Diana. She was diagnosed from an early age with ADHD, along with significant language difficulties. The following is a portion of a long letter she wrote to her mother. The original letter was filled with spelling and grammatical errors, which were indicative of her objective language difficulties. I will present it here with correct phrasing and spelling to make it easier for us to understand the content.

Diana throws accusations at her mother regarding her new partner:

"... *You never protect me, and always let him do whatever he wants, and always deny or justify what he does. You always call me a liar, even if it is really his fault. I tell you that I truly love you, but I can't be with you and your boyfriend, because he discriminates between his children and us, and I won't tolerate it ...*"

This letter is indicative of a genuine emotional issue Diana has with her mother, and other, genuine emotional difficulties have emerged from it, which require processing with a professional, regardless of ADHD and objective language difficulties.

Nonetheless, it is important for the emotional therapy used in this situation to also incorporate these objective difficulties.

In other words, **the selected treatment must address all sources of the difficulty—the emotional difficulties together with the many emotional ramifications of the attention disorder and the hyperactivity, as well as of the language difficulties.**

For example, "*You are very sensitive in general, and do not tolerate injustices done to you, or people misunderstanding your genuine objective difficulties. You speak up for yourself ... You do this, too, when you feel your mom's partner discriminates between you and his own children ...*"

Adapting Emotional Therapy to Children and Adults with ADHD

Despite all the progress made in ADHD research and the various different therapeutic methods, we are still living in a time when the therapeutic perspectives for ADHD are narrow. Professionals specializing in specific fields each stick to their narrow specialization without referring to the wider picture generated by ADHD. This is why, when an emotional difficulty exists, professionals, let alone the parents, often fail to link it to ADHD. The situation is much like a Japanese puppet show in which each character is operated by several puppet masters—the first operates the face; the second—the hands; and the third—the legs. If one of them is asked to fill in and operate the other part, he cannot do so, because he is not familiar with the part. These professionals are much like the Japanese operators—each of them is responsible for the field in which they are an expert (occupational therapy, adaptive teaching, medication, emotional therapy and so forth), and they focus on providing treatments in this field without fully understanding the complexities—or seeing the child with the ADHD as a whole entity.

This situation is very confusing for the parents. Moreover, it makes it difficult for the child to fully understand herself.

A holistic therapeutic approach is imperative when several professionals are involved in treating the child, and each has their own specialty. It is important that one of them functions as the case manager and coordinate between the therapists, making decisions and directing the parents, who can "get lost" among all the various treatments, and above all consistently taking care of the big picture of the child's world, in a holistic fashion.

Sometimes parents are capable of functioning as case managers for their own child. They organize the information, coordinate the various therapists, prioritize and lead the process.

Coordinating between various professionals, the child and the parents helps organize the various therapies around the primary cause—the ADHD. It enables an optimal division of labor between the various professionals, prevents conflicting messages or treatment methods, and ensures a successful therapeutic outcome.

Even when the case manager is not one of the parents, the iron rule is that the parents are active partners throughout. The parents are the most important adults in the child's life, and they are therefore the first who need to understand the complex significance of ADHD, internalize what it means to have ADHD and mediate it to their child. They need to participate in specific, professional parental guidance programs, learn about ADHD thoroughly, observe and explain the wide and varied gaps within the behavior of their children.

Beyond this, it is important that they themselves receive support, since raising a child with ADHD can be a very challenging and exhausting task.

ADHD frequently confuses parents, but it can also confuse experienced therapists who are not sufficiently familiar with the subject.

Here are two examples:

The parents of a child with ADHD, who was also being treated medically, participated in a workshop for parents that I led. They returned to me for a one-time consultation after several years, due to finding it difficult to accept the diagnosis of an emotional therapist who had treated their son. The mother was upset and concerned at the words of the experienced therapist who had explained the unease of her son as an expression of his *"difficulty with finding himself in the family."* The father, who had studied ADHD thoroughly after participating in the workshop, and who was extremely active in the treatment of his son, was sternly opposed to the therapist's diagnosis, as he felt strongly that the child was loving and loved in the family. He added: *"It is true that the child's restlessness has led the family to be angry at him recently, but I refuse to accept the therapist's diagnosis."* The mother agreed with her husband and explained that she even tried to challenge the therapist and ask him why he thought this but had not received a satisfactory answer.

I helped them refocus on the initial diagnosis – ADHD – and reminded them that the child was being treated successfully with appropriate medication. I requested that they recall the principles of the CHAMP model, in order to understand and be convinced that the restlessness was the result of hyperactivity. I encouraged them to return and speak with their son and his brother about the "coil spring;" discuss again the issue with the entire family; and later, if necessary, turn to a doctor to reexamine the type and dosage of the medical treatment. They called several weeks later, thanked me for the advice, and reported that they were back on track.

This example illustrates how even a professional can link a child's behavior to an emotional factor, whereas the primary causative factor is neurodevelopmental.

The adoptive parents of a five-year-old child came to me for consultation regarding the continuation of her emotional therapy.

The child was in emotional therapy for about a year, and the parents could not see any progress in the treatment. Although the child presented no resistance to the therapy, it was very expensive, and both felt that the therapist was missing the core issue by referring primarily to the issue of adoption.

This was a child who had been diagnosed with ADHD but had not been treated medically due to his young age—yet, did receive occupational therapy for a brief time. The parents came to me for emotional therapy since the child found it difficult to sit in group meetings, was restless, in a frenzy, hassled other children in the

kindergarten, wandered around the yard without any clearly defined purpose, and refused to participate in any creative activities
requiring painting or drawing skills. He gave out-of-context answers to questions, found it difficult to focus, refused to listen to
stories and gave up quickly when he had to deal with challenges.
When he did manage to rally himself to a task, he demanded a lot
of himself, was very harsh to and critical of himself and tore the
pages when he was not satisfied, especially when he compared his
work to the work of other children. I explained to the parents that
he was experiencing clear difficulties with attention, hyperactivity
and impulsivity alongside difficulties with fine motor skills. He
was indeed behaving in a frenzied manner and finding it difficult
to listen, which was why he had found it difficult to sit in groups.

These difficulties led him to avoid dealing with his issues, and
give up. When he tried, despite his difficulties, his high basic intelligence led him to feel severe self-criticism regarding his work.
He compared his own work to the other children's and felt frustrated and disappointed.

I added that I thought he should be helped to improve his
performance, so that he might experience success that would increase his motivation to cope. At this point, the father admitted
that he was confused and frustrated with the various pieces of
advice he had received and said: *"How do I know that my son's
tendency to give up is not a problem with his personality or a result
of the adoption?"*

I understood his confusion and doubt, and tried to explain to
these parents that the child was experiencing a specific difficulty
with issues of competence and lack of control. I expanded upon
the gap between his high basic intelligence and his poor ability
to perform and complete tasks; I continued to explain and insist

that, while these gaps were apparent to his parents and me, the child was also intuitively aware of the gap between his basic intelligence and his inability to perform and succeed in the way he himself expected of himself. I explained that we adults need to take responsibility over the situation, particularly in the case of such a small child. I insisted on helping them to understand the boy's objective difficulties and help him strengthen his graphomotor ability, while addressing his ADHD.

I recommended consulting with the kindergarten teacher and, if necessary, with the kindergarten psychologist, and to prepare a specific therapeutic plan customized to his needs, which would include occupational therapy to improve his ability to function with fine motor skills, as well as parental guidance for his ADHD. I also recommended they consider martial arts or swimming, or any other such extracurricular activity that the child might choose and persist with. I strongly recommended that the entire therapeutic program, including the regular kindergarten activities and the extracurricular classes, should take into account, above any other consideration, the specific difficulties with attention, hyperactivity and impulsivity. The therapy should be adapted specifically to their child, and coordinated between the different professionals and adults responsible for him; hence, I recommended appointing a case manager who would assess, throughout the process, the whole picture, and would involve and guide the parents. The case manager would also address the parents' anger and disappointment with themselves, and help them to express and let go of their feelings, but also to understand and draw in the child. If necessary later, the case manager could also recommend emotional therapy for the parents, to help them cope with the difficulties of adoption or any other relevant topic.

As in the case above, this example illustrates that where the presenting factor for a referral to emotional therapy is actually the result of ADHD and other objective developmental difficulties, such as fine motor skills, these difficulties must be addressed first. It may well be that later, it will also be necessary to treat purely emotional issues, such as adoption, divorce, single motherhood/fatherhood, death and so forth; but, in most cases, where there is a diagnosis of ADHD or other objective developmental issue, the therapy must be adapted accordingly.

This example also illustrates the all-too-common confusion and disputes that exist between different professionals, and sometimes between parents as well. Many parents are not aware of the need to coordinate between the professionals, and this leads different professionals with different goals and ideas to treat the same child at cross purposes. The result is confusing, ineffective therapy; an unpleasant atmosphere; and a feeling of helplessness. Therefore, it is critically important that there be a single competent professional that will serve as case manager. She must have a knowledgeable, direct, focused and targeted **holistic** perception of the entire picture.

PART TWO
THE ESSENCE OF EMOTIONAL THERAPY ACCORDING TO THE 'TALKING ADHD' THERAPEUTIC APPROACH

The emotional therapy which is incorporated into the CHAMP terminology refers to the oscillations of attention and energy. It is intended to assist us with coping with difficulties in the fields of attention, in general, and executive attention, in particular, with or without impulsivity and hyperactivity. It also addresses the complex emotional ramifications of ADHD. This kind of therapy is holistic, performed in practice by the parents and the adults who are responsible for the child, who live and meet with the child on a daily basis, with the assistance and accompaniment of a professional who understands the field. Since you, the parents, become the primary therapists, it is important to first be freed from feelings of guilt, anger, confusion and frustration, so that you can be truly available to provide support for your child. It is important that you understand your child's experience so that you can accept it. You must, therefore, in the first stage, learn the neurodevelopmental basis of ADHD. In the second stage, you must learn about its complexity, while referring to its unique expressions by your child. The therapy is based on the acquisition of a new and precise language, the CHAMP terminology, which will become a way of life for both you and your child. My hope is that this language construct will teach you how to observe without judgment or anger, trying to explain, or being quick to punish or criticize. It will enable you to listen, slowly and gradually increase your awareness, and encourage you to observe and be mindful of the diverse characteristics of ADHD. Utilizing this language, you will be able to help your child get to know a part of her that is integral to who she is, resist it and control it—on her own.

Using this new language construct, you will be able to help your child learn to discover her **specific difficulties** in the areas of attention, impulsivity and hyperactivity-"wandering" attention, hyperactivity, impulsivity, executive attention, and compensatory attention in accordance with the professional diagnosis. It is important to re-emphasize that this approach **does not replace medical therapy or any other therapy but needs to be integrated into it,** while adopting the CHAMP terminology into every setting in which there is a conversation with a child or adult coping with ADHD symptoms. My experience has shown me that incorporating the *Talking ADHD* approach into the various therapies is what enables the child to understand herself better, and become fulfilled in the most successful manner.

Early in the book, I noted that this therapeutic approach is well-reflected in the words of Albert Einstein, who proposed searching for a guiding principle within the confusion and seeing an opportunity in every challenge.

We need to look for a central and specific principle or characteristics that are present in the child, to learn about them with the intention of raising awareness about them and identifying them. Through this, the child will learn to gradually recognize these characteristics, to control and channel them, and to create opportunities for success with this knowledge and new capacity. I firmly believe that the *Talking ADHD* approach is, indeed, emotional therapy. **This is a long-term therapy, focused and direct, which is intended to develop awareness and mindfulness, empower the "self" and enable an individual to narrate his life story accurately**. As mentioned, there are various processes and principles interlaced with this; and the professional therapist in this sort of therapy is active – she teaches, mediates, provides solutions, determines the path, directs and serves as a model – first, for the parents, and when necessary, for the other therapists. The professional therapist acts as case manager and guides the parents and/or the other adults responsible for the child. After the case manager completes the parental guidance, and helps them become the primary therapists of the child, she stays in the background, to assist, provide counsel or mediate, and tackle specific problems as required. Extensive experience and knowledge combined with the right tools greatly contribute to understanding, drawing in the child and practicing control. An active and direct therapeutic approach, unlike psychodynamic therapy, is intended to imbue knowledge about a specific field so that the individual will be aware of it. The therapist or responsible adult directly explains and points out the characteristics of attention oscillations, impulsivity and hyperactivity that are unique to each individual; helps individuals to see themselves from the outside looking in; and helps them develop awareness of things that are so integral to them that may be completely unfamiliar or unknown to them. Unlike dynamic therapy, the therapist does not encourage talk of subconscious or unconscious conflicts in an attempt to "interpret" the **significance of the content**, but helps the adult or child with ADHD, and the child's parents, to understand the context of ADHD for this particular issue. To illustrate, in the case of tactlessness, the therapist does not interpret, explain or seek to treat subconscious conflicts. Rather, she explains the so-called lack of tact as a difficulty with mediating a response that comes impulsively. At the next stage, the therapist helps the individual identify, understand and internalize these ideas, develop mindfulness, and gradually improve her ability to delay her reactions. The therapist then continues to show her how impulsivity is expressed under other circumstances and helps her develop awareness and to practice in order to acquire the ability to keep her life under control more effectively.

This focused discourse uses **metaphors** and imagery which are known to play an important psychological role. They **connect between knowledge and understanding and emotions,** and lead to **insights.** They enable the child to "play," to feel understood and to decrease their tendency to anxiety, depression and/or loneliness; and the child is available to focus on gradually improving their ability to function.

The guiding principle is that the emotional difficulties described are a direct outcome of the objective difficulties deriving from ADHD.

Psychological therapy, which does not consider the neurological basis and is not active, by nature, may well increase anxiety and loneliness, generate resistance and perpetuate the child's feeling that she is not understood.

Many parents approach me, asking me to take care of their child, and I explain to them that a precondition for accepting a child for therapy is for the parents to first undergo **specific** parental guidance in relation to ADHD.

The responses to this approach are varied: Some parents think the problem is their child's, not theirs.

Some respond with disappointment and even slam down the phone. Some ask, *"What? Don't you need to meet the child before you speak to us?"*

Others doubt my ability to teach parents to handle their child without me treating the child herself, but are willing to set an appointment for an introductory meeting. Some parents say,

"The child needs to take responsibility for herself."

And some parents are excited, and immediately understand the logic behind my pre-condition. They very much wish to study the topic deeply in order to become their child's main therapist. **In fact, all parents understand inwardly that there is no other way,** since ADHD is a way of life and dealing with the world, which requires the daily attention of a parent (however **"they naturally still want shortcuts or quick help in dealing with the heavy burden"**).

Who are the children or adults who need therapy?

You surely understand now that there is hope—**many people among us with ADHD have been able to channel their attention "deficit," or surplus attention and energy, in creative and original directions,** which enables them to succeed on the developmental path they have chosen.

This **positive result** is a function of the fact that the unique qualities which distinguish this group enable many of them to fulfill their goals. They are sensitive, empathic, sometimes very intelligent, very purposeful, and have excellent intuition and internal integrity. They are curious, energetic, charismatic, opinionated and stubborn. They are also practical, resourceful and have excellent powers of improvisation and imagination, are prepared to take risks and live the moment. These are the same people who intuitively, or with the help of those around them, have been able to direct themselves in the positive direction that they have wanted. Some have been very successful; others describe a disappointment-, misunderstanding – and frustration-filled struggle, but they are proud that they have been able to overcome. Some feel a certain sense of missing out, but have managed to cope overall and very much wish to learn about ADHD and spare their children the path of thorns they themselves have gone through.

In contrast, there are many children and adults who do not understand themselves and remain unpredictable to themselves and to those in their environment. They are no less wise or successful, and need help in various fields: educational, behavioral, social and emotional. Above all, **they feel a lack of control, ability and capability.** This lack leads them to feel decreased self-esteem. They **find it difficult to control and regulate themselves.** Their frustration threshold is low; and they respond with outbursts of anger, frustration and weeping. They find it hard to not react and respond immediately, sometimes in a way that is inappropriate to the situation. They tend to exaggerate, to get swept away, to be rambunctious, to be irritated and to lock down. They find it difficult to remain engaged with any given activity, fail or experience a lack of satisfaction, are disappointed with themselves or demand too much of themselves. They frequently find it difficult to listen, and hence are avoidant, fearful, resistant and ashamed; they hide away and develop low self-esteem to such an extent that they find it difficult to fit into society.

Children, much like many adults, **who are not aware of themselves and are insufficiently understood by themselves and the environment**, constitute an irritant to themselves and to those in the environment, and therefore require help on both the functional and the emotional levels. I wish to emphasize that when ADHD symptoms, such as restlessness, rashness, daydreaming and distractedness, are expressed even partially, or else when an ADHD diagnosis exists, **such emotional difficulties** are usually **a direct outcome of neurodevelopmental** difficulties with attention, impulsivity and hyperactivity-regulation, and require a focused, unique and specific treatment, as described in this chapter.

Understanding the Gaps in Functioning Throughout Life

As I described in previous chapters, the life story of a child with ADHD is characterized by confusing gaps and conflicts, ups and downs that are not understood by them or their environment, and often make them seem immature or childish as compared to their peers. The more we manage to "talk ADHD" via the CHAMP model, the more these gaps narrow, which is why it is always better to start as early as possible. Still, it is never too late. Nevertheless, gaps in functioning are apparent between different fields of life (for example, between studying in school and participating in a recreational soccer class), within a given field (for example, between history and art studies) and throughout one's life.

This can be a very frustrating factor, both for the child and for those in his environment, but we must try to non judgementally understand, be empathic, embrace, and refer to it as part of the treatment of the child, as well.

For the child, and for adults with ADHD, the frustration is twice as great, and these gaps are often translated into emotional difficulties. So it is, for example, that there is inconsistency in their ability to do simple tasks on different days or in different situations: The child manages to read the instructions of a new game she received but finds it hard to read a book. She knows how to solve a mathematical exercise very easily but finds it difficult to solve the very same formula as part of a verbal question in mathematics. A child or an adult is able to get up for work on certain days, and get organized on time, but is unable to do so consistently. Most children, parents and adults report a sense of frustration, disappointment and missing out, given the many gaps they find difficult to bridge.

> As one of my patients told me: "We have walked a long way together and you have taught me many things. I can pass this knowledge on to others. I have invested a great deal of time and thought, and really try hard, but the problem is that, by the time I reach the store, somehow the price has already risen ..."

The more intelligent the child is, the more these gaps are pronounced and the greater their frustration. Often, children ask themselves or those around them:

"Why don't I understand what I read?"

"Why am I always responding by bursting out, instead of raising my finger?"

"Why is it hard for me to sit quietly like everyone else?"

As adults who have not studied the subject deeply, and who do not understand the child, we tend intuitively to explain, criticize, judge and get angry, misinterpreting rather than comprehending these ways of behaving or speaking. The child feels misunderstood, and responds with intense, powerful bursts of frustration or anger. Sometimes, she also acts defiantly, pulling away and rejecting others, arguing and even turning to violence. When she does not understand herself, she tends to withdraw, oppose and avoid others.

On a deeper level, feelings of embarrassment, fear, anxiety and depression arise, harming her motivation to deal with the difficulty. She compares herself to others and feels different and inferior. Outwardly, the child's situation seems to stem from emotional difficulties, and this leads the parents and those around her to feel anger and confusion, but mostly helplessness.

The following is a poem written by a talented, sensitive and intelligent 8-year-old boy. He implores us not to whitewash anything, but rather, to make do with the fact that he is special and different, but he requests that we explain what he is experiencing. Not every child knows how to express himself so eloquently, but this does not mean that other children do not feel similar things.

"I dream of being a regular child,
But I am special and different, I try to cope and don't always succeed.
I am angry and cry, disappointed and do not understand,
Even though all I wanted was to be a regular boy —
To peel a regular orange, to play with a regular friend, next to a regular computer.
And this is odd, because I am special and different,
I am angry and cry, disappointed and do not understand.
Can anyone explain to me **what** is different about me?"

As we have already learned, one can liken a child with ADHD to an incomplete puzzle. The child does not understand the gaps and conflicts in her own behavior and feels as if there are pieces within her that do not fit together. She has good moments also—soon followed by not-so-good moments. Days of successful behavior—and then a fall! The child is effectively forced to join these pieces together without a guiding principle, without understanding the connection between them, without understanding the full picture. Her gaps in functioning often form because she knows what she must do but does not know how to do it, and so she finds it difficult to understand the connection between what she wants to do and how to do it—in other words, between the "what" and the "how." Furthermore, she finds it difficult to understand the connection between her actions and their consequences. This is why she is unpredictable, even to herself; does not control herself; and often conducts herself based on momentary impulses, without directing herself clearly and definitively. Our role, as adults, is to provide her with a big picture view, so that she will be able to successfully deal with the challenges of life from a fair starting point.

Since unexpected and inconsistent functions, and the resulting gaps, are part of the lives of any child or adult with ADHD, there is no point in telling her *"but you just said"* or *"a few days ago you were able to do this."* It is completely wrong to punish her, certainly. In order to perform her various life tasks, this child, more than others, requires **mediation** and guidance in the area of "how." She needs to be provided with an explanation that will make it clear to her what exactly she is having difficulty with concerning the performance of necessary activities. Precisely here is where the gap lies, between her high basic potential and the mostly inferior outcomes. We, the adults, who are aware of these gaps and contrasts, are charged with genuinely and empathically understanding, accepting and embracing this inconsistency. We, unlike our child, know that this lack **derives from the gap between her basic, good abilities and the impairment of her performance caused by the difficulties with regulating her attention and impulses.**

The situation can be likened to a child finding it hard to find the right "button" to push in order to succeed in a task. Every time we are able to provide her with an explanation **which accurately reflects what she is experiencing**, it becomes possible for her to recognize the correct "button," and that is how an important piece in her "puzzle" finds its place. The accurate and "right" feeling of "Bingo! I am understood!" is the significant turning point that enables the process of change. This is the essence of empathy—which serves as the fertile substrate for the child's connection to the environment. This is where the adult, who reflects the situation to the child, needs to be able to observe accurately. "Accurately"—because this child has sharp intuition; she is **extremely sensitive to "faking."** When the description, reflection or explanation provided by the adult is generalized or vague, interpretive or critical, the child experiences it as an empathic failure, a lack of genuineness or even honesty. For the child to be able to continue to recognize her difficulty, to be mindful and, later on, to develop the ability to control herself, or at least prepare for the next unexpected event, the explanation and the mediation need to be exact. Through this, she will learn how to function well, including under pressure, and will feel good about herself.

Gaps, retrogression and less-good moments are particularly prominent when the child needs to deal with changes or transitions in life. At such crossroads, children with ADHD often experience retrogression in performance and behavior, and many parents tend to be disappointed and frustrated at such retrogressions. They forget the diagnosis and its nature—**life with ADHD is like being on a rollercoaster—unexpected and filled with ups and downs.**

This is what happened to the parents of a boy we will name Dan, who was diagnosed with ADHD. Dan was able to control his "coil spring" thanks to the instruction and good work of his parents, without any additional treatment, but when he was seven years old, his parents returned to me, disappointed and frustrated. They told me that things had returned to the way they had been before. After being questioned and delving deeper, they reported that they had relocated to a different city following workplace changes. During the move, the house had been in a state of unrest and they were not available to continue to work with Dan consistently and systematically. I helped them understand that the move had changed the family's routine, and this could certainly be a trigger for Dan's coil spring being released with such strength. In addition, these parents were not sufficiently available to help Dan gain control of his coil spring. I helped the parents recollect the ADHD diagnosis and focus on it, "forgive" themselves and return to work with the child as they had previously done, successfully, according to the principles of the CHAMP model. And this is what happened.

Here is another example of backsliding, not necessarily due to transitions:

David was a nine-year-old boy who was diagnosed with ADHD and was successfully treated in a children's group. In parallel, his parents participated in a parents' workshop. A year later, they returned to me frustrated and disappointed, since their son's behavioral disturbances in class had gotten worse. In response to my questions, the parents explained that David insisted on driving a toy car on the table during the classes. He got carried away, made loud noises and constituted a disruptive factor in class. The parents disagreed about how to deal with David—the mother would softly explain to him that he had to stop, while understanding his need to vent his energy—but without discussing this with him. The father, on the other hand, would grow irritated and angry, dole out punishments, and forbid him to meet with friends or have screen time. I repeated the need to remind David of the excess energy he needs to release, but that it is better for him to do so in a non-disruptive manner (for example, by scribbling in a notebook or crushing a rubber ball in his hand). As I spoke, the father raised his voice and said: *"I am sick of this—we have already discussed all this! Do you mean to tell me that he doesn't know?"* I explained once again that both the child and the parents knew, but that routine often wears down and makes us forget the CHAMP principles.

It is always important to remember to "lower the volume," recall everything you have learned, calm down, and go back and talk with the child (David, in this case) about the "coiled spring" and his need to release his pent up energy. During each period, the CHAMP talk should be adjusted to the child's age. Now, David needed to be helped to understand that his behavior with the car was simply unsuitable for the requirements of the class. David and his parents had to choose a solution which would be acceptable to the teacher, as well, and would help him let out energy in the classroom, in order to return to attention. He needed to consider the need of the other children in the class for quiet, so that they too would be able to concentrate during the lesson. I explained again that ups and downs are part of the diagnosis and are no reason to give up or to punish David. His behavior is not controllable—the intensity of a child's impulses and ability to pay attention change with age; the practice of the CHAMP talks with the child is forgotten, and one must return to it and make use of it.

After the meeting, the parents explained to their child what I had said and returned to "talking ADHD" as they had learned in the parents' and children's workshops, adapting the language to David's age; and I was happy to hear from them that he not only managed to reroute his excess energy in more desirable directions but also to prepare a presentation and explain to his classmates what he experiences.

A Change in Approach

Emotional therapy, therefore, begins with parental instruction—and only after we adults learn the subject do we look to direct the children. This very study and development of understanding enable us to change our approach and engage the children. We manage to face feelings of anger, criticism and judgment better, and instead of wandering helplessly in search of empathic mothers online, we begin to understand, internalize, embrace, and equip ourselves with the tools we need to focus and observe with precision, thereby enabling ourselves to explain to the child what she is experiencing .It is important that both parents understand the subject in order to prevent disagreements and also to strengthen each other, because the path forward can be long and exhausting. Throughout the journey, many parents identify their own attention disorder, impulsivity or hyperactivity, and the parental experience is a topic in and of itself. Sometimes the parent with ADHD (regardless of whether it is diagnosed) identifies and manages to display patience and empathy towards her child, whereas at other times she is not at ease with herself, due to the difficulty of dealing with her own attention disorder, and projects her anger and self-criticism onto her child. There are also cases in which the parent is so preoccupied with her own feelings and emotions that she is not fully available to care for her child. In this case, it is up to the other parent to take up the responsibility and to bring in his or her spouse later. The parents also need to recruit those in the child's environment and educate them about ADHD. In so doing, the parent and the teacher become the child's primary caregivers and, using the CHAMP model, can teach her about herself, gradually but consistently. Let us re-emphasize the main principles:

- Children **express resistance** at first. This is because, over the years, they have absorbed a significant amount of criticism, and they feel anxious and misunderstood. This is why, before anything else, a comfortable environment must be created, and the child must be given an explanation about why we want to talk to her using the CHAMP terminology. In other words, a lot of time needs to be invested in preparing the ground and resolving resistance. In order to do these things, we need to normalize the phenomena and bring ourselves and the child closer by explaining that parents have similar difficulties and that "we will all work together" on "getting better." At the basis of the explanation is the principle that understanding ourselves – our strengths and our weaknesses – is an advantage. In this context, I warmly recommend discussing the issue with all the family members, and explaining that our job, as parents, is to teach the children about themselves. Knowledge is power, and if they know themselves, they will be able to manage themselves in the best possible manner. In this way, the diagnosed child is not tagged as "problematic" by the family.
- We need to find a **"friendly" metaphor**, which will enable us to discuss specific manifestations of their ADHD. I will remind you that the metaphor I have chosen to use over the past few years is the **"smartphone"**—children are like the latest model of the "smartest" phone in existence, and they must learn all of their applications in order to operate the phone in an optimal way. I have gone on to develop the metaphor and explain that knowledge is power, and those who know themselves – and know how to operate themselves – succeed.
- We need to provide the child with explanations when she is quiet and

calm, **not when** she is restless or hyperactive. Each time, we need to explain to her about one specific phenomenon, out of the slew of manifestations related to her non-regulation of attention and hyperactivity.

- We need to help the child understand that **our job as adults and parents is to help her understand and be aware of what she is experiencing**. Only in this manner will she be able to observe different aspects of herself from an external perspective, with our mediation, without judgment or criticism.

- It is important to speak of the **positive sides** of the phenomena and help her understand when they serve her and when they interfere.

- She should be helped to understand that **different people respond differently to the same phenomenon**, which is why it is so confusing.

- Once the child develops awareness and manages to identify a specific phenomenon, she should be taught gradually how to explain it to herself and the environment, but **not as a "get out of jail free" card**. Furthermore, she **needs to learn how to control it**.

- Once she learns and manages to control a specific manifestation, she should be empowered and motivated to learn about another manifestation. It is advisable to start with a manifestation that is relatively easier or simpler to explain and deal with. **Motivation is a function of success,** and coping successfully with a simpler manifestation of the child's difficulties will increase her motivation to learn more about herself.

- We, the parents, need to assist and mediate, to protect her and to explain her situation to those in the environment, until the child can do so independently. **The more the child's functioning improves and the more the gaps narrow, the more capable she will feel, the better her self-esteem will be, and hence, the better her self-confidence, as well.**

We adults need to change our perspective, understanding and attitude in order to help the child behave effectively. To do so, I will linger on things I have said throughout the book and explain the significance of the instruction to "observe, reflect, redefine, identify and control," which is supposed to change our intuitive responses—the criticism, anger, explaining away, judging and quickness to punish.

How many times have we all heard these sentences?

"You need to focus on schoolwork because that is what matters."

"You must sit quietly and be polite."

"Take a deep breath before you speak."

"Think about yourself first before you criticize."

"When will you learn to give up?"

"Remember to check the test before you hand it in."

"Think first, then act."

"It is time for you to grow up ..."

These sentences, as corny as they are, are educational and help most of the population. Why don't they help, and even irritate, children with ADHD? It is hard for "regular" people to understand this, and they get even angrier:

"What is so hard to understand? It is so simple! You just need to stop!"

When children have **uncontrollable difficulties with regulation they cannot choose to stop. They do not know their "stop option."** Even if they understand that there is a need to stop, they don't know how to do it.

"What does that mean? How do others do this? Why can't we succeed?" they ask. The remarks which help most children to stop, think, plan and act cannot help the child with impulsivity and attention-regulation difficulties. Instead of using these familiar comments, the parents and adults should first help her learn about "brakes," in general, intentionally focus on her brakes, identify when she is able to brake and when she fails or only partially succeeds. The adults in the environment must teach the child to comprehend her difficulty and internalize it, and only by so doing will she be able to learn to control a component which is so much part of her—the difficulty with stopping.

In order to bring about a change, we must increase understanding and awareness, and provide relevant information in accordance with the principles of the CHAMP model as detailed in the previous chapters. It is only natural that, despite our awareness of these principles, we grow confused in real scenarios, and automatically, without any malicious intent, tend to criticize, grow angry, punish, judge or interpret in a skewed way. This is why a "rule of thumb" should first of all be to calm down and count to 10—and only then to try to simplify things within these moments of chaos by using one of our chosen metaphors.

Even if this metaphor is not super accurate at first, it "neutralizes" criticism, and the moment the child experiences empathy rather than a negative response, she will agree to continue to talk to us. When a dialogue starts, it is important to encourage the child to use precise metaphors to match the specific manifestations of her dysregulation. The adaptation and re-adaptation of the metaphor to the child is extremely important, as the continual use of an inaccurate metaphor will be interpreted by the child as "pestering." These are four metaphors that have already been described in the book; you can start with them:

- **"Coil spring"** (an expression of hyperactivity)
- **"Stop sign" or "brakes"** (an expression of impulsivity and the need to mediate or "delay" one's response)
- **"Balloon"** (an expression of attention which tends to wander)
- **"Complicated attention"** (an expression of the difficulty with using the executive attention system)

What do I mean? That we need to exchange the critical, angry, interpretive, judgmental sentences we use with remarks that convey genuine,non judgemental, empathic understanding.

x— sentences expressing criticism	✓ — sentences expressing understanding or comprehension, enabling reflection and identification
"If you don't slack off, you will succeed."	"This balloon has flown away now. Let's take a short break."
"Jumping around like that all the time is not nice."	"Looks like the coil spring jumped out of place. Let's try to put it back."
"It isn't nice to tell a neighbor he is fat, even if it is true."	"You say the first thing that pops into your head. Even if it's true, it's not always a good idea to say it, because it can be insulting. This is why you need to learn to press your brakes and pause for a moment before you say what you feel."

x — sentences expressing anger	✓ — sentences expressing understanding or comprehension, enabling reflection and identification
"Sit down quietly already! Can't you see that everyone is sitting quietly?"	"I know that it is very difficult for you, but please pay attention to your 'coil spring' and try to control it. If you can't overcome it, then it is better you step out for a bit, because everybody else is sitting down quietly now."
"What is so difficult? I only asked you to do two things!"	"You got lost with two instructions. This is precisely the 'complicated attention' we talked about."
"How many times have I told you not to talk like that?!"	"You forgot about your stop sign."

✗ — interpretive sentences	✓ — sentences expressing understanding or comprehension, enabling reflection and identification
"You do not like this teacher and don't have any patience with her. This is why you have outbursts whenever you run into her."	"I know that you are feeling sorry and did not want to harm the teacher, but you insulted her, because you were unable to stop before saying the first thing that popped into your head. Try to use your brakes."
"Once again, you decided not to do what is required of you."	"Your 'balloon' has floated away, and you are having difficulty starting your task. This is why you are procrastinating. Let's take a short break."
"You can't sit still even for a second."	"Your 'coil spring' is out of control," or "You are spinning around like a spinning top."

✗ — judgmental sentences	✓ — sentences expressing understanding or comprehension, enabling reflection and identification
"Is this how you behave at home as well?!"	"Pay attention — your 'coil spring' is jumping all over the place."
"Your achievements are low, and you lack the abilities required to fit into the program you wanted."	"I want you to always remember that you are an intelligent child with a 'balloon.' If their 'balloon' escapes, even the smartest person in the world can't be at their best. This is why it is very important to me that we learn how to try and take hold of the balloon and not let it fly away from us."
"Politeness requires restraint, and until you learn this you are suspended from school!"	"You need to adjust your brakes, whatever it takes, because you are suffering from making terrible accidents."

PART THREE
HOW TO CONDUCT CHAMP-BASED THERAPY?

Each child manifests ADHD uniquely. Once we adults have studied ADHD in depth, we find it easier to understand children with ADHD and cope better with feelings of anger, criticism and judgment. We enable ourselves to receive the tools that will help us focus and explain to the child what she is experiencing. When there is a diagnosis or symptoms of ADHD, we need to break down the general terms – attention, hyperactivity and impulsivity – into their specific manifestations and expressions, explaining them to ourselves and to the child while referring to the **direct** consequences of these difficulties on her behavior, and the associated emotional consequences.

The characteristics, as we know them, are many and varied, but for the most part only some of them exist in any given child with ADHD. For example, some children seem more impulsive and some seem more "spaced out" or indifferent; some children are hyperactive and some children are quiet; some tend to be rigid and over-focus on minor details, and some find it hard to get organized and study; some "lock up" and some are easily irritated, erupt, are infuriated or cry often; some run amok or suffer outbursts of various intensities; for some, social positioning is particularly difficult, and they are constantly occupied with trying to please their friends or with comparing themselves to others; some tend to exaggerate their difficulties, whereas others, more shy, hide the difficulties they are experiencing or are ashamed of them; many of them are shy, quiet, anxious and fearful; for most, **the central conflict (with both themselves and the environment) revolves around their abilities to perform, and these are translated into problems with self-esteem and self-image.**

Other such children feel that they, and only they, know what is good for them. They tend to express themselves with stubbornness, argumentativeness, contrariness and sometimes even haughtiness, insisting on only doing things their way. It is for this reason that I repeat my position that the general title of ADHD is insufficient. ADHD is an extremely varied phenomenon, which requires precise assessment to identify the unique characteristics of each child, out of the diverse manifestations of ADHD within this population. Only by breaking down the array of manifestations unique to each child and identifying them via precise assessment and comprehension will you, the parents, be enabled to help your child learn to know herself, and identify the difficulty involved in making the requisite change.

How do you talk to your child according to the CHAMP model?

The therapeutic discourse taken from the CHAMP model develops gradually and according to the child's ability to progress. CHAMP terminology is suitable to anyone who meets with the child or works with her. It is based on deep and precise understanding of the neurodevelopmental phenomenon; this is translated into code names, metaphors and imagery from the daily life of the child. This open discourse can also include humorous references to "mess-ups." It is permitted and even recommended to laugh with the children—sometimes even laughing at their "mess-ups" and sometimes at yourselves, especially if you too have ADHD. Since there is a genetic component to ADHD, you should use this opportunity to teach yourselves and understand yourselves better, even as you develop the child's awareness. This also generates a new closeness between you and your child, based on your common experience. The new terminology is an experiential language which offers the entire family a chance to engage in positive communication.

As such, it also speaks about the children's experience via precise assessments.

I must reiterate that the child was born with certain characteristics, knows herself as she is, and has no idea that she is different or suffers from any particular difficulty. Much of our work is to help her see herself as others see her. In other words, our job as adults is to teach the children about themselves, until they can observe themselves from the outside looking in and become aware of themselves.

I am mindful of the fear of many parents regarding directly raising these issues with their children, lest their words be interpreted as criticism and hurt their children. I am also mindful of the impatience of many parents undergoing prolonged processes and their need to arrive at a rapid solution.

I completely understand this need, since it derives from the frustration and difficulty they experience when engaging with their child due to their inability to help her. This is where I and my fellow therapists come in—it is our job to help you, parents, to be patient with the process, even when it stretches on and on, to accompany you through its various stages, to strengthen you and to support you.

Some children, for various reasons, are unprepared to cooperate. Most feel misunderstood by those in the environment or else experience severe criticism, and at a very young age become quite opinionated. These are the children who make declarations such as: *"Only I understand myself, and only I will decide for myself ..."* For such children, basic trust, along with the acceptance of parental authority, needs to be built up. This is the only way to secure their consent to cooperate with the process. These children need to be convinced that the discourse being shared with them has changed. Only when they feel that their parents have begun to speak to them differently do they lower their defenses and agree to cooperate.

We need to remember that the child was born this way and knows nothing else, and hence, that this is a very sensitive topic for her.

If she feels that we are demanding she change who she is, she will tend to resist us immediately. To explain the experience of a child with ADHD, I see fit to make use of a poem named "BLACK", which was written by an African child and was nominated by the U.N. as the best song of 2006.

> When I born, I black
> When I grow up, I black
> When I go in Sun, I black
> When I scared, I black
> When I sick, I black
> And when I die, I still black
> And you, white fellow—
> When you born, you pink
> When you grow up, you white
> When you go in sun, you red
> When you cold, you blue
> When you scared, you yellow
> When you sick, you green
> And when you die, you gray
> And you calling me colored?

Much like the black child, the child with ADHD was born this way and knows nothing else. She does not understand what people want with her when she is asked to change her behavior. Many children and adults repeatedly say:

"What are you actually trying to tell me? After all, everybody is like me."

We need to remember this and invest considerable time in helping a child or adult with ADHD to successfully see themselves from the outside looking in, through the eyes of the other. This is an extremely sensitive stage, and to secure cooperation, this should be done without criticism or judgment; one should explain the purpose of pure, mindful, neutral observation.

In Chapter 4, I described how I suggest speaking to the child. In the current chapter, I demonstrate the integrative process of emotional therapy and guidance according to the CHAMP model. For this, I will present two typical examples:

Jonathan's Case:

A seven-year-old child, whom we will call Jonathan, is a second-grader diagnosed with ADHD. He manifests hyperactivity and impulsivity, and finds it difficult to listen and pay attention. Jonathan's father met me for our initial discussion, in which he described his son as frenzied and restless. The father came to consult with me after extensive reading, which led him to realize that he and his wife might be wronging Jonathan when they displayed anger when he was out of control. The child was already undergoing emotional therapy, but the father decided to stop the therapy, because he felt it was not useful. Jonathan had a very low frustration threshold and could shift his mood from placid to outraged in a second. Jonathan entered his school like "a king," and the father did not understand how it was possible that two weeks before meeting me, a group of violent children had shoved him into the restroom and beat him. The father did not want the bullies to torment his son, and also did not want his own child to become a bully. Jonathan would try to play the "class clown," which the father thought was the result of insecurity and not being able to find his place among his classmates. He was also very extreme in the way he treated his friends—he either loves them or hates them. Jonathan was extremely clever, sharp, charming and handsome; his thoughts were quick and associative, and he made all the right connections. He had a very well-developed memory, and he could sail to far shores in his imagination and come up with many stories. However, he did not know how to use these good qualities to his advantage. The father felt that the child did not know how to defend and explain himself, and did not want him to be labeled as different. He had already been expelled from the afternoon childcare facility, but the punishment did not result in an improvement. The father added that Jonathan did not notice, for example, when he kicked someone on the bus; when he would stand in line at the supermarket, he would be restless and impatient and constantly complain: *"What now? When can we move on?"* Finally, when he would arrive home, he would go completely wild; he was opinionated and assertive and would cling to his position in an argument, and he did not know how to let go. He liked Lego very much, and built models from complicated designs, showing that he was capable of immersing himself and focusing. In contrast, he seemed lazy when it came to reading and writing, and avoided such tasks as much as possible; he would solve math problems swiftly, but refused to write down his solutions, and would find it difficult to solve word problems. When he would encounter difficulties, he tended to put things in his mouth. He required strong contact, and was very sensitive to certain fabrics. In response to my question regarding fears, dreams, negative thoughts towards himself, personal hygiene habits, eating habits and the like, the father responded that Jonathan fears nothing. He recalled that recently he had decided not to eat fruits and vegetables because they are "too healthy." At the same time, he added that his son was not at all picky about his food and could enter a luxury, gourmet restaurant and eat special dishes. The father added that Jonathan suffers from quite a few negative thoughts about himself: He would declare that he was not smart, and when he would have an outburst, he could say things he would later regret. I was very impressed with the sensitivity and precision with which the father described his son and said as much to him. The father immediately shared with me that he identified with his son, for he too had been such a child, and he very much wanted to understand and help him. I told him that I favored guiding parents in order that they be the ones who helped the child. I recommended that we diagnose Jonathan, and started by handing the parents and teachers questionnaires which I requested they fill out. I explained to the father that the reasons which led him to come to me seemed to be his son's emotional difficulties, but that my assessment was that the symptoms he described were a direct consequence of ADHD in a very intelligent, strong-minded, vulnerable and sensitive child with intense intuition, emotions and reactions, who was finding it difficult to accept the many gaps in his behavior. I added that there were many gaps in Jonathan's behavior, which were confusing to the parents, to Jonathan and to those around him, and that it was our job to understand their essence.

Jonathan arrived at the second meeting with his father, and the meeting took place, as is my custom, in the presence of the father. Jonathan entered the room in a turbulent state, like a restless motor, and found it difficult to sit in the chair. I pointed to the big, plush beanbag and suggested he use it. He sprawled over it, moving his entire body. At first, he did not participate in the conversation and, instead, took up my invitation to check out the many toys in the room. Soon, however, he lost interest in them and began throwing them around. I told him that I understood that he was no longer interested in the toys and that that was why he was tossing them, but requested that instead of throwing them, he return them to the shelves. He indeed stopped throwing the toys, and explained that these were toys for babies, and that he preferred to build with Lego, per his imagination. I asked him what he liked to build, for example, and he confidentially but impatiently responded that he had built a time machine. Later in the conversation, Jonathan's intelligence and alertness to everything happening around him became apparent, but he was restless, opinionated and swift to correct anything I said.

I examined the questionnaires filled out by both parents and the teacher. The questionnaires were quite similar. Jonathan met four criteria for inattention (he found it difficult to maintain a suitable degree of attention, found it difficult to listen to others, did not notice details and was easily distracted by external stimuli). He also met nine criteria for hyperactivity and impulsivity. He was described as restless, found it difficult to sit quietly, was in constant motion and boisterous, found it difficult to keep quiet, behaved as if driven by a motor, found it difficult to wait his turn, was impulsive, invaded the personal space of others, and constantly chattered.

He also met four other criteria for compensatory attention—argumentativeness, rejectionism, was irrationally overanxious, and exhibited a tendency towards impulsive behavior and to cling to his own opinion, not listening to the opinion of others.

I explained to the father that Jonathan had many strengths, which were mostly expressed in amplified impulses. **These strengths were essentially positive, as they were a source of strength and dynamism** and, **in the long run, would serve him.** But at present, they were a disruptive influence in the classroom, since Jonathan did not know how to channel them to his benefit.

I added that Jonathan did not meet the six criteria required to diagnose attention difficulties, but I believed they existed, and that he was managing to disguise him due to his sharp intelligence.

Jonathan also partially met the criteria for compensatory attention. This fact hinted that he was trying to rally his ability to listen
but was unable to do so over time and gave up. The use of this
strategy of compensatory attention might also explain his partial
awareness about the vast gaps in his behavior, which expressed
themselves in excess worrying, a tendency to be opinionated and
argue, and only acting as he pleased. I encouraged the father not
to dwell on the correctness of the diagnosis but to begin learning
about the subject, and to understand the specific issues and difficulties in order to address them and handle them appropriately.
At this point, having won the father's trust, I decided to also try
recruit the mother to the task, and I invited both parents to learn
about the subject, and to make up their own minds as to whether the general diagnosis I had suggested made sense to them. I
explained that I thought we should begin therapy as quickly as
possible, to prevent, as much as possible, misunderstandings,
empathic failures, frustration, unhelpful labeling and anger. The
therapy would help strengthen the relationship between Jonathan
and his parents, would improve the family environment and
would help Jonathan improve his behavior away from home, as
well. I recommended they read the book *My Mind Races*,[2] which
describes in light and catchy poems the difficulties as well as the
emotional experiences of a child. I suggested they use the book to
initiate a relaxed, free-flowing conversation with Jonathan.

I suggested two treatments in parallel—first, occupational therapy,
to help with the sensory sensitivity and gradually help Jonathan
to sit down and focus; the second—a group workshop guiding
the parents. I explained that parental guidance was particularly
important for young children, since a young child is unable to understand such a complex issue as an ADHD disorder. Instructions

enable the parents to achieve non judgemental understanding, and mindfulness,a change in their perception, and an ability to explain to the child in an empathic manner what was she was experiencing.

Both parents fully cooperated—they accepted the therapeutic path I recommended, and identified with many of the poems they read in the book *My Mind Races* This made it easier for them to accept the diagnosis in part, and understand that they were in the right direction, even if they were not of one mind regarding the diagnosis. They expressed their consent to send Jonathan to occupational therapy and signed up for the parents' workshop.

Let's track all the stages of Jonathan's emotional therapy:

Gaps: At the beginning of the parents' workshop, I explain the issue of the many gaps which differentiate these children and confuse their parents and others in the environment. I ask all the parents to write down the particular gaps which differentiate their child, and we work in the group on explaining these gaps (many of which are common), first, to the parents. In Jonathan's case, he possessed particularly high intelligence, which led to considerable frustration—he did not know how to explain even to himself what he was experiencing. As mentioned, he easily solved math problems without writing his calculations down, but found it difficult to solve word problems, which are more complex and require reading, together with a greater mobilization of attention, in general, and executive attention, in particular. He was extremely verbal and articulate but found it hard to get started and rally the attention reserves necessary to put his knowledge down into writing. The task overwhelmed him, and he would give up before he even got started. He could be immersed and concentrate on his Lego block construction, which he loved because it was "hands on" but failed to rally his strength to read a monotonous, required text. He was a very talented child but felt insecurity and "played the class clown" to try and attract positive attention from among his peers, and disguised the difficulties he could not explain even to himself. He intuitively felt the objective difficulties which were not under his control, and they would translate into a lack of self-confidence. On the one hand, he was opinionated and assertive, but on the other, he had a tendency to be locked into negative thoughts. At his essence, he was loved and loving, but he was socially labelled as a "troublemaker" for reasons he did not understand. He, and his parents needed to study each of the different issues precisely, so that he would be able to learn to see himself as others do and understand what leads to the wide variance in his behavior. The more his parents understood these gaps and what caused them, the more they would be able to explain them to Jonathan. The more he understood and accept these gaps, the more he would be able to understand and accept himself, and formulate a stronger, more powerful and healthier sense of self. This would also enable him to explain himself and defend himself when confronting the environment and also would improve his behavior.

Break-up: At the next stage, I tend to "break down" ADHD into its various components and help parents identify the manifestations that are unique to their child. In Jonathan's case, we began with hyperactivity, which is a source of strength and is expressed both in the body and the mind.

Physical hyperactivity is expressed via restlessness, considerable frenziedness, a difficulty with sitting still and boundless energy. The child with physical hyperactivity tends to chatter rapidly. He acts as if he is driven by an engine, unable to stop. Cognitive hyperactivity is defined by thoughts oscillating between under-activity and over-activity. Most of the time, the mind is burdened with racing or jumping thoughts. His thoughts are associative; he is constantly distracted; and he has difficulty with distinguishing between the essential and the superfluous. Deduction and inference of conclusions happen rapidly, and often incorrectly, but not due to a lack of understanding. Jonathan did not choose to be hyperactive. Rather, he had an objective, neurobiological difficulty with regulation, and the hyperactive manifestations were merely how his body and mind compensated and dealt with neural under-activity.

The task of the parents is also to understand extreme behaviors. Jonathan intuitively felt the under-activity and would transition to over-activity to balance himself out. In such situations, he might show interest in sports, extreme behavior, self-risk or pestering his siblings or classmates. When he would complain of boredom, that would be the point where he would lose interest and would be looking for some stimulus to jumpstart him. As such, many children manage to focus or cope in an exemplary manner when they are doing something interesting that breaks their routine—getting organized for a hike, participating in a competition or throwing a party. In contrast, they lose interest when faced with routine, "boring" tasks, such as doing their homework or getting organized in the morning.

At the next stage, we learn how to develop the new terminology with the children—we learn how to 'Talk ADHD':
According to the discourse methods described in Chapter 4, Jonathan's parents began to discuss with him differences in general and between people in particular: There were tall and short people; there were dark-skinned and light-skinned people; some people speak rapidly and loudly, and some speak softly and shyly. Some naturally walk, and even act, slowly; others are fast. Difference is a blessing as long as it is not disruptive. We need to notice the other's pace of speaking and understand that everyone is born different, and that this difference offers us variety and enriches us. Directing attention to the differences between people enables a child to notice his unique qualities, including his own pace, **and helps him look at himself from an external perspective;** while, at the same time, we remember that this is how he was born and that he mostly does not notice that he has a different rhythm than others. I ask parents to go back to their child's specific list of terms and to

explain to him all of the positive qualities of hyperactivity and of a rapid pace. After one speaks about the subject in general, one can start speaking about its positive qualities and normalizing the phenomenon. Only then is it possible to choose a specific manifestation from the list and treat it according to the CHAMP model:

Differentiation and the Use of Metaphor: Jonathan's parents chose a single manifestation they wished to make him more aware of, thereby, improving his performance—they chose his excessive frenziedness, and together with Jonathan, decided to call it a "tumbler." This name helped Jonathan develop awareness about this specific manifestation and differentiate it from the other characteristics of his ADHD, enabling him to better identify it when it manifested. Once he had developed the ability to identify it more easily, the family added the "stop sign" metaphor, and used it when they wanted to remind Jonathan what he had to do while the "tumbler" was in play. They explained that his natural mode was to be a tumbler, but with awareness and decisiveness, he could make a conscious effort to hold steady.

Active Adult Approach: Jonathan's parents began to help him understand the "tumbler" metaphor—they showed him that he was skipping from topic to topic without stopping or growing tired. They explained to him how vital this quality was in soccer, which he loved so much, and showed him that he was able to succeed in soccer by thinking quickly and responding immediately.

They encouraged him to continue to vent out his excess energy through running or any other sport, even when he was not at practice. Then they showed him that he was jumping on the bed, drumming on the table during meals and sometimes getting up and disappearing suddenly; they even photographed him frequently changing positions as he slept. When Jonathan was calm, they explained to him, without any hint of criticism, that the "tumbler" sometimes gets loose and goes wild, disrupting the environment. They frequently emphasized that he was a good, playful and happy child, and did not mean to be disruptive. His tumbler simply felt he had to be active to keep from being bored, but people around him could interpret this as a lack of consideration, because it could sometimes be disruptive. In a personal conversation with his parents, I helped them connect all of these varied expressions of hyperactivity and understand that it was Jonathan's difficulties with regulation which led him to go from "zero to one hundred" in a split second, like a tsunami hitting the shore without any warning. His difficulties with regulation explained the restlessness, impatience, tendency toward extremes, opinionatedness and argumentativeness.

Help with Reflection, Repetition and Redefinition: Jonathan's parents were careful to explain and reflect to him different situations in a very precise manner. They repeated their message many times while redefining things—the "tumbler" did not allow Jonathan to sit down quietly, because he was born this way, not because he had any ill intentions. In one of the parents' guidance meetings, they even recounted how Jonathan had told his grandmother: *"Have you noticed that I am a good boy? And that it is pleasant to spend time with me now?"*

The parents completely abandoned anger, criticism and punishments, since they now understood what Jonathan was experiencing when he grew frenzied. This understanding brought Jonathan and his parents closer, and he developed greater trust in them. Thanks to this trust, they continued to teach him to identify and control his energy, and to route it in desirable directions. They helped him understand that he could channel his frenziedness into activity which would serve him or else vent it at home or in other places where it would not be environmentally disruptive.

Practice Makes Perfect: The "practice stage" is the longest and most important. Jonathan's parents continued to talk to him about the "tumbler," linked it to various situations in which it was "active" and presented various manifestations of it to him. They began to share with the members of the extended family, and frequently made it into a game. Sometimes they played the game they called "Three Points": At family get-togethers, anyone who identified the "tumbler" got three points; whereas, if Jonathan identified it on his own, he got six points.

The winner of each get-together would get the biggest slice of the coveted cake Grandma had baked. At home, the parents played the "statue" game. Through it, they showed him he could put on the brakes and stop his frenzied behavior, even though it took some effort on his part, since stopping his behavior was not natural to him. Jonathan's parents continued to praise his every attempt to identify this behavior and put on brakes in his daily life, even if he was not always perfect at it, and even when his self-control abilities had retrogressed. They acknowledged the fact that there were ups and downs, and when retrogression occurred, remembered that punishment was fruitless, and that they needed to return to the principles of the CHAMP model.

Later, they expanded the language of metaphors and practiced the discourse around other expressions of hyperactivity, and only after a considerably long period, moved on to tackle the subject of impulsivity.

The improvement of Jonathan's ability to regulate his hyperactivity and impulsivity led to a considerable improvement in his behavior at school and at home. His parents encouraged him to vent his excess impulses and energy at home in an appropriate manner, and to control them at school as much as was possible. Use of the "tumbler" and "stop sign" metaphors helped him be calmer, and successfully sit and listen to the teacher in class and to friends during recess. The teacher was aware of the need to help him vent his frenzied feelings through deliberate breaks, and so had given him a special job—he was her helper, and every time she needed something that was outside the class, Jonathan would run to get it. In this manner, she enabled Jonathan to take deliberate breaks in which he could operate the "tumbler" in a positive manner. She also gave him considerable positive feedback and noted, at every opportunity, his effective use of the "stop sign" and the improvement in his behavior deriving from it.

In a follow-up meeting, I praised the parents for how they had mobilized, and their great success in handling their child, and equipped them with several recommendations: extracurricular sports to help reroute his excess energy; a martial arts class to help him control himself; the gradual addition (from easy to more difficult) of ADHD manifestations, according to the same model; and a follow-up regarding Jonathan's attention difficulties, which the parents had learned less of during the workshop, since it hadn't been as relevant to them.

When Jonathan was in fourth grade, his parents called me and told me that, though he was managing to control and regulate himself reasonably well, and was very intelligent, his difficulties at school were growing. I scheduled a meeting with them, where they described a gap between Jonathan's social and behavioral successes and his difficulties in various classes at school, whose root cause they were unable to identify. I pointed out that "wandering" attention and executive-attention difficulties had grown with the increase of academic demands. I reminded them that, at first, they had focused on the area of hyperactivity-impulsivity, and now they needed to expand the treatment to the field of general attention and executive attention. I explained that Jonathan lacked study habits, and that he was able to survive thanks to his intelligence and many strengths, but that he was unable to fully realize his abilities and was beginning to hate learning, and that this was a shame.

I asked them to rejoin the parent workshop to study the issues of "wandering" attention and executive attention in depth and to implement them with the CHAMP model. Following the positive experience and success with Jonathan in the behavioral-social field, they did indeed do so and began to talk with him. They explained to him that, until now, he had been successful thanks to his compensatory attention and that this was admirable. They also discussed and explained to him his current difficulties to rally and direct attention to routine tasks, and regarding his distractedness, associativity and difficulty with separating the essential from the peripheral. Together with Jonathan, they fine-tuned his learning strategy; set him on track in the areas of attention; guided the teacher, as well; and were able to help him cope, as a very good student in his class. When they called me to announce their success, I was impressed yet again with their determination and strength.

I now asked them to continue to follow Jonathan's attention difficulties while carefully watching over him and providing him with adaptive education. I suggested they contact me every six months to update me.

And indeed, they kept up phone contact with me over the years. Difficulties grew considerably at the age of 14, when his impulses grew and left him exposed and unprotected. Jonathan began to run wild and was at risk of dropping out of school. I invited the parents, together with Jonathan, for three meetings, and explained that the impulses had grown greatly with age, and recommended they consider medication. They accepted my recommendation. Jonathan was able to connect with his many strengths and learned how, and especially when, to use the medication. When he had completed his studies, he achieved a very good matriculation certificate, enlisted in the army and was accepted to the unit he wanted. Thanks to his awareness and the determination of his parents and himself he was able to move himself into the position that was appropriate for him in the army, without needing to rely on any additional medication.

During the therapeutic accompaniment process, our goal is to help the child get to know himself, identify his strengths and his difficulties, accepting and embrace them rather than fearing, resisting or hiding them. Upon familiarizing himself with them and accepting them, his chances of developing emotional, social and behavioral difficulties decline. The more the child identifies his ADHD characteristics, understands and directs them, the more the danger that his self-confidence, feelings of self-worth and self-esteem will be impaired declines. He will learn to better control himself and respond with less rashness, anger, outbursts, argumentativeness and "rudeness." The more he realizes that others in the environment understand him, and the more he improves his behavior, the less he will insist on doing things his own way, the more he will learn to take responsibility for his difficulties and the more flexible his positions and behavior will be. In the same manner, his tendency to blame others for his own difficulties will also decline, and he can focus on improving his behavior.

Jasmine's Case

Jasmine is an 11-year-old girl with attention difficulties—no hyperactivity. She had been referred to me for emotional therapy by her parents, after her mother had participated in a parent workshop I had directed. The family came to me with the psycho-didactic evaluation report Jasmine had undergone, a very detailed and professional report that had raised the suspicion of inattention ADHD—in other words, Jasmine had presented primary difficulties with attention, without hyperactivity or impulsivity. The report recommended that Jasmine undergo emotional therapy.

I have chosen to present to you a short portion of the diagnostic report, which accurately describes the emotional consequences of attention disorders:

"She is partially aware of her difficulties and, as a result, feels anxiety, and does not trust herself, which has created an emotional difficulty with dealing appropriately with *the challenges she faces at her age. She presents high motivation for academic success, but sometimes backs away and presents insecurity and a low feeling of capability. In difficult situations, her work style is sometimes hesitant, and her frustration threshold is low. She is disappointed with herself and tends to give up in the face of adversity. She requires considerable support and encouragement in order to motivate herself and cope with her difficulties."*

At my urging, the mother added additional details, naming the reasons for which she had asked that her daughter undergo emotional therapy:

"It is clear to me that she is suffering from an attention disorder, but I am concerned because she is losing faith in herself and is beginning to please friends and does not understand social codes, and sometimes other children take advantage of her kindness and

innocence. I notice that she finds it difficult to follow a shifting conversation, has no patience to participate in it, and tends to be passive and not express her own mind. When she recalls something, she immediately says it, even if it is completely irrelevant, and then she gets laughed at. The school staff have hinted that what the child needs is medication, but that simply isn't going to happen."

I explained to the mother that she was describing very precisely and sensitively what her daughter was experiencing and that she was quite right to be concerned about her emotional and social state. I explained that her diagnosis also precisely describes objective difficulties with attention, along with their emotional consequences. Jasmine was beginning to lose faith in herself, was hesitating and pleasing others, and her kindness was being exploited, all against the backdrop of her feeling a lack of competence, which was stemming from her attention difficulties. I reminded the mother about the issues discussed in the parents' workshop, emphasizing that Jasmine's emotional difficulties are a direct outcome of objective attention difficulties. Jasmine was a very positive child, who challenged herself and desired with every fiber of her being to succeed. She therefore demanded a lot of herself but was disappointed and frustrated when she was unable to function in spite of her fierce will. I explained to the parents that her attention difficulties were making it hard for her to cope and were being translated into difficulties with her social life and self-confidence, including a feeling of low self-competence and general emotional difficulties. This was why, what needed to be treated were the attention difficulties rather than the emotional symptoms. I added that the school saw the objective attention difficulties as the source of her difficulties, and this was why it was pushing for the use of medications. Medication certainly might help Jasmine focus and succeed in her studies, which would help her feel more confident in herself and her abilities.

After meeting with Jasmine, I added that she very much wanted to understand, and help, herself but was unable to motivate herself and explained that she was having genuine difficulties with attention, which naturally lead to difficulties with motivation. She needed the help of her parents, and perhaps medication as well. Since her parents opposed medication, I recommended that they start implementing the CHAMP model, and if they should fail to see any progress, I strongly recommended they consider medication nevertheless. I also recommended that they read Mel Levine's first book, *A Mind at a Time*,[3] which describe attention difficulties in detail. I found myself repeatedly emphasizing to the parents that Jasmine's lack of success was not the result of a lack of motivation, but of her attention difficulties. She was not doing well at school or with her friends, because she was unable to control her inattention not because of the lack of motivation. This was why I saw no need to treat the motivation or other emotional difficulties—rather, it was her attention difficulties I wanted to address and treat.

We will now follow the CHAMP model as it was implemented in Jasmine's family:

Separation Between the Manifestations and the Use of Metaphor:
Jasmine's parents began talking with her when she was quiet and attentive, not when she expressed disappointment or frustration. They helped her understand and grow convinced that she was a very clever girl. They explained to her what "wandering" attention was, and that these difficulties were what was making her feel unsure of herself. At first, they spoke with her about

attention in a general sense, and then began to show her when she phases out, grows confused or makes mistakes because of her lack of attention.

In the next stage, Jasmine and her parents chose the **"balloon"** metaphor in order to illustrate the attention difficulties.

Attention is like a balloon Jasmine holds in her hand, and it should be under her control. It may happen that the "balloon" suddenly floats high, **without any warning or control.** This is an unpleasant and embarrassing situation, but if she is aware that attention does not always behave as expected, and that this can happen, she will not be stressed out, and the attention (the balloon) will likely return. If not, she can ask a friend to help her and to remind her of what she had just said, so that she will be able to pick up where she had left off, or else can ask the teacher to repeat her instructions, so that she will be able to understand what she needs to do, and the like. Her parents helped her understand that, if she does not succeed in spite of her awareness and attempts to cope with genuine difficulties with attention, she can and should use mediation, which can prove very helpful for her.

Active Adult Approach:

In Jasmine's case, the active adult approach is extremely important, because she is not a hyperactive girl. This means, in fact, that she is increasingly less able to push herself. Reading the book *A Mind at a Time*[3] contributed to the parents' understanding of their daughter's difficulties, and they asked recommendations for additional books. I directed them to another book by the same author, Mel Levine[4]. Jasmine's parents decided to undertake the project, and moved heaven and earth to help their daughter, taking a very active role in the mediation process. They understood that their role was to follow, reflect, monitor, redefine, learn to identify and develop Jasmine's awareness in a specific and focused manner, until she proved capable of doing so on her own and assuming responsibility for herself. They invested considerable time in identifying issues and empathically raising awareness, being greatly involved in the process.

They asked her to notice all the situations in which "her balloon flies away" and write them down. They helped her identify these moments in her daily life, and in school as well—in doing her homework or organizing her notebooks.

The parents began to reflect and explain to Jasmine the many **gaps** in her performance—she was extremely witty and intelligent, and it was precisely this fact which led her to grow disappointed, for she did not understand why she did not always succeed. She did not like being confronted with embarrassing situations caused by the attention disorder and found it hard to answer questions concerning it.

On the other hand, when she associatively recalled something, she would "speak her thoughts" easily and at length, even when they were not relevant. Children and adults in her environment would not understand these gaps and sometimes even mocked her. Jasmine and her parents learned to identify situations in which the lack of attention severs the continuity of thoughts in an unexpected manner. For example, when she would start talking and then "forget" what she wanted to say. Later on, they helped her connect between these issues and understand that the thoughts that disassociate or "jump" make it difficult for her to maintain "**continuity**" in situations in which she is required to write or formulate her ideas in a sequence. This is why she would grow confused and find it hard to preserve the sequence and organization of a statement.

They explained that attention sometimes breaks off, but at other times "jumps" or is distracted, and pointed out all the situations in which she would be distracted, such as getting ready in the morning or a family talk over supper. The goal was for Jasmine to understand herself by developing a precise self-awareness, so she would feel confident about herself, and be able to protect herself and defend herself when necessary. The parents helped her to understand this and identify the associative thoughts that "popped up in her mind" and actively helped her discern between them and distracting thoughts. Such a familiarity with thought patterns would help her understand that sometimes a spontaneous thought is suitable, creative and productive, but sometimes is disruptive when it is not relevant, and hence, she must learn how to stop herself before she shares this thought.

They helped her internalize the imagery of the runaway balloon, identify it and make associations with sentences such as

"You are lost now; you phased out when I explained to you how to place the dairy products in the fridge. This is exactly what happens to you when you watch television; you suddenly lose connection with what has happened and ask: 'What was that? What did he say?' This is precisely what happens when you space out for a moment and find it hard to follow the rules of the game ... This is also what happens when you think you do not understand why "1/2" = "3/6". You must be convinced that your ability to understand is excellent, but if you space out for a moment and lose your attention, you feel like you don't know. This embarrasses you and you begin to doubt your abilities. If you manage to remember that it is the balloon that is flying away, and don't stress out over it, you can ask for help and return to attention. The main thing is that you believe in yourself and remember that it is all right—you simply lost track of your attention for a brief moment! We will help you identify the situations in which you find it difficult to hold this balloon, and the situations in which you have a hard time with complex instructions, hard texts, fractions or mathematical formulas, due to difficulties with a more complex system of attention—executive attention."

Every time the parents noticed an improvement, even a minor one, in Jasmine's forgetfulness or spacing out, if she was able to maintain continuity or executive attention, they pointed it out and encouraged her to continue in this manner. Over time, they saw that identification and encouragement contributed to an improvement in her capability and self-confidence at home, as well as at school and with her friends.

The parents showed Jasmine that the balloon floated away unexpectedly because her attention was not consistent. It was not her fault. Nonetheless, Jasmine also understood that stressful situations increased her attention difficulties. During exams, for example, she tended to make mistakes deriving from the lack of attention, whereas in her homework, which she did in her quiet room, she made fewer errors. Over time, as Jasmine's awareness grew, she became convinced that her difficulties were indeed to do with attention, not comprehension, and she was able to understand them, leading to a decreased incidence of such stressful situations. At this stage, her parents reflected to her that her frustration level had declined, and she was able to be disappointed in herself less. She began to identify certain patterns and situations in which her attention tended to "escape" more—before meeting a large group of friends, before making a presentation in class and so on.

This enabled her to prepare in advance, relax and remember to exercise control. It also helped her understand how much mediation helped her, which meant she did not need to be ashamed of her need for it. In parallel, they also explained to the staff and teachers at her school that Jasmine gives up sometimes due to a real objective difficulty, not because of insecurity or anxiety, and that mediation helps her a great deal and does not generate dependence from her.

Reflection, Repetition and Redefinition:
The more we continue to reflect and identify the specific situations in which attention "jumps," gets distracted, or "flies away like a balloon," the more we will see a general improvement in function, which results in an improvement in self-confidence and the desire to cope. Jasmine's parents did this, repeatedly telling her: "We have noticed that you show greater courage and are more prepared to raise your hand and participate in class rather than being afraid of being wrong. You dare more now because you understand attention difficulties full-well, and are focused on improving your attention abilities.

"You are surer of yourself, and so are less hesitant; you feel less of a need to withdraw or surrender. You manage to analyze situations in which you are disappointed, insulted or feel misunderstood."

They helped her explain herself instead of withdrawing inward once they had realized that she felt misunderstood but was insufficiently aware of this beforehand to explain to herself what had happened.

Over a long time, the parents continued to be active in mediating for Jasmine, and in parallel, explained Jasmine and her particular manifestations of her attention difficulties to her schoolteachers, her Scouts' counselor and her extended family, and actively guided and instructed them all. Throughout the process, I reminded them that this was a long process and that it was important to continue to observe Jasmine solely, in order to stay on track and to avoid wasting their efforts or seeking other causes for her problems, or ways to help her.

As part of developing awareness of her attention difficulties and transferring responsibility to Jasmine, her parents encouraged **her to speak to herself in a focused manner** in order to identify the attention difficulties and treat them. **This, in fact, enabled her to become an expert and assume responsibility for her own emotional therapy.** Throughout the process, Jasmine's parents redefined the reason for her hesitancy and lack of confidence. They helped Jasmine understand that if she would focus on the attention difficulties, rather than on the anxiety, frustration or disappointment with her lack of self-confidence, which are the byproduct, or result, of the attention difficulties, her chances of overcoming and succeeding would be higher.

Practice Makes Perfect:

The practice stage requires constant training until the use of the CHAMP model becomes automatic. In the practice stage, we repeat all the previous components of the model and reflect the positive and desired changes as much as possible. Jasmine's parents had helped convince her that the more aware she was of her difficulties and the more she understood their source, the more she would be able to cope with them. As time passed, they pointed out that she was no longer hesitant and doubtful of her strengths. The more she developed awareness and identified, internalized and comprehended her difficulties, the less scared she was, the more her anxiousness declined, and the more room and energy she was able to make available to deal with her difficulties in a practical, matter-of-fact and productive manner. They repeatedly reminded her that she was good at challenging herself and had always been motivated, but that she did not know how to help herself, because she, and they, did not understand objective difficulties with attention and their many consequences.

Following this process, Jasmine became the own expert of her attention disorder. As the expert on the topic, she began to explain and advocate for herself outside the home as well. The parents updated me that the more she did so, the more her self-confidence and self-image improved, and the better she was able to deal with various situations.

Thanks to the persistence of her parents, Jasmine was able to advance herself. In one of the update meetings, I explained to Jasmine's mother that she still needed to assist Jasmine and watch her closely, speaking to her often, continuing to be mindful of the specific complex issues, and being able to explain to her the various gaps that would inevitably crop up down the line. I explained to Jasmine's mother that she was able to cope today thanks to being a positive girl who challenged herself, thanks to her mental fortitude and her essentially good cognitive ability. She had also succeeded thanks to her supportive family network; and, for this, both Jasmine and her parents were worthy of great appreciation. Nonetheless, Jasmine's academic achievements needed to be followed and monitored. If, despite her fierce desire, she would find it difficult to realize her great cognitive abilities, then adaptive education or medication, or both, should be considered, to enable her to express her abilities and perform in accordance with them. I asked that they keep in touch with me and that they seek specific consultation and focused direction whenever Jasmine required it.

In Jasmine's case, as in many other cases, I served as a professional guide who actively accompanied the parents until they were able to serve as "therapist" to their own child. They, in turn, served as Jasmine's coaches and therapists until Jasmine was able to understand, identify and treat herself.

These two cases have been described at length to explain how to provide emotional therapy to children with ADHD. At the center of the therapy are the objective difficulties deriving from ADHD, as a result of which the social, behavioral, emotional and academic ramifications develop. This therapy emphasizes the development of gradual and precise assessment, mindfulness, raised awareness and finally the instillment of control in order to improve performance and self-perception, and strengthen the self-esteem and self-confidence of the child.

In many cases, the parents have stridently opposed medication for the attention disorder and prefer to send the child to emotional therapy or other treatments. Flinching away from reliance on medication is natural, but it is important we remember that **medication is meant to improve performance when the child is unable to achieve optimal improvement on his own or via alternate means. However, medication must be accompanied by the development of awareness and understanding to help the child understand**

himself and feel whole within himself. In other words, sometimes the combination of medication and emotional therapy is the winning treatment. Every child presents a complex and varied picture that depends on many factors—the intensity of her objective difficulties, her innate intelligence, her strengths, her recreational activities, the mobilization of her family and others in her environment, the existence of learning disabilities or additional emotional difficulties, and the like. All these, influence the functioning of the child and her ability to rally the necessary strength to change. This is why the adaptation of the therapy for the child needs to occur after referring to all the variables and their influence upon the child and upon one another.

PART FOUR
ADAPTING EMOTIONAL THERAPY TO DIFFERENT ADHD COMPONENTS

Adapting Emotional Therapy to Impulsivity

Emotional therapy which does not consider the complex ramifications of ADHD will not result in the desired improvement in performance and awareness. Emotional therapy must include several components: mediation and raising awareness of the specific difficulties with attention, hyperactivity and impulsivity; mediation for controlling them; and mediation for linking them to various aspects of daily life. Through these, the emotional therapist helps the patient to feel competent, achieve independence and raise her self-confidence.

In the case of impulsivity, the inability to control impulses among children with ADHD results in "serious accidents" and it is important to remember this genuine lack of control and to explain it to the parents and to their child. These children are used to suffering severe criticism and to being punished, but the punishment is of no avail. Their impulsive behavior only repeats itself—because they are unaware of the fact that it is uncontrolled. This is why we are obligated to explain to the children how the impulsivity is expressed and to teach them to control it—to help them be aware of what it is they are experiencing, so they can learn to observe and direct themselves.

A very positive child, whom I will call Ben came to my clinic with his parents. Ben and his parents had received guidance from me in the past. The parents entered the room, and Ben stayed outside. They whispered to me that they were ashamed to say that Ben was stealing from their wallet. As I was speaking with them, Ben impatiently burst into the room and asked: *"When will you be done already?"* I asked him to wait for a few minutes and he began to comply, but as he closed the door, he heard his parents talking about him, reentered the room, and shouted:

"What? You told her"? We said we don't talk about this … When will you understand that I am not a thief?!"

I asked him to come into the room and I embraced him tightly. I told him in all honesty that I was very happy to see him, and I knew that he was a wonderful and intelligent boy with a lot of grace and humor. I told him that it was obvious to me that he was not a thief, but if he could not wait, but burst like this into the room where we were talking, he might also not have been able to restrain himself and "burst into" his father's wallet, because he "had" to do that at that moment, and the **result** was theft.

Ben smiled in relaxation. I reminded both him and his parents of the content of the workshop, of the "stop sign" and the "I must" that we had spoken about so much. I asked that they only remember these two metaphors and go back to using them, and I invited Ben for two follow-up sessions, which I wrote down in my appointment calendar in his presence.

A little more than a week later, the mother called, thanked me for the meeting, but asked to cancel the two appointments we had set up. She told me that the metaphors had worked like "magic" and that Ben's condition had greatly improved.

This example illustrates well that when a child is diagnosed with ADHD, we are obliged to address his impulsivity, and not judge and interpret the behavior and actions of the child as something bad or attribute them with grave, deep emotional significance. Since such "accidents" are extremely commonplace, I will present you with another example of desirable treatment of typical impulsive behavior—the sort which is tactless or even untruthful.

Impulsive children and adults quickly say the first thing that comes to mind, for they find it difficult to withhold their responses. Such situations can be gravely insulting to those around them or else get the "lying" person in trouble. In such cases, we must first reach an understanding with the child concerning the consequences of their actions:

*"You say the first thing which comes to mind because you feel a need to unburden yourself, but the result is tactlessness or even a lie. We are convinced that you have no intention of lying or being rude. You are not an untrustworthy or rude child, but lies and tactlessness create unpleasant situations and **are completely unacceptable to us.** This is why we need to help you identify these situations, in which you cannot contain your thoughts, so that you can **stop** and weigh your words."*

In these cases, as well, there is no need to refer to the content of what has been said, because this will only confuse, frustrate and make the impulsive person feel even less understood. Use of words such as "rude" or "liar" will only increase the resistance and hostility of the child, because he will feel that no one can help him understand the real reason for his behavior. It is almost superfluous to note that, in the same manner, when some children diagnosed with ADHD respond disproportionately, curse, erupt, argue, hit, break things or pester other children, it is the impulsivity which needs to be treated, not the "violence."

And indeed, many parents approach me and ask for emotional therapy for their children following violent behavior at school. I will now present a therapeutic plan which constitutes the emotional therapy when "violence" is the outcome or an accompanying phenomenon of a child's ADHD.

Reason for Referral — A 10-year-old boy we will call Marty was suspended several times from school due to violent incidents. As a condition for his non-expulsion, the educational staff required him to receive emotional therapy. Marty is a very intelligent boy, who was diagnosed with ADHD. He was not realizing his abilities, but the school staff was not concerned, thinking that when his emotional condition improved, he would be able to narrow the gaps that had formed. The staff found it hard to explain the gaps in his performance, and especially his lack of control and his urge to fight other children to extremes, sometimes even injuring those around him.

While the school staff provided a precise description of his symptoms, the teachers needed to receive instructions which would increase their awareness of the ADHD diagnosis — Marty had many difficulties with regulation; he was extremely impulsive; his frustration threshold was low; he had a temper; and he did not control his responses.

Emotional therapy needs to **first** focus on impulsivity. It needs to start by **explaining the phenomenon to the adults in the environment**; the staff and the parents need to be told that Marty does not control his urges, and that he has a real and objective difficulty with everything related to regulation. The perceived violence is the result of the lack of control of his impulses, not the result of evil will or a desire to inflict harm. In other words, the therapy begins with the psychological education of the adults responsible for him, which is why it is so important for parents to participate in parent workshops where the topic is dealt with in depth, and where they will learn how to speak with the child as a form of emotional therapy. Only once they are convinced that the source of the problem is Marty's objective difficulty with controlling his urges, due to difficulties with regulation, will they be able to understand and comprehend – in other words, change – how the parents and teachers see the child, so that he will also be able to see himself differently. The staff should receive an explanation that traditional emotional therapy, which addresses anger, violence or any other **content** is not useful in any way, but might rather increase oppositional and uncooperative behavior. Even if a child does not know how to explain himself, an attempt to address the content of his actions, or interpret his behavior, will lead him to feeling misunderstood. His difficulty derives from his inability to contain his urges and control them, not from a deeper emotional burden troubling him. This is why, in this case, Marty felt misunderstood and did not cooperate with the emotional therapy he had received to date. Instead of being made to address the content of his ADHD manifestations, he should be made aware of the characteristics of ADHD – in this case, a lack of control over amplified impulses – so that he would feel better understood and learn self-control. In this manner, he would be able to improve his performance and behavior, and feel better about himself and his place in society. Parents and teachers must be instructed to help them help the child.

In moments of calm, rather than at the time of the event, Marty should be told that he is not violent, but if he cannot control his reactions and hits other people, he constitutes a source of disturbance and even danger, and will be suspended in order to protect the other children around him. This is why he needs to be helped to identify his urges and control his responses.

Marty should be told that he responds quickly, and that this has many advantages—rapid thinking, wittiness, creative thinking or the ability to think outside the box, spontaneity, charisma, improvisation, a well-developed imagination, good intuition, an opinionated nature and determination. Often, he fires off the correct answer, responds in a humorous fashion and spreads optimism to those around him.

Nonetheless, it should be made clear to Marty that every trait has two sides, and the less positive side of impulsivity is that it interferes with his ability to stop and exercise judgment before he responds. He should be told that sometimes he responds with the first thought that comes to mind, at the cost of tact; sometimes, he argues and clings to his position, excessively opinionated, without taking the position of the other party into account; sometimes he strikes another child without explaining why he is upset. He must also be told that his low frustration threshold also stems from the difficulty to restrain his response. His tendency to curse, argue, erupt, fixate, slam doors, immediately respond "no," run away or break objects—all of these behaviors are expressions of this very same difficulty to stop when he feels uncomfortable.

He should be told that we must treat these cases, in which his behavior is not desirable and results in "malfunctions" within the environment. It can be explained to him that such malfunctions are like a small stain on a beautiful shirt—it labels him and distances him socially. This explanation must be accompanied with a reminder that he is a sociable, kind and intelligent boy, and that his friends desire his company but want him to control his urges. Although his natural tendency is to not control them and to respond instantly, we must make clear to him that it is possible, with willpower and practice, to learn to control these undesirable situations and to respond appropriately. It is important to encourage the child and to explain to him why this control is desirable and even necessary.

In order to ease things for "Marty" and nurture the CHAMP terminology in discussions with him, we need to help him find a friendly metaphor which describes the specific phenomenon we had chosen to address. In this case, we need to find a metaphor for impulsivity. If he chooses, for example the "bottle" metaphor, then we should come to an agreement with him that we will learn to identify the bottle as it fills up, and learn what fills it up. We will learn to identify when the fluid approaches the point of exploding, and practice how to drain the bottle way before it gets to the point where it explodes or squirts out. A simulation can be performed at home—when the child grows angry, the moment when he seeks to instantly respond can be illustrated. After that, additional moments in which he responds impulsively with his family at home can be pointed out. Later, he should be helped to identify similar situations, at school or with his friends, in which the bottle fills up.

Every time Marty reports situations in which he wanted to respond and was able to restrain himself, wholly or in part, he will accumulate points and be praised. This specific expression should be continually practiced without judging or punishing the child, and the staff at school should get his teachers involved to act similarly. The child should be praised and reinforced with every step of improvement.

In parallel, it is recommended that the siblings and classmates of the child should be provided with an explanation of his uncontrollable behavior, to enable them to help him to practice discerning the level of water in the bottle. The more the child manages to recognize his expressions of impulsivity and control them, the more we should continue to point out improvement on the personal, family and social levels. The family and the staff of the school should be helped to understand that as Marty grows, his requirements and urges grow, and the challenge to control them grows greater, as well. This is why oscillations are to be expected, and there will be situations in which the child once again loses control to such an extent that the environment will believe the entire process was for nothing. The ups and downs in Marty's condition are part of the characteristics of ADHD. In conditions of reduced performance, it is important to recall the principles of therapy, to repeatedly practice and persist in them, in order to re-adapt every time to the new reality. It is very important to also teach his educational and social contexts to persist in the use of the CHAMP model, rather than falsely assuming the difficulties will pass with time or turning to some other emotional therapy.

Beyond this, it is important to remember that the original diagnosis is ADHD, which means that, in addition to the hyperactivity and impulsivity that generated the behavioral difficulties, there are also attention difficulties—a lack of attention, a high level of distractedness and difficulty with maintaining attention. This is why, even should the aggressive, or even seemingly violent behavior be curtailed (he is not a violent child – violence is a mere symptom of the difficulties which brought the child to therapy), Marty needs to be carefully observed and supported to ensure that his attention difficulties do not impair his good academic abilities. These attention difficulties may hinder him as the complexity level of his academic tasks and life increases, even if the child had been able to overcome them when he was younger. It is therefore essential to follow up with the child, focusing on the ADHD manifestations which might be expressed differently and pose an **obstacle at every stage of his life**. Only if they do not succeed alone should they approach an ADHD expert who will help the child and his family control impulsivity and attention.

There are also children dealing with ADHD who declare that

"I have had enough," that *"life is pointless;"* *"I want to run away from home;"* *"I want* to die."

They say the first thing which pops into their head, or get carried away, but "along the way," they manage to push every red button and alarm their environment. This can happen often, and be irritating, especially if others in the environment know that these responses are not serious. Nonetheless, harsh statements such as *"I want to die"* require a professional examination, in order to conduct a differential diagnosis and make sure that the children are not in emotional distress.

Sometimes the two components – emotional and impulsive – coexist and require appropriate integrated treatment.

A young, beautiful girl, whom we will call Leila, is over-occupied with her appearance, as is common during adolescence. She feels she "must" go to the mall with her friends almost every day. She makes disproportionate purchases, freely uses her doting father's credit card. He is happy he can afford her pampering herself in this manner. Her mother, on the other hand, is furious that her closet is bursting with new clothes that Leila has never worn, not even once.

I spoke to Leila openly and directly about the phenomenon. I reflected and said that at that moment "she felt she had to," a feeling which was bigger than her. We expanded the "must" feeling with other examples—she "had to" send all sorts of text messages, "had to" scoop every last bit of the ice cream container, and so forth.

I gave Leila various therapeutic tasks, but she did not apply herself much to them. To make progress with the therapy, I decided to use a story, which much like metaphors or imagery, enables distancing and "play," and so is a useful therapeutic tool. I told her that I had thought about her this week and that I wanted to share a personal experience: "I went out with a group of friends – men and women – for an outing in the mall. Right from the start, we decided to split up, men and women separately, and decided to meet up at a certain time at a café. We, the women, so much enjoyed our shopping that we lost track of the time and arrived at the café an hour late. Packed with bags and enthusiasm, we sat around the table, and the men asked: *What are you so happy about? What did you buy that you needed so much? How do the sales always manage to tempt you in this way?*"

I talked to Leila about shopping in general, about differences between people in general, and about men and women, in particular. We laughed at men who never need anything, in comparison to men who actually enjoy accompanying their women on shopping trips. We discussed people who love to shop because they feel a lack, some women "must" have a certain colorful shirt, and some run to the store at the very mention of the word "sale."

The stories I told Leila reached her and excited her, and so, were able to secure her cooperation. Leila understood that she "had to," both because she felt herself an inferior student, and because she found that *"this attention and concentration difficulty"* made her social life difficult.

We took our time and discussed the sensitive topic over several encounters.

After she opened up to me, we discussed low frustration thresholds, the significance of compensation, jealousy and the advantages of "must." I explained to her that great strength underlay the "must"—when she decided she "must," then no power in the world could stand in her way. She had the strength to invest and nurture herself in anything that she felt she really wanted to achieve.

In other words, in order to motivate Leila to take a productive and positive direction, the therapy focused on addressing attention and impulsivity characteristics, as well as the emotional difficulties generated over the years. Indeed, a year later, Leila updated me that she had found work suitable for teenagers, which incorporates the love of shopping but moves it towards positive activity.

Adaptation of Emotional Therapy to Attention

Inattentiveness, daydreaming, forgetting and spacing out are difficulties that are "quiet" and confusing and can easily be misinterpreted as stemming from emotional difficulties. I will reiterate that these attention difficulties are expressed in daydreaming, shyness, introvert-like behavior, withdrawal, scatter-mindedness and forgetfulness, passivity, and as difficulties with motivation and taking initiative. These can be accompanied by difficulties with studies or social relationships, self-criticism or a lack of motivation. These are children who seem tired, depressed or lazy, lacking a sense of self confidence and competence. These difficulties are confusing and require a differential diagnosis, which dictates the method of therapy. An inattention-ADHD diagnosis will refocus the discussion and the therapy onto attention, whereas the lack of a diagnosis might lead the child to emotional therapy which will not take the characteristics of attention oscillations into account, and hence will not be beneficial to her.

Children, being children, do not always know how to point out specific difficulties, but we still need to listen carefully to their often wise words.

The mother of a first grader, a boy we will call Glenn, arrived at my clinic because he had begun to express fierce opposition to going to school in the morning early in the school year. When I met him, he said simply:

"It isn't fun." I encouraged him to talk, and he added: "I don't know … I want to go back to kindergarten … I am not doing as well here as I do in kindergarten … I am not proud of myself anymore."

Later in the meeting, Glenn said that he found it hard to read because

"All of the letters jump all over the page," but added that he found it hard at recess, as well:

"I am picked on; they ask me to play with them, but I don't know how to play. I don't remember their rules."

This smart boy, from a very young age, was intuitively aware of having difficulties with general attention and executive attention but did not know how to give them names or how to deal with them.

I diagnosed Glenn with an inattention-ADHD diagnosis (without hyperactivity or impulsivity), with difficulties with executive functions. I described these difficulties to his parents, explaining to them that Glenn was an intelligent, quiet child who was easily distracted and found it difficult to maintain his attention over time. In addition, he suffered difficulties with his executive functions—his working memory, and ability to plan and organize. These difficulties impaired his feelings of capability and competence. He was somewhat passive and tended to give up on himself too easily, but we needed to understand the source of his difficulties and help him, because he had many strengths and he understood himself well. The focus of his therapy, therefore, were the difficulties with general attention and executive attention, and the goal was to raise awareness of them and help him cope with them effectively. Had this process not had satisfactory results, then medication might have had to be considered.

This example illustrates that attention difficulties without hyperactivity can appear and be disruptive even at the beginning of school, in first grade. They can be mistakenly interpreted as emotional difficulties, for the child refuses to go to school; but when one understands their neurodevelopmental source, the focus of the therapy changes and can be more useful. Another example of attention difficulties without hyperactivity and impulsivity

A nine-year-old girl we shall call Mary was quiet, polite, sensitive and intelligent, and was never disruptive in class. Accordingly, the teacher did not see any problem in her functioning, reporting her to be popular and accepted in class. In contrast, the parents noticed difficulties with her social functioning. When I asked Mary direct questions, she reported that she found it hard to follow the instructions given in games, made mistakes and lost. In group games, her friends were angry at her, because they thought she did not try hard enough, and the team would be disqualified because of her.

I diagnosed her with inattention ADHD (without hyperactivity and impulsivity). Mary was able to disguise her difficulties in class thanks to her emotional and cognitive intelligence, but her difficulties were nonetheless expressed in her social interactions.

I explained to her parents that by understanding the source of the difficulty, which is inattention, we can realize that what we need to address are the attention difficulties and their consequences, and not social difficulties, shyness or social-function withdrawal. All these are the outcomes of attention difficulties. Holistic understanding of attention, together with improving performance, will bring about the strengthening of the child's self-confidence, more active participation, and enable her to understand and explain herself.

Mary's parents joined a workshop, where they better understood the source of her difficulties, shared their experiences with other parents and gained tools that would help their child develop awareness of her "wandering" executive-attention difficulties.

Later, I suggested we meet individually, and I expanded upon her emotional difficulties, and discussed with them at length

the connection between attention difficulties and possible difficulties in class—the inattention would make Mary hesitate
and so she would not raise her hand, for she was not certain
she would know the answer. In such situations, she would be
very disappointed when another child gave the answer she had
thought of. I agreed with the parents that there was no **immediate** need for medication, but it was necessary to closely follow
her level of performance.

Over the previous year, Mary had been satisfied with her performance, because she had progressed and was able to cope better.
In the follow-up meeting with the family, I reviewed her report
card and felt that she was not realizing her abilities. Her parents
and I discussed this and decided that she could also benefit from
adaptive education, which would focus on providing her with
personally customized educational strategies, which would help
her become more familiar with the difficulties which marred
what should be a sound and effective experience with attention.
I also recommended she be medically assessed for her suitability
for medication. I explained that medication can sometimes work
immediately but that sometimes one must try out several options,
until one hits on the accurate medication and dosage. The parents
fully cooperated, and the combination of the parents' therapy, the
medication and adaptive education did indeed have impressive
results. Mary felt very good about herself and was very successful
both socially and as a student.

This example illustrates that the appropriate treatment was to explain to
the parents about their daughter's attention difficulties and focus upon
them, rather than addressing her social or emotional difficulties as would

be done in "conventional" emotional therapy. Difficulties are expressed first around self-confidence, and disturb her personally, and are then expressed in her ability to function socially. In addition, this therapy can be gradual or branched. It begins with raising her awareness about her attention difficulties, but as she grows older, its focus can change. In our case, as Mary matured, the focus moved to adaptive education, and the child also made use of medication.

Another example is that of a boy we will call Nat, a gifted 14-year-old adolescent, who had written a letter to his parents—a letter which led them, eventually, to me.

Dear Mother and Father,

"Recently, something weird has been happening to me. I am doing worse at school and can't manage to stop the decline. I tried as much as I could to change this situation, but I am not managing to do so. I keep on thinking about what to do, but I can't find a solution. Maybe I am simply a lazy child, and not really gifted as you say … I need help; I feel I have no hope. My life is worthless."

The letter is a clear cry for help from a positive, loved and loving boy with high emotional intelligence, who is feeling challenged at school. This letter can be interpreted as a "suicidal" letter, which is why the parents came to me —to see if Nat really could hurt himself.

In my conversation with him, I first explained to him that writing such a letter requires considerable insight and strength. I asked a little about his academic history, and he told me that in the past he had "cheated" a little. He had done well in elementary school, because he remembered verbatim everything they had learned in class, and so did not need to study for tests, even though he sometimes understood that he wasn't really listening to what the teacher was saying. Now he was disappointed with himself, sorry and regretful for putting on airs in front of his classmates; because now he was worse off than all of his friends, and he felt lost. He knew he should not give up, but it was "too much for him." Instead of investing his efforts in studying, he would spend all of his time with his friends.

I decided to perform a comprehensive psycho-didactic diagnosis to get a full picture of his IQ, his performance in practice, and his mental strength and suicidal intentions.

The diagnosis revealed that Nat did indeed have an extremely high IQ, that he was very popular and loved by his social circle, and that no depression or suicidal symptoms were present, but it did emerge that he was dealing with an attention deficit disorder. In the feedback meeting, I explained to him and his parents that he was able to mobilize his powers of attention in elementary school via his compensatory attention system, and paid a certain price for it. However, as the academic demands had increased, his strength had been overwhelmed and he could no longer mobilize himself for the many new tasks. I explained that his high intelligence did not benefit him—rather, it made the gaps between his excellent abilities and the subpar performance unbearable. I invited Nat to a short series of personal discussions, where I reflected on his various abilities and difficulties. I made clear to him that he was a positive and social boy, and I emphasized that social interactions were very important to him. I told him that my impression was that he was a strong, intelligent, mature, in-dependent, responsible young man, who had demanded much of himself in elementary school, and was able to recruit his powers of attention to deal with school tasks admirably.

The price he had paid was inflexibility, giving up social activities, and the investment of a lot of time. I explained to him that the letter he had written his parents took a great deal of strength and emotional intelligence. Moreover, it indicated the good relation-ship he had with his parents and his trust in them. We discussed the subject of attention, and he described the efforts he had in-vested in studying. We spoke about his current feelings of lack of control, and his need to demonstrate control outwardly—in his case, to be somewhat arrogant with his friends. We spoke of his tendency to see things in black and white—either it was all pos-sible, or it was all lost. I helped him understand that intermediate situations were also possible. We spoke about his disappointment with himself and the criticism he had internalized, which had reached a level of self-flagellation.

In parallel, Nat's parents also participated in a parents' workshop. Their and Nat's internalization and understanding of his attention difficulties helped reduce his anxiety and self-flagellation, and directed his many strengths towards growth. The more Nat grew convinced of the answers to the questions that had been troubling him, the easier he found it to go back to investing and succeeding in school, with no need for any additional therapies.

Motivation

The question regarding motivation often reoccurs, and so it is worth addressing. Motivation is a function of success—a child who succeeds in a given thing wants to experience it again. The lives of children dealing with ADHD are accompanied by much more frustration than success. When they are not aware of themselves, they do not function at their expected level, academically and socially, but they are also anxious and tense for fear that they will act in a manner they themselves cannot expect—and will fail. Some children develop a variety of emotional difficulties—from anxiety and depression to defiance and refusal to cooperate or deal with things. Emotional difficulties develop, expand and begin to dominate, obscuring the hyperactivity, impulsivity and attention difficulties, which are their source.

Raising awareness of the subject comprises emotional therapy—it helps the children understand that unexpected behaviors are a **core** part of ADHD. Anxiety and stress simply make the child more tense and make it even harder for her to function. Understanding and internalizing the source of the difficulty help to reduce anxiety and frustration, and clear space and strength to deal with the objective difficulties with attention and energy.

By so doing, the children learn to recall the source of the difficulty (regulation) every time anew, neutralizing their anxiety, and manage to have their attention restored. If they don't, they learn that they can rely on a friend or an adult who will help them by repeating what they have missed. This will enable them to continue onwards and not "get stuck." Understanding the source of the difficulty and dealing with it effectively will increase their success rate. There are also cases in which I advise the adults responsible for the child to initiate and ensure their success, in order to keep the children motivated to continue to learn about themselves and cope.

If, despite the learning and awareness, the children prove unable to pay sufficient attention and accumulate gaps in understanding or behavior, or operate beneath their potential, then medication should be considered, since, to reiterate, it constitutes a specific solution to objective difficulties with attention. It can relieve attention oscillation symptoms, helping the child succeed. In this way, the motivation of the child will increase. Later, if she is convinced that she has a specific difficulty with attention regulation, she will be motivated to learn more about the subject.

Sometimes parents are unwilling to consider medication, and they search for emotional and other therapies in order to nurture the child's sense of motivation. They provide support via private lessons, adaptive education and more. The child manages to "survive," but at the cost of much effort, which increases over the years insofar as the educational demands increase; and sometimes as they develop dependency on the external help they have received. Frustration and tension grow in some, and they do not enjoy the learning process. They do not function at their best and do not learn to rely on themselves. In such situations, not only does motivation not increase, but it also even declines, to the point where there are children who drop out of school, or don't reach higher education, since they think they are incapable.

Parents who oppose medication therapy are often parents who refuse to accept the ADHD diagnosis. They repeatedly say that the child is lazy, procrastinating, lacks motivation, does not have faith in himself and perhaps is also jealous of his sibling. They might add:

"When he wants to, he succeeds, but most of the time he acts contrarily and wants to wear us down." Some parents prefer to ignore the diagnosis and believe *"everything will work out over time."*

These are parents who "argue" with written reports. They have in hand the reports of professionals, which explicitly describe attention difficulties, but insist that the professional said the child had no attention difficulty, or else that the difficulty is borderline and requires no treatment.

Dear parents, accepting the diagnosis is indeed difficult and disappointing, and dealing with a child who has ADHD is sometimes a huge challenge. Nonetheless, opposing the diagnosis or the professionals only harms your child. Opposition prevents treatment or else results in the wrong treatment. It does not advance your child but further harms his motivation, and over time, we will witness retrogression in his functioning.

Accepting the diagnosis from an early age, internalizing and developing awareness about it, together with focused work over the years, does much to contribute to success and increase the child's motivation to continue to learn about himself and cope with the challenges in his life. The consistent mediation and follow-up of the parents and adults responsible are particularly important when the child is not hyperactive or impulsive, because these children do not push themselves forward or fight for themselves.

As for professional readers, many parents "get lost" with each professional they meet, who speak in general terms about ADHD without explicitly stating that they require specific counseling on the subject, or that the child requires development of awareness and specific mediation in the area of attention, or else requires medication to address their attention difficulties. There are also cases when the child or adult are diagnosed as dealing with ADHD but receive emotional therapy for anxiety, depression, self-confidence, or other emotional difficulties, without taking into consideration the possibility that their source is ADHD. It is the manifestations of ADHD which have not been addressed and have created a feeling of lack of control and low self-competence, anxiety, and depression.

A case manager must be appointed, due to the great confusion that might result. The case manager must be proactive and direct, explicitly addressing the issues of attention, impulsivity and hyperactivity, linking the definition to its manifestations from a holistic perspective, and directing the parents to focus on the areas of attention, which is the source of emotional difficulties—difficulties with motivation, capability, anxiety, depression, resistance and so forth.

Terminating Therapy

Emotional therapy for children with ADHD is focused and matter of fact. Its purpose is to strengthen the child and her parents, to increase their awareness and provide them with tools to cope in order to successfully **"Talk ADHD".**

The end of the therapy is an important stage in the process. It should be addressed explicitly, rather than being left vague. The professional therapist should summarize the process the parents and children have undergone; the responsibility for the child's therapy should be handed over to the parents; and there should be created an opening for a later continuation of the therapist's guidance, as required.

At the conclusion of the guidance process with parents and children, I use the metaphor of a "train station manager":

"Children, you are like very advanced, fast trains, operated by your parents. I am the station manager, and I am very happy to hear about your performances. Some of you travel very quickly; others sometimes go over the top a little and assess their boundaries; some drive slowly and with great joy, and make many stops along the way ... it is all right. The important thing is that you are moving forward! When there is some kind of accident, malfunction or collision, or when you get derailed, I am here to get you back on track!"

This metaphor enables many children to call me themselves and continue the "game":

"Have you derailed, or did you have an accident?" I ask, "Tell me what happened exactly?" and then I decide if there is a need to invite them for a check-up and a quick discussion, or whether it is better to talk to them or their parents on the phone.

In this manner, the mother of a nine-year-old child called and asked to schedule an urgent meeting. When they arrived, the child ran toward me and embraced me. I congratulated him and asked what the problem was.

"I went over the top, I really did, but mom freaked out. She needs therapy ..."

Another eight-year-old boy was in group therapy and was able to advance himself well. After six months, he asked to meet me again, on his own initiative. They arrived for the first meeting without him but noted that he had equipped them with a note he had insisted on writing on his own, in his nearly illegible scrawl: *"Hello Esther, I need to find a way to not be so vulnerable."*

When children (and their parents) learn to be aware and to" Talk ADHD", they cope better and can also describe themselves more accurately, so they know how to define the problem and ask for focused and effective help. The path of children and adults with ADHD is long and challenging, but also interesting and unconventional. It is most important that we understand and remember along the way that this is ADHD—not bad behavior or emotionally based difficulties. The child is not "stupid" or "crazy." Nor is she a "liar" or "lazy."

I hope that I have helped you understand that when the source of the difficulties is ADHD, and we know how to identify the behavioral and emotional consequences deriving directly from it, then it is ADHD which needs to be treated. I wholeheartedly believe that to reach the soul of a child or an adult dealing with ADHD we must **"Talk ADHD"!**

TO MY PARENTS

I am grateful, dear parents, that you understand,
The wherefores and whys that I sometimes crash land;
That it's not that I'm rude, or wild, or lazy;
And I'm not disrespectful, violent, or crazy.
Thanks for telling my teacher that, God forbid,
I never want to make trouble and disturb all those kids!

When you help me to see why I do what I do,
I can upgrade my brakes, unload my truck too;
Assemble my puzzle and relax my spring,
Reel in my balloon and hold on to its string;
Be my own great detective and unlock the code,
Ease the valve on my bottle before I explode;
To connect and to focus, to take part and learn,
Respect boundaries and rules and wait for my turn,
Slow down my race car, check my homework once more,
Then silence the devil, with the angels to soar;
Drink from a full cup and make use of my sieve,
And discover and share all the gifts I can give.

I wish to conclude this chapter with an ancient Buddhist teaching from *The Tibetan Book of Living and Dying*, which summarizes the educational-therapeutic process—a gradual, mindful, focused and consistent process, which we must undergo when dealing with ADHD.

AUTOBIOGRAPHY IN FIVE CHAPTERS:

Sogyal Rinpoche's *The Tibetan Book of Living and Dying*

1. I walk down the street.
   There is a deep hole in the sidewalk.
   I fall in.
   I am lost … I am hopeless.
   It isn't my fault.
   It takes forever to find a way out.

2. I walk down the same street.
   There is a deep hole in the sidewalk.
   I pretend I don't see it.
   I fall in again.
   I can't believe I'm in the same place.
   But it isn't my fault.
   It still takes a long time to get out.

3. I walk down the same street.
   There is a deep hole in the sidewalk.
   I see it is there.
   I still fall in … It's a habit.
   My eyes are open.
   I know where I am.
   It is my fault.
   I get out immediately.

4. I walk down the same street.
   There is a deep hole in the sidewalk.
   I walk around it.

5. I walk down another street.

APPENDIX A

Developmental Deviations: Temperament and Learning Difficulties

"You have a different and special child."

- **Why does my daughter not know how to approach those around her?**
- **Why does my son conduct himself so slowly?**
- **Why does it take my daughter more time to learn than her classmates or even her brother?**
- **Why is it so hard for my son to catch a ball and why can't he ride a bicycle?**
- **Why is my daughter's grasp of language so inadequate and confused?**
- **Why does my son chatter endlessly and is not able to listen to the teacher like the other children?**

Such questions are quite common among parents, and they touch upon developmental patterns and developmental variances. Many people get confused between Attention Deficit Hyperactivity Disorder (ADHD), which is the developmental variance explored in this book, and temperament and learning difficulties, which are also types of developmental variance. These phenomena are indeed similar, but they are not identical. They can simultaneously exist in the same children, but one can also be present without the other. Accordingly, and since the principles of treating both is, according to my view, similar, I have chosen to expand here somewhat on what temperament and learning difficulties are, on how they influence the child's personality and on how they are distinct from ADHD .

What are Developmental Patterns?

A parent knows how his child, from a very young age, will respond to suggesting another child play with her; how she will behave when she loses her pacifier; and how she will ask to be fed. These patterns are called developmental patterns, since they define the child's development in various fields such as communications, motor skills, coordination, visual and spatial perception, audial perception, body regulation, temperament and more.

These patterns influence the individual's natural **path** of communication with her environment. Developmental patterns are **innate** and can usually be discerned at an early age. They derive from neurobiological difficulties and are expressed under the influence of the environment which shapes them.

Knowledge about developmental patterns and their influence on the personality and behavior of individuals has only begun to be accumulated over the past few decades. Today, we know that developmental patterns distinguish each and every child and influence their developing personalities.[1] They shape the characteristics of the individual and how they communicate and conduct themselves in the world.

What is Developmental Variance?

In some cases, a parent feels that her child is different from other children. She notices various differences, such as the child's lack of success in forming relationships with other children, or the child's slower pace as compared to her peers. There may also be significant differences between the abilities of the child in different fields (without any connection to other children). For example, a child with very high language skills may suffer from difficulty with motor skills, which prevents her from learning how to ride a bicycle, or even gaps within a given ability, such as social skills—a child who, in spite of being very sociable and desirous of the company of others, finds it difficult to initiate social connections. These situations, in which a difficulty exists in one or more developmental fields, are developmental variance. Hence, the term refers to a broad range of innate developmental patterns which are not normative.

Developmental variance can appear in any aspect of human development—cognitive, physical, motor, social, language and communication, emotional and so forth. I will focus on the innate components of two fields—**temperament and learning ability.** These components are closely linked and reciprocally influence each other and are not readily visible. This is why they cause much confusion to external observers, as well as to the individual herself. When development is sound, they enable the individual to function normatively, but developmental variance in these areas may also have an impact on their functional and emotional development. We will now get to know them and distinguish between them and difficulties with attention and hyperactivity.

Temperament is the natural way an individual behaves from infancy. Some people have a slow pace and others are faster; some are easily distracted and some less so; some tend to approach other people easily, whereas others tend to keep their distance.

In the 1970s, Thomas and Chess defined nine components of temperament: pace and activity level, adaptability, reaction intensity, persistence, sensory sensitivity, self-regulation, approach-avoidance, listening ability and tendency to distractedness. These tendencies are, as mentioned, innate, and are present in every individual somewhere on the spectrum between excess and deficit. The unique combination of the various components of temperament in every individual define their temperament type, and hence the variation in temperament between different individuals, and the variations in the emotional influence of the temperament type on the individual. Although temperament is, as mentioned, an innate trait, it is influenced by the attitude of the environment towards the individual. In fact, the way the environment addresses the temperament, in combination with the child's strengths and natural intelligence, is what will eventually determine her personality as an adult.

An environment which accepts and embraces the child's temperament will help her become an individual who channels her temperament into positive channels. The key is an awareness of the fact that the temperament is part of the innate package of the child. A mother who understands that her son's "difficult" temperament is the result of an innate tendency, rather than a desire to irritate or rebel, will be able to help him develop into an adult with more positive feelings toward himself and others in his environment.

A child with a difficult temperament might confuse others in her environment from infancy, thus influencing the initial bond formed between her and her parents. A mother who does not succeed in regulating her child or instilling in her appropriate sleep and feeding habits may well be frustrated and think she is a not-good-enough mother (especially if the child is her first). If she understands that the situation is the result of an innate tendency of her child, rather than the child's own ill intentions or the mother's inadequate caring for her, she will be able to contribute to her child developing in a more healthy way. If that mother is aware of the temperament of her child and of her own temperament, and if she is able to accept her child without criticism, then the initial bonding stage required for continued sound development should be completed. In contrast, should she not be aware of her child's temperament and misinterpret their behavior, then the initial bonding processes will face difficulty.

Like ADHD, temperament influences **how** individuals address their environment and is not related to the **content** they wish to express.

It may well be, for example, that an infant has many desires to be in contact with her environment (and this is the content she wishes to express), but since her temperament tends to flinch and withdraw, she does not know how to approach those around her. Her difficulty is in how she wants to approach the environment, not in the desire to approach it. This way of relating to the environment will have long-term effects—few people around the child will want to be close to her, which may result in problems in forming connections when the child grows older. This infant – child – adult wants to form connections but cannot show others that she is indeed interested in being in a relationship with them. Likewise, a child with a high intensity of responsiveness might want to greet another person in order to form a connection with them, but she will do so with exaggerated enthusiasm. She will, for instance, pump the other's hand too hard, unaware of her own strength, so that she will eventually cause others to back away.

Temperament may, of course, have emotional, physical and social consequences. A rash child, with a high activity level, who has trouble regulating herself, will find it hard to fit in in society. Another, different child, one with too many inhibitions and barriers, will not approach others, and hence, others will stay away from her. She might therefore experience loneliness, and even develop anxiety or depression.

A parent to an infant with a demanding temperament must first understand that this is an innate characteristic; the child is restless, because this is how she was born, not because the parent is not functioning adequately. It is important to **study** the neurological data in order to **understand** the child better, and, when necessary, to even approach a professional to learn more about this data. Nonetheless, the more the parent takes upon herself responsibility for the continued healthy development of her child, the greater the chances are for her child's sound emotional development and her success. A child whose parents have successfully accepted her innate, unique differences and demanding temperament without criticism, and who manage to help her develop in accordance with what is expected of her in accordance with her age and the developmental stage she is in, will help her develop a healthy sense of self.

Should the parent not display the appropriate sensitivity, a certain disorder might develop from infancy. The role of the parent, therefore, is to understand and be aware of the innate burden on the child, to accept, hold and love without judging or comparing, or trying to change the child. The parent must communicate, explain positions, express demands and make decisions. She must listen and respect the opinions of the child, while, at the same time, insisting upon boundaries. It is very important to understand that difficulty is not a "get out of jail free" card, and, conversely, that accepting the child is not giving up on him in any way.

One may understand that the characteristics of their temperament define how the infant or child experiences the world and responds to it. Furthermore, they influence responses of others in the environment to the child, expressed in relation to the level of adaptation of the child to her environment. However, temperament, unlike ADHD, is not a defined clinical symptom, and hence is not included in the list of psychiatric definitions, as a diagnostic, clinical symptom. Nevertheless, the consequences of the temperament on personal development, on the ability to adapt and on the possible development of emotional difficulties require addressing during the diagnostic and treatment process.

Another aspect of developmental variance is expressed in the **learning ability**. The ability to learn basic and simple things is not self-evident. This is a complex activity which depends on innate tendencies and abilities—specific and unique to every child and every adult. Some children and adults learn better by hearing, and so pick up information well through speech and listening.

In contrast, some children and adults perceive the world visually, and they tend to study better through images and visual metaphors. Some children and adults have a logical-analytical way of thinking, whose preferred method of learning will be focused on performing experiments, making calculations, asking questions and raising doubts. Learning can also be aided by movement, music, interpersonal interactions or self-observation processes. Every individual has several ways of learning she tends toward more strongly and other modes of learning which she finds more difficult. Just as there are different modes of learning, there are also different and specific learning difficulties. Before I describe them, I will clarify the difference between the concepts of "gap," "difficulty" and "disability":

A child may have a **gap** in her ability to function in a certain area, such as perception, motor skills, cognition, mathematics, language development and so forth. In other words, her performance in this field is lower than that of her peers. This child might narrow the gap on her own, and later function just like the rest of her age group.

A difficulty is a situation in which the gap versus her peers, or else the gap between certain abilities of the child to others, does not close. In this situation, the environment needs to seek the specific necessary professional intervention, or assistance, to help the child acquire the skills she is having a hard time developing.

A difficulty will be defined as a **disability** only after significant efforts have been made to assist the child, but the difficulty yet remains. This does not mean that a child with a disability shall receive no benefit and make no progress through professional aid which is adapted to her specific needs.

One must be careful, therefore, not to rush to define a child with a disability, as sometimes it is no more than a gap or a learning difficulty, which can be resolved with appropriate encouragement or therapy.

Learning difficulties are many and varied, and though it is customary to link them with formal learning in school, in practice, they are much broader and influence many fields of life. One can liken their influence to a stone which is stuck in one's shoe and interferes with the child's ability to smoothly and naturally walk to her destination. A certain learning difficulty may result in the child being unable to express herself in conversation, another will lead the child to be unable to learn to walk alone from her house to her friend's house. Some difficulties will lead the child to be unable to read a street sign, or to find it hard to calculate how much change she should receive in the grocery store.

It is customary to classify learning difficulties into primary difficulties and academic difficulties:

Primary difficulties are difficulties in different fields that show up at a young age, and when they are severe, they may impair the child's ability to study formally. These difficulties are divided into two categories: verbal and nonverbal difficulties.

Verbal difficulties :

- **Communication difficulties**: a significant difficulty with initiating and maintaining a conversation; a difficulty with understanding jokes, metaphors and expressions; a tendency to stereotyped speech in which the same phrases are repeated, etc.
- **Language difficulties**: a difficulty with pronouncing, processing and taking up the phonetics and structure of the language, which may harm the ability to call things by their name and expand one's vocabulary;
  1. a difficulty with understanding the grammatical structure of the language or difficulties with the organization of expressions to verbally express ideas.
  2. Significant difficulties with language can interfere with the ability of the child to acquire verbal information from the environment, and to express her thoughts appropriately, and sometimes may also cause difficulties with memory, given the difficulty to process verbal information and store it in memory.
- **Difficulties with higher abstract thinking processes**: difficulties with the ability to discern and act, assemble and disassemble verbal information, compare data, distinguish between the essential and the nonessential, infer conclusions and arrive at a level of verbal abstraction.

Nonverbal difficulties:

- **Gross motor and fine motor skills**: difficulties with coordination and clumsiness (such as awkward running, frequent falls, difficulty with climbing, finger dexterity, graphomotor skills such as writing and drawing, difficulties separating fingers, inefficient pencil gripping, difficulties holding and using scissors and cutting, difficulty with threading beads, opening bottles and the like.)
- **Difficulties with learning motor sequences**, which are required to do various activities, such as the ability to perform gymnastic exercises, to use a computer, or to navigate applications on a smartphone.

- **Visual or visual-spatial difficulties:** difficulties with the ability to process visual information, which influences the ability to recognize faces, facial expressions, size, direction, location and distance. Difficulties with understanding pictures and graphs; reading the dial of a clock; recognizing and drawing objects, patterns and symbols; and assembling puzzles.
- **Sensory regulation difficulties**: difficulties which will usually be expressed in over-sensitivity or under-sensitivity to touch, smell, light or noise. These are experienced by children who don't want to play in the sandbox in kindergarten, avoid touching hand paint or prefer certain types of clothes, due to sensitivity to the feel of certain types of fabric on their body. These can also be the children who hug too strongly, constantly seek sensory stimulation or do not flinch at pain. Such difficulties might make it difficult for a child to take part in experiences contributing to learning, and even make it difficult for her to fit in to social situations.
- **Mathematical disabilities** : basic **disability** with understanding the concept of numbers or quantities (even very small groups, such as four or five items); with addressing amounts and the ability to assess amount; with distinguishing between sizes, understanding a numerical sequence and understanding basic calculations. Children with severe mathematical disabilities find it difficult to develop mathematical skills from their very first moments in first grade.
- **Social skill difficulties:** difficulties with understanding nonverbal behaviors, such as facial expressions, body language, gestures and eye contact; difficulties with understanding social situations and social messages (that do not stem from ADHD). Children with social skill difficulties will find it difficult to adequately function in society, to enjoy talks and social interactions, or to initiate social interactions spontaneously.

Academic difficulties are difficulties that emerge at school ages, often derived from the primary difficulties detailed above. They include:

- **Reading and literacy difficulties:** initial language difficulties can often lead to difficulties with learning the rules of the written language –spelling, reading comprehension and written expression – and difficulties with learning a new language.
- **Writing difficulties:** difficulties with unresolved fine motor skills will impair the graphomotor ability and result in difficulties with the technical aspect of writing—the pencil grip will be defective, the shaping of letters will not be sound, and there will be difficulty with maintaining the rules of writing, as well (writing on the line, maintaining spaces between words and so forth).
- **Mathematical difficulties:** unresolved difficulties in mathematics impair the ability of children to learn adding, subtraction, multiplication and division. They will find it difficult to memorize and learn the multiplication table. Accordingly, these children will continue to use their fingers to make basic calculations even at advanced ages. These difficulties will influence the area of mathematics throughout their school years.
- **Non-verbal learning difficulties,** such as ongoing difficulties with visual-spatial perception, make learning basic mathematics, as well as mathematical fields based on spatial perception, such as geometry, function equations, etc., very difficult.

When one speaks of learning difficulties or learning disabilities, they are all too often described in general terms: math difficulties, reading difficulties or writing difficulties. However, in most cases, the difficulty is only in a very **specific** portion of these areas. For example, the ability to write is an extremely complex ability, which relies on several specific abilities. It includes verbal learning, which depends on knowledge of spoken and written language, and nonverbal learning, which is dependent on motor skills as well as executive abilities. Writing requires a certain level of motor-muscular maturity: development of the shoulder and upper back muscles, upright posture of the body and maturity of the fine motor skills—all these are required simply to hold the pencil or pen correctly. Also required is visual-spatial maturity: The child needs to be capable of maintaining the proper direction of the writing, a uniform letter size, uniform spaces and the application of sufficient pressure to the pencil. In order to write and express herself, the child must be able to use the symbols of the written language. In other words, she needs to be able to translate the sounds of words into written symbols – letters – to express herself fluently.

Furthermore, the child also requires executive abilities: she must be capable of organizing her thoughts, using working memory to avoid forgetting what she wants to write, and perform quality control during and after she writes. It is enough for the child to have a difficulty with even one of these specific abilities to make writing a nightmare for her (and for anyone forced to decipher her scrawl). The smarter she is, the greater the anger and frustration she will likely feel at her difficulty. Such a child will be able to write, but will genuinely suffer from the writing process, since any writing assignment will place an obstacle in her path. A parent who is not aware of the genuine, specific difficulties of her child, and who sees that she is capable of writing but stubbornly insists not to do so, may think that her child is simply lazy. The parent's lack of knowledge prevents her from understanding that her child has a specific difficulty which trips her up, and that she is not being contrary.

It is important to clarify that this is not a behavioral characteristic of bad parenting—even a parent with the best possible intentions can fall victim to this trap of blaming the child and thus amplify the difficulty. In such situations, the child does not enjoy writing, to put it mildly, and will usually complain and do everything to avoid the task. In other words, an expansive writing difficulty can develop on the basis of very narrow and specific writing difficulties—and may also generate a **behavioral** problem. The child will choose to "cheat" or disguise her difficulty—she might, for example, adopt the role of the "class clown" rather than admit her vulnerability. Alternatively, she may choose to lie or deny having any difficulty:

"I don't have a problem. I can write very easily; I just don't feel like writing."

She can also say,

"*I don't know*," every time she is asked to write something, to avoid a task that is difficult for her, until she eventually internalizes the expression "*I don't know*," and says it about everything. By so doing, an emotional problem develops—the child comes to believe that she does not know, develops low self-confidence and self-esteem, and may adopt a passive approach. There are, therefore, different types of difficulties and learning disabilities. These difficulties usually require professional adaptive education, occupational therapy or speech therapy. As important as these may be, they are not the topic of this book. Nonetheless, it is very important to be aware of their existence, and to distinguish between them and ADHD. As a general rule of thumb, when the child's academic performance is not consistent – sometimes she can solve a mathematical problem and sometimes she cannot – then her struggles probably derive from general attention or executive-attention difficulties. If, in contrast, her difficulties are consistent, then they usually derive from learning difficulties or a learning disability. Furthermore, a child dealing with ADHD may have a hard time in school **because** of difficulties with her attention and energy—she has a hard time with the way (the "how"), not the content (the "what").

In contrast, a child with a learning difficulty will have a hard time in school due to a difficulty in a specific field (mathematics, reading or writing)—her problem is with the content (the "what"), and not necessarily with the way (the "how"). This is a child who can be attentive and focused over time, but who finds it difficult to cope with the academic skills expected from her age group. In many cases, children deal with both a learning difficulty and an attention disorder, which is why their therapy must start with a differential diagnosis that will clearly distinguish between learning difficulties and attention difficulties, and which will pinpoint the specific difficulty. Such a diagnosis will lead to a more precise and appropriate therapy.

The therapy and management of the learning difficulties are performed according to the same principle on which this book is based—that this is a given neurological difficulty which must be studied, accepted and coped with, as efficiently as possible. In cases of a genuine disability in any particular area, the child should be encouraged to accept and understand it and taught only basic skills or even be exempted from a subject.

Such custom-tailored diagnoses and therapies may streamline the learning process and reduce the chances for the development of emotional and behavioral difficulties on the basis of the learning difficulties.

I strongly recommend Mel Levine's book *A Mind at a Time*[3] to anyone seeking to learn more about learning and attention difficulties. In addition to temperament, attention and learning abilities, there are many different types of developmental variances. However, I feel the need to understand, address and integrate them into our interactions with children in the same way.

We will raise the same questions with regard to each of the different types of developmental variance.

1. What is the difficulty? How is it expressed?
2. When is the difficulty expressed? How does it influence the child's developmental stage?
3. What difficulties and coping mechanisms does the child develop to cope with the difficulty?
4. How do others in the environment interpret the difficulty, and how does the difficulty influence them?
5. How does the difficulty influence the child's connection with their environment?
6. What are the emotional ramifications of the difficulty on the child and her environment?

Let us take, for example, a child with spatial orientation difficulties, and consider all aspects of this difficulty. The spatial orientation difficulty is a primary, nonverbal, difficulty, which can manifest as early as two to four years of age, when the primary emotional developmental task of the child is to begin to separate from her mother.

As a result of her spatial orientation difficulties, this child may find it hard to separate from her mother, and, as a result, develop over-dependence on her. The child's difficulty may have additional, **emotional** ramifications. For instance, when she grows up a bit, her mother may instruct her to meet her at the mall near the local McDonald's. It's likely the child will not trust herself and will not want to go there alone, in contrast to a child without any spatial orientation difficulties, who will not have a problem being separated from her mother for an hour before arriving at a specified rendezvous point.

In order to cope with the difficulty, the child may develop various defenses at a very early age—she may try to conceal her feelings, make excuses, camouflage, lie and argue, or she might manifest a tendency to burst into tears at the slightest provocation, throw herself to the ground or present over-dependence due to her lack of faith in her ability to be independent.

When the environment is not aware of this child's difficulty, and does not understand it, the environment will tend to label her as cowardly, dependent or spoiled, but this is not the case. The child is only afraid or contrary in very specific cases—cases which confront her with her difficulty with spatial orientation.

The environmental attitude to which the child will be exposed may lead her to serially withdraw from her environment, until her behavior is eventually considered odd. The approach detailed throughout the literature examines ADHD in a holistic manner. This approach is also suitable for examining the **entire range** of developmental variation characteristics. Through this, we can see and understand the entire experience the child and her environment have undergone. This holistic understanding is the foundation of this book, enabling us to understand how even a small, specific neurological difficulty can lead to behavioral, emotional and social difficulties.

These small neurodevelopmental difficulties are often not readily apparent, and we often don't always notice their existence. However, **the awareness of the possible connection between things** can trigger the understanding within us, **that a neurodevelopmental difficulty may underlie the emotional, behavioral or social difficulties of a child. This understanding will enable us to treat the neurological difficulty accurately, and this treatment**

will help relieve the symptoms in these other areas.

To explain this idea to children, or to help parents explain this to their children, I use the fairytale of the princess and the pea:

" *There was once a very sensitive princess who wanted to go to sleep, but something in her back bothered her and prevented her from falling asleep. To block her from what was bothering her, a mattress was added to her bed, and then another and another, until she was lying on top of a tall pile of mattresses, but the small pea continued to disturb her sleep.*"

In a similar way, developmental variance, in all its possible manifestations, disturbs the child at a young age, and to deal with it, she tries to cover it, or find various other ways to distract those around her from her difficulty. However, eventually a situation forms in which it is not just the initial variation that is disruptive. Her attempts to ameliorate the problem are now also disruptive and are expressed in the form of emotional, behavioral and social difficulties.

Many parents come to me disturbed and confused, asking if the child's difficulty derives from emotional or innate neurological reasons. These questions are quite understandable, for we are used to thinking in binary terms, of pinpointing the source of problems to resolve them. When we are dealing with developmental variation, however, whether with ADHD, difficult temperament, learning disabilities, or any other neurological impairment, **there are behavioral, social and emotional difficulties that are a direct function of objective difficulties. In other words, the difficulties are a byproduct.** For example, a social-emotional-behavioral difficulty, which is often a direct spinoff of ADHD is low self-esteem, or a difficulty with following instructions, and outbursts of anger. These in turn result in social difficulties.

A child with learning difficulties will often develop a harsh resistance or hostility towards school and will get up each morning with stomachaches; a person with a difficult temperament will develop considerable frustration around her ability to create and preserve social relationships, and will feel incompetent in this field.

Nonetheless, it is always possible that, in addition to the emotional difficulties deriving from innate difficulties, there are emotional difficulties for which the background is different and not innate. For example, a child who is concerned with the fact that her parents are constantly fighting lacks the resources to apply herself to her studies and will therefore find it difficult to concentrate and perform the tasks required of her in school; another child might be naturally anxious, regardless of any neurological difficulties. It is therefore important to investigate every case on its own merits, and to **perform a differential diagnosis** between solely emotion-based difficulties and emotion-based difficulties directly deriving from objective and innate neurological difficulties.

THE FLAME

There are things in this world that just drive me crazy:
The tick tock of a clock, a noise that is hazy.
A hug that's too tight, or a door that goes clack,
A tag in my shirt when it sticks in my back,
A kiss that is wet, or a pinch on my cheek,
A seatbelt so tight that I just want to shriek!
The seams on my socks that bother my toes,
When a hair from Mom's head lands and tickles my nose.
These things hit me hard, drive me right up a tree,
Make me want to run off, make me just want to flee.
It's not that I'm fussy or spoiled or a shrew—
My body feels feelings more fully than you!

My senses are fierce; my nerves are a-churning,
Like a lighter turned up with is brightest flame burning;
So these real irritations that you think are so small,
For me they are awful, can't stand them at all;
So please understand and then help me out so,
I can turn down the flame to a nice, pleasant glow.

APPENDIX B

Diagnosis of ADHD

So many professionals have written about the diagnostic process that I was not sure whether I should address it in this book. Nonetheless, since diagnosis is a fundamental part of the therapeutic process, I decided to write about it, based on my experience as a clinician who treats and diagnoses many children, emphasizing common parental dilemmas. Another issue, which is very important to me, is the transition from the stage of accepting the results of the diagnosis to the therapy stage. This is a very important transition for both the child and her parents, and I will address it as well in this chapter. Many parents flinch at diagnosing ADHD, due to the speed and ease in which diagnoses are currently performed, and given the ready availability of medication-based therapy. Nonetheless, avoidance of diagnosis may well keep parents from truly understanding the phenomena their child is experiencing, and from coping with the situation. In the absence of a diagnosis, the parents will not acquire the correct tools required to improve the performance and raise the self-esteem of their child, tools which will lead to genuine improvement in her quality of life. I have seen fit to detail the central issues in the diagnostic process in order to address the vital steps in understanding the *Talking ADHD* approach, out of the informed observation on which this book is based. This is, as mentioned, an approach which speaks to the child and enables her to identify the experience she is undergoing, to better understand herself and develop a greater feeling of competence and self-worth.

I hope that reading this book has persuaded you of the premise of this chapter: ADHD is a clinical diagnosis, which addresses a genetic neurological phenomenon. Although it is innate, its neurological and behavioral expressions in different people are distinct and influenced by the environment. Nonetheless, many people still present many doubts and questions concerning this diagnosis. I will try to address some of them:

1. Many parents question the diagnosis and claim that *"all children today have some attention difficulties."* This is not the case. Between five and 10 percent of children are diagnosed with ADHD. True, the pace of life has certainly changed over the past decades: It seems we are all more hurried, impatient and rash, dislike reading, do not dive deeply into books, get bored quickly, find it difficult to sit quietly, need a lot of stimuli and are addicted to screens, out of a "fear of missing out" on something—but these symptoms in themselves are insufficient to diagnose ADHD.

2. There are several people with attention oscillations and irregularity of impulses, who live among us and have been able to understand themselves intuitively. These people have been able to reroute their "excess attention and energy" in creative and original directions, which has enabled them to succeed. This positive outcome is a result of the fact that the unique qualities which define these people enable many of them to fulfill their goals.

   They are sensitive. Empathic. Sometimes with higher-than-average intelligence. Purposeful, with integrity and innate honesty. They are curious, energetic and charismatic. Sometimes they are opinionated and stubborn, but also practical and resourceful, with high improvisational skills and well-developed imaginations, prepared to take risks and live in the moment. When we understand who we are and do not let our innate qualities interfere with what we want to do, but instead recruit them to serve our purposes, no disorder develops. Irregular attention is considered a "disorder" when it interferes with the ability of the individual to function adequately in her academic, family, social, emotional or workplace environment. It is considered a disorder when it is translated into difficulties around self-competence and self-worth, or when it disturbs the environment. In such cases, it is important to conduct a diagnosis, which will aid us in understanding the specific difficulties and route them in desirable and correct directions. When the ADHD is not diagnosed or misdiagnosed (whether by professionals or by parents), we miss out on the opportunity to discover the strengths of this individual and the possibilities of their development, and worse, we will sometimes misinterpret, criticize, judge, grow angry and punish, instead of trying to help.

3. ADHD is not caused by bad parenting, nor by the atmosphere at home, school or the neighborhood. It is not generated by faulty education, a lack of discipline, the child's personality, emotional problems or trauma. It has nothing to do with I.Q. It is a neurological disturbance and is mostly genetic. Nonetheless, this does not mean it is not influenced by the environment. People diagnosed with ADHD, especially, need an understanding, supportive and embracing environment. This environment can be of great aid in promoting individuals in the direction they require. In contrast, a family or social framework that is not supportive, or harsh life circumstances, can amplify difficulties, and even lead an individual to seek aid, comfort or solutions in undesirable places (many criminals, and alcohol and drug addicts, have undiagnosed or untreated ADHD). A few more words about the environment—children with innate irregularity of attention and drives have poor internal boundaries and, hence, must make use of external limits and discipline. In other words, their family and educational frameworks need to be clear and well-defined in addition to being accepting, embracing and understanding.

4. When an ADHD disorder that interferes, even slightly, with daily life is not treated or addressed, it may well develop into a significant difficulty which usually does not fade away with time.

5. It seems that the considerable over-preoccupation with ADHD derives from the fact that it is insufficiently understood. This is why it is important for **parents** to ensure professional diagnoses, and receive correct and

precise guidance, so that they can understand the essence of their own child's ADHD. The diagnosis will enable them to cope with it, reroute it in more desirable directions and make the most out of its manifestations. Emotional or other difficulties can amplify the disorder, but they are not the reason for its formation. A differential diagnosis is the first step in improving the quality of life of a child or individual with ADHD, and this therapy, like any therapy, begins with a correct diagnosis.

6. I will shortly explain what ADHD is from a physiological-structural perspective. This explanation is intended for you, the parents, and is usually not suitable for children.

    Functions of attention and the ability to regulate urges take place in the forebrain, by neurons, cells with electrical conductivity abilities. They regularly receive messages or stimuli from the sensory organs and transmit these messages onwards to other neurons in the brain. The transmission of messages from cell to cell is performed by the release of chemical substances in one cell, and their intake into the next cell, which continues to transmit the message. One of the main substances which is secreted for transmitting the stimuli is dopamine. The dopamine is sometimes absorbed, and dopamine intake in people with ADHD is unpredictable and irregular; hence, the transmission of messages between neurons suffers irregular downturns. Absorption of dopamine, or irregular absorption, is expressed in distractedness or spacing out repeatedly, sometimes accompanied by an inundation of impulses leading to an irregular ability to pay attention, and to hyperactivity and impulsivity—hence ADHD. Medications to improve attention and restrain urges, such as Ritalin, increase dopamine availability, and generate a more stable, regular environment of electric conduction between neurons, and hence, control the attention and impulses. This raises the level of attention and reduces the level of distractedness or spacing out, enabling the child to focus, and to better control her urges.

ADHD is an extremely broad phenomenon. As mentioned, something between five to 10 percent of all children experience it, boys more than girls (more girls tend to be inattentive and not hyperactive; they compensate, and go undiagnosed), and it has many components and characteristics, which change between one individual to another. Just as every individual is different and unique, so the expressions of the phenomena are different and unique in every individual with ADHD. But despite this variance, there are three main, common components, which have been detailed at length throughout the book: attention oscillations, hyperactivity and impulsivity. I will go over them again briefly, here:

- Unregulated attention is expressed in oscillations of attention and a difficulty with maintaining a regular sequence of focused attention over time.
- Hyperactivity is expressed with an overload of increased physical and mental activity because of multiple stimuli, thoughts and impulses which simultaneously "race through the mind" at the same time without respite.
- Impulsivity is a situation in which the individual finds it difficult to regulate her drives or urges, and to stop before a reaction (verbal or physical). In other words, the individual finds it difficult to stop and delay a response, think and exercise discernment, and is genuinely sorry and often humiliated afterwards, as she was not in control.

The title "disorder" is not suitable for all cases of the phenomena. Unregulated attention is actually inconsistency of the ability to pay attention. After all, some people manage to channel the characteristics of their ADHD into advantages so that this is no "disorder" to them. The word "disorder" has a negative and pessimistic connotation which does not encourage the child to learn about herself. Therefore, based on extensive therapeutic experience, I choose to call the phenomenon "an overload, abundance or excess of attention and energy," especially when I work with parents and children.

Diagnosis of an Attention Disorder:

The updated diagnosis manual of the APA (*DSM-5*)[1] currently defines three "types" of ADHD:

1. ADHD — Inattentive Presentation In this subtype difficulties with regulating attention are dominant.
2. ADHD — Hyperactive/Impulsive Presentation In this subtype, the hyperactivity and impulsivity characteristics are dominant.
3. ADHD — Combined Presentation In this presentation, both the inattention and the hyperactivity and impulsivity are dominant.

In order to determine a formal diagnosis of ADHD, the child's behavior should present at least six of the nine criteria for at least six months (see the DSM questionnaire at the end of this chapter). An ADHD diagnosis is performed via extensive conversations with the parents and the child, together with a questionnaire or questionnaires that the parents and teachers fill in. This is a professional, sometimes multistage diagnosis, and when questions exist regarding the child's performance, or gaps in performance, or when her performance is inconsistent for some unclear reason, an additional, differential diagnosis between several possible sources of difficulties is recommended. These difficulties are also apparent with regard to the feelings of competence and issues of control.

Parents often begin to understand that the child is different from her siblings or other age-group peers prior to the decision to do a formal diagnosis. Sometimes, some of the signs of the lack or excess of attention and/or urges are conspicuous already in kindergarten.

Parents report that the child has a hard time sitting and listening (to a conversation or to a story), and finds it difficult to take part in a social activity, including communication with other children. *"She hits other children"* or *"frequently complains that she is bored"*. When I meet her or diagnose her, I often discover she is a bright child, and could be a good student *"if she* *only wanted to,"* but says *"school "isn't my thing,"* and she would rather play basketball or hang out with her friends—which her parents are fine with, because they want her to be happy. When I ask a specific question about the realization of her abilities, the parents immediately agree that *"she is not realizing her potential."* At this point, I suggest that they ask why this bright child is not enjoying the learning process. It is often the case that a parent reports "regular rambunctiousness" or frequent injuries, which occur during sports or simply when the child moves around. The parents sometimes explain the child's *"lack of interest because she is very intelligent, and school does not stimulate her."* In other cases, the child is very intelligent, has unique strengths, is loved and supported by her family and environment, is not hyperactive, impulsive or disruptive, and manages to cope with her excess/deficit in attention, and disguise it, until she can no longer do so. Difficulties can begin to crop up when she enters elementary school, middle school or high school, when the requirements demand greater attention resources, prolonged sitting and patience, and when the material she is required to study becomes more complex and abstract. Then, "all of a sudden," difficulties emerge where seemingly none existed beforehand. The fact that these difficulties were not noticed previously does not necessarily indicate that this is not a diagnosis of ADHD, but that the child was somehow able to disguise her difficulties or "bypass" them, until this point in time, when the demands rose beyond the child's resources and ability to cope adequately.

Teachers in schools and kindergartens report the difficulties the child has in sitting quietly in gatherings or lessons, with great forgetfulness and a need to *"try harder than others."* They speak of a difficulty with understanding instructions, opening notebooks on time, writing down the content of the lesson or homework in an orderly manner. Sometimes they report disturbances—the child chatters; gets distracted; pesters; "plays the clown;" bursts into the conversations of others; does not wait her turn; is impulsive, easily irritated and violent, or sensitive and easily offended; does not understand social codes; and finds it difficult to naturally fit in socially.

Often, the teachers raise the suspicion that the child may be coping with ADHD and recommend she be diagnosed. It is important to clarify that a school counselor, teacher or kindergarten teacher is not qualified to perform a formal diagnosis of ADHD on their own or to define children as hyperactive or suffering from attention disorders, and can certainly not recommend medication. Nonetheless, their experience over many years can certainly help them identify difficulties which are indicative of the existence of ADHD, and they should be thanked and encouraged for devoting attention and care to the child's difficulties. It is worth listening to them and, following their reports, to turn to a professional qualified to perform diagnoses—a children's neurologist, a children's psychiatrist, a psychologist or other professionals specializing in ADHD.

The child herself frequently reports about her difficulties, and it is very important to listen to her, because she is intelligent, sensitive, has good intuition and knows herself well. Many children repeat such statements as:

"*I don't like going to school because it is boring.*"

"*I am not as successful as other children.*"

"*I only like recess.*"

"*The teacher does not like me.*"

"*I am suspended from school again because I hit someone.*"

"*I erupted when I lost a game, and also cursed and spoiled things for my friends.*"

"*I knew the answer but was afraid to raise my hand.*"

"*No one wants to come visit me at home; I have no friends.*"

"*Everyone is against me.*"

"*I never succeed.*"

"*My answers are only 'almost' right.*"

"*People are always angry at me, and I don't even know why.*"

"*You don't understand me!*"

"*Ahhh!!! I've had it! I can't live like this!*" (*Facing a seemingly trivial frustration*)

It is often the case that the children know how to describe their situation in a very precise way:

"Recess lets my brain freshen up."

"I hate reading! The lines 'jump around' before my eyes."

"I lift my hand to answer the question, and suddenly think of something else and forget what I was about to say."

"Mother, I think I have difficulties with attention and concentration!"

As mentioned, there are many cases in which the child does not present difficulties in kindergarten, or cases when the parent does not address (or notice) difficulties at a young age. Only with the transition to first grade in elementary school does the parent notice that the child finds it difficult to study, that she responds with anger and outbursts of rage, that her frustration threshold is low and that she avoids studying and practicing, that she has social difficulties and that she complains about being bored and not enjoying school. It is often the case that following a recommendation by the kindergarten teacher, children in the kindergarten are sent for diagnosis or therapy by a professional, such as an occupational therapist or speech clinician. The professional raises the suspicion that ADHD exists, but some of the parents "do not hear" what they are told, or else think that the child's behavior matches her age, and hence they seem inattentive or "energetic." These parents, who deny the inattention and hyperactivity symptoms in kindergarten, will find it harder to deny them when their child is at school, as these difficulties will generally multiply and grow.

Even parents who do not deny the diagnosis often find themselves confused, and ask themselves whether the child's behavior does indeed constitute a "disorder." After all, many of us have this or that characteristic of inattention and rambunctiousness, and we are not diagnosed as people suffering from ADHD.

When questions arise, and the symptoms are intense and constitute a disturbance to the child and her environment, then it is recommended to turn to a professional for a diagnosis.

In some cases, the child and the parent are referred to the kindergarten psychologist or the school counselor. In other cases, the family is referred to a child neurologist or a child psychiatrist.

Many parents show up at the doctor with high expectations of getting a serious diagnosis and are disappointed when in practice the professional merely speaks with the child and the parents, performs a medical review, asks the parents and the educational staff to fill out several questionnaires, confirms the suspicion of the parent or educational staff, and determines that the child does indeed have ADHD.

Doubts, accusations and anger, with considerable criticism of the short and "superficial" examination often follow.

A frenzied search online and in the archives for more information is launched. At this point, it is important to know and understand that there is no way to diagnose ADHD conclusively and unambiguously. There are no relevant medical examinations, such as blood tests or brain scans, so there is no reason to expect the child to be referred to them by the doctor (save in cases where he wants to rule out other disorders or diseases). It is also worth keeping in mind that a well-qualified and experienced professional can often make the correct diagnosis quickly—and immediately recommend beginning treatment.

I believe that the real difficulty is with certain professionals who do not understand the topic sufficiently and miss making a correct ADHD diagnosis, rather than professionals who do understand the phenomenon well and do not hesitate to diagnose it.

When the individual performing the diagnosis is a skilled professional, **I recommend the parents accept the findings of the diagnosis. Professionals know how to make a diagnosis, and I encourage the parents to accept it, or if absolutely necessary, to seek a second opinion and then focus on the therapy, which begins with understanding and accepting the phenomenon.**

From my experience, deeper understanding of the phenomenon enables parents to accept the diagnosis with fewer reservations.

There are two types of diagnoses:

1. **Clinical diagnoses** These are performed by a physician or psychologist specializing in the field of ADHD. This diagnosis is conducted based on a medical examination, in-depth questioning, interviews with the parents and with the child, and a collection of data from questionnaires. A few physicians also make use of computerized diagnostic tests, but this tool is not sufficient in and of itself (I will explain more about this later in this appendix).

2. **Psychological clinical evaluations** The professional speaks with the parents and the child, and clinically examines the child on several parameters—in this diagnosis, the examiner clinically observes the child, and her ability to regulate herself, to focus and pay attention, and to regulate and control her urges. She also evaluates her intelligence, personality, strengths, defenses, coping mechanisms, conflicts, judgment, self-esteem, etc.

Procedures for Performing a Comprehensive Diagnosis:
1) It is highly recommended that the child be examined by her pediatrician before she is examined by an ADHD specialist. The pediatric examination should include routine blood tests, as well as refer to the child's medical history, which includes information about the pregnancy and their birth, childhood diseases and family diseases, unusual events in the child's life and so forth. The pediatrician should also refer the child to a sight and hearing examination. The purpose of this examination is to rule out the existence of problems which may seem to be ADHD but derive from other reasons, such as a lack of vitamins, sleep disorders, hearing or speech impairment and the like. If the pediatrician rules out the existence of other medical conditions, but there are still symptoms of attention deficit and hyperactivity, the child is referred to an examination with an ADHD specialist.

2) Examination by a specialist — a children's psychiatrist, children's neurologist or **ADHD-specialist** pediatrician performs a differential diagnosis between different difficulties, which can have similar manifestations, such as reactions to changes in family settings, bedwetting, defiance, behavioral problems, oppositional and conduct disorders, rejection of authority, anxiety, depression, physical or sexual abuse, trauma, learning and communication disorders, autism and other disorders on the spectrum. **Each of these can co-exist with and exacerbate the ADHD.** The examination includes, as mentioned, the collection of a great deal of data about **the behavior of the child in different situations.**

This is done based on an extensive interview with the parents and with the child, as well as by reviewing questionnaires filled out by the kindergarten teacher or schoolteacher about the child's performance in the classroom and her academic, emotional, social and behavioral conditions.

The data is also based on a review of academic material, such as notebooks and report cards, and a review of her medical file.

The filling out of questionnaires by various figures in the child's world is meant to determine whether the behavior, which is characteristic of ADHD, exists in more than one life environment. A diagnosis of ADHD requires that such behavior exist in at least two environments.

The collected data must also include information regarding **the developmental history of the child**—if his development was sound in the motor, cognitive, language emotional and social categories. In addition, the **medical and general history of the family** needs to be examined as well: One should examine whether other family members have been diagnosed with ADHD or with other diseases, as well as identify significant events experienced by the family or the child, such as a harsh response to the death of a family member, divorce, trauma, abuse and so forth. The collection of data regarding the history of the child and her extended family is extremely important in order to determine whether there was atypical development of ADHD, and in order to rule out alternative explanations of the child's behavior. As mentioned, there is a high probability that ADHD is genetic, and if ADHD exists in the family, then the probability that it occurs in the child as well is higher. In certain cases the physician may refer the child to a C.T. or EEG scan, or for certain blood tests, prior to providing a final diagnosis.

3) Psychodidactic Evaluation

In cases where the ADHD symptoms are accompanied by academic, emotional, social or behavioral difficulties, or if a parent is not convinced about the diagnosis of ADHD, it is recommended one perform an extensive formal psychological or psycho-didactic evaluation. This is performed by an expert psychologist in the field (an educational, clinical, neurodevelopmental or developmental psychologist). The psycho-didactic diagnosis is also performed by a psychologist who specializes in the field and can also be performed by **two professionals** – a psychologist and a professional who diagnoses learning disabilities – each a specialist in his or her own field. In this manner the diagnosis can be reliable and go in depth.

In the psychological portion of the diagnosis, the I.Q. of the child is assessed. This is an objective measurement which also measures potential and enables us to determine whether a gap exists between the intellectual potential of the child and the relatively low realization of her abilities. This gap can also be explained by ADHD. In addition, an emotional evaluation is performed, during which the emotional state is examined—the psychological strengths of the child, her defenses, her style of coping, her compensation mechanisms, her personality type, her mental health, any tendency to anxiety, depression or obsession, and the like.

In the didactic portion of the psycho-didactic diagnosis, the cognitive mechanisms, which are the foundations of learning functions are assessed— visual or audible perceptions, graphomotor ability, general attention and executive attention functions, processing procedures, memory function and language ability, as well as nonverbal abilities, such as spatial, motoric, communication and social abilities.

These functions are the foundations of learning and can explain learning difficulties (in schoolchildren) or difficulties in preparing for school (in kindergarten children).

From the first grade onwards, academic functions are tested as well—the acquisition and mastering of reading skills, reading comprehension processes, writing processes and mathematical functions, which include arithmetic understanding, mathematical thinking and the mastery of learned mathematical procedures.

The integration of the information in the psychological and the didactic portion of the assessment enables us to discover and explain dispersion and gaps existing between the basic cognitive potential and its realization in reality. One of the explanations for this lack of realization of potential is ADHD, and the higher the intelligence, the greater the frustration.

In addition, a differential diagnosis exists between the existence of primary learning disabilities and learning disabilities which appear as a result of attention irregularities, hyperactivity and impulsivity. If a diagnosis of ADHD is made, the child is referred to a child neurologist or child psychiatrist (if this has not yet been done) to examine whether an associated illness exists, and to determine whether treatment with medications is required. In cases where the child has already undergone a medical assessment, it is recommended to return to the attending clinician to update her regarding the findings of the evaluation and for the purpose of continued follow-up. The goal of the psychological evaluation and diagnosis is also to rule out additional emotional factors that are not related to attention and hyperactivity, which might explain the child's difficulties. For example, a child might lack the ability to concentrate on her studies since she is thinking about her father leaving home, or since she is flooded with anxiety or immersed in depression. These reasons can offer an alternate explanation for behavior which seems like ADHD but is derived from purely emotional difficulties.

This **differential diagnosis** is absolutely necessary for referring the child to the appropriate treatment.

Language difficulties can also often be interpreted as ADHD difficulties. A child who finds it hard to come up with the correct words to express herself, or who finds it difficult to organize a sentence in a coherent manner, may seem restless (a typical symptom of ADHD), but her restlessness may derive from frustrations with her difficulties with expressive language.

The opposite situation is one in which difficulties with organizing sequential and coherent sentences, which may seem like language difficulties, are actually derived from difficulties with general attention and executive attention. This differential diagnosis, between language difficulties and attention difficulties, is important to determine the nature of the appropriate therapy and its characteristics.

A psycho-didactic evaluation is much longer than an ADHD diagnosis performed by a physician. It is supposed to include a familiarization meeting of the diagnosticians with the parents, several meetings with the child to perform the various tests, and a concluding meeting with the parents. This meeting will summarize the findings and include in-depth explanations of the extensive written report, alongside recommendations for treatment, as well as specific recommendations and adaptations.

The medical diagnosis – a clinical examination with an M.D. who is an ADHD specialist – is an absolutely **necessary** stage to diagnose ADHD. The psychological or psycho-didactic evaluation is imperative only where specific questions exist regarding intelligence (which can be used to determine potential), cognitive functions, learning abilities and personality issues.

In addition, there are **computerized tests,** which are nowadays common to perform when there is suspicion of the existence of ADHD. These tests examine the ability of the child to sit and stay active with a monotonous task over time, to focus their attention, to defer their reactions and to exercise mental flexibility in various tasks. It is important to note that these tests are not an exclusive means to diagnosis ADHD, but an **additional tool**, with which the diagnostician can secure more information regarding certain aspects of the ADHD disorder.

These tests, of which the best known are TOVA, BRC, MOXO and Conners CPT, were originally designed to assess the effectiveness of medication therapy, such as Ritalin, on attention and hyperactivity.

In the first part of the examination, the tested individual is required to perform a simple task, which measures various parameters of attention, impulsivity, hyperactivity and control. She then takes medication and is required to perform the same task about an hour later. In this way, the effectiveness of the medication use is measured in relation to a certain child, and a professional decision can be made regarding whether it is desirable that she take the medication and at what dosage. The test can be repeated with different dosages to reach the most effective dosage.

The computerized test can be used with or without medication, when parents are hesitant about using it, or when the child reports that the medication does not help her. Some parents cling to doing the computerized test, because it seems to them that it is objective and scientific. Nonetheless, it is important to understand that these tests cannot be the primary or exclusive tool in diagnosis. Many children with ADHD manage, for various reasons, to pass the first stage of the test even without using medication, and then the diagnosis is immediately written off, despite the existence of an ADHD disorder (a false negative). In contrast, a false positive can also occur if an ADHD diagnosis is made based on subpar functioning that was the result of, for example, a high level of anxiety during the test. The use of these tests as an exclusive diagnostic tool leads those children who have ADHD, who were not identified in the evaluation, to be denied their proper treatment, whereas children who were misdiagnosed with ADHD receive inappropriate treatment.

Studies have shown that these tests have a high error rate and, hence, repeatedly warn against relying on them as an exclusive or primary means of diagnosing ADHD.

Accepting the Diagnosis

This phase can and should be undergone with a professional, via individual or group guidance of the parents. In this way, it will be possible to learn about ADHD deeply, understand it and be convinced that this is indeed ADHD. Via the guidance process, many parents learn to accept the diagnosis, to understand their child and, moreover, to understand themselves, and even notice clear symptoms of ADHD in themselves.

The diagnosis and the discovery relieve the parents of a great burden, freeing them. They begin putting the puzzle together, and some retell their own life story to themselves. The spouses also undergo a process of in depth non-judgmental understanding, acceptance, and ability to embrace the child following the insight. When the parents begin to "deconstruct" the term, they usually realize that there is no need to fear the diagnosis, and they can rally themselves to help their child realize what was not explained to *them* when *they* were children.

In some situations, the diagnosis does not provide a clear, unambiguous diagnosis (even if sometimes the symptoms are clear). In these cases, as well, I help the parents understand that the "emotional" difficulties they describe, such as avoidance, frustration, anxiety, fear, social difficulties, anger, out-bursts, fixation, lack of confidence and low self-esteem, are very common and characteristic symptoms. They are the result of difficulties in the areas of attention, hyperactivity and impulsivity, even if an ADHD disorder is not unambiguously diagnosed since its severity is slight.

This is the chance to clarify that ADHD exists at various degrees of sever-ity, from slight to extreme. This continuum dictates the medical recommen-dations to be provided following the diagnosis. This fact contrasts with the prevailing opinion according to which doctors distribute Ritalin to anyone who seeks it.

Conversely, it is a shame to miss out on an opportunity to help a child with low-severity ADHD. It is important to remember that even at a slight severity, ADHD has many ramifications, and it makes it harder for the child or adult to fully realize their ability. An ADHD disorder which has not been diagnosed at all, or that has been diagnosed as "borderline," or that is not conclusively and unambiguously diagnosed, will often be interpreted as an educational, behavioral or emotional difficulty.

I will repeat that the diagnosis is primarily important in order to under-stand how to treat the child, and the most important initial treatment is, in my view, counseling the responsible adults – parents, teachers, therapists and instructors – so that they can understand the phenomenon precisely and deeply. Let us consider, for example, a child who finds it difficult to write extensively and continuously, or to listen in class or study for a test. Such a child, whose difficulties derive from undiagnosed ADHD, can develop resistance to learning, or even anxiety from studying and tests. In such a case, it is incorrect to treat the anxiety. Rather, what needs to be addressed is the element causing the child's difficulties – the ADHD – provided that the behavioral, emotional and academic difficulties are the outcome of difficulties with ADHD.

There are also children who match the hyperactivity and impulsivity criteria, but only partially meet the criteria for attention difficulties, since they are able to compensate for, or conceal their attention difficulties for a certain length of time, or at an emotional price. Accordingly, even in cases where the child does not formally meet all criteria procedurally required to diagnose ADHD, but a significant portion of the symptoms appear to be uncontrollable, I recommend that the parents study the phenomenon.

One typical difficulty occurs when parents resist accepting the diagnosis and insist that the doctor told them it was "borderline," because they immediately connect the diagnosis with the need for medication. In such cases, I help them understand that ADHD is not synonymous with medication and, once again, encourage them to study the entire phenomenon and make an informed decision.

Some parents oppose the diagnosis as they fear labeling their child. I explain to them that there is a real diagnosis called ADHD, and that labeling will occur precisely *if* they fail to diagnose the ADHD and address it specifically and treat the child.

In summary, it is very important to diagnose, and accept a diagnosis made by a competent professional. Professionals know how to diagnose, and we can rely on their diagnoses. I warmly recommend accepting the conclusions of the diagnosis, recognizing them and – moreover – not dwelling on them, but moving onwards, as rapidly as possible, to the stage of therapy. The therapy, as detailed throughout the book, is to help parents and responsible adults understand, so they can help the child understand—and be understood. The primary tool is to "Talk ADHD" by learning focused and precise discussions which raise awareness and mindfulness, and gradually enable the child to identify and direct their attention and impulses. When the parents begin the therapy, they learn about ADHD in depth, understanding it holistically, and can then wholeheartedly accept the diagnosis, speak with the child at every opportunity, and mostly help the child accept herself and realize her abilities. In so doing, she will be able to improve her quality of life and the connection between herself and the environment.

The DSM-V Questionnaire[1] to determine the diagnosis of ADHD

The behaviors described in the questionnaire are normal among children, but there is significance to their intensity and duration. In order to determine that a certain factor is manifesting within a child, it must be conspicuous and essential to her behavior, exist over time in a manner that is not expected from children this age, and significantly interfere with the soundness of a child's performance in a number of life environments.

The questionnaire is divided into two parts:

In the first part, six or more of the symptoms of inattention must exist in two life environments or more, for at least six months, at an intensity that impairs adaptation and which is unsuitable for the developmental level:

1. Frequently finds it hard to persist in tasks or games (for example, finds it difficult to focus during homework, conversations or prolonged reading)
2. Frequently does not listen when she is addressed directly (for example, her mind wanders even in the absence of external distractions)
3. Frequently fails to follow instructions and does not finish doing her homework, tasks or workplace assignments), not due to resistance or difficulty with understanding instructions. For example, initiates a task but loses focus rapidly, getting easily distracted)
4. Frequently finds it difficult to organize activities and tasks (for example, finds it difficult to organize continuous sequential tasks, such as getting organized in the morning and arranging various items in place, is messy, manages time ineffectively, does not meet deadlines)
5. Frequently avoids or withdraws from action in tasks which require continuous mental effort (such as homework or school tasks), or else resists them

---

1 Frequently does not notice details or makes careless mistakes when doing homework, working or in other activities (for example, ignores details or misses some of them, works in an imprecise manner)

6. Frequently loses things required for tasks or activities (toys, homework, pencils, books, devices, keys, cell phones)
7. Is easily distracted by external stimuli (or inner thoughts)
8. Frequently tends to forget things during daily activities (for example, housework, homework)

In the second portion, six or more symptoms of **hyperactivity-impulsivity** must exist in two or more life environments, for at least six months, at an intensity that impairs adaptation and is not suitable for the child's developmental level, for an ADHD diagnosis to hold:

1. Frequently, restlessly tosses arms or legs or squirms in her chair
2. Frequently rises from her seat in class, or other situations in which she is required to remain seated (a lesson in class, a family meal)
3. Frequently runs about or climbs in inappropriate situations (teenagers and adults suffer restlessness instead)
4. Frequently finds it difficult to play or act quietly in recreational activities
5. Is frequently in motion and seems to be "driven" by an engine (for example, is unable to sit calmly for a prolonged period of time, so that she is perceived by others as restless)
6. Frequently speaks, or chatters, a great deal
7. Frequently answers before the question is complete (or completes the sentences of others); does not wait for his turn in the conversation
8. Frequently finds it difficult to wait when standing in line
9. Frequently interrupts others or pesters them (for example, bursts into a conversation or game, plays with the belongings of others without permission)

- The first six parameters in the second part of the questionnaire are indicative of hyperactivity, whereas the latter three are indicative of impulsivity.

THE DETECTIVE

Help! I need a detective to solve this mystery:
The disappearance of the notebook I use for history,
And two pencils that have fled from my pencil case …
Plus, I'm missing a sweater and my sneaker's shoe-lace;
My erasers appear to be erasing themselves,
And five schoolbooks have vanished right off of their shelves!
Tell me, does it really seem normal to you,
That I'm wearing one brown sock, but the other turned blue?
How come all these things have to happen to me?
I need a detective immediately!

And it's not only objects that treat me this way;
Names, words, and ideas in my head will not stay;
What I learned from my teacher just flies far away;
My mind's full of riddles. And why? I can't say.

What was I saying? For what was I looking?
Where'd I put the red ladle that Mom needs for cooking?
Why'd my homework get torn, all messed up and crinkled?
Why's this shirt that Dad bought me already so wrinkled?
I need that detective to crack all these cases
To seek what I've left in all the wrong places.

What?! You say no detective's available for me;
Then I'll figure it out, you can just wait and see.
I'll solve all those mysteries and locate my stuff.
And then try to make order when the going gets tough.

REFERENCES

Chapter 1: The Story of My Life

1. Goldberg, E., and Zagury-Cohen, K. *My Mind Races.* (Hebrew) Amazia Publishing House, 2016.

2. 2 Aleksandrowicz, D. R., & Aleksandrowicz M. K. *The Injured Self: The Psychopathology and Psychotherapy of Developmental Deviations.* Routledge, 2011.

Chapter 2: The Development of the *Talking ADHD* Approach

1. Hoffman, H. "Shockheaded Peter." In The English Struwwelpeter, or Pretty Stories and Funny Pictures, translated and published by Frederick Warne & Co., Inc., New York, 1844.

2. Still, G. F. Some abnormal psychical conditions in children: excerpts from three lectures, 1902. *The Lancet, 96,* 1008-1012.

3. *See for illustration*: Laufer, M. W., & Denhoff, E. "Hyperkinetic behavior syndrome in children." *The Journal of Pediatrics, 50*(4), 463-474, 1957.

4. *See for illustration*: Wender, P. H. *Minimal brain dysfunction in children.* Wiley Interscience, 1971.

5. Douglas, V. I. "Stop, look and listen: The problem of sustained attention and impulse control in hyperactive and normal children." *Canadian Journal of Behavioral Science, 4*(4), 259-282, 1972.

6. Hallowell, E. M., & Ratey, J. J. *Driven to Distraction: Recognizing and Coping with Attention Deficit Disorder from Childhood Through Adulthood.* Touchstone, 1994.

7. Hallowell, E. M., & Ratey, J. J. *Delivered from Distraction: Getting the*

Most out of Life with Attention Deficit Disorder. Ballantine Books, 2005.

8. Lavoie, Richard, "How difficult can this be? The F.A.T. city workshop You Tube

Chapter 3: Who is the ADHD child?

1. Russell Barkley Taking charge of ADHD : The Complete Authoritative Guide for Parents Guilford Press 2020

2. Hallowell, E. M., & Ratey J. J. (2005). *Delivered from distraction: Getting the most out of life with attention deficit disorder.* Ballantine Books.

3. Hartmann, T. (1994). *Attention deficit disorder: A different perception.* Underwood Books.

4. Goldberg, E. and Zagury-Cohen,K .(2016). My Mind Races. (Hebrew) Amazia Publishing House

Chapter 8: Executive Attention

1. Altemeier, L. E., Abbott, R. D., & Berninger, V. W. "Executive Functions for Reading and Writing in Typical Literacy Development and Dyslexia." *Journal of Clinical and Experimental Neuropsychology, 30*(5), 588-606, 2008. DOI: 10.1080/13803390701562818

2. Tsal, Y., Shalev, L., & Mevorach, C."The Diversity of Attention Deficits in ADHD: The Prevalence of Four Cognitive Factors in ADHD Versus Controls. *Journal of Learning Disabilities, 38*(2), 142-158, 2005.

3. Miyake, A., Friedman, N. P., Emerson, M. J., Witzki, A. H., Howerter, A., & Wager, T. D. "The Unity and Diversity of Executive Functions and Their Contributions to Complex 'Frontal Lobe' Tasks: A Latent Variable Analysis." *Cognitive Psychology, 41*, 49-100, 2000.

4. Diamond, A. "Executive Functions." *The Annual Review of Psychology, 64*, 4, 135-168, 2013.

5. See for example: Merkel, R. L., Nichols, J. Q., Fellers, J. C., Hidalgo, P., Martinez, L. A., Putziger, I., Burket, R. C., & Cox, D. J. "Comparison of On-Road Driving Between Young Adults With and Without ADHD. *Journal of Attention Disorders, 20*(3), 260-269, 2016.

6. Baddeley, A., & Hitch, G. "Working Memory." In G. A. Bower (Ed.), *The Psychology of Learning and Motivation,* 47-89. Academic Press, New York, 1974.

7. See for example: Leon-Carrion, J., Garcia-Orza, J., & Pérez-Santamaría, F. J. "Development of the Inhibitory Component of the Executive Functions in Children and Adolescents." *International Journal of Neuroscience, 114,* 1291-1311, 2004.

8. Kendeou, P., Van den Broek, P., Helder, A., & Karlsson, J. "A Cognitive View of Reading Comprehension: Implications for Reading Difficulties." *Learning Disabilities Research & Practice, 29*(1), 10-16, 2014. DOI:10.1111/ldrp.12025.

9. Gilor, O., & Gazal, O. (2019(."GAG' Model: Representation of the Multi-Component Nature of Reading Comprehension. *Dash Bareshet (Hebrew) (The Israeli Speech, Hearing and Language Association's Journal)*, Vol. 38, 59-92, 2019,(Hebrew)

Chapter 9: Compensatory Attention

1. Kinsbourne, M. "Overfocusing: An Apparent Subtype of Attention Deficit-Hyperactivity Disorder. In Amir, N., Rapin, I., & Branski, D., (Eds.): *Pediatric Neurology: Behavior and Cognition of the Child with Brain Dysfunction, 1,* 18-35. Karger Publishing, 1991.

2. Amen, D. G. *Healing ADHD.* Berkley Publishing House Penguin Group, 2001.

3. Goldberg, E., and Zagury-Cohen, K. *My Mind Races.* Amazia Publishing House, 2016. (Hebrew)

Chapter 10: Emotional Therapy

1. Nylund, D. *Treating Huckleberry Finn: A New Narrative Approach to Working With Kids Diagnosed ADD/ADHD.* Jossey-Bass, 2000.

2. Goldberg, E., and Zagury-Cohen, K. *My Mind Races. Amazia Publishing House, (Hebrew) 2016.*

3. Levine, M. D. *A Mind at a Time.* Simon and Schuster, 2002.

4. Levine, M. D. *Developmental Variation and Learning Disorders*. Educators Publishing Service, 1987.
5. Nelson, P. "Autobiography in Five Short Chapters." In C. Whitfield. *Healing the Child Within: Discovery and Recovery for Adult Children of Dysfunctional Families*. Health Communications, 1989.
6. Riponche, S. *The Tibetan Book of Living and Dying*, 1993.

Appendix A — Developmental Variance, Temperament and Learning Difficulties

1. Aleksandrowicz, D. R., & Aleksandrowicz, M. K. *Developmental Deviations and Personality*. Gordon and Breach Science Publishers, New York, 1989.
2. Thomas, A., & Chess, S. *Temperament and Development*. Brunner & Mazel, 1977.
3. Levine, M.D. *A Mind at a Time*. Simon and Schuster 2003.

Appendix B — Diagnosing Attention and Hyperactivity Disorders

1. *The Diagnostic and Statistical Manual of Medical Disorders*, 5th edition (DSM-5). American Psychiatric Association, Washington, D.C., 2013.

Made in the USA
Las Vegas, NV
24 February 2024

86118216R00265